HOPE AGAIN

Publications by Charles R. Swindoll

BOOKS

Active Spirituality
The Bride
Come Before Winter
Compassion: Showing We Care in a Careless
    World
Dear Graduate
Dropping Your Guard
Encourage Me
The Finishing Touch
Flying Closer to the Flame
For Those Who Hurt
The Grace Awakening
Growing Deep in the Christian Life
Growing Strong in the Seasons of Life
Growing Wise in Family Life
Hand Me Another Brick
Improving Your Serve
Intimacy with the Almighty
Killing Giants, Pulling Thorns
Laugh Again

Leadership: Influence That Inspires
Living Above the Level of Mediocrity
Living Beyond the Daily Grind, Books I and II
Living on the Ragged Edge
Make Up Your Mind
Man to Man
Paw Paw Chuck's Big Ideas in the Bible
The Quest for Character
Recovery: When Healing Takes Time
Sanctity of Life
Simple Faith
Standing Out
Starting Over
Strengthening Your Grip
Stress Fractures
Strike the Original Match
The Strong Family
Three Steps Forward, Two Steps Back
Victory: A Winning Game Plan for Life
You and Your Child

MINIBOOKS

Abraham: A Model of Pioneer Faith
David: A Model of Pioneer Courage
Esther: A Model of Pioneer Independence

Moses: A Model of Pioneer Vision
Nehemiah: A Model of Pioneer
    Determination

BOOKLETS

Anger
Attitudes
Commitment
Dealing with Defiance
Demonism
Destiny
Divorce
Eternal Security
Fun Is Contagious
God's Will
Hope
Impossibilities

Integrity
Leisure
The Lonely Whine of the Top Dog
Moral Purity
Our Mediator
Peace . . . in Spite of Panic
Prayer
Sensuality
Stress
Tongues
When Your Comfort Zone Gets the Squeeze
Woman

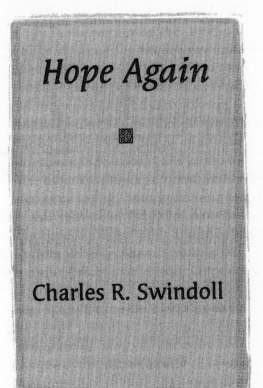

Hope Again

Charles R. Swindoll

W PUBLISHING GROUP™

www.wpublishinggroup.com

A Division of Thomas Nelson, Inc.
www.ThomasNelson.com

W Publishing Group
1996

Unless otherwise indicated, Scripture quotations used in this book are
from the New American Standard Bible NASB © 1960, 1962, 1963, 1968, 1971, 1972,
1973, 1975, 1977 by The Lockman Foundation. Used by permission.
The King James Version of the Bible (KJV). *The Living Bible* (TLB),
copyright 1971 by Tyndale House Publishers, Wheaton, Ill. Used by permission.
The Message (MSG). Copyright © 1993. Used by permission of NavPress
Publishing Group. The Holy Bible, New International Version (NIV).
Copyright © 1973, 1978, 1984 International Bible Society. Used by
permission of Zondervan Bible Publishers. J. B. Phillips: The New Testament
in Modern English, Revised Edition (PHILLIPS). Copyright © J. B. Phillips
1958, 1960, 1972. Used by permission of Macmillan Publishing Co., Inc.

Book design by Mark McGarry
Set in Monotype Dante

Library of Congress Cataloging-in-Publication Data
Swindoll, Charles R.
Hope Again / Charles R. Swindoll
p. cm.
ISBN 0-8499-1132-X (hardcover)
ISBN 0-8499-3994-1 (foreign edition)
ISBN 0-8499-4088-5 (trade paper)
1. Suffering — Religious aspects — Christianity. 2. Hope — Religious
aspects — Christianity. 3. Consolation. 4. Bible. N.T. Peter,
1st — devotional literature. I. Title.
BV4909.S95 1996 248.8'6 — dc20
96-8962
CIP

Printed in the United States of America.

2 3 4 PHX 9 8

I dedicate this book to two of my closest colleagues and
faithful friends on the leadership team at
Dallas Theological Seminary:

Dr. Wendell Johnston
and
Dr. Charlie Dyer

Without their invaluable assistance, there is no way these
recent years could have been so satisfying and
rewarding. These men have given me
fresh encouragement to press on . . . to finish strong
. . . to hope again.

Contents

Acknowledgments

I WANT TO ACKNOWLEDGE, with great gratitude, my longstanding friendship with several important people.

First, my friends on the leadership team at Word Publishing: Byron Williamson, Kip Jordon, Joey Paul, and David Moberg. There are others I could name, but these four have been especially encouraging and helpful on this particular project. Thank you, men, for continuing to believe in me and for knowing how to turn dreams into books.

I also want to express my gratitude to writer Ken Gire for his excellent work many years ago on our Insight for Living study guide on 1 Peter. I found several of his insights and illustrations helpful as I worked my way through this volume.

Judith Markham has again proven herself invaluable to me as my editor. Her ability to transform my primitive lines and disjointed phrases into understandable sentences and meaningful paragraphs is something to behold! I am especially grateful for her wise and seasoned counsel throughout this process. Without her help this book would have been twice as long and half as interesting.

Although I've already mentioned them in my dedication, I want to repeat my thanks to Wendell Johnston and Charlie Dyer for giving me hope again and again on numerous occasions since I began my work as president of Dallas Theological Seminary back in the summer of 1994. The Dallas heat during that July was enough to wilt the most stouthearted, but there they were right from the start, smiling, serving, and sweating alongside me, giving constant affirmation and providing plenty of wind beneath my wings. Without their whole-hearted commitment and assistance, rather than soaring like an eagle, I would have wandered around those halls like a turkey wondering where to roost. So thank you, men, for your faithful and supportive presence.

Finally, I want to acknowledge the encouragement of my wife, Cynthia, and express my thanks for her unswerving loyalty and compassionate understanding. We have been through a whale of a transition (we're still in it!), but because I haven't had to travel alone, the journey hasn't been nearly as difficult as it could have been. Having her by my side and knowing she is always in my corner and excited about my work has freed me up to finish what I started, regardless of the time and effort required. Thanks to her, I never felt the challenging task of finishing another project this extensive was hopeless.

CHUCK SWINDOLL
DALLAS, TEXAS

The Old Fisherman's Letter

HOPE IS A wonderful gift from God, a source of strength and courage in the face of life's harshest trials.

- When we are trapped in a tunnel of misery, hope points to the light at the end.
- When we are overworked and exhausted, hope gives us fresh energy.
- When we are discouraged, hope lifts our spirits.
- When we are tempted to quit, hope keeps us going.
- When we lose our way and confusion blurs the destination, hope dulls the edge of panic.
- When we struggle with a crippling disease or a lingering illness, hope helps us persevere beyond the pain.
- When we fear the worst, hope brings reminders that God is still in control.
- When we must endure the consequences of bad decisions, hope fuels our recovery.

- When we find ourselves unemployed, hope tells us we still have a future.
- When we are forced to sit back and wait, hope gives us the patience to trust.
- When we feel rejected and abandoned, hope reminds us we're not alone . . . we'll make it.
- When we say our final farewell to someone we love, hope in the life beyond gets us through our grief.

Put simply, when life hurts and dreams fade, nothing helps like hope.

Webster defines hope: "Desire accompanied by expectation of or belief in fulfillment . . . to desire with expectation of obtainment . . . to expect with confidence." How vital is that expectation! Without it, prisoners of war languish and die. Without it, students get discouraged and drop out of school. Without it, athletic teams fall into a slump and continue to lose . . . fledgling writers, longing to be published, run out of determination . . . addicts return to their habits . . . marriage partners decide to divorce . . . inventors, artists, entertainers, entrepreneurs, even preachers, lose their creativity.

Hope isn't merely a nice option that helps us temporarily clear a hurdle. It's essential to our survival.

Realizing the vital role hope plays in life, I decided several years ago to do a serious, in-depth study on the subject. To my surprise, one of the best sources of information was a letter located toward the end of the New Testament that was written by the old fisherman himself, Peter. He should know the subject well, having found himself in great need of hope at a critical moment in his own life—when he failed miserably.

And so . . . here it is, a book for all who sincerely search for ways to hope again . . . when your life hurts and when your dreams fade.

Hope Beyond Failure

The Broken
Man Behind
the Book

THIS IS A BOOK ON HOPE. *Hope*. It is something as important to us as water is to a fish, as vital as electricity is to a light bulb, as essential as air is to a jumbo jet. Hope is that basic to life.

We cannot stay on the road to anticipated dreams without it, at least not very far. Many have tried—none successfully. Without that needed spark of hope, we are doomed to a dark, grim existence.

How often the word "hopeless" appears in suicide notes. And even if it isn't actually written, we can read it between the lines. Take away our hope, and our world is reduced to something between depression and despair.

There once lived a man who loved the sea. Rugged, strong-willed, passionate, and expressive, he did nothing halfheartedly. When it came to fishing, he was determined—and sometimes obnoxious. But he was loyal when it came to friendships . . . loyal to the core, blindly courageous, and overconfident, which occasionally caused him to overstate his commitment. But there he stood, alone if necessary, making promises with his mouth that his body would later be unable to keep.

3

As you probably realize by now, the man's name was Peter, not just one of the Twelve, but the spokesman for the Twelve (whether they liked it or not). Once he decided to follow Christ, there was no turning back. As time passed, he became all the more committed to the Master, a devoted and stubborn-minded disciple whose loyalty knew no bounds.

Ultimately, however, his commitment was put to the test. Jesus had warned him that Satan was hot on his heels, working overtime to trip him up. But Peter was unmoved. His response? "Lord, with You I am ready to go both to prison and to death!" (Luke 22:33). Jesus didn't buy it. He answered, "Peter, the cock will not crow today until you have denied three times that you know Me" (Luke 22:34). Though that prediction must have stung, Peter pushed it aside . . . self-assured and overly confident that it would never happen.

Wrong. That very night, Jesus' words turned to reality. The loyal, strong-hearted, courageous Peter failed his Lord. Deliberately and openly he denied that he was one of the Twelve. Not once or twice but three times, back to back, he turned on the One who had loved him enough to warn him.

The result? Read these words slowly as you imagine the scene.

And the Lord turned and looked at Peter. And Peter remembered the word of the Lord, how He had told him, "Before a cock crows today, you will deny Me three times." And he went out and wept bitterly. (Luke 22:61–62)

No longer loyal and strong, far from courageous and committed, the man was suddenly reduced to heaving sobs. What guilt he bore! How ashamed he felt! Words cannot adequately portray his brokenness. Emotionally, he plunged to rock bottom, caught in the grip of hopelessness; the effect on Peter was shattering. Every time he closed his eyes he could see the face of Jesus staring at him, as if asking, "How could you, Peter? Why would you?" That look. Those words. The man was haunted for days. The Savior's subsequent death by crucifixion must have been like a nail driven into Peter's heart.

The one thing he needed to carry him on was gone . . . gone forever, he thought. *Hope.* Until that glorious resurrection day, the first Easter morn, when we read not only of Jesus' miraculous, bodily resurrection from the dead but also those great words of grace, "Go, tell His disciples and Peter . . . " (Mark 16:7). *And Peter!* The significance of those two words cannot be overstated.

They introduced hope into the old fisherman's life . . . the one essential ingredient without which he could otherwise not recover. Upon hearing of his Savior's resurrection and also his Savior's concern that *he* especially be given the message, Peter had hope beyond his failure. Because of that, he could go on.

And, not surprisingly, he would later be the one who would write the classic letter of hope to those who needed to hear it the most . . . those who were residing "as aliens, scattered" across the vast landscape of the Roman Empire (1 Pet. 1:1).

Between his earlier failure and his writing this letter, Peter had been used of God as the catalyst in the formation of the early church. But having been broken and humiliated, his leadership was altogether different than it would have been without his failure. Now that he had been rescued by grace and restored by hope, he had no interest in playing "king of the mountain" by pushing people around. Rather, he became a servant-hearted shepherd of God's flock.

I like the way Eugene Peterson describes Peter in his introduction to 1 and 2 Peter:

> The way Peter handled himself in that position of power is even more impressive than the power itself. He kept out of the center of attention, he didn't parade his power, because he kept himself under the power of Jesus. He could have easily thrown around his popularity, power, and position to try to take over, using his close association with Jesus to promote himself. But he didn't. Most people with Peter's gifts couldn't have handled it then *or* now, but he did. Peter is a breath of fresh air.[1]

I cannot speak for you, but I certainly can for myself—this is a time when I could use some of Peter's "fresh air" in the form of a big dose of hope! These past two and a half years of my life and ministry have been anything but relaxed and settled. Having left a thriving, flourishing church where I had ministered for almost twenty-three years with a staff many would consider among the best in the country, and having stepped into a whole new arena of challenges—including endless commuting, facing the unknown, and accepting responsibilities outside the realm of my training, background, and expertise—I have found myself more than ever in need of hope. Solid, stable, sure hope. Hope to press on. Hope to endure. Hope to stay focused. Hope to see new dreams fulfilled.

And so it follows naturally that a book with this title has begun to flow from my pen. I trust that you who once smiled with me as we learned to laugh again by working our way through Paul's words to the Philippians are ready to travel with me through Peter's words as we now learn to hope again.

The journey will be worth the effort, I can assure you. We'll find hope around the corner of many of life's contingencies: hope beyond suffering and temptation . . . hope beyond immaturity and bitterness and the realities of our culture . . . hope beyond our trials and beyond times of dissatisfaction, guilt, and shame, to name only a few.

Best of all, we'll be guided on this journey by one who knew hopelessness firsthand, thanks to his own failures . . . and who experienced, firsthand, what it was like to hope again and again and again.

If that sounds like the kind of journey you need to take, read on. It will be a pleasure to travel with you, to be your companion on a road that leads to the healing of hurts and dreams fulfilled.

A Prayer for Hope Beyond Failure

Dear Father, every person reading these words, including the one writing them, has experienced failure. It has left us broken

and disappointed in ourselves. And there are times when a
flashback of those failures returns to haunt us. How sad it
makes us when we recall those moments! Thank You for the
remarkable transformation made possible by forgiveness.
Thank You for understanding that "we are but dust," often
incapable of fulfilling our own promises or living up to our
own expectations.

Renew our hope—hope beyond failure—as we read and
reflect on the words of Peter, with whom we can so easily
identify. Remind us that, just as You used him after he had
failed repeatedly, You will also use us, by Your grace.

May we find fresh encouragement from his words and new
strength from his counsel as we journey together with Peter as
our guide. We look to You for the ability to hope again, for
You, alone, have the power to make something beautiful and
good out of lives littered with the debris of words we should
never have said and deeds we should never have done.

Our only source of relief comes through Your grace. Bring it
to our attention again and again as we discover the truths You
led the old fisherman to write so many years ago. In the
gracious name of Jesus, I ask this.

AMEN

2

Hope Beyond Suffering

How We Can Smile Through Suffering

WE DON'T LOOK ALIKE. We don't act alike. We don't dress alike. We have different tastes in the food we eat, the books we read, the cars we drive, and the music we enjoy. You like opera; I like country. We have dissimilar backgrounds, goals, and motivations. We work at different jobs, and we enjoy different hobbies. You like rock climbing; I like Harleys. We ascribe to a variety of philosophies and differ over politics. We have our own unique convictions on child-rearing and education. Our weights vary. Our heights vary. So does the color of our skin.

But there is one thing we all have in common: We all know what it means to hurt.

Suffering is a universal language. Tears are the same for Jews or Muslims or Christians, for white or black or brown, for children or adults or the elderly. When life hurts and our dreams fade, we may express our anguish in different ways, but each one of us knows the sting of pain and heartache, disease and disaster, trials and sufferings.

Joseph Parker, a great preacher of yesteryear, once said to a group of aspiring young ministers, "Preach to the suffering and you will never lack a congregation. There is a broken heart in every pew."

Truly, suffering is the common thread in all our garments.

This has been true since the beginning, when sin entered the world and Adam and Eve were driven from the Garden. It shouldn't surprise us, therefore, that when the apostle Peter wrote his first letter to fellow believers scattered throughout much of Asia Minor he focused on the one subject that drew all of them together. Suffering. These people were being singed by the same flames of persecution that would take the apostle's life in just a few years. Their circumstances were the bleakest imaginable. Yet Peter didn't try to pump them up with positive thinking. Instead, he gently reached his hand to their chins and lifted their faces skyward—so they could see beyond their circumstances to their celestial calling.

> Peter, an apostle of Jesus Christ, to those who reside as aliens, scattered throughout Pontius, Galatia, Cappadocia, Asia, and Bithynia, who are chosen according to the foreknowledge of God the Father, by the sanctifying work of the Spirit, that you may obey Jesus Christ and be sprinkled with His blood: May grace and peace be yours in fullest measure. (1 Pet. 1:1–2)

The men and women Peter wrote to knew what it was like to be away from home, not by choice but by force. Persecuted for their faith, they had been pushed out into a world that was not only unfamiliar but hostile.

Warren Wiersbe, in a fine little book entitled *Be Hopeful*, says this about the recipients of the letter:

> The important thing for us to know about these "scattered strangers" is that they were going through a time of suffering and persecution. At least fifteen times in this letter, Peter referred to suffering; and he used eight different Greek words to do so. Some of these Christians were suffering because they were living godly lives and doing what was good and right. . . . Others were suffering reproach for the name of Christ . . . and being railed at by unsaved people. . . . Peter wrote to

encourage them to be good witnesses to their persecutors, and to remember that their suffering would lead to glory.[1]

Take another look at the beginning of that last sentence: "Peter wrote to encourage them to be good witnesses to their persecutors." It is so easy to read that. It is even easier to preach it. But it is extremely difficult to do it. If you have ever been mistreated, you know what a great temptation it is to retaliate, to defend yourself, to fight back, to treat the other person as he or she has treated you. Peter wants to encourage his fellow believers to put pain in perspective and find hope beyond their suffering.

While most of us are not afflicted by horrible persecution for our faith, we do know what it means to face various forms of suffering, pain, disappointment, and grief. Fortunately, in the letter of 1 Peter we can find comfort and consolation for our own brand of suffering. Just as this treasured document spoke to the believers scattered in Pontius or Galatia or Cappadocia or Asia, so it speaks to us in Texas and California, Arizona and Oklahoma, Minnesota and Maine.

The first good news Peter gives us is the knowledge that we are "chosen by God." What a helpful reminder! We aren't just thrown on this earth like dice tossed across a table. We are sovereignly and lovingly placed here for a purpose, having been chosen by God. His choosing us was *according to His foreknowledge, by the sanctifying work of the Spirit, that we may obey Jesus Christ, having been sprinkled with His blood.* Powerful words!

God has given us a purpose for our existence, a reason to go on, even though that existence includes tough times. Living through suffering, we become sanctified—in other words, set apart for the glory of God. We gain perspective. We grow deeper. We grow up!

Can you imagine going through such times without Jesus Christ? I can't. But frankly, that's what most people do. They face those frightening fears and sleepless nights in the hospital without Christ. They struggle with a wayward teenager without Christ. Alone, they endure the awful words from a mate, "I don't want to live with you any longer. I want my freedom. I don't love you any more. I'm gone." And they go through it all without Christ.

For souls like these, life is one painful sting after another. Just imagining what life must be like without Christ, I am surprised that more people who live without hope don't take their own lives. As appalled as I am by Jack Kevorkian and his death-on-demand philosophy, I am not surprised. What surprises me is that more people don't simply put an end to it all.

Yet if we will only believe and ask, a full measure of God's grace and peace is available to any of us. By the wonderful, prevailing mercy of God, we can find purpose in the scattering and sadness of our lives. We can not only deal with suffering but rejoice through it. Though our pain and our disappointment and the details of our suffering may differ, there is an abundance of God's grace and peace available to each one of us.

These truths form the skeleton of strong doctrine. But unless the truths are fleshed out they remain hard and bony and difficult to embrace. Knowing this, Peter reminds his readers of all they have to cling to so that they can actually rejoice in times of suffering, drawing on God's grace and peace in fullest measure.

Rejoicing Through Hard Times

As I read and ponder Peter's first letter, I find six reasons why we as believers can rejoice through hard times and experience hope beyond suffering.

We Have a Living Hope

> Blessed be the God and Father of our Lord Jesus Christ, who according to His great mercy has caused us to be born again to a living hope through the resurrection of Jesus Christ from the dead. (1 Pet. 1:3)

As difficult as some pages of our life may be, nothing that occurs to us on this earth falls into the category of "the final chapter." That chapter will not be completed until we arrive in heaven and step into the presence of the living God. Our final meeting is not with the antagonist in our life's story but with the author Himself.

"Who can mind the journey," asks the late, great Bible teacher James M. Gray, "when the road leads home?"

How can we concern ourselves that much over what happens on this temporary planet when we know that it is all leading us to our eternal destination? Peter calls that our "living hope," and he reminds us that it is based on the resurrection of Jesus Christ. If God brought His Son through the most painful trials and back from the pit of death itself, certainly He can bring us through whatever we face in this world, no matter how deep that pit might seem at the time.

Do you realize how scarce hope is to those without Christ? One cynical writer, H. L. Mencken, an American newspaperman during the early half of this century, referred to hope as "a pathological belief in the occurrence of the impossible."

To the unsaved, hope is nothing more than mental fantasy, like wishing upon a star. It's the kind of Disneyland hope that says, "I sure hope I win the lottery." . . . "I hope my boy comes home someday." . . . "I hope everything works out OK." That's not a living hope. That's wishful thinking.

But those who are "born again" in the Lord Jesus Christ have been promised a living hope through His resurrection from the dead.

So if you want to smile through your tears, if you want to rejoice through times of suffering, just keep reminding yourself that, as a Christian, what you're going through isn't the end of the story . . . it's simply the rough journey that leads to the right destination.

"Hope is like an anchor," someone has said. "Our hope in Christ stabilizes us in the storms of life, but unlike an anchor, it does not hold us back."

We Have a Permanent Inheritance

Blessed be the God and Father of our Lord Jesus Christ, who according to His great mercy has caused us . . . to obtain an inheritance which is imperishable and undefiled and will not fade away, reserved in heaven for you. (1 Pet. 1:3–4)

We also can rejoice through suffering because we have a permanent inheritance—a secure home in heaven. And our place there is reserved under the safekeeping, under the constant, omnipotent surveillance of Almighty God. Nothing can destroy it, defile it, diminish it, or displace it. Isn't that a great relief?

Have you ever had the disconcerting experience of finding someone else in the theater or airplane seat you had reserved? You hold the proper ticket, but someone else is in your seat. At best it's awkward; at worst it can lead to an embarrassing confrontation.

Have you ever made guaranteed reservations at your favorite hotel for a "nonsmoking" room and arrived late at night to find they have given it to someone else? What a disappointment! You give them your guaranteed reservation number and they punch endless information into the computer, then they look at you as though you've just landed from Mars. Your heart sinks. You force a smile and ask to speak to the manager. He comes out, stares at the same computer screen, then gives you the same look with a slightly deeper frown. "Sorry," he says. "There must be some kind of mistake."

Well, that's not going to happen in glory! God will not look at you like, "Now, what did you say your name was again?" The living God will ultimately welcome you home to your permanent, reserved inheritance. Your name is on the door.

I don't know what that does to you, but it sure gives me a reason to rejoice. The more difficult life gets on this earth, the better heaven seems.

We Have a Divine Protection

[We] . . . are protected by the power of God, through faith for a salvation ready to be revealed in the last time. (1 Pet. 1:5)

Under heaven's lock and key, we are protected by the most efficient security system available—the power of God. There is no way we will be lost in the process of suffering. No disorder, no disease, not even death itself can weaken or threaten God's ultimate protection over our lives. No matter what the calamity, no matter what the disappointment or depth of pain, no matter what kind of destruction occurs in our bodies at the time of death, our souls are divinely protected.

Our world is filled with warfare, with atrocities, with terrorism. Think of those men and women, especially those precious, innocent children, whose lives were shattered in an instant on that April 1995 morning in Oklahoma City when the world blew up around them. What happens in such times of tragic calamities? Is our eternal inheritance blown away with our bodies? Absolutely not. Even through the most horrible of deaths, He who made us from the dust of the earth protects us by His power and promises to deliver us to our eternal destination.

"God stands between you and all that menaces your hope or threatens your eternal welfare," James Moffatt wrote. "The protection here is entirely and directly the work of God."

Two words will help you cope when you run low on hope: *accept* and *trust*.

Accept the mystery of hardship, suffering, misfortune, or mistreatment. Don't try to understand it or explain it. Accept it. Then, deliberately *trust* God to protect you by His power from this very moment to the dawning of eternity.

We Have a Developing Faith

In this you greatly rejoice, even though now for a little while, if necessary, you have been distressed by various trials, that the proof of your faith, being more precious than gold which is perishable, even though tested by fire, may be found to result in praise and glory and honor at the revelation of Jesus Christ. (1 Pet. 1:6–7)

Here is the first of several references in Peter's letter to rejoicing. The words "even though" indicate that the joy is unconditional. It does not depend on the circumstances surrounding us. And don't overlook the fact that this joy comes *in spite of* our suffering, not because of it, as some who glorify suffering would have us believe. We don't rejoice because times are hard; we rejoice in spite of the fact that they are hard.

These verses also reveal three significant things about trials.

First, trials are often necessary, proving the genuineness of our faith and at the same time teaching us humility. Trials reveal our own helplessness. They put us on our face before God. They make us realistic. Or, as someone has said, "Pain plants the flag of reality in the fortress of a rebel heart." When rebels are smacked by reality, it's amazing how quickly humility replaces rigidity.

Second, trials are distressing, teaching us compassion so that we never make light of another's test or cruelly force others to smile while enduring it.

How unfair to trivialize another person's trial by comparing what he or she is going through with what someone else has endured. Even if you have gone through something you think is twice as difficult, comparison doesn't comfort. It doesn't help the person who has lost a child to hear that you endured the loss of two.

Express your sympathy and weep with them. Put your arm around them. Don't reel off a lot of verses. Don't try to make the hurting person pray with you or sing with you if he or she is not ready to do that. Feel what that person is feeling. Walk quietly and compassionately in his or her shoes.

Third, trials come in various forms. The word *various* comes from an interesting Greek term, *poikolos*, which means "variegated" or "many colored." We also get the term "polka dot" from it. Trials come in a variety of forms and colors. They are different, just as we are different. Something that would hardly affect you might knock the slats out from under me—and vice versa. But God offers special grace to match every shade of sorrow.

Paul had a thorn in the flesh, and he prayed three times for God to remove it. "No," said God, "I'm not taking it away." Finally Paul said, "I've learned to trust in You, Lord. I've learned to live with it." It was then God said, "My grace is sufficient for that thorn." He matched the color of the test with the color of grace.

This variety of trials is like different temperature settings on God's furnace. The settings are adjusted to burn off our dross, to temper us or soften us according to what meets our highest need. It is in God's refining fire that the authenticity of our faith is revealed. And the purpose of these fiery ordeals is that we may come forth as purified gold, a shining likeness of the Lord Jesus Christ Himself. That glinting likeness is what ultimately gives glory and praise and honor to our Savior.

We Have an Unseen Savior

And though you have not seen Him, you love Him, and though you do not see Him now, but believe in Him, you greatly rejoice with joy inexpressible and full of glory. (1 Pet. 1:8)

Keep in mind that the context of this verse is suffering. So we know that Peter is not serving up an inconsequential, theological hors d'oeuvre. He's giving us solid meat we can sink our teeth into. He's telling us that our Savior is standing alongside us in that furnace. He is there even though we can't see Him.

You don't have to see someone to love that person. The blind mother has never seen her children, but she loves them. You don't have to see someone to believe in him or her. Believers today have never seen a physical manifestation of the Savior—we have not visibly seen Him walking among us—but we love Him nevertheless. In times of trial we sense He is there, and that causes us to "greatly rejoice" with inexpressible joy.

Some, like the struggling, reflective disciple Thomas, need to see and touch Jesus in order to believe. But Jesus said, "Blessed are they who did not see, and yet believed" (John 20:29). Even though we can't see Jesus beside us in our trials, He is there—just as He was when Shadrach, Meshach, and Abednego were thrown into the fiery furnace.

We Have a Guaranteed Deliverance

. . . obtaining as the outcome of your faith the salvation of your souls. (1 Pet. 1:9)

How can we rejoice through our pain? How can we have hope beyond our suffering? Because we have a living hope, we have a permanent inheritance, we have divine protection, we have a developing faith, we have an unseen Savior, and we have a guaranteed deliverance.

This isn't the kind of delivery the airlines promise you when you check your bags. ("Guaranteed arrival. No problem.") I'll never forget a trip I took a few years ago. I went to Canada for a conference with plans to be there for eight days. Thanks to the airline, I only had my clothes for the last two! When I finally got my luggage, I noticed the tags on them were all marked "Berlin." ("Guaranteed arrival. No problem." They just don't guarantee when or where the bags will arrive!) That's why we now see so many people boarding airplanes with huge bags hanging from their shoulders and draped over both arms. Don't check your bags, these folks are saying, because they probably won't get there when you do.

But when it comes to spiritual delivery, we never have to worry. God guarantees deliverance of our souls, which includes not only a deliverance from our present sin but the glorification of our physical bodies as well. Rejoice! You're going to get there—guaranteed.

Rejoicing, Not Resentment

When we are suffering, only Christ's perspective can replace our resentment with rejoicing. I've seen it happen in hospital rooms. I've seen it happen in families. I've seen it happen in my own life.

Our whole perspective changes when we catch a glimpse of the purpose of Christ in it all. Take that away, and it's nothing more than a bitter, terrible experience.

Nancy and Ed Huizinga in Grand Rapids, Michigan, know all about this. In December 1995, while they were at church rehearsing for the annual Christmas Festival of Lights program, their home burned to the ground. But that wasn't their only tragedy that year. Just three months earlier, Nancy's long-time friend, Barb Post, a widow with two children, had died of cancer. Nancy and Ed had taken her two children, Jeff and Katie, into their home as part of their family, something they had promised Barb they would do. So when Ed and Nancy's house burned to the ground just before Christmas, it wasn't just their home that was lost; it was the home of two teenagers who had already lost their mother and father.

As circumstances unfolded, irony went to work. The tragedy that forced the Huizingas from their home allowed Jeff and Katie to move back to theirs. Since their home had not yet been sold following their mother's death, they and the Huizinga family moved in there the night after the fire.

On the following Saturday, neighbors organized a party to sift through the ashes and search for anything of value that might have survived. One of the first indications they received of God's involvement in their struggle came as a result of that search. Somehow a piece of paper survived. On it were these words: "Contentment: Realizing that God has already provided everything we need for our present happiness."

To Nancy and Ed, this was like hearing God speak from a burning bush. It was the assurance they needed that He was there . . . and He was not silent.

Nancy's biggest frustration now is dealing with insurance companies and trying to assess their material losses. Many possessions, of course, were irreplaceable personal items such as photographs and things handed down from parents and grandparents. But her highest priority is Jeff and Katie, along with her own two children, Joel and Holly. The loss has been hardest on them, she says.

"They don't have the history of God's faithfulness that Ed and I have. We've had years to make deposits in our 'faith account,' but they haven't. We've learned that if you fail to stock up on faith when you don't need it, you won't have any when you do need it. This has been our opportunity to use what we've been learning."

While the world might view this as a senseless tragedy, deserving of resentment, Nancy and Ed have seen God reveal Himself to them and refine them through this fire as He pours out a full measure of grace and peace.[2]

Suffering comes in many forms and degrees, but His grace is always there to carry us beyond it. I've lived long enough and endured a sufficient number of trials to say without hesitation that only Christ's perspective can replace our resentment with rejoicing. Jesus is the central piece of suffering's puzzle. If we fit Him into place, the rest of the puzzle—no matter how complex and enigmatic—begins to make sense.

Only Christ's salvation can change us from spectators to participants in the unfolding drama of redemption. The scenes will be demanding. Some may be tragic. But only then will we understand the role that suffering plays in our lives. Only then will we be able to tap into hope beyond our suffering.

A Prayer for Hope Beyond Suffering

Lord, mere words about hope and encouragement and purpose can really fall flat if things aren't right in our lives. If we're consumed by rage and resentment, somehow these words seem meaningless. But when our hearts are right, we hear with new ears. Then, rather than resisting these words, we appreciate them, and we love You for them.

Give us grace to match our trials. Give us a sense of hope and purpose beyond our pain. And give us fresh assurance that we're not alone, that Your plan has not been aborted though our suffering intensifies.

Help those of us who are on our feet right now to maintain a compassion for those who aren't. Give us a word of encouragement for others living in a world of hurt.

Let us never forget that every jolt in this rugged journey from earth to heaven is a reminder that we're on the right road.

I ask this in the compassionate name of the Man of Sorrows who was acquainted with grief.

AMEN

3

Hope Beyond Temptation

Staying Clean in a Corrupt Society

WOULDN'T IT BE wonderful if God would save us and then, within a matter of seconds, take us on to glory? Wouldn't that be a great relief? We would never have any temptations. We would never have to battle with the flesh. We would never even have the possibility of messing up our lives. We could just be whisked off to glory—saved, sanctified, galvanized, glorified! Trouble is, I have a sneaking suspicion that many, if not most, would wait until fifteen minutes before takeoff time to give their lives to Christ and then catch the jet for glory.

Since that's not an option and since it's clearly God's preference that we prove ourselves blameless and innocent and above reproach, we obviously have to come up with an alternative route. Some have suggested sanctification by isolation, believing the only way to keep evil and corruption from rubbing off on you is to withdraw from the world. After all, how can you walk through a coal mine without getting dirty? The logic seems irrefutable.

But God, in His infinite wisdom, has deliberately left us on this

27

earth. He has sovereignly chosen to give many of us more years *in* Christ than *out* of Christ—many more years to live for Him "in the midst of a crooked and perverse generation, among whom you appear as lights in the world" (Phil. 2:15). Or, as one of my mentors, the late Ray Stedman, so succinctly put it, "Crooked and perverse simply means we are left in a world of crooks and perverts." That's the kind of world God left us in on purpose.

Don't think for a minute, however, that the Lord has made a mistake leaving us here. We are His lights in a dark world. In fact, just minutes before Jesus' arrest and ultimate death on the cross, He prayed this for His disciples and for us:

> I have given them Thy word; and the world has hated them, because they are not of the world, even as I am not of the world. I do not ask Thee to take them out of the world, but to keep them from the evil one. (John 17:14–15)

Think about that. "I'm not asking You to take them out from among the midst of a crooked and perverse generation," Jesus said. "But I do ask You to guard them, to protect them." Jesus doesn't ask the Father to isolate His disciples from the world but to insulate them, "to keep them from the evil one."

He has left us in the world on purpose and for His purpose. In a world where the majority are going the wrong way, we are left as lights—stoplights, directional lights, illuminating lights—as living examples, as strong testimonies of the right way. We are spiritual salmon swimming upstream.

The Seductive Cosmos Mentality

Few things are more awesome than pictures of earth the astronauts have taken from space. Our big, blue-and-white marble planet stands out so beautifully against the deep darkness of space. However, that's not the "world" Jesus has in mind here. He's not talking about the visible planet named Earth; He's talking about a philosophy that envelopes earthlings. It's not a place but a system—a system that finds its origin in the Enemy himself. It's a figure of speech that encapsulates the mind-set and morality of the unregenerate. It's what John calls the *cosmos*.

> Do not love the world, nor the things in the world. If anyone loves the world, the love of the Father is not in him. For all that is in the world [the *cosmos*], the lust of the flesh and the lust of the eyes and the boastful pride of life, is not from the Father, but is from the world. And the world is passing away, also its lusts; but the one who does the will of God abides forever. (1 John 2:15–17)

The physical world upon which we have our feet planted is visible. It can be measured. It can be felt. It has color and odor and texture. It's tangible . . . obvious. What is not so obvious is the system that permeates and operates within lives on this earth. It is a world-system manipulated by the pervasive hand of Satan and his demons, who pull the strings to achieve the adversary's wicked ends. If we are ever to extricate ourselves from those strings, we must be able to detect them and understand where they lead.

So what is this system? What is its philosophy? What is the frame of reference of the *cosmos*—its thinking, its drives, its goals?

The first thing we need to know is that it is a system that operates apart from and at odds with God. It's designed to appeal to us, to attract us, to seduce us with its sequined garb of fame, fortune, power, and pleasure. God's ways are often uncomfortable, but the world-system is designed to make us comfortable, to give us pleasure, to gain our favor, and ultimately to win our support. The philosophy of the world-system is totally at odds with the philosophy of God.

Greek grammarian Kenneth Wuest wrote:

> *Kosmos* refers to an ordered system . . . of which Satan is the head, his fallen angels and demons are his emissaries, and the unsaved of the human race are his subjects. . . . Much in this world-system is religious, cultured, refined, and intellectual. But it is anti-God and anti-Christ.

. . . This world of unsaved humanity is inspired by "the spirit of the age," . . . which Trench defines as follows: "All that floating mass of thoughts, opinions, maxims, speculations, hopes, impulses, aims, aspirations, at any time current in the world, which it may be impossible to seize and accurately define, but which constitutes a most real and effective power, being the moral, or immoral atmosphere which at every moment of our lives we inhale, again inevitably to exhale."[1]

You want to know what we are inhaling? Pay close attention to the commercials on television and observe what they're advertising and how virtually every word, picture, and sound is designed to pull you in, to make you dissatisfied with what you have and what you look like and who you are. The great goal is to make you want whatever it is that is being sold.

But it's not just on television. The world-system, the cosmos philosophy, is everywhere. It's going on all the time, even when you can't see it, and especially when you're not thinking about it. It's whistling its appeal, "Come on. Come on. You'll love it. This is so much fun. It'll make you look so good. It'll make you feel so good." It motivates us by appealing to our pride and to that which pleases us, all the while cleverly seducing us away from God.

And over all this realm, don't forget, Satan is prince.

A Challenge to Be Different

The pull of the world is every bit as strong and subtle as gravity. So invisible, yet so irresistible. So relentlessly there. Never absent or passive.

Unless we realize how strong and how subtle the world's influence really is, we won't understand the passion behind Peter's words.

Living in Holiness

Therefore, gird your minds for action, keep sober in spirit, fix your hope completely on the grace to be brought to you at the revelation of Jesus Christ. As obedient children, do not be conformed to the former lusts which were yours in your ignorance, but like the Holy One who called you, be holy yourselves also in all your behavior; because it is written, "You shall be holy, for I am holy." (1 Pet. 1:13–16)

Reading these statements, we can't help but catch something of Peter's assertive spirit. He seems to be saying that this is no time to kick back; this isn't a day to be passive. In fact, I think Peter really bears down with his pen at this point. Look at the forcefulness of his phrases: "gird your minds for action" . . . "keep sober" . . . "fix your hope." He spits them out in staccato form. Today we might say, "Straighten up!" . . . "Get serious!" And then the clincher command from God, saying, in essence: "Be holy like I am."

It's easy to let the world intoxicate us and fuzz our minds. But if we're to shake ourselves out of that dizzying spell, we must resist the power it exerts on us.

I think Peter is saying, "You have to realize that even though you're living in the cosmos, your mind, your eyes, *your focus* must be beyond the present." Kenneth Wuest suggests this: "Set your hope perfectly, unchangeably, without doubt and despondency."

That goes back to what we were thinking about in the previous chapter. No matter how bad things get, fix your mind beyond what's happening around you and what's happening to you. Otherwise you'll erode into the cosmos mentality.

I love the way verse 14 begins, "As obedient children. . . ." Isn't that affirming? Rather than coming down on his fellow believers, assuming they're disobedient, Peter assumes just the opposite here. "You're obedient children."

Through the years, my wife, Cynthia, and I found that if we referred to our children as good kids, obedient kids, kids we were proud of, that attitude instilled in them a sense that Mom and Dad had confidence and trust in them. And that's the attitude Peter employs when he tells the believers scattered throughout the ancient world: "As obedient children, do not be conformed." This also reminds me of Paul's words to believers in Romans 12:2: "And do not be conformed to this world, but be transformed. . . ."

How easy it is to allow the world, the cosmos, to suck you into its system. If you do, if you conform, then you are adopting the kind of lifestyle that was yours when you were in ignorance, when you didn't know there was another way to live. That was back when the cosmos was your comfort zone.

Have you been in Christ so long that you have forgotten what it was like to be without Him? Remember, He has called us to follow in His footsteps—to be *holy* "like the Holy One who called you, be holy yourselves also in all your behavior; because it is written, 'YOU SHALL BE HOLY, FOR I AM HOLY.'" We have a Father who is holy, and as His children, we're to be like Him.

But what does it mean to be *holy*? That's always a tough question to answer. Stripped down to its basics, the term *holy* means "set apart" in some special and exclusive way. Perhaps it will help if we think of it in another context. In holy matrimony, for example, a man and a woman are set apart, leaving all others as they bond exclusively to each other.

When I was a young man and a young husband serving in the marines, I was eight thousand miles away from my wife. I knew Cynthia existed. I could read her letters and occasionally hear her voice on the phone, but I couldn't see her or touch her. I had only the memory of our standing together three years earlier before God and a minister who had pronounced us husband and wife, setting us apart exclusively to each other for the rest of our lives. We were wed back in June 1955, but regardless of how long ago it was, we stood together and committed ourselves to a *holy* intermingling of our lives. To be intimate with another woman would break that holy relationship, that exclusive oneness. Remembering that helped keep me faithful to my wife while we were apart those many months . . . and it still helps over forty-one years later!

Church ordinances or sacraments, such as baptism and communion, are often called *holy*. In Holy Communion, for example, the bread and wine are set apart from common use and set aside to God alone. The same meaning lies behind the word *sanctify* in 1 Peter 3:15: "But sanctify Christ as Lord in your hearts." I love that. We are to "set Him apart" as Lord in our hearts.

What a successful way to deal with the cosmos! To begin the morning by saying, "Lord, I set apart my mind for You today. I set apart my passion. I set apart my eyes. I set apart my ears. I set apart my motives. I set apart my discipline. Today I set apart every limb of my body and each area of my life unto You as Lord over my life." When we start our day like that, chances are good that temptation's winks will not be nearly as alluring.

Walking in Fear

And if you address as Father the One who impartially judges according to each man's work, conduct yourselves in fear during the time of your stay upon earth. (1 Pet. 1:17)

Another secret of living a godly life in the midst of a godless world involves the way we conduct ourselves hour by hour through the day. Peter says we are to do it "in *fear*." We don't hear much about the *fear* of God today, and when we do, some may think only of images of a fire-and-brimstone preacher pounding a pulpit. We need a better perspective. Perhaps the word *reverence* gives us a clearer picture of what Peter means here. In fact, the New International Version translates this phrase "live your lives as strangers here in reverent fear." The point is, if we're going to address God as Father, then we should conduct ourselves on earth in a way that reflects our reverence for Him as our Father.

Also, if you're going to address Him as your Father, if you're going to have a one-on-one relationship with Him in fellowship and in prayer, then conduct yourself as one who knows that you will someday have to account to Him for your life. Why? Well, in case you didn't know, "each one of us shall give account of himself to God" (Rom. 14:12).

When we die, we will be brought before the judgment seat of Christ where we will independently account for our lives before God. He will see us as our lives pass in review, and He will reward us accordingly. It's not a judgment to see if we get into heaven. That's taken care of. As we saw in the previous chapter, we can't lose our salvation. We can, however, lose our reward. At the judgment seat, Christ will judge our works and determine whether they were done in the power of the Spirit or in the energy of the flesh. We will all give an account of the deeds we have done in this life, and God will "test the quality of each man's work" (1 Cor. 3:13). That thought, alone, will instill a big, healthy dose of the fear of God in us!

We don't know how God is going to do this, but it helps me to put it into an everyday image we can understand. So I picture myself in the future standing there all alone before my heavenly Father. Along comes an enormous celestial dump truck, piled high with stuff. The truck backs up, the bed lifts up, and the whole load is dumped out in front me. The Lord and I talk about all the wood, hay, and stubble that's piled there, and then He begins digging through it. "Oh, there's a piece of gold," He says. "Hmm, here's some silver." With that He begins setting aside all the precious and permanent stuff. Then, *whoosh!* The wood, hay, and stubble are gone, instantly consumed by fire. Only the gold, silver, and precious stones that remain are rewarded.

In the 1988 Summer Olympics in Seoul, South Korea, Ben Johnson of Canada won the one-hundred-meter dash, setting a new Olympic record and a new world record. Our American contender, Carl Lewis, came in second, and most were shocked that he hadn't won the gold. After the race, the judges learned that Johnson had had an illegal substance in his body. He ran the race illegally, so the judges took away his medal. Though he ran faster and made an unforgettable impression, he did not deserve the reward.

Though the world and even our fellow Christians may be impressed with and applaud our deeds, let's not forget that God is the final judge! He searches our hearts; He alone knows our motivation. And He will be the One to say, "This deserves a reward. Ah, but that does not."

That's why we conduct ourselves in fear. That's why we walk in reverence. Because we know that He is checking for illegal substances. He knows whether down deep inside we have gotten sucked into the cosmos, whether we have bought into the system. He knows whether our noble acts and deeds are done out of pride and self-aggrandizement or whether they have been carried out in the power of the Spirit. He knows whether our inner, unseen thoughts and motives match our external words and works. He is pleased when our lives honor Him—inside and out. He is grieved when they do not. And it is *His* smile we want. It is *His* reward, not the reward of this world, not the applause of those around us, not the superficial spotlight of fame or fortune or power.

This Christian life is a tough fight. Earlier in this century, Donald Grey Barnhouse, a well-known minister and radio preacher, wrote an entire book on this subject, *The Invisible War*. This conflict is not a war fought with Uzis or tanks or smart bombs or ground-to-air missiles. The land mines, ambushes, and traps set by our enemy are much more subtle than that—and even more deadly, for they aim at the soul. And they are everywhere.

But with the pride and pleasures of the cosmos so alluring, how can weaklings like us run the race without being disqualified and forfeiting our reward? How can we win the battle over an enemy we can't see? The solution to that problem rests within our minds.

Focusing Your Mind

. . . knowing that you were not redeemed with perishable things like silver or gold from your futile way of life inherited from your forefathers, but with precious blood, as of a lamb unblemished and spotless, the blood of Christ. For He was foreknown before the foundation of the world, but has appeared in these last times for the sake of you who through Him are believers in God, who raised Him from the dead and gave Him glory, so that your faith and hope are in God. (1 Pet. 1:18–20)

I'm convinced that the battle with this world is a battle within the mind. Our minds are major targets of the Enemy's appeal. When the world pulls back its bowstring, our minds are the bull's-eyes. Any arrows we allow to become impaled in our minds will ultimately poison our thoughts. And if we tolerate this long enough, we'll end up acting out what we think. So the third technique for counteracting that poison, for dealing with the seduction of the cosmos, the world around us, is to focus our minds on Christ. We can do this by remembering what our Savior has done for us. Or, to paraphrase 1 Peter, "remember what your inheritance cost your Savior."

The first thing Christ did for us was to deliver us from slavery—slavery to a "futile way of life." Whether we knew it or not, we were trapped in a lifestyle that had only empty pleasures and dead-end desires to offer. We were in bondage to our impulses spawned from our sinful nature. In such a condition, we were hopelessly unable to help ourselves. The only way for us to be emancipated from that slavery was to have someone redeem us. That ransom price was paid by Christ, not with gold or silver, but with His precious blood. In doing so, He broke the chains that bound us to this world. He opened the door and said, "Now you're free to live for Me and serve Me." That single emancipation proclamation made possible a life of hope beyond temptation.

The second thing Christ did for us was to come near and make Himself known; He "appeared in these last times for the sake of you who through Him are believers in God . . . so that your faith and hope are in God" (vv. 20–21). That makes the whole thing personal, doesn't it? He realized the enormity of our earth-born emptiness. He knew our inability to free ourselves. And He willingly stepped out of His privileged position in heaven to pay the ransom . . . for us! He gave Himself, not only so we could become free, but so we could be secure, with our faith and hope resting not precariously on our own shoulders but securely on His.

What is life like without Christ? Look at 1 Peter 4:3–4.

> For the time already past is sufficient for you to have carried out the desire of the Gentiles, having pursued a course of sensuality, lusts, drunkenness, carousels, drinking parties and abominable idolatries. And in all this, they are surprised that you do not run with them into the same excess of dissipation, and they malign you.

That's a pretty vivid description of the futile lifestyle of the lost. That's what we see around us every day—a lifestyle promising to satisfy, to bring happiness and pleasure and contentment. Yet it brings just the opposite. This lifestyle leads only to another hangover or another bout with guilt—if there is even enough conscience left for guilt. It's one "happy hour" (strange name!) after another. One high after another. One snort after another. One drug after another. One affair after another. One abortion after another. One partner after another. It's life lived for the highs, which are nothing more than temporary breaks in the lows. It's empty. It's hollow. It's miserable. It's exactly as Peter describes it: a "futile way of life."

And we've been redeemed from that, not with silver or gold, "but with precious blood, as of a lamb unblemished and spotless, the blood of Christ."

Techniques to Remember

When we're in the comfortable conclave of Christian fellowship, it's relatively easy to be holy, to conduct our lives in the fear of God, and to focus our minds on the Savior (at least externally). But when we're out in the world, when we're in the minority, it's different, isn't it?

If you want to stay clean, even when you're walking alone in the dark, low-ceilinged coal mine of the corrupt and secular culture, you need to remember a few practical things—four come to mind.

First, pay close attention to what you look at. This takes us back to verse 13, where we are told to gird our minds for action, keep sober in spirit, and fix our hope completely on the grace that's revealed in Jesus Christ.

Our eyes seem to be the closest connection to our minds. Through our eyes we bring in information and visual images. Through our eyes we feed our imaginations. Through our eyes we focus on things that are alluring and attractive and, don't kid yourself, extremely pleasurable for a while . . . *for a while.* Remember, the Bible says that Moses, by faith, gave up the "passing pleasures of sin" to walk with the people of God (Heb. 11:24–26). The cosmos offers pleasures, no doubt about it, but they are passing. . . .

If then you have been raised up with Christ, keep seeking the things above, where Christ is, seated at the right hand of God. Set your mind on things above, not on the things that are on earth. (Col. 3:1–2)

Second, give greater thought to the consequences of sin rather than to its pleasures. One of the characteristics of the cosmos is that nobody ever mentions the ugly underside of pleasurable sins. If you're thinking about having an affair, if you are getting caught in that lustful trap, I strongly suggest that you walk through the consequences in your mind. Stroll slowly . . . ponder details. Think through the effects of that act in your life and in the lives of others whom your life touches.

In a *Leadership* magazine article titled "Consequences of a Moral Tumble," Randy Alcorn says that whenever he is feeling "particularly vulnerable to sexual temptation," he finds it helpful to review the effects such action could have. Some of things he mentions are:

- Grieving the Lord who redeemed me. . . .
- One day having to look Jesus . . . in the face and give an account of my actions. . . .
- Inflicting untold hurt on . . . your best friend and loyal wife. . . . losing [her] respect and trust.
- Hurting my beloved daughters. . . .
- Destroying my example and credibility with my children, and nullifying both present and future efforts to teach them to obey God. . . .
- Causing shame to my family. . . .
- Creating a form of guilt awfully hard to shake. Even though God would forgive me, would I forgive myself?
- Forming memories and flashbacks that could plague future intimacy with my wife.
- Wasting years of ministry training and experience for a long time, maybe permanently. . . .

- Undermining the faithful example and hard work of other Christians in our community.

- Bringing great pleasure to Satan, the enemy of God and all that is good. . . .

- Possibly bearing the physical consequences of such diseases as gonorrhea, syphilis, chlamydia, herpes, and AIDS; perhaps infecting [my wife] or, in the case of AIDS, even causing her death.

- Possibly causing pregnancy, with the personal and financial implications, including a lifelong reminder of my sin. . . .

- Causing shame and hurt to my friends, especially those I've led to Christ and discipled.[2]

And that's just a partial list of the consequences! It doesn't even begin to factor in the consequences for the other person in the affair and the number of people affected by his or her sin.

Take a realistic look at the other side of a moral tumble. For a change, force yourself to give greater thought to the painful consequences than to the passing pleasures of sin.

Third, begin each day by renewing your sense of reverence for God. Start each new day by talking to the Lord, even if that early-morning talk has to be brief.

"Lord, I'm here. I'm Yours. I want You to know that I'm Yours. Also I want to affirm that I reverence You. I give You my day. I will encounter strong seductive forces that will allure me. Since I am frail and fragile, I really need Your help."

If you know of some challenges you'll be facing that day, rehearse the areas of need. If you know a real test is coming, talk to the Lord about it. Then trade off with Him. Hand over your fragility and receive His strength in return. Reverence Him as the source of your power.

Fourth, periodically during each day focus fully on Christ. In his book *Spiritual Stamina*, Stuart Briscoe cites a good example of this:

It's fun watching young men in love. It can be even more fun when the romance is long distance.

You can predict what will happen. There'll be hours of late-night, heart-pounding telephone conversations. The postal service will be overrun with love notes crossing each other in the mail. Pillows will be soaked with tears.

But the most telling symptom is the glazed, faraway look in Romeo's eyes. I'm sure you've seen it. You ask the man a question and you get a blank stare. He's not at home. He's elsewhere. He's in another land. He's with his sweetheart.

You might say his heart is set on things afar, where Juliet is seated right by the telephone.[3]

That's being focused fully on another person. I challenge you to do this with your Lord. Deliberately set aside a few minutes every day when your eyes glaze over, when you don't realize where you are, when a telephone ring means nothing because you are focusing fully on Christ. Imagine Him as he walks with His disciples, touching those who were sick, praying for them in John 17, going to the cross, sitting with His disciples at the seashore and having broiled fish for breakfast. Then imagine Him as He is thinking about you, praying for you, standing with you, living in you.

These four techniques will help you stay clean in a corrupt society—to be in the world but not of it.

A Prayer for Hope Beyond Temptation

Thank You, Father, for Your truth preserved through the centuries. Thank You for the careful concern of a man like Peter who knew both sides of life on planet Earth: what it was to live in this old world and what it was to walk with the Savior, Your Son.

Lord, since You don't save us then suddenly take us home to glory, hear our prayer this day as we ask You to bring to our attention those things that will assist us in staying clean in a corrupt world. Give us an intense distaste for things that displease You and a renewed pleasure in things that bring You honor and magnify Your truth. As You do this, we will have what we need so much, hope beyond temptation.

I ask this for the honor of Him who consistently and victoriously withstood the blast of the Devil's temptations without relief, Jesus our Lord.

AMEN

4

Hope Beyond Division

Reasons for
Pulling Together

BEFORE ANDREW JACKSON became the seventh president of the United States, he served as a major general in the Tennessee militia. During the War of 1812 his troops reached an all-time low in morale. As a result they began arguing, bickering, and fighting among themselves. It is reported that Old Hickory called them all together on one occasion when tensions were at their worst and said, "Gentlemen! Let's remember, the enemy is over *there!*"

His sobering reminder would be an appropriate word for the church today. In fact, I wonder if Christ sometimes looks down at us and says with a sigh, "Christians, your Enemy is over there! Stop your infighting! Pull for one another. Support one another. Believe in one another. Care for one another. Pray for one another. Love one another."

One of the most profound comments made regarding the early church came from the lips of a man named Aristides, sent by the Emperor Hadrian to spy out those strange creatures known as "Christians." Having seen them in action, Aristides returned with a mixed report. But his immortal words to the emperor have echoed down through history: "Behold! How they love one another."

How often do we hear such words today from those who don't know Christ but who have watched those of us who do? I'm inclined to think that it's much more likely that they say, "Behold! How they hurt one another!" . . . "Behold! How they judge one another!" . . . "Behold! How they criticize one another!" . . . "Behold! How they fight with one another!"

This is the generation that has given new meaning to the shameful practice of brother-bashing and sister-smashing. You would think we were enemies rather than members of the same family. Something is wrong with this picture.

The mark of the Christian should be a spirit of unity and genuine love for others, but the church today rarely demonstrates those qualities. We are looked on by the world as self-seeking and factious rather than loving and unified. You question that? Just step into a Christian bookstore and scan the shelves. What impression do you get? Do the books reflect love and unity within the body of Christ? Or do they reflect polarization, criticism, and judgment of one another? Better yet, sit back and observe what's going on in your own church. Are you overwhelmed with the love and unity that exudes from your local body of believers? Or are you saddened and disappointed by the political power plays and petty disagreements that block our ability to get along with one another?

Unity: An Almost Forgotten Virtue

To underscore this important quality, let's consider Jesus' words in John 13, where we find Him with His twelve disciples for the last time. They have met together for a meal in a second-floor room in the city of Jerusalem. Jesus notices that the men have come into the room with dirty feet—not surprising in that rocky, dusty land. What must have been disappointing was that none of the Twelve had voluntarily washed the others' feet. So during supper Jesus arose from the table and poured water into a basin and proceeded to go around the table and wash the disciples' feet.

What a scene it must have been! To this day, I shake my head when I imagine the Savior washing the dirty feet of His disciples.

> And so when He had washed their feet, and taken His garments, and reclined at the table again, He said to them, "Do you know what I have done to you?" (John 13:12)

Understand, He wasn't fishing for the obvious answer, "You've washed our feet, Master." He was looking for the answer He has to explain to them a few moments later:

> You call Me Teacher and Lord; and you are right, for so I am. If I then, the Lord and the Teacher, washed your feet, you also ought to wash one another's feet. For I gave you an example that you also should do as I did to you. (John 13:13–15)

I think most of Jesus' disciples would have gladly returned the favor and washed *His* feet. Peter out of embarrassment. John out of devotion. That would be easy to do. After all, they loved Him. Why wouldn't they take an opportunity to wash His feet—if only to make a good impression? But that is not what Jesus told them to do. Instead He said, *"Wash one another's feet."*

Then, a bit later, in their final hours together, He changed the subject from washing feet to showing love.

> A new commandment I give to you, that you love one another, even as I have loved you, that you also love one another. By this all men will know that you are My disciples, if you have love for one another. (John 13:34–35)

It's easy to love Christ for all He is, for all He's done. It's not so easy, however, to love other Christians. Yet that is the command we have been given. That compelling mark of the Christian will be a powerful witness to non-Christians. It has nothing to do with talking to the lost about their spiritual condition. It has everything to do with how we treat one another. If you want to make an impact on the world around you, this rugged society that is moving in the wrong direction more rapidly every year, He said, "love one another." That's how they'll know that you're different. Your love will speak with stunning eloquence to a lost world.

Then, as the oil lamps flickered away the last hour before His arrest and trial, Jesus prayed to the Father on behalf of His disciples.

I do not ask in behalf of these alone [the disciples], but for those also who believe in Me through their word [that's you and me]; *that they may all be one*; even as Thou, Father, art in Me, and I in Thee, that they also may be in Us; that the world may believe that Thou didst send Me. And the glory which Thou hast given Me I have given to them; that they may be one, just as We are one; I in them, and Thou in Me, that they may be perfected in unity, that the world may know that Thou didst send Me, and didst love them, even as Thou didst love Me. (John 17:20–23, italics mine)

Look at that! Believe it or not, He was praying for us during those final hours. He was praying that you and I might make an impact on the world because of our unity with Him and with each other.

The margin notes of the New American Standard Bible gives this literal translation: "That they may be perfected *into a unit*." A unit is a team, folks. No more brother-bashing. No more sister-smashing. No more ugly gossip groups. No more sarcastic, judgmental put-downs. Jesus prayed that we would support and encourage and love and forgive each other until we are perfected into a unit.

Unity. That's what He desires for us. Not uniformity, but unity; oneness, not sameness. We don't have to look alike. We don't even have to think alike. The body is made up of many different parts. He doesn't even pray for unanimity. We can disagree. Every vote doesn't have to be 100 percent. But we must be a unit: our eyes on the same goal, our hearts in the same place, our commitment at the same level. And we must love each other.

If there is anything that would keep me away from Christ these days, if I were lost, it would be the attitude Christians have toward one another. That would do it. While there is much wonderful fellowship in the church where the fire of friendship warms and affirms us, there are still too many places where for the life of me I don't know how people stay in ministry. The conditions in which some men and women labor are occasionally beyond belief.

Paul wrote to the Philippians:

Do nothing from selfishness or empty conceit, but with humility of mind let each of you regard one another as more important than himself; do not merely look out for your own personal interests, but also for the interests of others. (Phil. 2:3–4)

Selfishness and conceit and pride are the things that break down our fellowship and erode our unity. Everything you need to know about getting along well in a family, to say nothing of getting along well in a church, is right here in these verses.

If you're on a church board and you're wondering what's going wrong, what's missing, what's happened to the unity you once had, I'll guarantee somebody isn't abiding by these verses.

You want to pull together as the family of God? It's merely a matter of obeying Philippians 2:3–4. Stop looking for credit. Stop looking for what you can get out of it. Think about the other person instead of yourself. Don't be selfish. Sounds like something a teacher would say to a roomful of kindergartners, doesn't it? Yet how many adult problems could be solved if the elementary truths woven into these two verses were the driving force in our relationships with one another? How many committees could resolve their disputes? How many couples could reconcile their marital differences?

Love: A Never-to-Be-Forgotten Command

With the teachings of Christ and Paul as a backdrop, we are better able to understand and appreciate Peter's comments about love and unity. Remember, he was writing to hurting people. They were scattered, many of them far from home (see 1 Pet. 1:1). They were "distressed," living in extreme situations (1:6). They were being "tested" by "various trials" (1:6–7). Some of them were running for their lives. With the madman Nero on the throne in Rome, it was a dangerous time to be a Christian. Some, no doubt, were tempted to conform, compromise, or give up altogether.

When I was a kid and an argument broke out in our home, my dad always used to say, "We may have a few differences inside these walls, but just remember, we're family. If your brother or your sister needs you, you take care of 'em. You love 'em. You pull for 'em." Good advice for the church as well!

When people hurt—and we've all been there—it's easy to get a little thin on love. But that's what these people needed. They needed to pull together and support each other. They needed a community where they could find acceptance and unity. They needed to conduct themselves as members of the family of God.

Following his strong words encouraging fellow believers to live holy lives, Peter gives them a pep talk, explaining exactly how they have been freed to support each other. He says, in effect, "You have everything you need that makes it possible; you don't have to live in lonely isolation." Read his counsel carefully:

> Since you have in obedience to the truth purified your souls for a sincere love of the brethren, fervently love one another from the heart, for you have been born again not of seed which is perishable but imperishable, that is, through the living and abiding word of God. (1 Pet. 1:22–23)

As we read Peter's uplifting words, we see that he specifies three things that encourage mutual support. First, obedience to the truth. Second, purity of soul. Third, a lack of hypocrisy.

Being obedient to the truth means that we don't have to look at others through the distorted lenses of our own biases. We can see them as God sees them and love them as He loves them. This has a purifying effect on us. It purges us, not only from a limited perspective, but from prejudice, resentment, hurt feelings, and grudges. Such purity of soul helps us love each other without hypocrisy and with a sincere love. It doesn't blind us to each other's faults; it gives us the grace to overlook them.

The glue—the bonding element—that holds all this together is love: "Fervently love one another from the heart." Peter writes with a strong, emotional, passionate commitment that is difficult to pick up on in the English.

Two Greek words are used predominantly in the New Testament to describe love, and Peter uses both of them here. One is *philos*, which generally refers to a brotherly love or the love of a friend. That is the word he uses for "love of the brethren." The other is *agape*, a higher form of love, a more divine type of love, which is the word he uses for "love one another." Peter then intensifies both with passionate modifiers: "sincere," "fervently," and "from the heart."

> These Christians to whom Peter was writing already had a fondness and an affection for one another. . . . But if these Christians would blend the two kinds of love, saturate the human fondness and affection with the divine love with which they are exhorted to love one another, then that human affection would be transformed and elevated to a heavenly thing. Then the fellowship of saint with saint would be a heavenly fellowship, glorifying to the Lord Jesus, and most blessed in its results to themselves. There is plenty of the *phile* fondness and affection among the saints, and too little of the *agape* divine love.[1]

Maybe it's time to pause and take a look inside your own heart. Are you "fervently loving one another from the heart"? When I am snippy or negative, judgmental or ugly toward a brother or a sister, I look at myself with honesty, shining God's light of truth on my own attitude, and I invariably find that it's my heart that's not right. The old spiritual hymn says it well:

> It's not my brother nor my sister
> but it's me, O Lord,

Standin' in the need of prayer.
It's not the preacher nor the deacon
but it's me, O Lord,
Standin' in the need of prayer.

Support: Four Much-Needed Reminders

What kind of love and support do we need? What kind of love and support do we give? What about a "love one another" support group, in which we offer—and receive from—our brothers and sisters in the family of God this same kind of love and lack of judgmental spirit, this true affection, this arm around your shoulder, saying, "I'm in your corner"?

Many churches have support groups of various kinds in which individuals are actively involved in each other's lives. Through the years I've talked with lots of individuals who say they couldn't survive without such support groups.

Some are struggling through the backwash of a divorce, trying to gain self-respect and a sense of dignity again. Aided by the support of others who are going through, or have gone through, the same turmoil, they work through their feelings of rejection, sadness, and loneliness . . . then emerge stronger and more stable.

Some attend support groups because they are in the grip of an awful addiction. Right now they're clean or dry, but they realize they're just a day away, just an hour away, from the same old habit. The support of others keeps them strong and helps them hope again.

Most of these groups are not highly visible, but they're there for those who need them, week in and week out. With consistent regularity people keep coming because they find refuge in this safe and supportive harbor. They find love, acceptance, and a lack of judgmental spirit. They find tolerance and accountability. They find care and encouragement—and a word of affirmation from a sincere heart and an arm of support around the shoulder mean more than a thousand words from some frowning preacher.

What is it about the family of God that gives us this sense of oneness and support? Since we don't have to look alike and we don't all have the same temperament and we don't all vote the same way at election time, what is it that draws believers together?

We Are Children of the Same Father

For you have been born again not of seed which is perishable but imperishable, that is, through the living and abiding word of God. (1 Pet. 1:23)

In the human family, there are various kinds of birth experiences. But in God's family, everybody begins the same way. We are all adopted. We all have the same Father. We all come to Him the same way—through His Son, Jesus Christ. We are all members of the same family. Our background, our education, our social connections, our job, or how much money we have in the bank—all these things are irrelevant. We've all been born anew. We're all brothers and sisters in the Lord.

We Take Our Instruction from the Same Source

Not of seed which is perishable but imperishable, that is, through the living and abiding word of God. For,
"All flesh is like grass,
And all its glory like the flower of grass.
The grass withers,
And the flower falls off,
But the word of the Lord abides forever."
And this is the word which was preached to you. (1 Pet. 1:23b–25)

The seed is the Word of God, our reliable source of truth, and we all get our instruction from this source. But for that seed to grow and produce fruit in our lives, it must be embraced and applied.

There's nothing automatic about being exposed to the same source of truth. We may all hear the same Sunday morning message, but unless our ears are attentive and our hearts prepared, that seed will be picked up in Satan's beak and winged right out of our lives. You can sit and listen to truth being delivered, and it can change your life in a moment's time. Yet someone sitting right next to you, hearing the same insightful information, can go right on living against the will of God.

We have a responsibility, not only to hear the truth, but to apply it. Just being exposed to the truth will not change us. You can put me in a room with a dozen beautiful Steinway pianos and leave me there for hours, but I still won't be able to sit down and play. You could put an accomplished pianist at every one and expose me to hours of exquisite music, but even in that stimulating environment I wouldn't be able to sit down and play. Bringing beautiful music from those black-and-white keys takes work—commitment, dedication, private lessons, and untold hours of practice.

We Have the Same Struggles

> Therefore, putting aside all malice and all guile and hypocrisy and envy and all slander. . . . (1 Pet. 2:1)

In case you've ever wondered what breaks down the fellowship, what keeps us from pulling together, there's your list. Read each one slowly and form pictures in your mind: malice, guile, hypocrisy, envy, and slander. In weaker moments we fall back on them, but God says, "put them aside"—get rid of them. If you want to move beyond your divisions, beyond your differences, if you want to become one in the Lord, lose them. And, by His grace, let them go!

Let's return to this list and probe a little deeper.

Malice. The Greek word here is a general word for the wickedness that characterizes unbelievers entrenched in the world system. These are the sins that hurt and injure others.

Guile. The Greek word means two-facedness, deception, or trickery. In its earliest form, this word meant "to catch with bait." It refers to a deception that is aimed at attaining one's own end—a hidden agenda.

Hypocrisy. The Greek word here means to act a part, to hide behind a mask, to appear to be someone else. This is what happens when we try to be someone or something we are not.

Some family members have a tendency to be envious of those who are going through "good times." Others have a tendency to slander those who are going through a bad patch. The next two sins are kind of the flip side of each other, and we are told to put both aside.

Envy is not only hidden resentment over another's advantage, but wanting that same advantage for yourself. According to Webster, it is "painful or resentful awareness of an advantage enjoyed by another joined with a desire to possess the same advantage." In other words, someone has something you don't have and you long to have it yourself. Edward Gordon Selwyn comments on the Greek term, saying that this sin is "a constant plague of all voluntary organizations, not least religious organizations, and to which even the Twelve themselves were subject at the very crisis of our Lord's ministry."[2]

Slander is even more vicious. Literally the word means "evil speaking." It occurs most often when the victim is not there to offer a defense or set the record straight. Often disguised as rumor or bad news or just passing on information, slander is disparaging gossip that destroys one's confidence in another, discoloring or harming that person's reputation. It can be as mild as bad-mouthing or as vile as backstabbing. When the tongue is used for slander, it becomes a lethal weapon.

Peter commands us to "strip off" these five outdated garments that once belonged to our old natures! If all of us in God's family were mutually committed to such behavior, can you imagine the pleasure we could enjoy together? But it'll never happen until we "strip off" the old garments that keep us carnal.

We Focus on the Same Objectives

Like newborn babes, long for the pure milk of the word, that by it you may grow in respect to salvation, if you have tasted the kindness of the Lord. (1 Pet. 2:2–3)

What is the objective of all this? Maturity. "Grow up," Peter says. And our model? The Lord Himself.

For three and a half years Peter followed Jesus everywhere He went. Why? Because he had "tasted the kindness of the Lord."

Nourished by that kindness, Peter grew toward greater maturity, and so can we!

What do people think of after they have had a conversation or a meal with you? What do they think after they have worked alongside you? Do they think, "How kind he is. What a kind person she is"? Selflessly giving ourselves to one another is the key to unity. Our relationships with others are to be built upon the example of the selflessness Christ first demonstrated.

It's so basic, isn't it? It reminds me of Robert Fulghum's *All I Really Need to Know I Learned in Kindergarten*, which I read when it originated as an article in the *Kansas City Times*. In it he said, "Share everything. Play fair. Don't hit people. Put things back where you found them. Clean up your own mess. Don't take things that aren't yours. Say you're sorry when you hurt somebody. . . . And it is still true, no matter how old you are: When you go out into the world, it is best to hold hands and stick together."

Come on, let's pull together. Let's support each other. In doing so, remember Paul's closing words in Ephesians 4. I like the way Eugene Peterson paraphrases that final verse:

> Make a clean break with all cutting, backbiting, profane talk. Be gentle with one another, sensitive. Forgive one another as quickly and thoroughly as God in Christ forgave you. (Eph. 4:31 MSG)

Think of somebody in the family of God—just one person you know—who could really use a word of support. Then give it! Don't wait . . . give it this week. Don't just think about it or write it in your journal. Do it. *Do it today.*

Pray for that individual you were thinking about a moment ago. Ask God to give you just the right word, just the right method of approaching that person. Maybe you need to write a note. Maybe you need to make a phone call. Maybe you need to take the person out for a cup of coffee or invite him or her over for a meal. Who knows? Your action could be the catalyst that causes that individual to gain hope beyond division.

Remember, "The enemy is over *there!*" Behold! How we need to love one another!

A Prayer for Hope Beyond Division

Forgive us, oh, forgive us, our Father, for the hours we have spent in the wasteland of malice and guile, hypocrisy and envy and slander. What grimy garments we've worn! Show us the joy of kindness, the long-lasting benefits of unity, grace, and support. Remind us that it all begins with genuine love prompted by forgiveness. Start a work within us so that our love flows from a pure heart, not from a desire to win friends or impress people.

Most of all, Lord, make us like Your Son. Kind. Meek. Humble. Gracious. May we grow up into His kindness, may we model His meekness, may we walk with His humility. May we reflect His grace so that others gain new hope. What we're really asking is that You help us grow up!

We're so glad to be in Your family, so grateful for Your forgiveness. Use us this week, perhaps even today, to help someone else feel grateful that he or she, too, is a part of this family. Through Christ, who prayed for our unity.

AMEN

5

Hope Beyond Guilt

Becoming
Living
Stones

FOR SOME STRANGE REASON, those of us who have known the Lord since we were young have a tendency to outgrow a close friendship with Him. When we were children, we felt free and open with our heavenly Father. But when we became adults, we seemed to take a few giant steps backward in that relationship.

When we were young, we talked to Him freely. With a child's faith, knowing He loved us, we trusted Him with the details of our life. Nothing was too small and, for sure, nothing was too big to ask of Him. In unguarded innocence, we prayed for *anything*!

The ease with which we once approached God can be seen in the letters written to Him by children. See if the ones below don't take you back to a time of innocence and openness in your own relationship with Him.

Dear Lord,
    Thank you for the nice day today. You even fooled the TV weatherman.
                                        Hank (age 7)

Dear Lord,
   Do you ever get mad?
   My mother gets mad all the time but she is only human.
                                        Yours truly,
                                        David (age 8)

Dear Lord,
   I need a raise in my allowance. Could you have one of your angels
tell my father?
                                        Thank you.
                                        David (age 7)[1]

Dear God,
   Charles my cat got run over. And if you made it happen you have to
tell me why.
                                        Harvey

Dear God,
   Can you guess what is the biggest river of all of them? The Amazon.
You ought to be able to because you made it. Ha, ha.
                                        Guess who[2]

Wouldn't it be interesting to compile an assortment of adult letters to God? Undoubtedly the childhood innocence would be lost as
well as the candor and ease of approach. The words would be more
guarded. We would be sophisticated. Fear and feelings of worthless-
ness would underscore the halting sentences. Shame, guilt, and regret would punctuate the paragraphs. We have lost much, haven't
we, on the road to adulthood?

We can learn a great deal from children about simple faith and
simple hope. Yet we have had years to experience those truths. We
can look back at the many times He has taken our brokenness and
made something beautiful of our lives. Our greatest failures, our
deepest sorrows, have offered opportunities for the operation of His
mercy and grace. How can we forget that?

God's Appraisal of Us

The Bible is filled with reminders of how much God cares for us, His plans for our welfare, and what our relationship with Him should be. Take, for example, the familiar words of the psalmist. Though an adult, he writes of God with free-flowing delight.

> Bless the LORD, O my soul;
> And all that is within me, bless His holy name.
> Bless the LORD, O my soul,
> And forget none of His benefits;
> Who pardons all your iniquities;
> Who heals all your diseases;
> Who redeems your life from the pit;
> Who crowns you with lovingkindness and compassion;
> Who satisfies your years with good things,
> So that your youth is renewed like the eagle. . . .
>
> For as high as the heavens are above the earth,
> So great is His lovingkindness toward those who fear Him.
> As far as the east is from the west,
> So far has He removed our transgressions from us.
> Just as a father has compassion on his children,
> So the LORD has compassion on those who fear Him.
>
> For He Himself knows our frame;
> He is mindful that we are but dust. (Ps. 103:1–5, 11–14)

What a list! What a relief! Our Lord understands our limits. He realizes our struggles. He knows how much pressure we can take. He knows what measures of grace and mercy and strength we'll require. He knows how we're put together.

Frankly, His expectations are not nearly as unrealistic as ours. When we don't live up to the agenda we have set, we feel like He is going to dump a truckload of judgment on us. But that will not happen. So why do we fear it could? Because we forget that He "knows our frame; He is mindful that we are but dust."

What, then, is God's agenda for us? What does He want for us this afternoon, tomorrow morning, or next week? Well, His plans for us are clearly set forth. He wrote them originally to Israel, but they apply to us too.

> "For I know the plans that I have for you," declares the LORD, "plans for welfare and not for calamity to give you a future and a hope. Then you will call upon Me and come and pray to Me, and I will listen to you." (Jer. 29:11–12)

Isn't that wonderful? "I have plans for you, My son, My daughter," God says. "And they are great plans. Plans for your welfare and not for your calamity. Plans to give you a future and a hope." It is God's agenda that His people never lose hope. Each new dawn it's as if He smiles from heaven, saying, "Hope again . . . hope again!"

After the fall of Jerusalem, the prophet Jeremiah reminded himself of God's hope-filled plans.

> This I recall to my mind,
> Therefore I have hope.
> The LORD's lovingkindnesses indeed never cease,
> For His compassions never fail.
> They are new every morning;
> Great is Thy faithfulness.
> "The LORD is my portion," says my soul,
> "Therefore I have hope in Him."
> The LORD is good to those who wait for Him,
> To the person who seeks Him.
> It is good that he waits silently
> For the salvation of the LORD. (Lam. 3:21–26)

Right now you may be waiting for something from the Lord. Matter of fact, most people I meet are in some sort of holding pattern. (I certainly am!) They have something on the horizon that they're trusting God for. (I certainly do!) And their hope is not misplaced. He is good to those who wait for Him. He is good to those who seek Him. We have nothing to fear. And we certainly have no reason for living each day crushed by guilt or shame.

He has redeemed us, given us an inheritance, and shown us forgiveness. The most succinct summary of God's appraisal of our relationship as His children can be found in Romans 8:31–32. Many years ago I memorized the concluding paragraph in Romans 8, which begins with these two verses. I cannot number the times I have had my hope renewed by quoting these words to myself.

> What then shall we say to these things? If God is for us, who is against us? He who did not spare His own Son, but delivered Him up for us all, how will He not also with Him freely give us all things?

Contrary to popular opinion, God doesn't sit in heaven with His jaws clenched, His arms folded in disapproval, and a deep frown on His brow. He is not ticked off at His children for all the times we trip over our tiny feet and fall flat on our diapers. He is a loving Father, and we are precious in His sight, the delight of His heart. After all, He "has qualified us to share in the inheritance of the saints in light" (Col. 1:12). Think of it! He's put us in His inheritance!

Remember that the next time you think God is coming down on you. You have reason to give thanks. You don't have to qualify yourself for His kingdom. His grace has rescued you. He has already qualified you by accomplishing a great deliverance in your life. That brings to mind another verse I love to quote:

> For He delivered us from the domain of darkness, and transferred us to the kingdom of His beloved Son, in whom we have redemption, the forgiveness of sins. (Col. 1:13–14)

He has literally transferred us from the dark domain of the Enemy of our souls into the light of the kingdom of His Son. He considers us there with Him, surrounded by love, receiving the same treatment He gives His Son.

Sometimes it's encouraging just to thumb through the Scriptures and find all the promises that tell us what God thinks of us, especially in a world where folks are continually telling us all the things they have against us and all the things they see wrong with us.

God is not only "for us," according to Romans 8, He is constantly giving great gifts to us.

Every good thing bestowed and every perfect gift is from above, coming down from the Father of lights, with whom there is no variation, or shifting shadow. (James 1:17)

Literally, that last phrase means "shadow of turning." In other words, there is no alteration or modification in His giving, regardless of how often we may turn away. No shifting shadow on our part causes Him to become moody and hold back His gifts to us. Talk about grace!

God is for us. I want you to remember that.

God is for us. Say those four words to yourself.

God is for us.

Remember that tomorrow morning when you don't feel like He is. Remember that when you have failed. Remember that when you have sinned and guilt slams you to the mat.

God is for you. Make it personal: *God is for me!*

Never ever, ever tell your children that if they do wrong, God won't love them. That is heresy. There's no grace in that. Grace says, "My child, even though you do wrong, God will continue and I will continue to love you. God is for you, and so am I!"

I thought of this the other day as I was humming the children's tune, "Jesus loves the little children, all the children of the world." I thought, well, what about all the grownups? So I changed the words of that little song.

> Jesus loves His adult children,
> All the grownups of the world.
> Red and yellow, black and white,
> We are precious in His sight.

Jesus loves all the teens and adults of the world.
[Just thought I should include the teenagers too!]

Why do we think His love is just for the little children, innocent and disarming as they are? He loves all of His people. Let me repeat it once more: God is for us.

In Peter's letter, we catch a glimpse of the delight God takes in us as the apostle paints six beautiful word pictures of us, vivid pen portraits of God's children.

And coming to Him as to a living stone, rejected by men, but choice and precious in the sight of God, you also, as living stones, are being built up as a spiritual house for a holy priesthood, to offer up spiritual sacrifices acceptable to God through Jesus Christ. For this is contained in Scripture:
"Behold I lay in Zion a choice stone, a precious
     corner stone,
And he who believes in Him shall not be disappointed."
This precious value, then, is for you who believe. But for those who disbelieve,
"The stone which the builders rejected,
this became the very corner stone,"
and,
"A stone of stumbling and a rock of offense";
for they stumble because they are disobedient to the word, and to this doom they were also appointed. (1 Pet. 2:4–8)

We Are Living Stones in a Spiritual House

The metaphor woven through the fabric of this passage is that of a building, Christ being the cornerstone and we, His children, being the living stones that make up the building. (The apostle Paul uses this same image in Ephesians 2:19–22.)

Each time someone trusts Christ as Savior, another stone is quarried out of the pit of sin and fitted into the spiritual house He's building through the work of the Holy Spirit. And carefully overseeing the construction is Christ, who is the hands-on contractor of this eternal edifice.

We are His living stones, being built up as a spiritual house.

Think of it this way. There's a major construction project going on through time as Jesus Christ builds His family. It's called the *ekklesia*, the "church," those who are called out from the mass of humanity to become a special part of God's forever family. And you, as a Christian—a follower of Christ—have been picked, chosen, and called out to be one of them.

He has quarried you from the pit of your sin. And now He is chiseling away, shaping you and ultimately sliding you into place. You are a part of His building project.

All kinds of prophets of doom wonder about the condition of God's building. They see it as condemned property, worn out, dilapidated, and derelict rather than as a magnificent edifice that is being constructed on schedule. The truth is, God is the master architect, and every stone is being placed exactly where He designed it to fit. The project is right on schedule. Never forget, even on those blue days, we are living stones in a spiritual house. But there's more. . . .

We Are Priests in the Same Temple

Peter refers to us both as a "holy priesthood" and as a "royal priesthood." It's true that we're not all preachers or evangelists or gifted teachers. But we *are* all priests, belonging to a kingly order that has been set apart by God.

The role of priest implies more than meets the eye, for priests have specific responsibilities delineated in Scripture. Priests offer up prayers, bring spiritual sacrifices, intercede to God on behalf of others, and stay in tune with the spiritual side of life. All this applies to every believer, regardless of age, regardless of sex, regardless of social standing. Perhaps you never thought of this before, but it's really true; we are priests in the same temple. But there's more. . . .

We Are a Chosen Race

Our heads might have a tendency to swell at being chosen to be on God's team, so it might behoove us to take a quick glance at exactly why God chose the Hebrews to be His people. This will help us put the whole idea of being chosen by God into perspective. Here Moses is addressing the nation Israel, preparing them to enter the Promised Land.

> For you are a holy people to the LORD your God; the LORD your God has chosen you to be a people for His own possession out of all the peoples who are on the face of the earth. The LORD did not set His love on you nor choose you because you were more in number than any of the peoples, for you were the fewest of all peoples, but because the LORD loved you and kept the oath which He swore to your forefathers, the LORD brought you out by a mighty hand, and redeemed you from the house of slavery, from the hand of Pharaoh king of Egypt. (Deut. 7:6–8)

Why did God choose Israel? Because of their strength? No. Because of their numbers? Because of their mental or moral superiority? No. He chose them not because they deserved it, but simply because of His grace—a kindness shown to them entirely without merit on their part. Simply "because the Lord loved you."

Why did God choose us? For the same reason. Not because we did anything that impressed Him. It wasn't the size of our faith . . . or the sincerity. It wasn't the goodness of our heart . . . or the greatness of our intellect. It certainly wasn't because we first chose Him. It was entirely by grace. Grace prompted by love.

The Lord chooses us because He chooses to choose us. Period. He sets His love upon us because out of the goodness and grace of His own heart He declares, "I want you to be Mine."

I love that! Not only because it exalts the grace of God, but because God gets all the glory in it. We won't walk around heaven with our thumbs under our suspenders outbragging one another. Instead, we'll be absolutely amazed that we are privileged to be there.

John 15:16 says, "You did not choose Me, but I chose you." We didn't hunt Him down. He hunted us down. He is the eternal Hound of Heaven. We didn't work half our lives to find Him; He gave His life to find us. Being chosen by God says a lot more about Him than it does about us! He is the Good Shepherd who gives His life for the sheep. When you find yourself slumping in shame or giving way to guilt, remind yourself of this: You have been chosen by the Good Shepherd. He wants you in His flock. But there is more. . . .

We Are a Holy Nation

Holy can be an intimidating word. Though meant to be sacred, it can seem scary. Remember, earlier we explained that the word means "to be set apart." But let's look at it another way.

I'm sitting in my study right now, and I'm wearing a suit and a tie because I'm going to an important meeting in a couple hours. This morning when I was getting dressed, I looked on my tie rack and I selected a tie. I had a number to choose from, but I chose this particular one. I pulled it off the rack, put it around my neck, and tied the knot, and at that moment the tie became holy. Doesn't look holy. I can assure you, it doesn't feel holy. (As a matter of fact, I can see a small spot on it. Must have gotten some gravy on it when I wore it last.) But it's still the tie I set apart for this particular purpose. In the broadest sense of the word, the tie I'm wearing is "holy." It's set apart for a special purpose.

You and I are a holy nation. We make up a body of people set apart for a special purpose: to be ambassadors for Jesus Christ, the King of the church. We are a people set apart for His special purpose and glory.

If we seem out of step with the rest of the world, it is because we march to the beat of a different drummer. We sing a different national anthem and pledge our allegiance to a different flag—because our citizenship, our true citizenship, is in heaven. You and I are parts of His holy nation. But there's more . . . .

We Are God's Own Possession

Possessions of the powerful, wealthy, or famous, no matter how common, can become extremely valuable, even priceless. Napoleon's toothbrush sold for $21,000. Can you imagine—paying thousands of dollars for someone's cruddy old toothbrush? Hitler's car sold for over $150,000. Winston Churchill's desk, a pipe owned by C. S. Lewis, sheet music handwritten by Beethoven, a house once owned by Ernest Hemingway. At the Sotheby's auction of Jackie Kennedy Onassis's personal belongings, her fake pearls sold for $211,500 and JFK's wood golf clubs went for $772,500. Not because the items themselves are worthy but because they once belonged to someone significant.

Are you ready for a surprise? We fit that bill too. Think of the value of something owned by God. What incredible worth that bestows on us, what inexplicable dignity! We belong to Him. We are "a people for God's own possession" (1 Pet. 2:9).

I love that expression—"a people for God's own possession." And I'm glad this verse is correctly translated in the version of the Bible I'm using. For the longest time I used a version that said, "We are a peculiar people." (Actually, I saw all kinds of evidence of that around me, as if Christians were supposed to be odd or weird or strange.) But the correct rendering is far more encouraging. Weird or not, we're His possession . . . owned by the living God.

The price paid for us was unimaginably high—the blood of Jesus Christ—and now we belong to Him. We have been bought with a price. That's enough to bring a smile to anyone's face. But there is more . . . one more.

We Are a People Who Have Received Mercy

Have you lived so long in the family of God that your memory has become blurred? Have you forgotten what it was like when you weren't?

> . . . for you once were not a people, but now you are the people of God; you had not received mercy, but now you have received mercy. (1 Pet. 2:10)

As a result of God's mercy, we have become a people who are uniquely and exclusively cared for by God. The fact that we are the recipients of His mercy makes all the difference in the world as to how we respond to difficult times. He watches over us with enormous interest. Why? Because of His immense mercy, freely demonstrated in spite of our not deserving it. What guilt-relieving, encouraging news!

Of all the twelve disciples, none could have been more grateful than Peter . . . or, if he had allowed it, none more guilt-ridden. Called to serve his Savior, strong-hearted, determined, zealous, even a little cocky on occasion, the man had known the heights of ecstasy but also knew the aching agony of defeat.

Though warned by the Master, Peter announced before His peers, "Even though all may fall away . . . I will never fall away" (Matt. 26:33). And later . . . "Lord, with You I am ready to go both to prison and to death!" (Luke 22:33). Yet only a few hours later he denied even knowing Jesus . . . three times!

What bitter tears he wept when the weight of his denials crushed his spirit. But our Lord refused to leave him there, wallowing in hopeless discouragement and depression. He found the broken man and forgave him . . . and used him mightily as a leader in the early church. What grace . . . what mercy!

Charles Wesley beautifully captures the theology of such mercy in the second stanza of his magnificent hymn, "And Can It Be?"

> He left His Father's throne above,
> So free, so infinite His grace!

Emptied Himself of all but love,
And bled for Adam's helpless race!
'Tis mercy all, immense and free,
For, O my God, it found out me.

Our Lives Are Being Watched

Beloved, I urge you as aliens and strangers to abstain from fleshly lusts, which war against the soul. Keep your behavior excellent among the Gentiles, so that in the thing in which they slander you as evildoers, they may on account of your good deeds, as they observe them, glorify God in the day of visitation. (1 Pet. 2:11–12)

Peter begins his practical summary of this section with the words, "Beloved, I urge you." He feels passionate about this—and there's a warning here. Peter is telling us that in light of all that we are as God's children, in light of our roles as living stones in a building that will never be destroyed, and in light of our being these things he's described—a royal priesthood, a chosen race, a holy nation, a people for His own possession, those who have received mercy, we are to live in a certain way. Our earthly behavior is to square with our divinely provided benefits.

For unbelievers, earth is a playground where the flesh is free to romp and run wild. But for believers, earth is a battleground. It's the place where we combat the lusts that wage war against our souls. For the brief tour of duty we Christians have on this earth, we cannot get stalled in sin or, for that matter, incapacitated by guilt. To live the kind of life God requires, Peter offers four suggestions.

First, live a clean life. Don't think for a moment that it makes no difference to unbelievers how Christians live. We live out our faith before a watching world. That's why Peter urges us to abstain from fleshly lusts, "in order to get their attention" and to prove that what we believe really works.

You and I don't know how many non-Christians are watching us this very day, determining the truth of the message of Christianity strictly on the basis of how we live, how we work, how we respond to life's tests, or how we conduct ourselves with our families.

Every time I hear of a pastor or Christian leader or well-known Christian artist who has failed morally, it breaks my heart. Not just because it scandalizes the church and possibly destroys his or her family, although those are certainly tragedies enough. But I think of what it says to unbelievers who read it in the headlines or hear it joked about on television talk shows. Living a clean life isn't merely a nice option to consider; it's the least we can do to demonstrate our gratitude for God's deliverance.

Second, leave no room for slander. When the ancient Greek philosopher Plato was told that a certain man had begun making slanderous charges against him, Plato's response was, "I will live in such a way that no one will believe what he says."[3]

The most convincing defense is the silent integrity of our character, not how vociferously we deny the charges.

Third, do good deeds among unbelievers. It's easy for Christians to have such tunnel vision that we limit all of our good deeds to the family of God. But if you're driving along and see someone with a flat tire, you don't roll down your window and say, "Hey there . . . you with the flat tire! Are you a Christian?" . . . then determine if you should help. We would do well to extend our good deeds to those outside the family.

What makes the story of the Good Samaritan so compelling? The merciful deeds were done on behalf of a total stranger. That is how we win the right to be heard—not by a slick mass-advertising campaign but by our compassionate and unselfish actions.

Notice that Peter says, "on account of your good *deeds*," not your good *words*. The unsaved are watching our lives. When our good deeds are indisputable the unbeliever says, "There must be something to it." Chances are good that at that point the person will hear what we have to say.

Fourth, never forget—we are being watched. The world is watching us to see if what we say we believe is true in our lives. Warren

Wiersbe tells a brief but powerful story that illustrates this beautifully.

> In the summer of 1805, a number of Indian chiefs and warriors met in council at Buffalo Creek, New York, to hear a presentation of the Christian message by a Mr. Cram from the Boston Missionary Society. After the sermon, a response was given by Red Jacket, one of the leading chiefs. Among other things, the chief said . . .
>
> "Brother, we are told that you have been preaching to the white people in this place. These people are our neighbors. We are acquainted with them. We will wait a little while and see what effect your preaching has upon them. If we find it does them good, makes them honest and less disposed to cheat Indians, we will then consider again what you have said."[4]

Whew! That's laying it on the line. I wonder how many people are looking at us and saying to themselves, "I hear what he's saying. Now I'm going to watch how he lives. I'll see if what he says is what he does."

Let's Not Forget—God Is for Us

This has been a searching chapter to write. I've not attempted to soften Peter's words, lest we miss the punch in his points. For whatever it's worth, I've felt a few stinging reproofs as well. Sometimes an author has to swallow some of his own medicine . . . except in this case, God is giving the medicine through Peter's pen, not mine! And so, you and I both have taken it on the chin. Hopefully, it will make a difference.

But let's not forget the good news: There is hope beyond guilt! May I remind you of that oft-repeated line from Romans 8? "God is for us." In devoted love He chose us. In great grace He stooped to accept us into His family. In immense mercy He still finds us wandering, forgives our foolish ways, and (as He did with Peter) frees us to serve Him even though we don't deserve such treatment.

So . . . away with guilt! If you need a little extra boost to make that happen, read Eugene Peterson's paraphrase of Romans 8:31–19. Read it slowly, preferably *aloud*. As a good friend of mine once put it, "If this don't light your fire, you got wet wood!"

So, what do you think? With God on our side like this, how can we lose? If God didn't hesitate to put everything on the line for us, embracing our condition and exposing himself to the worst by sending his own Son, is there anything else he wouldn't gladly and freely do for us? And who would dare tangle with God by messing with one of God's chosen? Who would dare even to point a finger? The One who died for us—who was raised to life for us!—is in the presence of God at this very moment sticking up for us. Do you think anyone is going to be able to drive a wedge between us and Christ's love for us? There is no way! Not trouble, not hard times, not hatred, not hunger, not homelessness, not bullying threats, not backstabbing, not even the worst sins listed in Scripture:

"They kill us in cold blood because they hate you.
We're sitting ducks; they pick us off one by one."

None of this fazes us because Jesus loves us. I'm absolutely convinced that nothing—nothing living or dead, angelic or demonic, today or tomorrow, high or low, thinkable or unthinkable—absolutely *nothing* can get between us and God's love because of the way that Jesus our Master has embraced us. (Rom. 8:31–39 MSG)

A Prayer for Hope Beyond Guilt

Father . . . dear gracious Father, we're our own worst enemy.
We focus on our failures rather than on Your rescues . . . on
our wrongs rather than on Your commitment to making us
right . . . on our puny efforts rather than on Your powerful

plans for our good. Even our attempts at being devoted to You can become so self-centered. Turn our attention back to You.

- *Remind us of our exalted position in Christ.*
- *Refresh us with frequent flashbacks—"God is for us."*
- *Renew our spirits with the realization that we're your possession.*

Then, with those joyful thoughts to spur us on, slay the dragon of guilt within us so we might enjoy, as never before, your ultimate embrace. Through Christ I pray.

AMEN

6

Hope Beyond Unfairness

Pressing on

Even Though

Ripped Off

EVER BOUGHT A LEMON of a used car? Ever sent away for some marvelous $16.95 gadget displayed on an infomercial and ended up with about 85 cents worth of plastic?

Who hasn't been hoodwinked by a smooth-talking salesman with styled hair and patent-leather shoes? Who hasn't been burned by a glitzy ad campaign that promises more than it delivers? Who hasn't, at some point, been taken advantage of or "ripped off"?

Yet we recover relatively easily and quickly from ripoffs like those. What's really difficult to endure is the kind of abuse or victimization that gets personal—when someone slanders our reputations, pulls the economic rug out from under us, or even threatens our lives. It's hard enough to deal with the consequences of our own missteps, miscalculations, and stupid mistakes. But it seems unbearable to suffer the consequences of something that wasn't our fault or that we didn't deserve.

If you've ever been treated like that, you're in good biblical company. David was ripped off by Saul, Esau was duped by Jacob, Joseph was mistreated by his brothers, and Job was victimized by the Sabeans and Chaldeans.

David, as a young shepherd boy, killed Goliath and helped rout the Philistine enemy. After that, David became overwhelmingly popular among the people. He also became the object of King Saul's rage. David had done only good for Saul and his people. Therefore, the people appropriately sang their praises to David: "Saul has slain his thousands, and David his ten thousands" (1 Sam. 18:7). That popular song sent Saul into such a revengeful rage against the young hero that for more than a decade David ran for his life while Saul hunted and haunted him. David didn't deserve this, but it happened.

Joseph didn't ask to be his father's favorite, but when Jacob showed favoritism to his youngest son, Joseph's brothers, in a moment of absolute hatred, sold him into slavery. Although Joseph triumphed over his circumstances, he was initially ripped off by his brothers.

Earlier, Joseph's father, Jacob, had cheated his own brother, Esau, out of his birthright. Admittedly Esau was rash and irresponsible, but Jacob took advantage of his brother in a vulnerable moment.

And what about that good man Job? According to the Scriptures, he was "blameless" and "upright" and had taken unfair advantage of no one . . . but because Satan used him as a guinea pig, Job lost all his land, servants, possessions, and above all, his ten children.

While God ultimately used all these circumstances for the believers' good and His honor, initially all of these men could have said, "What is happening here? This is unfair! I don't deserve this!"

So while we may be in good company—and misery does love company—company doesn't alleviate the pain of unfair treatment.

Natural Reactions to Unfair Treatment

It's been my observation that when we're treated unfairly, we respond with three common, knee-jerk reactions.

First, there is the aggressive pattern: we blame others. This reaction not only focuses on the person who ripped us off and keeps a running tally of wrongs done against us, it also engineers ways to get back. This reaction says, "I don't just get mad, I get even." In the process, aggression grows from simple anger all the way to rage. It starts with the seed of resentment, germinates into revenge, and in the process nurtures a deep root of bitterness that tenaciously wraps around our hearts. When allowed to grow to full size, it leaves us determined to get back at *every* person who has done anything against us.

It's like the fellow who was bitten by a dog and was later told by his physician, "Yes, indeed, you do have rabies." Upon hearing this, the patient immediately pulled out a pad and pencil and began to write.

Thinking the man was making out his will, the doctor said, "Listen, this doesn't mean you're going to die. There's a cure for rabies."

"I know that," said the man. "I'm making a list of people I'm gonna bite."

It is probable that a few who read these words are making lists right now of people you're gonna bite the very next chance you get. Some of you are already engaged in doing just that. The blame game may temporarily satisfy an aggressive inner itch, but it doesn't lead to a lasting solution. Small wonder God warns us: "Never take your own revenge . . . 'Vengeance is Mine, I will repay,' says the Lord" (Rom. 12:19).

Second, there is the passive pattern: we feel sorry for ourselves. We throw a pity party, complaining to anyone who will lend a sympathetic ear. "Life just isn't fair," we whine. But if we wallow in this slough of despondency too long, we become depressed and immobile, living the balance of life with the shades drawn and the doors locked. Like quicksand, feeling sorry for ourselves will suck us under.

Though you may be holding back, there's a lot of anger in this passive pattern as well. Give in to this temptation, and I can assure you, you'll not be vulnerable to anybody ever again.

Reminds me of some fellows in the military who were stationed in Korea during the Korean War. While there, they hired a local boy to cook and clean for them. Being a bunch of jokesters, these guys soon took advantage of the boy's seeming naiveté. They'd smear Vaseline on the stove handles so that when he'd turn the stove on in the morning he'd get grease all over his fingers. They'd put little water buckets over the door so that he'd get deluged when he opened the door. They'd even nail his shoes to the floor during the night. Day after day the little fella took the brunt of their practical jokes without saying anything. No blame . . . no self-pity . . . no temper tantrums.

Finally the men felt guilty about what they were doing, so they sat down with the young Korean and said, "Look, we know these pranks aren't funny anymore, and we're sorry. We're never gonna take advantage of you again."

It seemed too good to be true to the houseboy. "No more sticky on stove?" he asked.

"Nope."

"No more water on door?"

"No."

"No more nail shoes to floor?"

"Nope, never again."

"Okay," the boy said with a smile . . . "no more spit in soup."

Even in a passive mode, you can spit in somebody's soup.

Third, there is the holding pattern: we postpone or deny our feelings. We might call this the Scarlett O'Hara syndrome: "I'll think about it tomorrow." Every boiling issue is left to simmer on the back burner over a low flame. On the surface all seems calm—"Doesn't bother me"—but underneath, our feelings seethe, eating away at us like acid. This failure to deal with the problem forthrightly leads only to doubt and disillusionment and weakens the fiber of our lives. Furthermore, it's physically unhealthy to sustain feelings of resentment.

An Alternative That Honors God

Though they are all very common, don't expect to find any of these reactions in Peter's wonderful letter where he informs us how to

84

have hope beyond unfairness. Expect instead an alternative reaction
to unfair treatment.

The Command

> Submit yourselves for the Lord's sake to every human institution,
> whether to a king as the one in authority, or to governors as sent by him
> for the punishment of evildoers and the praise of those who do right.
> (1 Pet. 2:13–14)

It's important to understand the historical context of this command. The Roman Empire, throughout which the readers of Peter's
letter were scattered, was not a benevolent monarchy. It was a dicta-
torship ruled by the insane demagogue Nero, who was especially
notorious for his wickedness and his cruelty to Christians. Many of
the believers who received Peter's letter had suffered persecution.
The bodies of their friends and loved ones had bloodied the sand of
the Roman coliseum. Their corpses, soaked in oil, had lit that vast
stadium. So it was altogether natural and fitting that Peter would
address the subject of unfair treatment. These believers had been the
target of the grossest kind of mistreatment by government, by their
fellow citizens, and by their neighbors.

Should these Christians pick up arms and resist a government
with such a leader at its helm? No, said Peter. Incredibly, in the midst
of all this, he had the audacity to say, "Submit."

God does not promote anarchy. Jesus said, "Render to Caesar the
things that are Caesar's and to God the things that are God's" (Matt.
22:21). And Paul exhorts us to pray for those who are in authority
over us (see 1 Tim. 2:1–2). Nowhere in Scripture is overt insurrection
against the government recommended. The believer was not put on
earth to overthrow governments but to establish in the human heart
a kingdom not of this world.

There may be instances, of course, when we must stand our
ground, when we must stand firm and disobey a law that is disobedient to the law of God. We are not to buckle under by compro-
mising our convictions or renouncing our faith. But those are the

exceptions, not the normal rule. Whenever possible we are to render unto Caesar the coin of civil obedience, pray for those in authority, pay our taxes, obey the laws of the land, and live honorably under the domain of earthly elected leaders.

The way to live honorably, Peter says, is to "submit." The Greek word is *hupotasso*, a military term that means "to fall in rank under an authority." It's composed of two words: *tasso*, meaning "to appoint, order, or arrange," and *hupo*, meaning "to place under or to subordinate." In this particular construction it conveys the idea of subjecting oneself or placing oneself under another's authority.

This recognition of existing authority, coupled with a willingness to set aside one's own personal desires, shows a deep dependency upon God. This submission to authority is not only in respect to God, the foremost human authority, but to lesser officials as well, such as kings and governors as well as law officers and teachers.

I'm convinced in my heart that if we were good students of submission we would get along a lot better in life. But I am also convinced that it is the one thing, more than any other, that works against our very natures, which argue, "I don't want to submit. I don't want to give in. I won't let him have his way in this." And so we live abrasively.

Let's get something very clear here. Our problem is not understanding what submission means. Our problem is doing what it says.

Because submission is so difficult, we need to look at the reason behind Peter's command.

The Reason

For such is the will of God that by doing right you may silence the ignorance of foolish men. (1 Pet. 2:15)

The Greek word translated "silence" here means "to close the mouth with a muzzle." You see, Christians in the first century were the targets of all kinds of slanderous rumors. "They're a secret sect," people said. "They are people of another kingdom." . . . "They follow another god." . . . "They have plans to overthrow us." Throughout the Roman Empire people gossiped about their secret meetings, their subversive ideologies, their loyalty to another kingdom, their plans to infiltrate, indoctrinate, and lead an insurrection. This kind of paranoia was common, all the way to Nero. To muzzle these rumors, Peter encouraged submission to the powers that be. By submitting, Peter said, by doing right before God, they would muzzle the mouths of those passing around such rumors.

Let's translate it into today's terms. We live in a city where the government is run by civil authorities. Our church building is located in that city. Now, those civil authorities have no right to tell us what to preach, what to teach, or which philosophy to adopt as a church. If they attempt to do that, we have a right—in fact, it's a duty—to rebel, because there is a higher law than their law, the higher law relating to the declaration of truth. However, they do have the right to say, "In this room you may put 150 people and no more. If you go beyond that you are violating the fire code and will be subject to a fine and possibly other penalties." It is neither right nor wise for us to break this civil law. It does not violate God's law and is, in fact, there for our protection. So we must submit to that law.

In the church I pastored in Fullerton, California, we had to abide by local laws, one of which stated that we could not use folding seats in the worship auditorium; the seats had to be fixed to the floor. Also, the local law mandated a certain predetermined ratio between how many cars were parked in a parking lot measured against how many people could sit in an auditorium. Any church that constructed a worship center had to provide parking for "X" number of people in the worship gathering. We agreed to cooperate with that.

By submitting to this civil authority, we muzzled any rumors that we were just a maverick group, that we did as we pleased, thank you. We would have gained nothing by rebelling against the civic authorities. In fact, we would have lost in many ways by doing so.

The Principle

Act as free men, and do not use your freedom as a covering for evil, but use it as bondslaves of God. Honor all men; love the brotherhood, fear God, honor the king. (1 Pet. 2:16–17)

It's important that we keep the right perspective on the principle here. We do not submit because we necessarily agree. We do not submit because deep within we support all the rules, codes, and regulations. At times they may seem petty and galling, terribly restrictive, and even prejudicial. We submit because it is the "will of God" and because we are "bondslaves of God."

Now, you see, the principle comes to the surface: "Do not use your freedom as a covering for evil." Do not use or abuse grace so that your freedom becomes a cloak for evil.

In little staccato bursts, Peter gives us several commands in verses 16 and 17: act as free men; honor all men; love the brotherhood; fear God; honor the king. And wrapped around the commands is that main principle: "Do not use your freedom as a covering for evil."

We must forever be aware of the temptation to abuse liberty. It's so easy to stretch it; so easy to make it work for ourselves rather than for the glory of God.

An Example and *the* Example

Servants, be submissive to your masters with all respect, not only to those who are good and gentle, but also to those who are unreasonable. For this finds favor, if for the sake of conscience toward God a man bears up under sorrows when suffering unjustly. For what credit is there if, when you sin and are harshly treated, you endure it with patience? But if when you do what is right and suffer for it you patiently endure it, this finds favor with God. For you have been called for this purpose. (1 Pet. 2:18–21a)

To understand the full import of what Peter is saying we must understand something of the nature of slavery in the time of the early church. William Barclay sheds some historical light on this.

In the time of the early church . . . there were as many as 60,000,000 slaves in the Roman Empire.

It was by no means only menial tasks which were performed by slaves. Doctors, teachers, musicians, actors, secretaries, stewards were slaves. In fact, all the work of Rome was done by slaves. Roman attitude was that there was no point in being master of the world and doing one's own work. Let the slaves do that and let the citizens live in pampered idleness. The supply of slaves would never run out.

Slaves were not allowed to marry; but they cohabited; and the children born of such a partnership were the property of the master, not of the parents, just as the lambs born to the sheep belonged to the owner of the flock, and not to the sheep.

It would be wrong to think that the lot of slaves was always wretched and unhappy, and that they were always treated with cruelty. Many slaves were loved and trusted members of the family; but one great inescapable fact dominated the whole situation. In Roman law a slave was not a person but a thing; and he had absolutely no legal rights whatsoever. For that reason there could be no such thing as justice where a slave was concerned. . . . Peter Chrysologus sums the matter up: "Whatever a master does to a slave, undeservedly, in anger, willingly, unwillingly, in forgetfulness, after careful thought, knowingly, unknowingly, is judgment, justice and law." In regard to a slave, his master's will, and even his master's caprice, was the only law.[1]

That was the reality of the first-century world when Peter addressed slaves and told them to "be submissive" to their masters. It would have been easy for slaves who became Christians to think that their Christianity gave them the freedom to break with their masters. Peter, under the Holy Spirit's inspiration, stated that this was not so.

Centuries later, Christianity pervaded the culture and overcame slavery, but it didn't happen in the first century. This is a good lesson for us regarding God's timing versus our timing, even when it comes to adversity. While He certainly commands us to be salt and light and thus bring about justice and change in our culture, His ultimate priority is changing the individual human heart.

It's difficult for us in America to read some of these verses. Our frame of reference is so different—so Western, so twentieth century—that we sometimes try to rewrite God's Word to make it fit us. We can't do that. We must let it speak for itself.

"Well, that's great if you have a good master," you say. It's wonderful if you're a slave of Saint Francis of America . . . or Mother Teresa of your community. If you're working for some marvelous, saintlike boss, everything is cool. You're happy to submit. But what if your taskmaster fits the description in the last part of the verse—what if you work for "those who are unreasonable"?

Do you have an uncaring boss? Do you have a supervisor or a manager who isn't fair? Do you have to deal with unreasonable people? You may not want to hear this today, but there is a lot of truth for you in verses 18 and 19, none of which will ever appear in your local newspaper or on a television talk show.

The natural tendency of the human heart is to fight back against unfair and unreasonable treatment. But Peter's point is that seeking revenge for unjust suffering can be a sign of self-appointed lordship over one's own affairs. Revenge, then, is totally inappropriate for one who has submitted to the lordship of Jesus Christ. Christians must stand in contrast to those around them. This includes a difference in attitude and a difference in focus. Our attitude should be "submissive," and our focus should be "toward God." And how is this change viewed by God? It "finds favor" with Him.

Our focus, then, should not be consumed with getting the raise at the office but with getting the praise from God, not with getting the glory for ourselves but with giving the glory to Him.

> For what credit is there if, when you sin and are harshly treated, you endure it with patience? But if when you do what is right and suffer for it you patiently endure it, this finds favor with God. (1 Pet. 2:20)

The contrast is eloquent. There's no credit due a person who suffers for what he has coming to him. If you break into a house and steal, you will be arrested, and you could be incarcerated. And if you patiently endure your jail sentence, no one is going think you are wonderful for being such a good and patient prisoner. You won't get elected "Citizen of the Year."

But if you are a hard-working, faithful employee, diligent, honest, productive, prompt, caring, working for a boss who is belligerent, stubborn, short-sighted, and ungrateful, and if you patiently endure that situation—aha! That "finds favor" with God! (I told you this wasn't information generally embraced by the public!) Actually another meaning for the word translated "favor" is *grace*. So when you endure, you put grace on display. And when you put grace on display for the glory of God, you could revolutionize your workplace or any other situation.

Can you see why the Christian philosophy is absolutely radical and revolutionary? We don't work for the credit or the prestige or the salary or the perks! We work for the glory of God in whatever we do. The purpose of the believer in society is to bring glory and honor to the name of Christ, not to be treated well or to have life be easy or even to be happy, as wonderful as all those things are. Again, this is not promoted in today's workplace.

> For you have been called for this purpose, since Christ also suffered for you, leaving you an example for you to follow in His steps. (1 Pet. 2:21)

You are "called for this purpose." That's the reason you're in that company. That's the reason you're filling that role. That's the reason these things are happening to you. Why? So that you might follow in the steps of our Lord Jesus, who suffered for us.

I deliberately left Christ off the list of biblical examples at the beginning of the chapter because I wanted to mention Him here. No one was ever more "ripped off" than our Savior. Absolutely no one. Jesus of Nazareth was the only perfect Man who ever lived, yet He suffered continually during His brief life on this planet. He was misunderstood, maligned, hated, arrested, and tortured. Finally, they crucified Him.

And Peter says we are to walk in the steps of Jesus.

> Since Christ also suffered for you, leaving you an example for you to follow in His steps, who committed no sin, nor was any deceit found in His mouth; and while being reviled, He did not revile in return; while

suffering, He uttered no threats, but kept entrusting Himself to Him who judges righteously; and He Himself bore our sins in His body on the cross, that we might die to sin and live to righteousness; for by His wounds you were healed. (1 Pet. 2:21b–24)

In these verses Peter shifts from *an* example of unfair treatment to *the* example we should follow—from that of a servant to that of the Savior.

John Henry Jowett writes of Jesus' perfection.

> The fine, sensitive membrane of the soul had in nowise been scorched by the fire of iniquity. "No sin!" He was perfectly pure and healthy. No power had been blasted by the lightning of passion. No nerve had been atrophied by the wasting blight of criminal neglect. The entire surface of His life was as finely sensitive as the fair, healthy skin of a little child. . . . There was no duplicity. There were no secret folds or convolutions in His life concealing ulterior motives. There was nothing underhand. His life lay exposed in perfect truthfulness and candour. The real, inner meaning of His life was presented upon a plain surface of undisturbed simplicity. "No sin!" Nothing blunted or benumbed. "No guile!" Therefore nothing hardened by the effrontery of deceit.[2]

That's the sinless Christ. But still they mocked Him and bruised Him and beat Him and *crucified* Him. When Peter tells us He is our example, that's saying something!

Consider His focus. He "kept entrusting Himself to Him who judges righteously."

That's a good thing to do throughout your day. "Lord, this is a hard moment for me. I'm having a tough time today. Here I am again, dealing with this unreasonable person, this person who is treating me unfairly. Lord, help me. I entrust myself to You. I give You my struggle. Protect me. Provide the wisdom and self-control I need. Help me do the right thing."

We must understand that the purpose of Jesus' suffering was different from ours. I know there comes a point where subjection to certain situations can become absolutely unwise and unhealthy. No argument there. But most of us don't get anywhere near that. We are so quick to defend ourselves. We are a fight-back generation. We know our lawyers' phone numbers better than we know verses of Scripture on self-restraint. Quick to get mad! Quick to fight back! Quick to answer back! Quick to threaten a lawsuit! "Don't you DARE step across that line . . . I've got my rights!"

When was the last time you deliberately, for the glory of Christ, took it on the chin, turned the other cheek, kept your mouth shut, and gave Him all the glory?

A Benefit That Accompanies Such Obedience

For you were continually straying like sheep, but now you have returned to the Shepherd and Guardian of your souls. (1 Pet. 2:25)

Staring in horror at the cross, one can't help but become dizzy from a swarm of questions. Why? Why should this innocent man endure such unjust suffering? Why should we? Why shouldn't we resist the thorns and the lash we are forced to bear? Why should we submit to the hammer blows, to the piercing nails, to the cross of unjust suffering?

Because it causes us to return to our Savior for protection rather than defending ourselves or fighting for "our rights." That kind of reaction has become so much a part of our lifestyle and culture that we don't even realize it when we react that way. We don't even recognize that we should be different from those around us.

By the way, see the words, "by His wounds you were healed"? Talk about vivid! Peter had seen firsthand the yoke of unjust suffering placed upon Jesus' shoulders. No doubt he was remembering. He could see it as clearly as though it were yesterday—that moment when he saw his Master's bruised and bleeding body staggering along the narrow streets of Jerusalem on the way to Golgotha. And as he remembered that scene, he said, "by that He heals us."

Are you feeling the splinters of some cross of unjust suffering? Has a friend betrayed you? Has an employer impaled you? Has a disaster dropped on your life that's almost too great to bear? If so, don't fight back. Unjust suffering can be a dizzying experience. To keep your balance in those times when things are swirling around you, it's important to find a fixed reference point and focus on it. Return to the protection and guardianship of the Good Shepherd who endured the cross and laid down His life . . . for you.

It was because David refused to take vengeance on King Saul that we remember his story to this day. It was because Joseph was so willing to forgive his brothers that we admire him to this day. And it was because Job did not waver in his faith, in spite of all those unfair calamities, that we are impressed to this day.

If you'd just as soon be forgotten because you lived consumed with blame and self-pity, keep fighting back. Get even. Stay angry.

But if you hope to be remembered, admired, and rewarded, press on even though you've been ripped off.

A Prayer for Hope Beyond Unfairness

*Dear Lord, find within us a yielded and quiet spirit of
submission. To make that happen, we need You to come in like
a flood. Occupy us as water finding empty spaces. Occupy
reserved portions of our lives where anger is festering and the
secret places where grudges are being stored. Sweep through
our houses . . . don't miss one room or a single area—cleanse
every dark closet, look under every rug. Let nothing go
unnoticed as You take full control of our motives as well as our
actions. Deep within our hearts we pray that You would sweep
us clean of blame and revenge, of self-pity and keeping score.
Enable each one of us to be big enough to press on regardless
of what unfair treatment we've had to endure. Take away the
scars of ugly treatment and harsh words. Forgiveness comes
hard . . . but it's essential. Help us forgive even those who*

never acknowledge their wronging and hurting us! Give us peace in place of turmoil and erase the memories that keep us offended. We need fresh hope to go on! I ask this in the name of Him who had no sin and did no wrong, but died, the just for the unjust: Jesus Christ our Lord.

AMEN

7

Hope Beyond "I Do"

The Give-and-Take
of
Domestic Harmony

A WEDDING IS ONE thing. A marriage is another. What a difference between the way things start in a home . . . and the way they continue.

In his book *Secrets to Inner Beauty*, Joe Aldrich humorously describes the realities of married life.

> It doesn't take long for the newlyweds to discover that "everything in one person nobody's got." They soon learn that a marriage license is just a learner's permit, and ask with agony, "Is there life after marriage?"
>
> An old Arab proverb states that marriage begins with a prince kissing an angel and ends with a bald-headed man looking across the table at a fat lady. Socrates told his students, "By all means marry. If you get a good wife, twice blessed you will be. If you get a bad wife, you'll become a philosopher." Count Herman Keyserling said it well when he stated that "The essential difficulties of life do not end, but rather begin with marriage."[1]

Marriage begins like a romantic, moonlight sleigh ride, smoothly gliding over the glistening snow. It's living together after the honey-moon that turns out to be rough backpacking across rocks and hot sand. For two people to live in domestic harmony, it takes a lot of give-and-take. If you need any confirmation of this outside your own life, just look at the statistics. No, forget statistics. Just look about you. On the job. In the office. Around your neighborhood. At church. Broken marriages. Separations. Divorces. Fractured homes. Some children have so many stepparents they can't keep track of them.

A wedding is one thing. A marriage is something else entirely.

I am a realist, not an idealist. I've been married for forty-one years, and they have been years of learning and growth, years of difficulty and ecstasy, years of delight and discovery, years of heartache and hardship, years of having children and losing children (two miscar-riages), years of growing together and, I must confess, some days in which it seemed we were growing apart.

At first, of course, deceived by the rose-colored glasses of roman-tic love, we didn't see any of this. And looking back through the fog of disappointment, we see very few things clearly.

In an essay on the theme of "arranged marriages," writer Philip Yancey offers these insights.

In the U.S. and other Western-style cultures, people tend to marry because they are attracted to another's appealing qualities: a fresh smile, wittiness, a pleasing figure, athletic ability, a cheerful disposition, charm. Over time, these qualities can change; the physical attributes, especially, will deteriorate with age. Meanwhile, surprises may surface: slatternly housekeeping, a tendency toward depression, disagreements over sex. In contrast, the partners in an arranged marriage [over half of all mar-riages in our international global village fit this description] do not cen-ter their relationship on mutual attractions. Having heard your parents' decision, you accept that you will live for many years with someone you now barely know. Thus the overriding question changes from "Whom should I marry?" to "Given this partner, what kind of mar-riage can we construct together?"[2]

Truthfully, that is the kind of attitude we need if we are going to move beyond romance into reality to build a strong and lasting life together. The apostle Peter gives us some helpful advice. He offers hope beyond "I do."

Tucked away in the heart of his letter is a little gem of truth, like a diamond in a ring. Without the right setting to enhance its beauty, this little gem would get lost; but viewed in its proper setting it becomes a sparkling delight. In the Bible, this setting is called the scriptural context.

The overall setting begins at 1 Peter 2:13 and continues through the end of chapter 3. These many verses challenge us to respond correctly, even in unfair circumstances. Some of those circumstances are briefly illustrated: citizens in various situations (2:13–17), slaves with unjust masters (2:18–20), wives with unfair husbands (3:1–6), and Christians in an unchristian society (3:13–17).

The key term in this context is the word *submit*, which we defined and analyzed in the previous chapter. You'll recall it is translated from a Greek military term meaning "to fall in rank under the authority of another . . . to subject oneself for the purpose of obeying or pleasing another." Some men have taken this word to the extreme in marriage, promoting cowering and servile behavior by women in the face of the worst kinds of abuse. Others have gone to the opposite extreme and labeled these passages dated and therefore culturally obsolete, saying that they apply only to the era in which they were originally written. The balance of the biblical position lies somewhere between these two poles.

Wise Counsel to Wives

The first six verses of our "gem of truth" passage refer to wives, and the seventh verse refers to husbands. One New Testament scholar gives a good explanation of this seeming inequity.

It may seem strange that Peter's advice to wives is six times as long as that to husbands. This is because the wife's position was far more difficult than that of the husband. If a husband became a Christian, he would automatically bring his wife with him into the Church. . . . But if a wife became a Christian while her husband did not, she was taking a step which was unprecedented and which produced the acutest problems.[3]

Despite that explanation, I know this passage is probably one of the hottest potatoes in Scripture, especially for women. Let me put some of you at ease. I do not believe this or any other part of Scripture admonishes a wife to stay in a situation where her health is being threatened or where her life—or the lives of her children—is in danger. That is not what submission is all about. So please don't run to that extreme and hide there, thinking you can avoid or deny the importance of submission in every other area or at any other level.

I find no fewer than three implied imperatives woven into the fabric of these important verses. They are reasonable and doable commands. They aren't culturally irrelevant. Best of all, they work!

Analyze Your Actions

In the same way, you wives, be submissive to your own husbands so that even if any of them are disobedient to the word, they may be won without a word by the behavior of their wives, as they observe your chaste and respectful behavior. (1 Pet. 3:1–2)

Many wives tend to view their roles as conditional; their behavior depends on the behavior of their husbands. "Sure, I'll be the kind of wife I should be if he's the kind of husband he should be." On the surface, that sounds great. Turnabout is fair play. There's only one problem: This passage isn't written just to wives who have husbands who play fair. Peter doesn't let us off the hook that easily. The passage is written to all wives, even those whose husbands are "disobedient to the word." In fact, by implication this paragraph is directed to women who live with disobedient husbands—husbands who are going their own way, husbands who care little about the things of God, husbands who would even mock the things of Christ. In short, these are husbands who aren't measuring up to God's standard.

Having to exhibit godly behavior under such circumstances can, however, cause wives to substitute secret manipulation for a quiet spirit. This may take many forms: pouting, sulking, scheming, bargaining, nagging, preaching, coercing, or humiliating. Wives who use this strategy are not trusting God to change their husbands' lives. They're trusting themselves.

You see, a wife is not responsible for her husband's life. She is responsible for her life. You cannot make your husband something he is not. Only God can do that.

I think it was the evangelist's wife, Ruth Graham, who once said, "It is my job to love Billy. It is God's job to make him good." I'd call that a wonderful philosophy for any wife to embrace.

Wife, it is your job to love your husband. It is God's job to change his life.

And wives who are truly obedient to Christ will find that He will honor their secure spirit. Yes, submission is a mark of security. It is not a spineless cringing, based on insecurity and fear. It is a voluntary unselfishness, a willing and cooperative spirit that seeks the highest good for one's husband.

"Well, that sounds like a dead-end street, Chuck," some of you might be saying. "If you only knew what I am living with, what a rascal, what a reprobate, what an ungodly man he really is."

But notice what Peter says: "they may be won without a word by the behavior of their wives, *as they observe your chaste and respectful behavior.*" The Greek term for *observe* suggests that this is a keen and careful observation, not a casual glance. As a "disobedient" husband observes his wife's godly behavior, his heart will eventually soften toward spiritual things. Such a lifestyle has been called "the silent preaching of a lovely life."

Watch Your Adornment and Your Attitude

And let not your adornment be merely external—braiding the hair, and wearing gold jewelry, or putting on dresses, but let it be the hidden person of the heart, with the imperishable quality of a gentle and quiet spirit, which is precious in the sight of God. (1 Pet. 3:3–4)

Obviously Peter is drawing a sharp contrast between inner beauty and outer beauty, or as Peter puts it, between outer adornment (verse 3) and inner adornment (verse 4).

It's easy in our shop-'til-you-drop culture to get carried away with the externals, ladies. Catalogs for every conceivable item of clothing pour into our homes, with their 800 numbers eager to take your order at any hour of the day or night. If that isn't convenient enough, we have entire television channels devoted to shopping and stores available on the Internet. Ready . . . set . . . *charge!*

The point of the contrast here is to restore the balance. Peter isn't prohibiting the braiding of hair or the wearing of jewelry any more than he's prohibiting the wearing of dresses. He merely wants to put those things in the background and bring the woman's character into the foreground. Perspective is the key.

Taken to an unrealistic extreme, you can really miss the mark in your external adornment. I have seen some women who think that it is a mark of spirituality to look like an unmade bed. That is not what God has in mind. On the other hand, if externals get overemphasized, appearance, cosmetics, and clothing take on too much significance. You can become preoccupied with your external adornment, and you can begin judging yourself and others solely by appearance, which is often what our culture does.

External beauty is ephemeral. Internal beauty is eternal. The former is attractive to the world; the latter is pleasing to God. Peter describes this inner beauty as "a gentle and quiet spirit." This might be paraphrased "a gentle tranquility." Without question, this is any woman's most powerful quality—true character. And such character comes from within—from the hidden person of the heart—because you know who you are and you know who you adore and serve, the Lord Christ. God values this kind of inner beauty as "imperishable" and "precious."

Outward adornment doesn't take a great deal of time. I've seen women do it in a few minutes on their way to work in the morning. (Ever been driving behind a woman putting on her makeup in the car as she's driving to work? It's an amazing process! And dangerous. I always cringe and wonder—what happens if she hits a pothole?) It may take only a few hours to prepare yourself for the most elegant of evenings, but it takes a lifetime to prepare and develop the hidden person of the heart.

Adornment is important but not nearly as important as attitude. If the internal attitude is right, it's amazing how much less significant one's external appearance becomes. Wise is the wife who watches both.

Evaluate Your Attention

For in this way in former times the holy women also, who hoped in God, used to adorn themselves, being submissive to their own husbands. Thus Sarah obeyed Abraham, calling him lord, and you have become her children if you do what is right without being frightened by any fear. (1 Pet. 3:5–6)

The fact that Sarah called her husband her lord (Gen. 18:12) reveals much about their relationship. It shows that she respected him, was attentive to his needs, cooperated with his wishes, and adapted herself to his desires.

Wives, are you patterning yourself after Sarah's role model? Take a look at where you place most of your attention, where you spend your time, what the focus of your prayer life is. Is your husband at the top of your earthly list?

I would encourage you wives to evaluate where you place most of your attention, and this is especially true for women who are busy raising a family. It is so easy in the press of caring for the constant needs of your children to put the needs of your husband on hold. Experience has taught me that is often where a breakdown in a marital relationship begins.

Peter says, "Sarah obeyed Abraham." A good paraphrase might be, "She paid attention to him."

★

Strong Commands to Husbands

You husbands likewise, live with your wives in an understanding way, as with a weaker vessel, since she is a woman; and grant her honor as a fellow heir of the grace of life, so that your prayers may not be hindered. (1 Pet. 3:7)

The final verse in this section turns the spotlight on husbands. It's short, but penetrating. I find that it is packed with three strong imperatives.

First, live with your wife. The Greek term here is a compound word composed of *sun* (with) and *oikeo* (to dwell/abide); put together they obviously mean "to dwell together." Now, you're probably thinking, "Well, certainly, I live with my wife. I'm *married* to her." But that is not what Peter is talking about. He's talking about a "close togetherness." *Sunoikeo* suggests much more than merely living under the same roof. There is a depth, a sense of intimacy, in the word. He is saying that husbands are responsible for that in the relationship. Providing a good living should never become a substitute for sharing deeply in life. The husband needs to be "at home with" his wife, understanding every room in his wife's heart and being sensitive to her needs. "Dwelling together" definitely means more than eating at the same table, sharing the same bed, and paying for the same mortgage.

Second, know your wife. Peter exhorts husbands to live with their wives "in an understanding way." That phrase literally means, "according to knowledge"—not an academic knowledge, but a thorough understanding of how your wife is put together.

"Oh, I know my wife," you may say. "Brown hair. Blue eyes. Weight. Height. I know what she likes for supper. Her favorite color is blue. I know where she likes to go for dinner." It's not that kind of knowledge either. Any man can know those things about her!

Your wife is a unique vessel, carefully crafted and beautifully interwoven by her Creator. To "know your wife" means you know the answers to those complex questions about her. What is her innermost makeup? What are her deepest concerns and fears? How do you help her work through them in the safety and security of your love? What does she need from you? Why does she respond as she does?

There's no handbook for those insights into her life. Even your father-in-law can't give you this inside information. You have to find it out in the intimacy of marriage and in the process of cultivating your life together. It takes time. It takes listening. It takes paying attention, concentrating, praying for insight, seeking understanding. Most wives long for that. Some of them die longing for it. Few things give a woman more security than knowing that her husband really knows her. That's what results in intimacy. That's what turns romance into a deep, lifelong love. That's what keeps her focused on and committed to you, longing to have you there, delighting in your presence, your words, your listening ear.

By the way, we need to address another phrase that occurs here: "living with your wife in an understanding way, *as with a weaker vessel.*" Now a word of caution: This has nothing to do with weakness of character or intelligence.

> The woman is called the "weaker vessel" (*skeuos*, lit., "vessel"); but this is not to be taken morally, spiritually, or intellectually. It simply means that the woman has less physical strength. The husband must recognize this difference and take it into account.[4]

Sometimes this is a bit difficult to comprehend when we consider what a woman goes through in bearing children. There's no doubt about the kind of strength women have within them when it comes to enduring pain. When my daughter gave birth to her second child, our fourth grandchild, she had natural childbirth. (Seemed strange to me—"natural" childbirth—and I was thankful I never had to go through that. I've never heard of anybody having a natural appendectomy or requesting a natural root canal!) What strength she demonstrated!

But when it comes to actual physical strength, Dr. Robert Kerlan, orthopedic surgeon and sports medicine specialist, says: "If the battle of the sexes was reduced to a tug-of-war with a line of 100 men on one side of the trench and 100 women on the other, the men would win." What makes the difference, he says, is muscle makeup.[5]

God's goal for us as husbands is to be sensitive rather than to prove how strong and macho we are. We need to love our wives, listen to them, adapt to their needs. We need to say no to more and more in our work so we can say yes to more and more in our homes . . . so we can say yes to the needs of our children and our families. (How else will your children learn what it means to be a good husband and father?)

Mind you, this is not to be a smothering kind of attention—the kind that says a husband is so insecure he cannot let his wife out of his sight. Instead, this is the kind of love that means your wife can't come back fast enough to your arms. Which brings us to the third imperative.

Third, honor your wife. To "grant her honor" is to assign her a place of honor. The same word translated "honor" here in 3:7 refers to the blood of Christ as "precious" in 1:19. I'd call that a rather significant analogy, wouldn't you?

Authors Gary Smalley and John Trent define this word well in their book *The Gift of Honor.*

> In ancient writings, something of honor was something of substance (literally, heavy), valuable, costly, even priceless. For Homer, the Greek scholar, "The greater the cost of the gift, the more the honor." . . .
>
> Not only does it signify something or someone who is a priceless treasure, but it is also used for someone who occupies a highly respected position in our lives, someone high on our priority list.[6]

That's how husbands are to treat their wives—to honor them by assigning them the top priority on their list of human relationships . . . in their schedules . . . and most importantly, in their hearts.

May I ask a few very personal questions? How do you treat your wife on an average day? Do you honor her? Do you give her a place of significance? Does she know she's your "top priority"? And do you communicate that in both actions and words? Honoring another is never something we keep to ourselves.

This is a magnificent truth, and you'll only get it from the Scriptures. It revolutionized my home. That's why I know it works. I didn't come from a model home and my wife didn't come from a home where her mother was honored. Cynthia and I knew that if we were going to make our marriage work, we had to go God's way, which meant we both had to be willing to change. We determined to do just that. And I'll freely admit, of the two of us, I have had to change more. About the time I think I've got things in good shape, another area emerges, and I have to deal with that! The journey toward marital maturity is a long one! And each year there are always some changes that must occur.

Let me summarize what Peter has written. Wives, your actions, your adornment, your attitudes, your attention are crucial in your marriage. Husbands, living with your wife, getting to know your wife, and honoring your wife are imperative if your marriage is going to be what it should be in God's eyes. Marriage is a two-way street. Both sides must be maintained.

A Promise to Both Partners

To seal this "heavenly bargain," Peter closes with a promise to both partners: "So that your prayers may not be hindered." This is an added incentive for husband and wife to live together in domestic harmony.

If you and your mate hope to cultivate an effective prayer life, the secret lies in your relationship with each other. Your prayers will not be hindered if you cultivate a close and caring relationship. Could that explain why your prayers are not being answered now?

A Project to Add Hope to Your Home

During the next week I'd like you to work on a very practical project. It will involve your doing two things. *First*, write down four qualities you appreciate most about your mate. After thinking them through, tell your spouse what they are and why they come to mind. Give examples. Take your time. Spell them out. Genuinely affirm your partner. *Second,* using this section of 1 Peter as your guide, admit the one thing you would most like to change about yourself. Don't be afraid to be vulnerable. Your mate will appreciate your willingness to be transparent.

Now don't get those two reversed. Don't mention four things you want your partner to change and the one thing you like most about yourself!

Talk truth. Refuse to blame. Guard against this becoming an evening of confrontation. Make it an evening of getting back together. Go ahead . . . be willing to risk.

You may be amazed to discover how quickly new hope for your marriage can return. The secret isn't that profound. A good marriage isn't so much finding the right partner as it is being the right partner.

And that starts with you.

A Prayer for Hope Beyond "I Do"

Lord, marriage was Your original idea. You hold the patent on this one. You brought the first couple together and gave Adam and Eve wise instruction on how to make their marriage flourish.

I believe You are still bringing men and women together . . . all around this big world. But today I pray specifically for those who read this chapter. For some, their hopes are dim. They don't know where to start or how to rekindle the flame that once burned brightly. For others, starting over seems too great a hurdle . . . too huge a mountain to climb . . . too much to face.

Somehow, Lord, break down the barriers. Bring back the "want to." Restore a glimmer of hope, especially in the lives of that one couple who think they will never make it. May Your Spirit miraculously renew their hope at this moment. I ask this in the name of Christ, in whom nothing is impossible.

AMEN

8

Hope Beyond Immaturity

Maturity Checkpoints

DURING MY MOST obnoxious years as a teenager I frequently received two admonitions. The first one was an abrupt, "Shut up!" The second was, "Grow up!"

Though I found it difficult on occasion, I usually managed to accomplish the first rather quickly. But I must confess, there are still days when I struggle with the second piece of advice.

En route to maturity, we all spill our milk, say things we shouldn't, and fail to act our age. At times we act like a two-year-old throwing a temper tantrum. At other times we pout like a pubescent child or go through sweeping mood swings like an awkwardly adjusting teenager.

This process is called "growing up." Let's not minimize the truth—it's painful. We struggle through it more by trial and error than by unfaltering charm-school grace. Consequently, every now and then we skin an elbow, bruise a knee, or bloody a nose from falling on our faces.

Growing up. Sooner or later we all have to do it. The sooner we do, the easier it will be to walk the uneven and sometimes uncertain sidewalks of faith.

Problem is, how do we determine whether we are grown up? Does it mean our hair starts to turn gray? No, that means we're growing older but not necessarily wiser. I've met people with snow-white hair who are still immature. Signs of aging do not necessarily mean we are showing signs of maturity.

If you think it's easier to tell from the inside out, forget it. How do you know that you are more mature this year than you were last year? Has living twelve months longer made any difference? We know we're growing older, but how do we know we're growing up? And is growing up something God even requires of us? Maybe He just wants us to live in His family, sort of exist between now and eternity, then He's planning to take us home. No, that's not the way it works. Growing up is a stated objective for every member of God's family. God says so in His Word.

The writer of Hebrews addresses this very matter when he takes his readers to task for their lack of maturity. They had grown older in the faith, but they had not yet grown up. Instead of building on the foundation laid by the apostles, they were still playing with blocks.

For though by this time you ought to be teachers, you have need again for someone to teach you the elementary principles of the oracles of God, and you have come to need milk and not solid food. For everyone who partakes only of milk is not accustomed to the word of righteousness, for he is a babe. But solid food is for the mature, who because of practice have their senses trained to discern good and evil.

Therefore leaving the elementary teaching about the Christ, *let us press on to maturity,* not laying again a foundation of repentance from dead works and of faith toward God, of instruction about washings, and laying on of hands, and the resurrection of the dead, and eternal judgment, and this we shall do, if God permits. (Heb. 5:12–6:3, italics added)

Do you notice the Lord's concern that some seem perpetually immature? "You have need *again* for someone to teach you the elementary principles of the oracles of God," says the writer (italics added). "You have come to need milk and not solid food." How interesting that he puts it like that. We would say, "You're back on baby food."

I've had grocers tell me that they sell more baby food to the aging than to the parents of infants in their community. As we get older, in many ways we revert back to childhood. Physically that can't be helped—as we age and grow infirm, our bodies deteriorate. But spiritually, immaturity is something we must not allow. God wants us to get beyond the elementary matters of the faith and set out on a lifelong pursuit of maturity. He longs for us to grow up in the faith.

Leave behind elementary teachings, says the letter to the Hebrews. Press on to maturity.

By "elementary teachings," the writer is very likely referring to the Old Testament signs and sacrifices. "We've gone beyond that now," he says. In today's terms we could say, "Move beyond the gospel. You have heard the gospel, you have responded to the gospel, you have believed the gospel, now go on. Grow up. Get into areas of teaching and learning that probe much deeper into your life." That kind of solid food results in spiritual strength. In fact, I've heard it rendered, "We are to leave the ABCs of the faith." In other words, we need to quit playing blocks and sucking milk from a bottle and wanting to be entertained. Leave the things that characterize infancy and get on with a grown-up lifestyle.

Few things are more pathetic to behold than those who have known the Lord for years but still can't get in out of the rain doctrinally and biblically. To put it succinctly, they have grown old, but they haven't grown up.

Do you feed yourself regularly on the Word of God or must you have the teaching of someone else to keep growing? Now, don't get me wrong; I don't decry teaching and preaching. How could I? That's my job security! All of us have a need for someone to instruct and exhort us in the things of God. But it isn't because we have no way of taking it in on our own. Teaching and preaching are more like nutritional food supplements.

Let me ask you several penetrating questions. Are you digging into the Word of God? Are you truly searching the Scriptures on your own? Are you engaged in a ministry of concerted and prevailing prayer? Can you handle pressure better than you could, say, three years ago? Are you further along on your own growth chart than you were a year ago, two years ago, five years ago?

Checkpoints for Maturity

How can we know we're growing up? Outwardly we have various signs of physical growth and aging. But when it comes to spiritual maturity, we need another kind of growth chart, and Peter, in his letter of hope, offers us a series of checkpoints to help us know we're growing up and getting on in spiritual life.

In the past three years I have flown on more airplanes than ever before in my life, commuting from California to Texas and back again, plus dozens of other destinations. When people ask Cynthia and me where we live, I sometimes reply, "Seats 16C and D, American Airlines." We're now on a first-name basis with many of the airline personnel.

As a result of this unusual transitional lifestyle, I have had ample occasions to watch the procedure pilots go through as they prepare for an upcoming flight. You may have observed it as well. The next time you're taking a trip, stand in the terminal and look out the windows into the cockpit of the airplane parked at the gate. You'll see the pilot sitting there with a clipboard, checking off all the instruments and systems. He'll also get out and check the outside of the aircraft, walking all around it. This is a seasoned pilot, with perhaps tens of thousands of hours in the air. Still, every time, before he takes that airplane up, he runs through his preflight checklist. We're thankful he does!

Look at 1 Peter 3:8–12, and you'll find another kind of checklist—a checklist for spiritual maturity. It helps us evaluate how we're doing on this pilgrimage from earth to heaven.

To sum up, let all be harmonious, sympathetic, brotherly, kind-hearted, and humble in spirit; not returning evil for evil, or insult for insult, but giving a blessing instead; for you were called for the very purpose that you might inherit a blessing. For,

> "Let him who means to love life and see good days
> refrain his tongue from evil and his lips from speaking guile.
> "And let him turn away from evil and do good;
> let him seek peace and pursue it.
> "For the eyes of the Lord are upon the righteous,
> and his ears attend to their prayer,
> but the face of the Lord is against those who do evil."
> (1 Pet. 3:8–12)

If I count correctly, there are no fewer than eight checkpoints in this section of Scripture. They help us determine how we're doing in our growth toward maturity.

Unity

The first checkpoint is unity: "Let all be harmonious." This refers to a oneness of heart, a similarity of purpose, and an agreement on major points of doctrine.

Please remember, this quality is not the same as *uniformity*, where everyone must look alike and think alike, form identical convictions and prefer the same tastes. That's what I call a cracker-box mentality. Peter isn't promoting uniformity. Nor is he referring to *unanimity*, where there is 100 percent agreement on everything. And it is not the same as *union*, where there is an affiliation with others but no common bond that makes them one at heart.

The secret to this kind of harmony is not to focus on petty peripheral differences but to concentrate on the common ground of Jesus Christ—His model, His message, and His mission.

How mature are you in the area of unity? Are you at harmony with other believers in the family of God? Are you one who works well *with* others?

Mutual Interest

The second checkpoint is mutual interest: "Let all be . . . sympathetic." The Greek root gives us our word *sympathy*, meaning "to feel with."

This means that when others weep, you weep; when they rejoice, you rejoice. It connotes the *absence* of competition, envy, or jealousy toward a fellow Christian.

Romans 12:15–16 states it well: "Rejoice with those who rejoice, and weep with those who weep. Be of the same mind toward one another. . . ." Believers who are growing toward maturity share in mutual feelings—mutual woes and mutual joys.

This is one of the best benefits of being part of the body of Christ and a major reason why we need to be involved in a local church. In that local community we have a context in which we can rejoice with each other and weep with one another. Think what happens when you move to a new community, a new home. Sadly you leave the church that has been your home, your spiritual family, where God has used you and encouraged you. But then He leads you to another. When you move to a new town or city, as a Christian one of the first things you do is search for a new church home, one where your new brothers and sisters welcome you and receive you into their fellowship and life. Right away you're surrounded by a family.

How's your maturity level on this second checkpoint? Can you truly say you enter the feelings of the other person? When others hurt, do you hurt? When they enjoy life, do you really enjoy it with them? When God blesses them with material prosperity or some significant award or promotion, do you rejoice with them or do you envy them? When they lose, do you feel the loss with them, or do you feel just a tiny pinprick of satisfaction?

I've heard it said, "Maturity begins to grow when you can sense your concern for others outweighing your concern for yourself."

Maturing believers care very much about the things others are experiencing.

Affectionate Friendship

The third checkpoint is friendship and affection: "Let all be . . . brotherly."

The word translated here as "brotherly" is from the Greek word *philos*, which has in mind the love of an affectionate friend. The poet Samuel Coleridge once described friendship as "a sheltering tree." When you have this quality, the branches of your friendship reach out over the lives of others, giving them shelter, shade, rest, relief, and encouragement.

Much has been written about the importance of friendship. James Boswell said, "We cannot tell the precise moment when friendship is formed. As in filling a vessel drop by drop, there is at last a drop which makes it run over; so in a series of kindnesses there is at last one which makes the heart run over." Longfellow wrote, "Ah! How good it feels, the hand of an old friend." Isn't that true!

Friends give comfort. We find strength near them. They bear fruit that provides nourishment and encouragement. When something troublesome occurs in our life, we pick up the phone and call a friend, needing the comfort he or she provides. I think there are few things more lonely than having no friend to call. Friends also care enough about us to hold us accountable . . . but we never doubt their love or respect.

Are you cultivating such friends? Are you being a friend? Are there a few folks who will stand near you, sheltering you with their branches?

Jay Kesler, my long-time friend and currently the president of Taylor University, has said that one of his great hopes in life is to wind up with at least eight people who will attend his funeral without once checking their watches. I love it! Do you have eight people who'll do that?

As we mature, it is healthy for us to have a circle of friends who lovingly hold us close, regardless . . . who care about our pain, who are there for us when we can't make it on our own. The flip side of that is equally healthy—our being friends like that to others. Works both ways. As we mature our friendships deepen.

Kindheartedness

The fourth checkpoint is kindheartedness: "Let all be . . . kindhearted." The Greek term here can also be translated "compassionate," and it is used in the Gospels to describe Jesus.

And seeing the multitudes, He *felt compassion* for them, because they were distressed and downcast like sheep without a shepherd. (Matt. 9:36, italics added)

As a good shepherd, Jesus looked at humanity's lost sheep who were scattered, frightened, and hungry. What He saw pulled at His heartstrings. He was full of tenderness for them. He had compassion for them. Just as these hurting people touched the heart of the Savior, so should hurting people today touch our hearts. If they do, it's a definite sign of spiritual growth. No one who is mature is ever so important that the needs of others no longer matter.

I've just finished reading a fascinating volume, *Character Above All*. It is a compilation of ten essays on the ten United States presidents from Franklin Roosevelt in the 1930s to George Bush in the 1990s, each written by people who knew those presidents well—friends, speechwriters, fellow politicians, and other colleagues who worked alongside them.

My favorite was the chapter on Ronald Reagan, who served our country from 1981–1989. His speechwriter, Peggy Noonan, wrote the piece and captured the essence of his character in twenty-two pages. Wonderful reading!

She concludes with a story about, in her words, "the almost Lincolnian kindness that was another part of Reagan's character . . . everyone who worked with Reagan has a story about his kindness." Before I retell that story, go back and read those eleven words. Wouldn't it be great if that could be said about each of us? Wouldn't it be wonderful to be remembered for our kindness?

In highlighting this quality in Reagan's character, Noonan tells the story of Frances Green, an eighty-three-year-old woman who lived by herself on social security in a town just outside San Francisco. She had little money, but for eight years she'd been sending one dollar a year to the Republican National Convention.

Then one day Frances got an RNC fund-raising letter in the mail, a beautiful piece on thick, cream-colored paper with black-and-gold lettering. It invited the recipient to come to the White House to meet President Reagan. She never noticed the little RSVP card that suggested a positive reply needed to be accompanied by a generous donation. She thought she'd been invited because they appreciated her dollar-a-year support.

Frances scraped up every cent she had and took a four-day train ride across America. Unable to afford a sleeper, she slept sitting up in coach. Finally she arrived at the White House gate: a little elderly woman with white hair, white powder all over her face, white stockings, an old hat with white netting, and an all-white dress, now yellow with age. When she got up to the guard at the gate and gave her name, however, the man frowned, glanced over his official list, and told her that her name wasn't there. She couldn't go in. Frances Green was heartbroken.

A Ford Motor Company executive who was standing in line behind her watched and listened to the little scenario. Realizing something was wrong, he pulled Frances aside and got her story. Then he asked her to return at nine o'clock the next morning and meet him there. She agreed. In the meantime, he made contact with Anne Higgins, a presidential aide, and got clearance to give her a tour of the White House and introduce her to the president. Reagan agreed to see her, "of course."

The next day was anything but calm and easy at the White House. Ed Meese had just resigned. There had been a military uprising abroad. Reagan was in and out of high-level secret sessions. But Frances Green showed up at nine o'clock, full of expectation and enthusiasm.

The executive met her, gave her a wonderful tour of the White House, then quietly walked her by the Oval Office, thinking maybe, at best, she might get a quick glimpse of the president on her way out. Members of the National Security Council came out. High-ranking generals were coming and going. In the midst of all the hubbub, President Reagan glanced out and saw Frances Green. With a smile, he gestured her into his office.

As she entered, he rose from his desk and called out, "Frances! Those darn computers, they fouled up again! If I'd known you were coming I would have come out there to get you myself." He then invited her to sit down, and they talked leisurely about California, her town, her life and family.

The president of the United States gave Frances Green a lot of time that day—more time than he had. Some would say it was time wasted. But those who say that didn't know Ronald Reagan, according to Peggy Noonan. He knew this woman had nothing to give him, but she needed something he could give her. And so he (as well as the Ford executive) took time to be kind and compassionate.[1]

In our high-tech, cyberspace era it is so easy to become distant. We can live our lives untouched and untouchable. In a fast-lane world it isn't difficult to become uncaring and preoccupied with our own agendas. The freeway of life requires that we keep moving, no matter what we see happening around us. The pace at which we travel does not allow us to stop easily. And even if we could, we've seen the stories in the news about people who stopped to help and were rebuffed, mugged, or carjacked—even murdered. So we learn to keep our eyes straight ahead and keep going . . . fast! The homeless person on the sidewalk? The mentally disturbed stranger at the mall? Hurry past. Just keep looking straight ahead, moving past them, down the road of life.

Of course, we need to be wise; we must use discernment. Still, is there no place for kindheartedness and compassion in our world? Is there no time for tender mercies?

Read again the words that appear at the end of Ephesians 4:

> And be kind to one another, tender-hearted, forgiving each other, just as God in Christ also has forgiven you. (Eph. 4:32)

Maturing people are tender people. How valuable they are in a busy society like ours!

Humility

The fifth checkpoint is humility: "Let all be . . . humble in spirit." The phrase "humble in spirit" literally means "lowly" or "bowed down" in mind. It speaks of an internal attitude rather than an external appearance. Humility isn't a show we put on; in fact, if we think we're humble, we're probably not. And in our day of self-promotion, self-assertion, spotlighting "celebrities of the faith," and magnifying the flesh, this quality—so greatly valued by the Lord Jesus—is a rare commodity indeed. Oswald Chambers writes of this so insightfully:

> We have a tendency to look for wonder in our experience, and we mistake heroic actions for real heroes. It's one thing to go through a crisis grandly, yet quite another to go through every day glorifying God when there is no witness, no limelight, and no one paying even the remotest attention to us. If we are not looking for halos, we at least want something that will make people say, "What a wonderful man of prayer he is!" or "What a great woman of devotion she is!" If you are properly devoted to the Lord Jesus, you have reached the lofty height where no one would ever notice you personally. All that is noticed is the power of God coming through you all the time.
>
> We want to be able to say, "Oh, I have had a wonderful call from God!" But to do even the most humbling tasks to the glory of God takes the Almighty God Incarnate working in us.[2]

If you are blessed with abilities, if you are gifted, if you are used by God, it is easy to start believing your own stuff. Yet one of the marks of a truly mature life is humility of spirit.

> It can be said without qualification that no human being can consider himself mature if he narrows the use of his efforts, talents, or means to his own personal advantage. The very concept of maturity rests on the degree of inner growth that is characterized by a yearning within the individual to transcend his self-concentration by extending himself into the lives of others. In other words, maturity is a stage in his development when to live with himself in a satisfying manner it becomes imperative for him to give as well as to receive.[3]

A truly humble person looks for opportunities to give himself freely to others rather than holding back, to release rather than hoarding, to build up rather than tearing down, to serve rather than being served, to learn from others rather than clamoring for the teaching stand. How blessed are those who learn this early in life.

Carl Sandberg once related the story about a mother who brought her newborn son to General Robert E. Lee for a blessing. The southern gentleman tenderly cradled the lad in his arms then looked at the mother and said, "Ma'am, please teach him that he must deny himself."[4]

Forgiveness

Thus far, Peter has written about how maturity affects how we think and how we feel. In his last three checkpoints, found in verses 9 through 11, he tells us how maturity affects *what we do and what we say.* In verse 9 he tells us not to return evil for evil. In other words, be willing to forgive.

> . . . not returning evil for evil, or insult for insult, but giving a blessing instead; for you were called for the very purpose that you might inherit a blessing. (1 Pet. 3:9)

Isn't that a great statement? It touches all the important bases regarding forgiveness. Just look at the four steps in it; observe the process.

First, when we have true forgiveness in our hearts, we refuse to get back or get even.

Second, we restrain from saying anything ugly in return.

Third, we return good for evil, "giving a blessing instead [of evil or insult]."

And fourth, we keep in mind that we were called to endure such harsh treatment.

It's easy to miss that last one, isn't it? I thought at first I was misreading it, and then I went back to chapter 2 and found that's what Peter says over there too. So he must mean it. Do you remember his earlier comment?

What credit is there if, when you sin and are harshly treated, you endure it with patience? But if when you do what is right and suffer for it you patiently endure it, this finds favor with God. For you have been called for this purpose. (1 Pet. 2:20–21a)

What is a sure sign that I'm growing up? When I stop fighting back. When I take the chip off my shoulder. When I stop working on my clever answer so I can punch back with a sarcastic jab.

Whenever the urge to get even comes over us, it's important for us to realize that retaliation is a sign of adolescence while restraint is a mark of maturity.

A Controlled Tongue

"Let him who means to love life and see good days
refrain his tongue from evil and his lips from speaking guile."
(1 Pet. 3:10)

You knew we'd get around to this one, didn't you? The tongue . . . what a battle! Warnings about the tongue are threaded throughout the Bible. In fact, in this verse and the one that follows Peter is quoting from Psalm 34:12–16.

Here he says to "refrain" your tongue from evil. Actually the psalmist used a little more forceful language: "Keep your tongue from evil." The idea is to get control of your tongue, or, as James puts it, put a bridle on it. It's the idea of holding it back from galloping headlong into greater evil (see James 3:1–10). Control your tongue!

Show me a person who has learned to refrain from gossip, to refrain from passing on confidential information, to refrain from making an unverified comment, and I'll show you somebody who is well on his or her way to maturity.

You really want to love life? You want to see good days? Gain better control of your tongue. Life will be happier for you. It'll even be easier for you. You'll see better days.

Some never learn this lesson. Remember the classic grave marker from jolly old England?

Beneath this sod,
this lump of clay,
lies Arabella Young,
who, on the 24th of May
began to hold her tongue.

Will it take death to control your tongue? It need not! Pray that God will control your tongue, starting today! Pray that He will muzzle your mouth when someone says, "Please don't share this with anyone else." When someone speaks to you in confidence, seal the information in the secret vault of your mind.

Believe me, I'm a preacher, and I know how tempting it is to use real-life examples in my sermon illustrations, especially family-related examples. I heard recently about a preacher up in the Northwest who pays his kids a royalty of a dollar every time he uses them in an illustration! He asks permission, they approve, he tells the story, they get a buck. That'll curb a loose tongue real quick!

A mark of maturity is a controlled tongue.

A verse in Psalm 141 puts all of this so clearly. It's from the ancient writings of David, and I've often thought of it as a great prayer with which to begin each day.

Set a guard, O LORD, over my mouth;
Keep watch over the door of my lips. (Ps. 141:3)

How are you doing on the checklist so far? Unity. Mutual interest. Friendship and affection. Kindheartedness and compassion. Humility. Forgiveness. A controlled tongue. Pretty convicting list, isn't it? But if we wish to have hope beyond our immaturity, these qualities are worth our time and attention. And there's one more twofold checkpoint.

Purity and Peace

"And let him turn away from evil and do good;
let him seek peace and pursue it.
"For the eyes of the Lord are upon the righteous,

And his ears attend to their prayer,
But the face of the Lord is against those who do evil."
(1 Pet. 3:11–12)

Look again at Peter's counsel. "Turn away from evil and do good."
That's purity. "Seek peace and pursue it." That's peace. And then he
tells us that the Lord is watching us and listening to us. Why? Because He cares about our modeling these qualities.

The eyes and ears of the Lord are emblematic of God's providential care for His people. What a wonderful reason for pursuing purity
and peace—the promise of God's providential care!

A Final Glance at the Checklist

That's quite a checklist, isn't it? Eight distinct notches to mark our
Christian maturity. How do you measure up?

We're told to grow up. We're told to press on to maturity. But
growing up is never easy. We all have areas of trouble, setbacks,
stumbling points along the way. (I don't know of one item on this list
that isn't a struggle for me at various times in my own life.) So those
are the things that we pray about, for "His ears attend to our
prayers."

Here's a practical suggestion. Go over that list at the end of every
month. Write it out and stick it where you will see it. Put it under a
refrigerator magnet. Tape it to your mirror. Ask God for strength in
these eight areas.

As children of God moving toward maturity, let's be committed to
harmony, to a spirit of unity. Let's engage in a mutual interest in
each other's lives. Let's develop friendships marked by affection, by
"touchable love"—love that is genuine and demonstrative. Let's be
kindhearted and compassionate. Let's exhibit humility of spirit and
a mind that is concerned about others instead of ourselves. Finally,
let's forgive, control our tongues, and pursue purity and peace.

I am grateful airline pilots take the time to check their lists before
we take off. I'm especially glad they don't shrug their shoulders when

they see a bulge on one of the tires and say, "Well, we'll just hope for the best." I'm glad they don't ignore the smallest detail, even though they've gone down the same list hundreds of times in their careers. I'm glad they don't take my life and safety for granted. That's why they are willing to return to that list again and again and again.

We dare not take our Christian maturity for granted either. That's why we must return to God's checklist again and again and again.

We dare not do any less if we hope to get beyond a life of immaturity.

A Prayer for Hope Beyond Immaturity

Father, thank You for the reminder today of things that are such an important part of our lives. Though none of these qualities is new, we continue to need the reminder. How often we have come asking for help in one or more of these areas. You've heard our pleas on many occasions. We so want to be growing toward maturity . . . but the journey takes forever! And so, this very moment, we thank You for the Lord Jesus Christ, our model and our master, who fulfilled each of these marks of maturity and dozens of other character qualities to perfection, though fully man. Thank You for the hope we have that Your Holy Spirit will be with us each step of our way on our road to maturity. We certainly need His empowerment to keep us going and growing.

I would ask, finally, that You give us hope beyond our immaturity. Guard us from discouragement as we look back over the checklist and realize how far we have to go. Remind us that we've come a long way toward the goal, by Your grace. Through Jesus Christ I pray.

AMEN

9

Hope Beyond Bitterness

When Life
"Just Ain't Fair"

AN OLD FRENCH fairy tale tells the story of two daughters—one bad and the other good. The bad daughter was the favorite of her mother, but the good daughter was unjustly neglected, despised, and mistreated.

One day, while drawing water from the village well, the good daughter met a poor woman who asked for a drink. The girl responded with kind words and gave the woman a cup of water. The woman, actually a fairy in disguise, was so pleased with the little girl's kindness and good manners that she gave her a gift.

"Each time you speak," said the woman, "a flower or jewel will come out of your mouth."

When the little girl got home, her mother began to scold her for taking so long to bring the water. The girl started to apologize, and two roses, two pearls, and two diamonds came out of her mouth.

Her mother was astonished. But after hearing her daughter's story and seeing the number of beautiful jewels that came out in the telling, the mother called her other daughter and sent her forth to get the same gift. The bad daughter, however, was reluctant to be seen performing the lowly task of drawing water, so she grumbled sourly all the way to the well.

When the bad daughter got to the well, a beautiful queenly woman—that same fairy in another disguise—came by and asked for a drink. Disagreeable and proud, the girl responded rudely. As a result, she received her reward too. Each time she opened her mouth, she emitted snakes and toads.[1]

How's that for poetic justice!

There's something in each one of us that longs for circumstances to be fair, isn't there? Maybe that's why fairy tales are so appealing. Good people receive their rewards and "live happily ever after" while bad people are soundly punished. Life works out, justice is done, and fairness reigns supreme.

Unfortunately, real life doesn't usually turn out that way. Every child needs to be taught, "Fairness is rare." Every epitaph could read, "Life is difficult."

Our lives are haunted by unfairness when we want fairness. Instead of justice we are surrounded by injustice. We want deceit exposed, dishonesty revealed, and truth rewarded. But things don't work out that way. At least not as we perceive them.

Some families have been racked by unfairness. A mate leaves a loving, faithful partner. Disease steals a loved one prematurely. An unfair situation at work or at school keeps escalating.

Life just doesn't turn out fair for some . . . for most!

Truly, life *is* difficult. But therein lies some of life's best lessons.

I was reminded of those words when I read this astonishing statement by a well-known British writer and radio personality:

> Contrary to what might be expected, I look back on experiences that at the time seemed especially desolating and painful with particular satisfaction. Indeed, I can say with complete truthfulness that everything I have learned in my seventy-five years in this world, everything that has truly enhanced and enlightened my existence, has been through affliction and not through happiness. In other words, if it ever were to

be possible to eliminate affliction from our earthly existence by means of some drug or other medical mumbo jumbo . . . the result would not be to make life delectable, but to make it too banal and trivial to be endurable. This, of course, is what the Cross signifies. And it is the Cross, more than anything else, that has called me inexorably to Christ.[2]

Now it is one thing to read those words from a man like Malcolm Muggeridge and almost be moved to tears. It's another thing to embrace them in our own lives. I know there isn't a person reading this who hasn't, at some point, had reason to become bitter because of the way you were treated by someone or because of some "unfair" affliction or experience. Everyone can blame someone for something!

As Christians we know that, ultimately, good will triumph over evil and that our God is just and kind and fair. But what can we do with the injustices and unfairnesses in the meantime? How can we keep pressing on in spite of such mistreatment?

Two Different and Distinct Perspectives

Our response to unfairness, as with all other issues, is based on our perspective—the particular vantage point from which we look at life. Basically, in this case, we have two perspectives to choose from: the human perspective or the divine.

The Human Perspective

Our natural, human perspective contends, "Since life isn't fair, I'm going to get my share. I'm going to look out for number one. I'm going to spend my energy getting my own back or setting things straight or making it right. I'm not going to take it any longer."

Our world is full of literature and counselors who will help you carry out this agenda. The problem is, you may get even but you won't get peace. You may feel better for the short term, but you won't get lasting satisfaction. You may find a way to channel your anger, but if retaliation is your major goal, you will not glorify God. Those who live their lives from this perspective are more likely to end their lives as bitter, cynical, hostile people. Tragically, I have just described how the majority of Americans choose to live.

The Divine Perspective

Fortunately, we do have another option, and we find it clearly spelled out for us in 1 Peter.

> "For the eyes of the Lord are upon the righteous,
> And His ears attend to their prayer,
> But the face of the Lord is against those who do evil."
> (1 Pet. 3:12)

The principle that Peter gives us is this: God misses nothing. He's looking out for us. He's listening to our prayers. And He is completely aware of the evil that is happening to us.

Don't ever think He has missed the evil. He sees, and He remembers. He may be long-suffering, but He doesn't compromise His justice. Not only is His eye on the righteous, His face is against evil. Ultimately, good will overcome evil. In the end, God wins!

But if this is true, we wonder, why doesn't He do something about evil? Why does He let it go on so long? Because God's time line is infinite—He doesn't close His books at the end of the month. It may take a lifetime—or longer—before justice is served. But in the end, count on it, *God will be just.* In the end, He will "work everything together for good" and for His glory.

That thought gives us hope beyond bitterness. If we don't believe that and if we don't focus on that, we become the loser. We spend our years like a rat in a sewer pipe, existing in the tight radius of cynicism and bitterness. Ultimately, we become, in our aging years, angry old men and jaded old women.

★

Some Helpful Insights and Techniques to Keep Hope Alive

Building on this divine perspective, Peter gives us five ways we can live in an unfair and inequitable world. But first there's a general principle we need to underscore.

A General Principle

And who is there to harm you if you prove zealous for what is good? (1 Pet. 3:13)

If we were to paraphrase this verse, we could say that those who live honest lives will not usually suffer harm. *Usually.* There are exceptions, of course, to almost every rule, as we will see below. But as a general rule, if you live a life of purity and integrity, in the long run you usually won't suffer as much as those who habitually traffic in evil.

For example, if you pay your debts, chances are good that you won't get into financial trouble. If you pay all your taxes on time, you probably won't have the IRS on your case. If you take care of your body—get sufficient exercise and sleep, watch your diet and your stress level—chances are good that you will live a healthier life than those who don't. If you help others, chances are good that when you are in need someone will be there to help you. To paraphrase Peter's principle, those who do what is right are usually not in harm's way. *Usually* that's the rule.

Occasional Inequities

However, to return to reality, because life is difficult, there are times when life "just ain't fair." So there will be times when, despite that general principle, despite your righteous life, despite your faithful walk with God, situations turn on you. And it's these exceptions to the rule that Peter is addressing in chapter 3, verses 11 through 17. He begins with a general summation of the condition.

But even if you should suffer for the sake of righteousness, you are blessed. (1 Pet. 3:14a)

Before going on, notice the words, "But even if you should." In New Testament Greek, there are four conditions introduced by the word *if*. Three were quite common. The first-class condition, meaning "assumed as true," was a common usage (see Matt. 4:3, 6); the second-class condition, meaning "assumed as not true," was also commonly used (see Gal. 1:10); the third-class condition, meaning "maybe, maybe not," was frequently employed by writers (as seen earlier in 1 Pet. 3:13). The fourth-class condition, meaning "unlikely but possible," is rarely used in Scripture. Interestingly, this is the condition Peter uses here in verse 14. It could be paraphrased, "It is unlikely that you should suffer for the sake of righteousness, but if you should. . . ." That, alone, ought to give us a boost of fresh hope!

Then Peter goes on to suggest five ways you and I should respond if this happens. Remember, this is not my advice; this is God's advice. Human advice says, "Kick 'em in the teeth. Get even." That's not good advice, but it's often heard. So we need to know what God has to say about how to respond when we have done what is right but wrong is done to us in return.

It might help if you wrote these responses down on a three-by-five card and keep them handy. I'd suggest that you look at the card at least once a day. You might want to stick it on your bathroom mirror or slide it under the glass of your desktop.

How are we to respond when the exception to the rule occurs?

First, consider yourself uniquely blessed by God.

As far as the injustice itself is concerned, Peter's surprising advice is, "Be happy! Consider yourself blessed!" James tells us something similar in the first chapter of his letter.

When all kinds of trials and temptations crowd into your lives, my brothers, don't resent them as intruders, but welcome them as friends! (James 1:2 PHILLIPS)

Sure sounds nice, you may say, but honestly now, how can we be happy and consider ourselves blessed when we've just been punched in the eye with the fist of injustice?

Well, we can do this by remembering two things: first, as we saw in chapter 6, we are called to patiently endure unfair treatment (see 1 Pet. 2:21; 3:9) so that when it comes we can know we're still experiencing God's plan and fulfilling our calling. Such treatment reminds us that God's hand is still on our lives. And second, someday we will be rewarded for our endurance of these undeserved trials (see Matt. 5:10–12; James 1:12).

Anybody can accept a reward graciously, and many people can even take their punishment patiently when they have done something wrong. But how many people are equipped to handle mistreatment after they've done right? Only Christians are equipped to do that. That is what makes believers stand out. That's our uniqueness. And, yes, there are occasions in life when we will be called for that very purpose. In the mystery of God's sovereign plan, we will be singled out. Then later, like Job, we will be rewarded for enduring those trials we did not deserve.

Remember Jesus' instruction?

"Blessed are those who have been persecuted for the sake of righteousness, for theirs is the kingdom of heaven. Blessed are you when men cast insults at you, and persecute you, and say all kinds of evil against you falsely, on account of Me. Rejoice, and be glad, for your reward in heaven is great, for so they persecuted the prophets who were before you." (Matt. 5:10–12)

Because of these promises (there are many similar ones throughout the Scriptures) Christians can do something different from all the rest of humanity. We can respond to injustice with a positive attitude. When we do, mouths drop open . . . and we're frequently given an opportunity to explain why we're not eaten up with revenge.

Second, don't panic and don't worry.

And do not fear their intimidation, and do not be troubled. (1 Pet. 3:14b)

It doesn't take a linguistic scholar to interpret that counsel. Peter puts his finger on two common responses. Panic and worry. I do both of those things when I operate in the flesh, don't you? But observe what Peter says.

First, look at the word *fear*. It comes from the original term *phobos*, from which we also get our word *phobia*. This kind of fear is the fear that seizes us with terror and causes us to take flight, running away from the pressure. Peter says, "Don't do that. There's no reason to run. Don't attempt to escape the trial. Don't panic."

In the second phrase he tells us that we don't need to "be troubled." The word *troubled* in Greek means "to be agitated, uneasy," the idea of feeling inner turmoil or agitation. Remember John 14:1, "Let not your heart be troubled"? Same root word here.

The energy and effort we expend worrying never solves a thing. In fact, it usually makes the situation worse for us, creating a terrible inner turmoil which, if allowed to intensify, can paralyze us.

Peter's counsel to us is that, even when trials are pressing in and people are trying to intimidate us, we can have a calmness of spirit. As far as the persecutor or instigator is concerned, we can be free from panic and worry. How? Why? Because we know that God is on our side.

Third, acknowledge Christ as Lord even over this event.

But sanctify Christ as Lord in your hearts . . . (1 Pet. 3:15a)

We often overlook the first phrase of this verse in our concentration on the second part:

. . . always being ready to make a defense to everyone who asks you to give an account for the hope that is in you. (1 Pet. 3:15b)

We usually apply those words to some public defense of the faith. While they may be used in that way, the verse actually appears in a context of wrong having come to us as a result of our doing what is right. And it says, "Do not fear . . . but in your hearts set apart [sanctify] Christ as Lord" (NIV).

You and I can do that in prayer. When we think a wrong has been done to us that we don't deserve, we can respond, "Lord, You're with me right now. You are here, and You have Your reasons for what is happening. You will not take advantage of me. You're much too kind to be cruel. You're much too good to be unjust. You care for me too much to let this get out of hand. Take charge. Use my integrity to defend me. Give me the grace to stay calm. Control my emotions. Be Lord over my present situation." In such a prayer, we "set apart Christ as Lord" in our hearts.

If I have prayed that sort of prayer once, I must have prayed it dozens of times. "Lord, there is no way I can set the record straight, it seems. It's getting more complicated and I find myself completely at Your disposal . . . at Your mercy. Take over, Lord. You be the sovereign Master over this moment. I can't change this person . . . I can't alter these circumstances. You be the Lord over this scene."

When our older daughter, Charissa, was in high school, she was on the cheerleading squad. One day at the church office I got an emergency call from her school. She had accidentally fallen from the top of a pyramid of the other cheerleaders during practice and landed on the back of her head. To her and everyone else's amazement, she couldn't move. It took me about fifteen minutes to drive from my study at the church to the school campus. I was praying that kind of prayer all the way. "Lord, You are in charge of this situation. I have no idea what I'm going to face. You be the Lord and Master. I am trusting You in all this."

When I got to the school, they already had Charissa immobilized on a wrap-around stretcher. I slipped to my knees beside her.

"Daddy, I can't move my fingers. My feet and legs are numb," she said. "I can't feel anything in my body very well. It's kind of tingling."

At that moment, I confess I had feelings of fear. But I leaned closer to Charissa and whispered in her ear, "Sweetheart, I will be with you through all of this. But more importantly, Jesus is here with you. He is Lord over this whole event."

Her mother and I were totally helpless. We had absolutely no control over the situation or over the healing of our daughter's body. She was at the mercy of God. I can still remember the deliberateness with which I acknowledged Christ as Lord in my heart and encouraged her to do the same. Cynthia and I waited for hours in the hospital hallway as extensive X-rays were taken and a team of physicians examined our daughter. We prayed fervently and confidently.

Today, Charissa is fine. She recovered with no lasting damage. She did have a fracture, but thankfully it wasn't an injury that resulted in paralysis. Had she been permanently paralyzed, we would still believe that God was in sovereign control. He would still be Lord!

A good example of someone who sanctified Christ as Lord in his heart is Stephen. When he gave an eloquent and penetrating defense of Jesus before the Jewish Sanhedrin, this infuriated many who heard him. Their hatred raged out of control. Do you remember his response?

> But being full of the Holy Spirit, he gazed intently into heaven and saw the glory of God, and Jesus standing at the right hand of God; and he said, "Behold, I see the heavens opened up and the Son of Man standing at the right hand of God." (Acts 7:55–56)

They wouldn't listen to him. They covered their ears and rushed upon him. They drove him out of the city and violently stoned him to death.

As Stephen died, "he called upon the Lord and said, 'Lord Jesus, receive my spirit!' And falling on his knees, he cried out with a loud voice, 'Lord, do not hold this sin against them!'" (Acts 7:59–60). And then he died.

Stephen didn't deserve their savage attack. He certainly didn't deserve death. Because of that, he could have died in bitterness and cynicism. He could have died with curses on his lips. Instead, he sanctified the moment to God and died with a prayer on his lips, asking forgiveness for those who so mercilessly killed him. When those men looked into Stephen's face, they didn't find their own hatred reflected back at them; they saw the reflection of the Savior's grace and love.

Like Stephen, we need to acknowledge Christ's control over our unfair circumstances and do our best to see that He is glorified in them. That is the only thing that will bring us lasting, peaceful satisfaction.

Fourth, be ready to give a witness.

. . . . always being ready to make a defense to everyone who asks you to give an account for the hope that is in you, yet with gentleness and reverence. (1 Pet. 3:15b)

I'm intrigued by this. Some of us are so anxious to give a witness that we press it on others even when it isn't appropriate or when the timing isn't right. But this says we are to be ready *when they ask us* to give an account. And believe me, if you are handling mistreatment or unfairness or suffering for the glory of God, people will ask.

"How do you do it?" . . . "How do you handle this?" . . . "How do you live with it?" . . . "Why is it you haven't lost your joy?" . . . "What keeps you on your feet?" . . . "Why haven't you just turned tail and run?" . . . "Why haven't you fought back?" Common questions from curious onlookers.

"Be ready to make a defense . . . to give an account." The word *defense* comes from the term *apologia*. We get our word *apology* from this Greek word. It refers to making a verbal statement of defense. And *account* comes from the word *logos*, translated elsewhere in Scripture, "the word." At such times we are to be ready to give a verbal witness . . . a gentle and yet pointed declaration of the truth.

Stop and consider. Mistreatment is a perfect platform for a witness. Your neighbors will want to know how you stay calm in the midst of it, how you go through it without strongly reacting. Your friend at work will want to know, "How do you pull it off?"

Be ready to make a defense, to give an answer, to witness to anyone who asks. Seldom will there be a more opportune time to share your faith than when you are suffering and glorifying Him through it. Others who know what you are enduring will listen. You have earned the right to be heard. But don't miss the way you should testify: "with gentleness and reverence." Wise counsel from Peter, a man who had been broken.

William Barclay gives an excellent explanation of what our "defense" and "account" should be like.

It must be *reasonable*. It is a *logos* [account] that the Christian must give, and a *logos* is a reasonable and intelligent statement of his position. . . . To do so we must know what we believe; we must have thought it out; we must be able to state it intelligently and intelligibly. . . .

His defence must be given with *gentleness*. . . . The case for Christianity must be presented with winsomeness and with love. . . . Men may be wooed into the Christian faith when they cannot be bullied into it.

His defence must be given *with reverence*. That is to say, any argument in which the Christian is involved must be carried on in a tone which God can hear with joy. . . . In any presentation of the Christian case and in any argument for the Christian faith, the accent should be the accent of love.[3]

And fifth, keep a good conscience.

Here Peter digs below the surface, turning up the rich soil of inner character. And what is the precious gem he is trying to unearth? *Integrity.*

And keep a good conscience so that in the thing in which you are slandered, those who revile your good behavior in Christ may be put to shame. (1 Pet. 3:16)

Nothing speaks louder or more powerfully than a life of integrity. Absolutely nothing! Nothing stands the test like solid character. You can handle the blast like a steer in a blizzard. The ice may form on your horns, but you keep standing against the wind and the howling, raging storm because Christ is at work in your spirit. Character will always win the day. As Horace Greeley wrote: "Fame is a vapor, popularity an accident, riches take wing, and only character endures."

There is no more eloquent and effective defense than a life lived continually and consistently in integrity. It possesses invincible power to silence your slanderers.

The Underlying and Unwavering Principle

For it is better, if God should will it so, that you suffer for doing what is right than for doing what is wrong. (1 Pet. 3:17)

Simply stated, the principle is this: Unjust suffering is always better than deserved punishment. And sometimes—though we cannot fully explain why—it is God's will that His people should suffer for doing what is right.

An old Hebrew story tells of a righteous man who suffered undeservedly. He was a man who had turned away from evil, took care of his family, walked with God, and was renown for his integrity. But suddenly, without warning, and seemingly without reason, he lost everything he had: his flocks, his cattle, his servants, his children, and finally his health. This old Hebrew story is no fairy tale. It is the real account of a real person—Job.

Though he suffered terribly, and though he could never have foreseen it himself or understood it when it happened, Job has been remembered down through the ages and to this very day as a model of patient endurance. "The patience of Job" remains one of our axiomatic phrases.

I would not wish the life of Job on anyone. But, then, I'm not God. I've never been too good at directing anyone else's life. I have a hard enough time keeping my own on track. But I have observed a few "Jobs" in my years in ministry. They come under that fourth-class condition: "If He should will it so . . . it's unlikely but possible."

If you are one of those modern-day "Jobs," don't waste your time trying to figure out *why*. Someday all will be made clear. For now, follow the five responses outlined by Peter.

Dr. Bruce Waltke was my Hebrew professor during three of my years at Dallas Seminary. He has since become something of a mentor and friend. He is a brilliant man with a tender heart for God. When I was going through a very difficult time in my senior year in seminary and wanted some answers to the *whys,* Bruce said something like this: "Chuck, I've come to the place where I believe only on very rare occasions does God tell us why, so I've decided to stop asking." I found that to be very helpful counsel. From that point on, I began to acknowledge that I am not the "answer man" for events in life that don't make logical, human sense. I'm now convinced that even if He did explain His reasons, I would seldom understand. His ways are higher and far more profound than our finite minds can comprehend. So I now accept God's directions, and I live with them as best I can. And frankly, I leave it at that. I've found that such a response not only relieves me, it gives me hope beyond bitterness.

If God has called you to be a Job—a rare calling—remember that the Lord is not only full of compassion, He is also in full control. He will not leave you without hope. He offers us His promises:

> "For My thoughts are not your thoughts,
> Neither are your ways My ways," declares the LORD.
> "For as the heavens are higher than the earth,
> So are My ways higher than your ways,
> And My thoughts than Your thoughts." (Isa. 55:8–9)

> When a man's ways are pleasing to the LORD,
> He makes even his enemies to be at peace with him. (Prov. 16:7)

Listen to the counsel of Peter. Calmly and quietly let these five bits of counsel sink in.

- Consider yourself uniquely blessed by God.
- Do not run in panic or sit and worry.

- Acknowledge Christ as Lord even over this event.
- Be ready to give a witness.
- Keep a good conscience.

A Prayer for Hope Beyond Bitterness

Our Father, as we acknowledge Your Son as Lord, it is with a sigh, because we cannot deny the pain or ignore the difficulty of earthly trials. For some who read these words, the reality of this is almost unbearable. But being sovereign and being the One with full capacity to handle our needs, it is not beyond Your strength to take the burden and, in return, to give us the perspective we need.

Quiet our spirits. Give us a sense of relief as we face the inevitable fact that life is difficult and that there will be those rare moments when it will not be at all fair. Erase any hint of bitterness. Enable us to see beyond the present, to focus on the invisible, and to recognize that You are always there. Remind us, too, that Your ways are higher and far more profound than ours.

Thank You for the joy of this day. Thank You for the pleasure of a relationship with You and a few good, caring, loving friends. And especially, Father, thank You for the truth of Your Word that lives and abides forever. In the strong name of Him who is higher, Jesus the Lord.

AMEN

10

Hope Beyond the Creeds

Focusing Fully
on
Jesus Christ

WHEN I WAS a little boy, my family moved to Houston, where my father had been hired to work at what was called, in those days during World War II, a "defense plant." Houston is a city of industry, and during those war years many of the industries retooled in order to manufacture implements, ammunition, and equipment for the war. The particular place where my father worked built transmissions for the rugged Sherman tank and landing gears for the powerful B-17 "Flying Fortresses."

We didn't see much of my dad during those five years because he was working ten to fifteen, sometimes even eighteen, hours a day, from six to seven days a week. Since our family had only one car, which Dad used each day to drive himself and several coworkers to the shop, the rest of our family had to walk to the grocery store, to school, and to church.

The closest church was a Methodist church at the end of our street. I still remember sitting in those wooden pews almost every Sunday. And every Sunday, as part of the worship-service liturgy of that particular Methodist church, we recited the Apostles' Creed.

I don't remember one sermon that was preached during those five years. I cannot recall any church-sponsored event that made an impact on me. But I clearly remember repeating the Apostles' Creed. In fact, I memorized that statement of faith in a matter of months simply because we repeated it Sunday after Sunday. You, too, may know these words well:

> I believe in God the Father Almighty, maker of heaven and earth;
> And in Jesus Christ, His only begotten Son, our Lord, who was conceived by the Holy Spirit, born of the Virgin Mary, suffered under Pontius Pilate, was crucified, dead and buried; He descended into hell; the third day He rose again from the dead; He ascended into heaven, and sits at the right hand of God the Father Almighty; from thence He shall come to judge the living and the dead.
> I believe in the Holy Spirit, the holy catholic church, the communion of saints, the forgiveness of sins, the resurrection of the body, and the life everlasting. Amen.

Even though I was only a small boy when I recited the creed, there were two statements in it that troubled me. My first concern was, "I believe in the holy catholic church." I knew our family wasn't Catholic, so how could I keep saying I believed in the Holy Catholic Church? Then, at some point, a youth worker explained to me that catholic (small "c") really meant "universal," so what we were really saying was, "I believe in the universal church." No problem.

More difficult to resolve, however, was the part where we said that Jesus Christ "descended into hell." That troubled me. There was nobody around who could answer that for me, not even my mother. Interestingly, it was almost twenty years later in a Greek class in seminary that I experienced a flashback to those days as a little boy in the Methodist church. We were digging into the text at the end of 1 Peter 3, and I came across the verse that described in Scripture what I had stated as a little boy but had never understood.

Let me remind you of the last five verses in 1 Peter 3:

For Christ also died for sins once for all, the just for the unjust, in order that He might bring us to God, having been put to death in the flesh, but made alive in the spirit; in which also He went and made proclamation to the spirits now in prison, who once were disobedient, when the patience of God kept waiting in the days of Noah, during the construction of the ark, in which a few, that is, eight persons, were brought safely through the water. And corresponding to that, baptism now saves you—not the removal of dirt from the flesh, but an appeal to God for a good conscience—through the resurrection of Jesus Christ, who is at the right hand of God, having gone into heaven, after angels and authorities and powers had been subjected to Him. (1 Pet. 3:18–22)

Isn't that a grand statement of faith? It's almost like another creed that we might recite in church from Sunday to Sunday.

Our Example

I have found in my study of the Bible that one of the best rules to follow if I'm going to understand any particular section of Scripture is to look at the whole scene (the context) before I try to work my way through each verse. Sort of like looking at the forest before examining the trees.

Following that rule, we first need to answer a primary question: What's the main subject of this paragraph? As you may recall from the subject we dealt with in chapter 9, it is unjust suffering. Remember the words of Peter?

For it is better, if God should will it so, that you suffer for doing what is right rather than for doing what is wrong. (1 Pet. 3:17)

If unjust suffering is the main subject, what's the point of the whole paragraph? Clearly, it is this: blessings follow suffering for well-doing.

Now at this point, immediately after Peter has written verse 17, the Spirit of God prompts him to mention the One who best exemplifies that truth. Who in every believer's mind would best exemplify blessing following unjust suffering? Obviously, Christ. And that's why Peter at verse 18 says, "For Christ." He doesn't say so, but we could insert in parentheses, "As an example."

> For Christ (as an example) also died for sins . . . the just for the unjust, in order that He might bring us to God . . . .

What is the blessing that came to us following Christ's unjust suffering? Our salvation. And what was the blessing for Him, personally, following His unjust suffering? His resurrection. That is stated at the end of verse 20.

The focus of attention here is Jesus Christ, not the recipients of the letter or those who would read it centuries later. It is Jesus Himself. He alone is the focal point. Look at this great statement of faith regarding the Lord Jesus.

Verse 18: He "died for sins." That's His *crucifixion*.

Verse 19: "He . . . made *proclamation*."

Verse 21: "through the *resurrection* of Jesus Christ."

Verse 22: "who is at the right hand of God . . . after angels and authorities and powers had been subjected to Him." That's *exaltation*.

What we have here, in brief, is a survey of the crucifixion, proclamation, resurrection, and exaltation of the Lord Jesus Christ. Peter is clearly and openly highlighting some major doctrines related to Jesus Christ. So far, so good. But the paragraph also includes a digression (see verses 19–21).

Sometimes while writing a letter you'll mention a subject that is important to you, which reminds you of something not as pertinent as the subject but since it completes the picture, you add it. It might take another paragraph to do so, or it might just take a sentence or two. In this instance, Peter completes the overall thought regarding Christ by adding some details . . . things seldom mentioned elsewhere in the Bible. In fact, there are two knotty issues here that every serious student of the New Testament struggles with. One of them has to do with Christ's "descent into hell" (see verses 19–20), and the other has to do with what appears to be an affirmation of baptismal regeneration, "baptism now saves you" (verse 21)—more about these later.

Our Entree

Having considered the overall context, then, let me come to the central theme of the passage. Look back again at verse 18. This is one of those all-encompassing verses that states the gospel in its briefest and most concentrated form. That concentrated statement concerning the Lord Jesus is beautiful: "Christ also died for sins once for all." We don't have to relive or redo the death of Christ. We don't have to anticipate His dying another time or several other times. He has died "once for all." It was the death of all deaths, permanently solving the sin problem.

When Christ came, He was the perfect substitute for sin. And as a lamb without spot and without blemish, He hung on the cross and died. His blood became the one-and-only, all-sufficient payment to God for sins. The anger of God was satisfied, because Christ's payment for sin settled the account, once for all. Furthermore, all the debt against us was wiped away as Christ's righteousness was credited to our account. It wasn't fair for Him to die. He was just. He died, "the just for the unjust."

You may not know it, but you're mentioned (by implication) in Scripture on a number of occasions. And here is one of those times. Your name could appear in the place of the words "the unjust."

Let me state it in my case: "For Christ also died for sins once for all, the just for Chuck Swindoll. . . ."

Or you could put *your* name there: "The just for [your name]."

Why did He do it? "In order that He might bring us to God." One very careful student of the New Testament calls this "an entree." Our Lord Jesus Christ, in dying on the cross, provided us with "an entree" into heaven. He gave us access. As a result of His death, the access to heaven is now permanently paved. It is available to all who believe in the Lord Jesus Christ.

He "was put to death in the flesh, but made alive in the Spirit." So what is He doing now? "He is at the right hand of God." Maybe you didn't know that—a lot of people don't know what Christ is currently doing. He has ascended from this earth, and He has gone back to the place of glory in bodily form. (He is the only member of the Godhead who is visible. God the Father is in spirit form. God the Spirit is in spirit form. The only visible member of the Trinity is the Lord Jesus Christ.) He sits at the right hand of God making intercession for us. He's praying for us. He is moved by our needs; He is touched with the feelings of our infirmities. He is there for us, His people, and He is interceding for us. Since He is at the right hand of God, there is no question of His place of authority.

The Apostles' Creed is correct when it says, "He ascended into heaven and sits at the right hand of God; from thence He shall come to judge the living and the dead." He will come to judge both, and that judgment awaits His return to this earth. What powerful truths are here! Peter knew his theology!

His Proclamation

All that is fairly clear . . . now the tough part. First of all, let's address the subject of Jesus' descent, as the creed calls it, "into hell." Referring to the Lord Jesus Christ, Peter tracks His itinerary following His crucifixion.

> . . . in which also He went and made proclamation to the spirits now in prison, who once were disobedient, when the patience of God kept waiting in the days of Noah, during the construction of the ark, in which a few, that is, eight persons, were brought safely through the water. (I Pet. 3:19–20)

What in the world does that mean? When exactly did this occur? Who were these spirits that He visited? And what is the "proclamation" that He made? Good questions.

Let me draw upon your knowledge of the Scriptures and ask you to remember a scene back in the days before the Flood. It's recorded in the sixth chapter of Genesis. (When you have time, you may want to go back and read it.) We are told that during this period the depravity of men and women reached an all-time high. Their wickedness was so severe that it grieved the heart of God—He was sorry He had even created humanity!

> Then the LORD saw that the wickedness of man was great on the earth, and that every intent of the thoughts of his heart was only evil continually. And the LORD was sorry that He had made man on the earth, and he was grieved in His heart. (Gen. 6:5–6)

If you read this in the context of the first four verses of Genesis 6, you learn of an amazing and seldom-mentioned series of events that had happened. There was sexual cohabitation at that time between spirit beings and women on this earth. It is believed that during the antediluvian era—the time prior to the Flood—these spirits came in bodily form and somehow had intercourse with human women. As a result, a generation of supernatural beings were born—admittedly a strange phenomenon rarely mentioned by preachers and therefore seldom taught to Christians.

When the Flood came, it put an end to that heinous lifestyle and that freakish generation. Also, God's judgment fell upon those spirits who cohabited with women, and He placed them in a location called, in the original, *Tartarus*. It was a special place, described here as "a prison." It was there Jesus made His victorious proclamation.

What was this proclamation? I find it helpful to know that this is not the word used for proclaiming the gospel. Rather, it is a word, *kerusso*, used to describe someone "heralding" a statement. It denotes one who proclaims that the king has made a decision or that someone is declaring a certain edict—actually, it can refer to a proclamation of any kind. Jesus openly and forthrightly proclaimed that He had fulfilled His mission. He had died for the sins of the world. The work of salvation was accomplished.

When I put all of this together, I come to the following conclusion. I believe verses 19 and 20 describe the time immediately after Jesus died. His body was taken down from the cross and placed in a grave, but His inner being, His soul and spirit, descended into the shadowy depths of the earth, into the place of Tartarus (the creed calls it "hell"), where the antediluvian wicked spirits were imprisoned. Once there, He proclaimed to them His victorious death over sin and His power over the enemy, Satan himself. It was this proclamation that caused them to realize their work of attempting to corrupt and confuse the human race had been in vain. All of their attempts to sabotage the cross, to keep it from happening, were null and void. He went to that place to proclaim His victory at Calvary.

Our Faith

That brings us to the second question raised by verse 21, where we read: "Baptism now saves you." What does this mean?

Again, we can't ignore the context. First, we must understand that the Flood is in Peter's mind. He has just said so (verse 20). It was the Flood that brought death and destruction to those who didn't believe. It was also the water that brought deliverance to those who did—eight of them. Imagine that. Though there were multiple millions of people, only eight got in the ark. Along with the animals, only eight human beings believed and lived!

It was the ark floating on the water that got them through the Flood, which became a beautiful picture to the early church. In fact, the ark was frequently used to describe salvation. Today, we see the cross as our ark. It is our way to life. It is the way we get through the death-like world about us. Thus, baptism became another beautiful expression or picture of just such a deliverance from death—through the water.

Baptism symbolizes deliverance, just as the ark did. In fact, look at the words in parentheses, which in my Bible, the New American Standard version, are placed between dashes:

And corresponding to that, baptism now saves you—not the removal of dirt from the flesh, but an appeal to God for a good conscience—through the resurrection of Jesus Christ. (1 Pet. 3:21, italics added)

Baptism doesn't cleanse anyone, either literally or symbolically. It does not cleanse us externally, as a bath does; nor does it cleanse us within. But, indeed, it is our appeal to God for a good conscience. That which saves us is faith in the Lord Jesus Christ, and this is what is illustrated beautifully in baptism as we come out of the water. The Living Bible, in 1 Peter 3:21, offers a fine paraphrase of this parenthetical section.

(That, by the way, is what baptism pictures for us: In baptism we show that we have been saved from death and doom by the resurrection of Christ; not because our bodies are washed clean by the water, but because in being baptized we are turning to God and asking Him to cleanse our *hearts* from sin.)

Now you understand why in a baptismal service each candidate testifies personally to his or her faith in Jesus Christ. Nothing in the waters of baptism cleanses the flesh or the soul, but the water does illustrate what has already happened in the life of the redeemed.

Practical Principles

As we wrap up our thoughts here, let me mention a couple of very practical principles we can draw from this section of Peter's letter.

First, when unjust suffering seems unbearable, remember the crucifixion. I know you've heard that before, but it is something we cannot be reminded of too often. It can be a wonderful comfort. It is remarkable how focusing on the Lord Jesus Christ's body hanging on the cross as a payment for sin really does help alleviate the pain in my life. About the time I start thinking my suffering is terribly unjust I turn my attention to what He endured; that does a lot to ease or even erase any sense of bitterness or resentment within me. And so, when unjust suffering seems unbearable, remember the crucifixion.

Second, when the fear of death steals your peace, remember the resurrection. There is nothing quite like the hope we derive from our Lord's resurrection. Every Easter we celebrate it. In fact, every Lord's Day we're to be reminded of it. Certainly the Apostles' Creed reinforces it. Which brings us back to where we began.

I believe in God the Father Almighty, maker of heaven and earth;

And in Jesus Christ, His only begotten Son, our Lord, who was conceived by the Holy Spirit, born of the Virgin Mary, suffered under Pontius Pilate, was crucified, dead and buried; He descended into hell; the third day He rose again from the dead; He ascended into heaven, and sits at the right hand of God the Father Almighty; from thence He shall come to judge the living and the dead.

I believe in the Holy Spirit. . . .

Despite the all-encompassing truths contained in these concise words, the most personal and crucial part of the creed is the first two words, "I believe." Without them, it's just a statement someone originated—a statement many worshipers recite every week without ever having any kind of personal relationship with Christ. A body of bright, godly, religious-minded men honed that statement to put in simple form the salient features of our faith. But without our faith, it's still just a creed—a statement of *their* faith. What we need most is a firm hope beyond any creed we may recite.

The question is, do I *believe* the truth of that statement? Do you *believe* it? If you do, there is hope for you beyond it or any other creed. And that hope is a heavenly home reserved for you.

A Prayer for Hope Beyond the Creeds

Father, thank You for the truth of Your Word, for its clarity and its simplicity. And, Lord, because it is so exact, there isn't any reason to doubt. We do believe. Freely and willingly and gratefully, we believe.

But our belief goes beyond any creed . . . far beyond any statement originated by humans, no matter how godly or sincere. With great faith, our Father, we believe in the Lord Jesus Christ who died for us. We believe He suffered unjustly. We believe His payment was sufficient to wash away sins. Our sins. And now that He has been raised and ascended, our Father, we believe that He is alive, interceding for us, and is coming again.

Because of Christ's crucifixion, proclamation, resurrection, and exaltation, give us a sense of peace when we face death. Give us a sense of hope when we suffer unjustly. Remind us that heaven is our ultimate hope. I pray in His matchless name, with great anticipation.

AMEN

Hope Beyond the Culture

How to
Shock the
Pagan Crowd

STEPPING ONTO FOREIGN soil and into the midst of another language and culture for the first time in one's life can be an uneasy experience.

It happened to me while I served in the Marine Corps in the late 1950s. Our troopship had carried us across the Pacific, and my comrades and I were about to step onto Japanese soil. We eagerly anticipated being on land after such a long time at sea. For many of us, it was our first visit to a foreign country. We were surging with excitement, imagination, and every other emotion you could think of due to those seventeen days on the same ship. We were ready!

Before we left the ship, however, our company commander called all of us together. He stood in front of us, looked around at the group, and then, staring deeply into our eyes, he said loudly and sternly, "I want all of you men to remember that for the first time in your lives, *you are the foreigners*. This is not your country or your culture. Now you are the minority. These are not your fellow citizens. They do not speak your language. They know nothing of your homeland except what they see in you."

It was one of those "behave yourself" pep talks, but it went beyond that. Our commander was also saying, "You, as individuals, are representing the entire United States. Don't blow it! Don't become another example of 'the ugly American.' Act in such a way that the Japanese people will gain a good impression of your country and what America must be like. Make us proud, not ashamed." Those words rang in my ears for many days.

As Christians, we face a similar situation. Since our citizenship is in heaven, planet Earth is really not our home. For us, it is foreign soil. We are citizens of another realm. We belong to the kingdom of God. Consequently, we need to be on our best behavior; otherwise, people will get a distorted perception of what our homeland is like. As a result of our behavior, they will either be attracted to or repelled by heaven, the place we call home.

The old gospel song is still right on target.

> This world is not my home.
> I'm just a passin' through.
> My treasures are laid up
> Somewhere beyond the blue.[1]

It's true! But it's easy to forget. Maybe this is a good time to be reminded . . . we live in a pagan culture, surrounded by people who embrace a pagan philosophy and a pagan way of life.

Just consider the latest Broadway fare being ecstatically hailed as "the breakthrough musical of the nineties" . . . "the most exuberant and original American musical to come along this decade." The play, *Rent*, is set "among the artists, addicts, prostitutes, and street people of New York City's East Village." The leading characters are "a drug-addicted dancer in an S&M club who is suffering from AIDS" and a rock singer who is HIV positive. "AIDS is the shadow hovering over all the people in *Rent*, but the musical doesn't dwell on illness or turn preachy; it is too busy celebrating life and chronicling its characters' effort to squeeze out every last drop of it." Those characters are a gay teacher, a transvestite, and a lesbian attorney, among others.[2]

A friend of mine would call that "being mugged by reality," but that's the world we live in. Our earthly culture is pagan to the core. Let's not forget that God has left us here on purpose. We're here to demonstrate what it is like to be a member of another country, to have a citizenship in another land, so that we might create a desire for others to emigrate. Our mission is to create a thirst and an interest in that land "beyond the blue."

In 1 Peter 4:1–6, the apostle gives some marching orders to Christian soldiers who are stationed on this foreign soil. He opens the subject by addressing a Christian's behavior before a watching world with the connective word, *therefore*.

> Therefore, since Christ has suffered in the flesh, arm yourselves also with the same purpose. (1 Pet. 4:1a)

Careful students of the Scriptures pay close attention to words, especially words that connect main thoughts. The word *therefore* is a word of summary that connects what the author is about to write with what he has just written. And what has he just written? Look back at 3:18 and 22.

> For Christ also died for sins once for all, the just for the unjust, in order that He might bring us to God, having been put to death in the flesh, but made alive in the spirit . . . . who is at the right hand of God, having gone into heaven, after angels and authorities and powers had been subjected to Him. (1 Pet. 3:18, 22)

Christ has suffered and died on our behalf, the just for the unjust. *Therefore* . . . Do you see how it all ties together? Since Christ has died for our sins, the just for the unjust, and since He has been seated at the right hand of God, and since all authorities have been subjected to Him, and since He has suffered in the flesh, *therefore*, we should arm ourselves with the same purpose He had when He was on this earth.

I like the way one scholar amplifies what was meant by "arm yourselves."

> [Peter] exhorts the saints to arm themselves with the same mind that Christ had regarding unjust punishment. . . . The Greek word translated "arm yourselves" was used of a Greek soldier putting on his armor and taking his weapons. The noun of the same root was used of a heavy-armed footsoldier who carried a pike and a large shield. . . . The Christian needs the heaviest armor he can get to withstand the attacks of the enemy of his soul.[3]

This word picture offers a blunt reminder that we Christians are not living on this earth as carefree tourists. We are not vacationing our way to heaven. We are soldiers on raw, pagan soil. Everywhere around us the battle rages. The danger is real, and the enemy is formidable. Christ died not only to gain victory over sin's dominion but to equip us for that fight—to give us the inner strength we need to stand against it. Therefore . . . we are to arm ourselves with the strength that Christ gives because our purpose in life is the same as His.

Martyn Lloyd-Jones's warning bears repeating:

> Not to realize that you are in a conflict means one thing only, and it is that you are so hopelessly defeated . . . you do not even know it—you are unconscious! It means that you are completely defeated by the devil. Anyone who is not aware of a fight and a conflict in a spiritual sense is in a drugged and hazardous condition.[4]

Transformation: Remarkable Difference in the Christian Life

Several years ago when I was preaching on First Peter, a man called me and said, "I just want to let you know, Chuck, that the message of First Peter is happening in my life." When I asked what he meant, he went on to describe some difficulties he'd been going through. As he did, he said, "The things you've been talking about recently came back to my mind."

He said he had felt a heaviness in his spirit . . . he called it "a dark oppression." We prayed together about his situation. A few days later when I saw him after the Sunday morning service, he said, "I just want you to know the cloud has lifted." He had sensed the beginning of deliverance from his private war in the realm of darkness.

Many of you live in the competitive jungle of the business world, and some of you may work for a boss who asks you to compromise your ethics and integrity. Pressured by the tension between pleasing your boss, who can fire you or demote you or just make your life difficult, and your commitment to Christ, you need the inner resources to stand firm. "Arm yourselves with the same purpose" is certainly applicable for you. The good news is this: you have it! The provision Christ gives will be sufficient for such a stress test.

> Therefore, since Christ has suffered in the flesh, arm yourselves also with the same purpose, because he who has suffered in the flesh has ceased from sin, so as to live the rest of the time in the flesh no longer for the lusts of men, but for the will of God. For the time already past is sufficient for you to have carried out the desire of the Gentiles, having pursued a course of sensuality, lusts, drunkenness, carousals, drinking parties and abominable idolatries. (1 Pet. 4:1–3)

Fortunately those who are "in Christ" have been transformed. This transformation brings with it at least four benefits that Peter mentions. We no longer serve sin as our master (verse 1b); we don't spend our days overcome by desires as we once did (verse 2b); we now live for the will of God (verse 2b); we have closed the book on godless living (verse 3).

We've sowed our wild oats. Most have had enough time to see the end result of this lifestyle of loose living. Peter calls that lifestyle "the desire of the Gentiles."

Before Christ entered our lives, we had no power to withstand sin. When temptation came along, we yielded. We were unable to do otherwise. When the weakness of the flesh appeared, we fell into its trap. Though we may have looked strong on the outside, we had no inner stability. But when Christ took up residence in our lives, He gave us strength so that we could cease serving sin as a master. (Romans 6 is a wonderful section of scripture on this subject.) Because Christ now lives within us, we have been released from sin's control. We are no longer enslaved to sin. We've been freed!

Observe how "the will of God" (verse 2) is contrasted with "the desire of the Gentiles" (verse 3). Notice, too, how "the desire of the Gentiles"—the old habits, practices, associations, places of amusement, evil motives, and wicked pastimes—are all scenes from the past. The list sounds like your average *Animal House* on some college campus:

- sensuality
- lusts
- drunkenness, carousals, and drinking parties.

The original terms are vivid. *Sensuality* refers to actions that disgust and shock public decency. *Lusts* go beyond sexual promiscuity and involve sinful desires of every kind, including the lust for revenge and the lust for money (greed). *Drunkenness, carousals, and drinking parties* describe a whole miserable spectrum of pleasure-seeking consumption, from wanton substance abuse to wild sexual orgies. And we thought these things represented twentieth-century wildness! When it comes to a shameless, pagan lifestyle, nothing is new.

What is so liberating about our relationship with Christ is that He fills the void in our lives that we once tried to fill with all that garbage. With the void filled, the gnawing emptiness that accompanied it is gone too. And with the emptiness gone, we no longer crave the things we used to crave.

That's where Christians are different from the world. That's where we stand out. That's where the light shines in the darkness. And invariably the darkness reacts to such a light.

*

Reaction: Angry Astonishment from the Unsaved World

While we may live in this foreign land, far from our ultimate home, we live for the will of God. As a result, there is a marked contrast between our lifestyle and the lifestyle of the pagans—people who do not know the Lord—around us. And when we don't partake of that lifestyle, we are considered "weird."

Make no mistake about it. If we don't participate in that lifestyle, you and I are weird. *We are really weird!* And they notice it. Again, Peter's words are as relevant as this morning's newspaper. Look how he describes the reaction of the unsaved world.

And in all this, they are surprised that you do not run with them into the same excess of dissipation, and they malign you. (1 Pet. 4:4)

Talk about the relevance of Scripture! Peter sounds like he is alive today! Any lifestyle of restraint, no matter how tactful we try to be, makes unbelievers uncomfortable. Sometimes it makes them defensive and angry, causing them to lash out at us as though in living our lifestyle we were judging theirs. I experienced this among fellow marines on numerous occasions—those who spent their lives in a realm of lustful drives and carousals and one drinking party after another. We see the same thing today in the after-hours of the corporate world. It's all part of the so-called "happy hour."

Beyond their discomfort and defensiveness, of course, is the inner emptiness they live with, day in and day out, the natural result of a life of lust and debauchery. What emptiness there is when the party's over and everybody goes home! They're left with the horrors of the sunrise and a head-splitting hangover, the guilt and even some shame as they crawl out of somebody else's bed, wondering what disease they might have gotten this time. And there's always that dark-brown taste in their mouth.

It's a horrible lifestyle! I don't care how beautiful the commercials look, it stinks! It doesn't last an hour, and it's anything but "happy!" But if they haven't any power to overcome it, the only thing they have to look forward to is the next "happy hour." And if they play the music loud enough and if there's enough booze and drugs, they think they can drown their troubles. Another lie of the Enemy. He's got a thousand of them.

Do you get the picture? The time already past is sufficient for you to have had your fill of "the desire of the Gentiles." You've tasted it. You've known it firsthand. But when Christ transformed your life, He filled the void and took away a lot of that drive. It's borderline miraculous, in fact, especially if He's enabled you to quick-kick an addiction.

But when that happens, you stand out like a sore thumb in your neighborhood . . . in your university dorm . . . at the office party. You're noticed. Even without saying a word, you're noticed. Even if you very quietly and graciously request a 7-Up instead of a cocktail, the word gets out.

Why? Because you've been transformed. You're no longer a helpless slave to sin. You're not overcome by your glandular drives. You are now interested in God's will; you have closed the door on godless living. And the pagan sits up like a doberman, eyes open, ears perked. "What in the world is wrong with Sam? Remember when we used to run around together? Now he's got religion." Or, "Suzy's gotten really weird . . . became a Bible-thumper. She was once a ton o' fun. Now she's Miss Goody Two Shoes. Next thing we know she'll become a televangelist!"

Brace yourself for such reactions if you're getting serious about Jesus and you've just broken off from a wild bunch of friends. The fact is, He is transforming you. Your old friends will not only be surprised, even shocked, at your new lifestyle, they might also actively ridicule and unjustly judge you for it as well. Expect it . . . it'll keep you from being "mugged by reality." You've just begun to experience hope beyond the culture.

Sometimes I wonder if they are really saying, "Look, misery loves company. If I'm gonna be this miserable, then you need to be miserable with me—like you used to. I don't want to do this alone."

The terrible irony of our unsaved friends' judgment is that they will themselves face the ultimate judgment . . . but that's the *last* thing they want to hear. Nevertheless,

. . . they shall give account to Him who is ready to judge the living and the dead. (1 Pet. 4:5)

Some of you have discovered that your close friends have changed now that you're in Christ. Regarding that, let me first warn you, and then I want to commend you.

First, I want to warn you about spending all of your time with Christians. If your entire circle of friends and acquaintances is nothing but Christian people, you will really get idealistic and unrealistic about the world. You really will get weird! Furthermore, how are the lost going to hear the gospel if all the saved stay clustered, sipping their 7-Ups and reviewing Bible verses together? We need to guard against our tendency to be with believers exclusively. The lost, deep down, are curious . . . and we need to be nearby when they start asking questions.

Second, I commend you for changing your circle of close friends. Some of your former friends do you no good, especially if you cannot withstand the lifestyle temptations they bring your way. Most people who fall into gross sensuality do not do it alone. They're usually prompted or encouraged by other people. You need to be wise and tactful about it . . . but before long, your change in lifestyle needs to be communicated.

There's a line in a country-western song sung by Alabama, "I'm Not That Way Anymore," that says it well: "Time has closed yesterday's door."

That's the way it is with Christians. You're not like that anymore. The fact is, my friend, Christ has closed yesterday's door. The way you are is different from the way you *were*. You won't be able to hide it . . . nor should you want to. Hopefully, however, you'll become a magnet of understanding, drawing others to the Savior rather than an offensive porcupine, driving them away.

Ideally, we want to be a fragrant aroma of Christ, winsomely attracting the unsaved to Jesus, the Savior. But Scripture, as well as our own experience, teaches us that what is fragrant to some is occasionally fetid to others.

Live an Authentic Lifestyle

The point of all of this? Once again we're back to the theme of Peter's letter: finding hope beyond unjust suffering. Enduring hardship. Seeing the reasons behind unfairness. Simply because you desire to live for Christ you will have people who once really enjoyed your company now talking about you behind your back, wondering if you've lost it . . . gone over the deep end. That is tough to take, because you know they aren't representing you fairly. But it's to be expected, looking at life strictly from their pagan perspective.

In fact, the longer I live, the more I see the value of having a thick skin but a tender heart. If you do, their cutting comments won't get to you. Furthermore, you won't feel the need to "set the record straight." Those maligning and ugly words kind of glance off, freeing you from an attack-back reaction.

Let me tell you what's happening. The pagan crowd will never tell you this, but down deep inside, many of them envy you. They wonder, *How does she do that? . . . How can he no longer do these things? . . . I'm not able to stop. . . . What in the world has made the difference?* And when you get them alone, it's remarkable how many of them will really listen as you tactfully and graciously tell them what has transformed your life. That's the joy of being left on foreign soil. You get to acquaint them with a life that is now yours and can be theirs, if only they'll genuinely and completely turn their lives over to Christ.

But let me warn you: Don't beat them up for their lifestyle. Nobody ever got saved because he was rebuked for his drinking or shamed for taking drugs or sleeping around. To tell you the truth, I'm surprised more in the pagan world don't do more of that to fill the void. So don't make an issue of their lifestyle. They can't help it.

They have no power to stop. Let grace and mercy flow. Relax . . . and leave the rebuking to the Lord.

Admittedly, there will be times that it will get to you . . . and you'll find yourself reaching the end of your tether.

One of the Bible teachers who used to lecture at Dallas Seminary when I was a student on campus was as tough as nails yet pure in heart. On one occasion while he was in the city to deliver a series of lectures, he went to a local barbershop to get a haircut. (A friend of mine happened to work there and overheard this conversation.) The barber, who didn't have the faintest idea who the man was, began talking about various issues of the day, giving his opinion, as barbers usually do. He peppered every phrase with an oath or a four-letter word. The teacher bit his lip as long as he could. Finally, he grabbed the barber's arm, pulled him around to the side of the chair, and looked the man right in the eye. Quietly but firmly he pulled on his own earlobe and said to the barber, "Does that look like a sewer?" The rest of the haircut was done in absolute silence.

I realize that such a reaction may not win many friends . . . but I understand the frustration.

Sometimes I just get my fill of it, too, don't you? Especially something as prevalent as blasphemous profanity. Throughout my months in the marines, I listened to that stuff till I thought I'd scream, so it's not that I haven't heard it before or that I can't handle it. I just occasionally reach the place where I have to say something. If it's handled right, even *that* can result in an opportunity to witness.

But in the final analysis, you cannot clean up anybody's lips until you've cleaned up his or her heart. And, ultimately, that's Christ's job. He's a master at it. So you stand it as best you can, realizing these are all simply signs of being lost. Such habits make the inhabitants of this pagan culture appear rough and rugged, but down inside they're often frightened little children. And they're scared to DEATH of death and what it might mean—whether they believe that to be nothingness or judgment.

Thankfully, the believer doesn't have to fear any of that. Our judgment is behind us . . . but their judgment is in front of them. Christ took our judgment, and He bore it on a cross. And He's given us the power He had now that we're in Christ. Remember the words of Isaac Watts?

> Am I a soldier of the cross?
> A follower of the Lamb?
> And shall I fear to own His cause
> Or blush to speak His name?
>
> Sure I must fight if I would reign:—
> Increase my courage, Lord!
> I'll bear the toil, endure the pain,
> Supported by Thy Word.

It's a great hymn. Even though it is almost 275 years old it is really up to date! It applies to businessmen and women who are facing verbal from their fellow employees. It applies to athletes today who refuse to live the lifestyle of the others on the team. It applies to those in the military service who love Christ but serve alongside those who don't. You're a soldier of the cross. What more can you expect? You're not a martyr. You're just taking a few verbal punches. It's good for you and me to be talked about like that. It drives us back to our knees before Christ and reminds us of our dependence on Him.

All believers owe it to themselves to read at least a portion of *Foxe's Book of Martyrs*, which traces the martyrdom of Christians throughout the centuries and demonstrates how viciously the world can act in its attempt to extinguish the light of Christlike character. There are some scenes that will make you shake your head. Talk about paying a price for one's faith!

Do you, like the brave saints of old, want to stand out like a bright light against the darkness of your world? Do you want to shock the pagan crowd? You don't need flamboyance or fanaticism. You don't need to fly a giant Jesus Saves flag over your house or to wag your finger and rail against others' lifestyles. You don't need put-down bumper stickers or T-shirts with big, bold messages. You certainly don't need to rely on sermons or shame. What you do need to do is live differently. And you need to be aware of the consequences of Christlike living. For some it may mean persecution; for others, it could mean death . . . as it did for John Hus, a Bohemian Reformer accused of heresy.

Prior to his appearance before the Council of Constance in 1414, Hus wrote to one of his friends,

> I shall not be led astray by them to the side of evil, though I suffer at His will temptations, revilings, imprisonments, and deaths—as indeed He too suffered, and hath subjected His loved servants to the same trials, leaving us an example that we may suffer for His sake and our salvation. If He suffered, being what He was, why should not we?[5]

I love that last sentence: "If He [Christ] suffered, being what He was [perfect, the ideal model], why should not we?"

You want to know how to really shock the pagan crowd? *Live an authentic Christian life.* No fanfare, of course. No need to wave John 3:16 signs at a ball game . . . or embarrass your colleagues by loudly spouting Bible verses to your unsaved friends at work. That's offensive, not winsome. They're lost, but they're not ignorant or beyond feelings. Just keep three things in mind—three simple but workable suggestions, not at all complicated.

First, continue living for Christ. That means being different on purpose. Let your integrity speak for itself. When opportunities occur for you to speak of your faith, do so graciously and kindly.

Second, expect to be misunderstood. Don't be surprised when ugly things are said or false accusations are made or twisted statements are passed along about your life. Your life will prove that they're wrong. Relax . . . and let the Lord defend you.

Third, keep your eyes fixed on Christ. Stay on a steady course. Keep on being different. Live an authentic godly life, and you'll blow the world away. This is especially true if you keep a healthy sense of humor! They will not be able to stay quiet about the difference between your life and theirs.

Never forget, this world is not your home . . . you're just passin'
through.

A Prayer for Hope Beyond the Culture

*Lord God, Your Son has closed yesterday's door, and we don't
live like that anymore. Not because we've been strong and good
and noble but because You have transformed our lives, Lord.
You've changed our course of direction. Even though You've
left us on foreign soil, we have a home in the skies. And
sometimes we get pretty homesick!*

*Hear the prayers of Your people as we call out to You. Give
us self-control on those occasions when we're tempted to
moralize and put people down. Make us aware that a godly
life, alone, preaches the most unforgettable message the
unsaved can be exposed to. Help us remember that we're
soldiers away from home, living in a culture that's lost its way
and is in desperate need of Jesus Christ. Keep us easy to live
with, strong in faith, unbending in our convictions, yet full of
grace toward those who are bound by sin and captured by
habits they cannot break. Enable us to shock this pagan
culture with lives that are real, that still have fun, and that
ultimately glorify You, O God . . . as Jesus did. In His name
I pray.*

AMEN

12

Hope Beyond Extremism

Marching Orders for Soldiers of the Cross

WHEN TIME IS short, things get urgent. And simplified. Something about the brevity of time introduces both urgency and simplicity to the equation of life.

When a friend or family member tells you he or she hasn't long to live, your time together becomes more urgent and your discussions return to the basics. When a hurricane is blowing in or the black funnel of a tornado looms on the horizon, you don't pull out a Monopoly game or begin preparing a gourmet meal. It's all about survival, and survival calls for simplicity. If you're driving to church and you see an accident happen and you are the only one there to assist, you don't worry about being late or about getting your Sunday clothes dirty or bloody. The situation is urgent. The mission is simple.

Jesus Himself modeled this for us. As long as there was time, He took time—to eat with His disciples, to train His disciples, to minister to individuals whenever and whatever their need. He would linger over a meal with friends. He would sit back and enjoy relaxed moments with close friends like Mary and Martha and Lazarus. But when the hour of the cross drew near, urgency gripped His voice and His attention focused on those few priorities that were in front of Him.

> From that time Jesus Christ began to show His disciples that He must go to Jerusalem, and suffer many things from the elders and chief priests and scribes, and be killed, and be raised up on the third day. (Matt. 16:21)

At that point, Peter—the same disciple who had just given a wonderful statement of faith—rebuked Jesus, saying, "God forbid it, Lord!" (v. 22), telling Him not to talk like that—that such things should never happen to Him.

Such audacity! Peter was planning on a kingdom. He was not planning on a cross.

But Jesus turned and said to Peter,

> Get behind Me, Satan! You are a stumbling block to Me; for you are not setting your mind on God's interests, but man's. (Matt. 16:23)

And then Jesus said to His disciples, in effect, "Let's get down to basics. Let's get down to the essentials, the simple requirements of discipleship."

> If anyone wishes to come after Me, let him deny himself, and take up His cross, and follow Me. (Matt. 16:24)

He was down to urgent, simple demands. Why? Because the hour was short.

During World War II, Winston Churchill encouraged and supported the people of Britain through endless dark hours. He made many memorable statements and speeches, but one rings particularly apt here. He was speaking to Parliament just after London had been bombed to smithereens, and he sensed the people were losing heart. It seemed as though Churchill never did. He must have had low moments, but his speeches don't reveal it. So he said to those people in Parliament, who were probably quaking in their spirits, "This is not the end. This is not even the beginning of the end. But it is, perhaps, the end of the beginning."

Jesus said the same sort of thing to His disciples, telling them, in essence, "When you see these things occurring, it isn't the end."

> And you will be hearing of wars and rumors of wars; see that you are not frightened, for those things must take place, but that is not yet the end. (Matt. 24:6)

If you live in the light of Christ's return each day of your life, it does wonders for your perspective. If you realize that you must give account for every idle word and action when you stand before the Lord Jesus, it does amazing things to your conduct. It also makes you recognize how many needless activities we get involved in on this earth. Sort of like rearranging the deck chairs on the *Titanic*. Don't bother! Don't get lost in insignificant details! He's coming soon! Recognize the urgency and the simplicity of the hour!

Peter seems to have gotten the message. He was a practical man. Prior to following Christ, his life consisted of very tangible, practical things: boats, nets, fish, supporting a family, hard work. And then he met the hard realities of the Master. Consequently, we should not be surprised that his personality and his prose followed suit.

Being neither scholarly nor sophisticated, Peter had little interest in theoretical discussions. Life was not meant to be talked about but lived out. If an urgent situation demanded action, Peter wasn't one to call for a committee to study the alternatives. He cut through the bureaucratic red tape and got down to business.

So when the big fisherman took up his pen to write about suffering saints, he cut to the chase. And when he addressed the reality of the end times, he summed up a game plan in a one-two-three fashion rather than waxing eloquent on the options. Pragmatic Peter at his best offers four commands and one goal to those of us who live nearer than ever to Jesus Christ's return. Simple. Direct. No beating around the bush.

Marching Orders for Soldiers of the Cross

Now remember, Peter is dealing with suffering saints, men and women who are being taken advantage of, men and women who can see no relief in sight. During days of suffering we often become even more intensely aware of the end—the final outcome, whatever that may be. And in writing to his brothers and sisters suffering in the trenches of persecution, Peter himself intensified his focus as he deployed the troops and briefed them for battle.

Observe the urgency and the simplicity in the words that follow.

> The end of all things is at hand; therefore, be of sound judgment and sober spirit for the purpose of prayer. Above all, keep fervent in your love for one another, because love covers a multitude of sins. Be hospitable to one another without complaint. As each one has received a special gift, employ it in serving one another, as good stewards of the manifold grace of God. Whoever speaks, let him speak, as it were, the utterances of God; and whoever serves, let him do so as by the strength which God supplies; so that in all things God may be glorified through Jesus Christ, to whom belongs the glory and dominion forever and ever. Amen. (1 Pet. 4:7–11)

Suddenly, with no relief in sight, Peter introduces the one thought that always helps people hope again: *the end of all things.* In doing so, he not only adds urgency to the moment, he also simplifies the game plan. He leaves his reader with four direct commands to obey and one clear goal to pursue in the midst of it all.

Four Commands to Obey

First, he says: *Use good judgment and stay calm in a spirit of prayer.*

> The end of all things is at hand; therefore, be of sound judgment and sober spirit for the purpose of prayer. (1 Pet. 4:7)

Be of sound judgment. Be of sober spirit. Be calm. Today we might say: Stay cool. Don't be filled with anxiety. Don't panic. Face life realistically. Realize God is in control.

Sober does not mean the opposite of *intoxication*. It means the opposite of living in a frenzy, in a maddening kind of extremism. For example, don't try to set dates regarding Christ's coming. That's an extreme reaction to prophecy. Here's another. Don't panic, as if things were out of control. And another. Don't be filled with anxiety. Don't quit your job, put on a white robe, and sit on some rooftop waiting for Christ to come back. That's extremism. And don't think you have to know every detail of the end times in order to feel secure, as Warren Wiersbe, in his book *Be Hopeful*, rightly notes.

Early in my ministry, I gave a message on prophecy that sought to explain everything. I have since filed away that outline and will probably never look at it (except when I need to be humbled). A pastor friend who suffered through my message said to me after the service, "Brother, you must be on the planning committee for the return of Christ!" I got his point, but he made it even more pertinent when he said quietly, "I've moved from the program committee to the welcoming committee."

I am not suggesting that we not study prophecy, or that we become timid about sharing our interpretations. What I am suggesting is that we not allow ourselves to get out of balance because of an abuse of prophecy. There is a practical application to the prophetic Scriptures. Peter's emphasis on hope and the glory of God ought to encourage us to be faithful today in whatever work God has given us to do (see Luke 12:31–48).[1]

The secret of maintaining the balance and calmness that my friend writes about is prayer. We don't need to parade through the neighborhood wearing a big signboard that says REPENT! THE END IS NEAR! Instead, Peter says, "Be calm, use sound judgment, and do it in a spirit of prayer." Such wise, reasonable counsel from a man who once was neither. Before, Peter would panic so easily. Now . . . he urges prayer.

We don't dream our way into eternity. We pray and watch. In fact, there is nothing quite like prayer to sharpen our awareness, to keep us alert, to make us more discerning, and yet to remind us who has the controls.

When I see a person who is all out of sorts, full of anxiety, on the ragged edge of extremism, I'm looking at a person who isn't spending enough time in prayer. Prayer calms your spirit, yet it doesn't make you indifferent. On the contrary, it reminds you: He has everything in control. Use sound judgment. Stay calm.

Let me go back, again, to yesteryear . . . a dark night in a garden near the edge of Jerusalem. Peter was one of the disciples who was told by the Lord in the Garden of Gethsemane to "Wait here and pray, while I go over there to pray." But when the Lord returned to them, he found Peter asleep. Sound asleep. And He said to Peter and the others, "Couldn't you have waited with Me for this hour?" That must have stung, especially since Peter was the disciple who, a few hours earlier, had bragged about his loyalty and commitment. You think Peter doesn't write with a sense of urgency and understanding here? You think he doesn't remember that rebuke? "I left you to pray, and you fell asleep." That's why Peter could add those words to his letter with a real sense of understanding.

Prayer was what allowed Jesus to submit to His arrest, and the lack of it was what made Peter resist.

The second command is: *Stay fervent in love for one another.*

Above all, keep fervent in your love for one another, because love covers a multitude of sins. (1 Pet. 4:8)

"Fervent" speaks of intensity and determination. It comes from the Greek word *ektene*, which literally means "strained." It's used to describe athletes straining to reach the tape at the finish line or stretching high enough to clear the bar.

When lean sprinters race around that last turn and are pressing for the tape, they'll get right to the end and then they'll deliberately lean forward. I've even seen runners fall on the track because they're pushing so hard to reach the tape before their competitors. That's "being fervent." It's the idea of stretching yourself. Those who do the long jump leap into the air and throw their feet forward as they stretch every muscle of their body to reach as far as they can. The same is true with the high jump or the pole vault. Athletes stretch to the utmost to reach the limit. All those actions describe "fervent." But here Peter applies it to love, not athletic events. He tells us to have fervency in our love for one another.

If there was ever a time when we needed to stay close, it is today. Don't play into the hands of the Enemy. This is the time to stick together. Don't waste precious time criticizing other Christians. Don't waste time criticizing another church or some pastor. Spend your time building up one another, staying fervent in love.

Look at how the verse begins: "Above all"—more than anything else. And then Peter gives them a compliment. He says, "Keep fervent." This implies that they already were fervent. Keep at it, he says. You're doing it already, so stay at it.

Because my schedule is already so full of regular responsibilities connected to both Dallas Seminary and our radio ministry, Insight for Living, I rarely accept invitations to minister elsewhere. But Cynthia and I have made an exception to this when it comes to the Christian Embassy in Washington, D.C., and a retreat they sponsor for many of the flag officers in the Pentagon and various members of Congress who serve on Capitol Hill.

On several occasions we have returned to this significant group of men and women to minister to them and spend some time getting to know their world better. Most of these generals and admirals are academy graduates who have spent many years in military leadership, some of which were during wars on land and at sea. The politicians are also seasoned veterans who have invested their time and effort serving the people of their states, standing for what is right and representing causes worth fighting for. Most who attend the retreat are Christians. They operate their lives on the cutting edge of our times. What amazing, admirable people they are!

As a result of our annual reunions, my wife and I have been able to see how these men and women have grown spiritually in their Christian walk (yes, there are *many* Christians in high places!). What stands out most eloquently to the two of us is their love for the Lord and their love for one another . . . as well as for us. Rather than being sophisticated and distant, these dear folks *fervently* express their love and *fervently* demonstrate compassion.

Peter would have been proud of them. They "keep fervent"—they stay at it, year after year.

If there's ever a time to stretch our love for one another to the limit, it's during the end times—*it's now*. And what is it that reveals this love? Forgiveness.

When Peter says that "love covers a multitude of sins," he's alluding to the principle in Proverbs 10:12:

> Hatred stirs up strife,
> But love covers all transgressions.

Nothing is a more compelling witness than the love and unity that Christians exhibit toward each other, and nothing is more disturbing or disruptive to the unity of the body than Christians who are stirred up against each other and experiencing strife. Nothing is a poorer witness.

Don't think the unsaved aren't watching when we bash our brothers and smash our sisters! They *love* it when we can't get along with each other. It makes news. They love to quote one Christian who is after another Christian. It's as if the journalist or pundit leans back and says, "Aha! Gotcha!"

Mahatma Gandhi, the Indian nationalist leader, once said, "I like your Christ but I don't like your Christians. . . . They are so unlike your Christ."[2]

What a rebuke. I deeply regret that his words are so often true!

And what is Christ like? He is characterized by love and forgiveness. An insightful person once said, "We are most like beasts when we kill. We are most like men when we judge. We are most like God when we forgive."

Let me repeat something I said earlier: I have never met a person who didn't have a reason to blame someone else. Every one of us can blame somebody for something that has happened in our lives. But don't waste your time. What we need most is a steady stream of love flowing among us. Love that quickly forgives and willingly overlooks and refuses to take offense.

Moffatt states that this passage "is a warning against loving others by fits and starts. It is a plea for steady affection, persisting through the irritations and the antagonisms of common life in a society recruited from various classes of people."

Some people are so easy to love that you just naturally fall into their arms. But others are so hard to love, you have to work overtime at it. There's something about their natures that's abrasive and irritating. Some are the opposite of magnets. They repel. Yet even they need our love, perhaps more than the others. How very important that we "stretch fervently" to love each other!

The third command Peter gives is: *Be hospitable toward one another.*

Be hospitable to one another without complaint. (1 Pet. 4:9)

Underscore the words "one another." It is the same phrase Peter uses in verses 8 and 10, and it doesn't refer just to those who are lovable or friendly or fun to be with. It refers to all who are in the body of Christ, even the unlovely and unfriendly.

Another little phrase tacked onto the end of verse 9 is a crucial one when it comes to showing hospitality—"without complaint."

What do you complain about when it comes to hospitality? About the time and trouble it takes? The energy it requires to invite someone into your home and entertain them? The expense? The mess? The clean-up? It's true that hospitality takes effort and planning, and it interrupts your privacy. But hospitality is never a problem when our priorities are in place, when love opens the door.

"True love is a splendid host," said the famous English preacher John Henry Jowett. In his excellent volume on the epistles of Peter, he writes with eloquence:

> There is love whose measure is that of an umbrella. There is love whose inclusiveness is that of a great marquee. And there is love whose comprehension is that of the immeasurable sky. The aim of the New Testament is the conversion of the umbrella into a tent and the

merging of the tent into the glorious canopy of the all-enfolding heavens. . . . Push back the walls of family love until they include the neighbor; again push back the walls until they include the stranger; again push back the walls until they comprehend the foe.[3]

When was the last time you entertained someone who was once your enemy? There is something about hospitality that disarms a foe.

Since the former head coach of the Dallas Cowboys, Tom Landry, has served on our Dallas Seminary board for many years, I have had the opportunity to get to know the man. My respect for him has grown, not lessened, as time and our mutual roles have linked us together.

I was told a wonderful story about Coach Landry that illustrates the level of his Christian love for others. Years ago, the late Ohio State coach, Woody Hayes, was fired for striking an opposing player on the sidelines during a football game. The press had a field day with the firing and really tarred and feathered the former Buckeye coach. Few people in America could have felt lower than he at that time; he not only lost control in a game and did a foolish thing, but he also lost his job and much of the respect others had for him.

At the end of that season, a large, prestigious banquet was held for professional athletes. Tom Landry, of course, was invited. Guess who he took with him as his guest? Woody Hayes . . . the man everyone was being encouraged to hate and criticize.

The quality of our love is determined by its inclusiveness. At the one extreme there is self-love; but at the other extreme there is philanthropy! What is the "tense," the stretch, of my love? What is its covering power? . . . "Love covereth a multitude of sins." Not the sins of the lover, but the sins of the loved! Love is willing to forget as well as to forgive! Love does not keep hinting at past failures and past revolts. Love is willing to hide them in a nameless grave. When a man, whose life has been stained and blackened by "a multitude of sins," turns over a new leaf, love will never hint at the old leaf, but will rather seek to cover it in deep and healing oblivion. Love is so busy unveiling the promises and allure-ments of the morrow, that she has little time and still less desire to stir up the choking dust on the blasted and desolate fields of yesterday.[4]

Are you hospitable . . . I mean *really* hospitable? Do you make room in your life to be interrupted? Do you allow people to be drawn by the magnet of your love because of Christ's presence? One more question: Would you have done what Tom Landry did?

There's something about sitting down with someone over a cup of coffee or a sandwich. Something about taking time . . . making time. I am fully aware that there are times when we need to be alone. *But not all the time.*

Have you ever opened your home for a traveling college choir or other strangers who need lodging? Remember how Jesus and His disciples always stayed in private homes when they traveled and preached? Is your home open to those in need?

I can't tell you how many times people have told me what a blessing it has been to open their homes. Many of these were folks who felt a little uneasiness or apprehension at first, letting strangers invade their most private domain. But there's an unforgettable job connected with hospitality. Folks never forget the warmth of a home . . . the joy of kids around the table . . . the pleasure of meaningful conversation. A friend of mine traveled with a musical group during her college days, over thirty years ago, and she says she can still remember homes she stayed in and Christian hospitality demonstrated on her behalf. Such expressions of hospitable love gave her numerous opportunities to hope again during the three decades that followed.

From the perspective of the guest, however, hospitality is not something we should ever abuse. Apparently this was happening in the first century, largely by people who were living unbalanced lives in response to prophetic teaching. They reasoned, "Since Christ is coming soon, why bother working? Why not liquidate all assets and live off others?" The apostle Paul speaks directly to this heretical reasoning in 2 Thessalonians 3:6–15. Peter speaks to it more indirectly in the next two verses by promoting involvement in the local church and the exercise of spiritual gifts.

In fact, verses 10–11 contain his fourth command: *Keep serving one another.*

> As each one has received a special gift, employ it in serving one another, as good stewards of the manifold grace of God. Whoever speaks, let him speak, as it were, the utterances of God; whoever serves, let him do so as by the strength which God supplies. (1 Pet. 4:10–11a)

Do you know, fellow Christian, that you have at least one—perhaps more than one—spiritual gift? Several sections of the New Testament talk about these gifts—special abilities God has given the body of Christ with which we minister until He returns. Each gift we have needs to be used in serving one another. That is how we become good stewards of our gifts.

Here's a list of some of the places where spiritual gifts are listed. Look them up and examine your own life in the light of them.

- Ephesians 4:11–12
- 1 Corinthians 12:28–30
- Romans 12:6–8

Make a list of these gifts and then ask yourself, where do I best fit in this list? You might approach it the way you would approach applying for a job. If you don't find your spot right away, keep pursuing it. Keep thinking about it. Ask other Christians—those who know you and have been around you during various experiences—what they think your gifts are. Then try them out. Put them into action as you serve others. You'll discover what you do well . . . then do that throughout the balance of your life.

But note the warning in verse 11 that goes along with exercising our gifts.

> Whoever speaks, let him speak, as it were, the utterances of God; whoever serves, let him do so by the strength which God supplies. (1 Pet. 4:11)

When we speak, we shouldn't be voicing our own opinions and

philosophies about life; we should be speaking "the utterances of God." And when we serve, we shouldn't be doing so in our own strength but "by the strength which God supplies."

When you speak for Christ, base your words on the Scriptures, not on your own opinions. You will be forever relevant if you do. And you'll never lack for a message! When you serve, serve in His strength, not your own. That way, He gets the glory.

Many of you have the gift of teaching. You can teach children, teenagers, or adults. You can lead a Bible study at work or in your neighborhood.

Many gifted people also serve behind the scenes, doing vital but perhaps not-so-visible jobs. You help, encourage, and pray. The body would be crippled without the many parts that are able to serve, to help, to encourage.

Others have the gift of showing mercy, of ministering to those who are laid aside or suffering. You visit hospitals and nursing homes. You spend hours listening, caring.

Still others have the gift of evangelism. With ease they communicate the gospel and lead people to Christ. It's a natural part of their lives. God uses them again and again as He harvests souls for His kingdom.

But all of these gifts—there are many others—have one thing in common. They come alive in serving other people. So get out of your own tiny radius. It will do wonders for your depression, for your pity parties, for those times when you sit alone and want to sing, "Woe is me. Woe is me. Woe is me." (That's a very dull song.)

Think of it this way: When we employ our spiritual gift(s), others benefit. Others are encouraged. Others gain fresh hope. Interestingly, so do we!

A Goal to Pursue

Verse 11 ends with a purpose clause that reveals the logical reason we should obey these four commands. Why stay calm and pray? Why be fervent in love? Why demonstrate hospitality? Why serve one another?

. . . so that in all things God may be glorified through Jesus Christ, to whom belongs the glory and dominion forever and ever. Amen.

In everything, God gets the glory. How many church conflicts could be resolved if God's glory were everybody's goal? How many egos would be put in their place if God's glory—not human glory—were at stake? How much extremism would be avoided if we did all for the greater glory of God?

"But that's so basic," you may say. "Why even spend time on it?" Because without that, your teaching becomes drudgery, your helping leads to burnout, your evangelism becomes either frenetic or self-glorifying.

When we keep His glory uppermost in our minds, it's amazing how much else falls into place. Since He gets the glory, we're more comfortable leaving the results with Him in His time. Since He gets the glory, our umbrella of love expands to cover others. Since He gets the glory, it's easier for us to show hospitality to others, for we're ultimately serving Him. Since He gets the glory, exercising our gifts is not a pain but a privilege. The benefits are endless when the glory goes to God!

A Concluding Thought

Let me bring this to a close by returning to a comment I made at the beginning of the chapter: Time is short. You and I don't have forever to put these things into action. Whatever needs to be simplified, *let's simplify*! Whatever it takes to remind us of the urgency of the hour, *let's do it*! Time is short. That means we need to move the words off the pages and slide them into our lives—*now*.

Need a little boost? One of the most encouraging promises in all the New Testament comes to mind:

For God is not unjust so as to forget your work and the love which you have shown toward His name, in having ministered and in still ministering to the saints. (Heb. 6:10)

Read that again, only this time *with feeling.*

Your effort is not in vain. Your love will not be overlooked. Your ministry—whatever it includes—will be rewarded. You will maintain a wonderful balance in the process. Keep your eyes on the Shepherd as you open your heart to His flock. And remember, He gets all the glory!

> The Bride eyes not her garment,
> But her dear Bridegroom's face;
> I will not gaze at glory
> But on my King of grace.
> Not at the crown He giveth
> But on His pierced hand,
> The Lamb is all the glory
> Of Immanuel's land.[5]

A Prayer for Hope Beyond Extremism

Our Father, keep us calm and cool in a spirit of prayer. Give us a fervency in our love for one another that has a way of covering a multitude of sins. Find us to be hospitable people who take time, who are accessible, available, and caring. And, Lord, as we put our gifts into action, use us to give a hope transplant to someone really in need. And may we do it all for Your glory.

May these words make a difference in the way we live, and may the difference be so significant that it is noticed, so that others have cause to give You praise . . . for You, alone, deserve all the praise and all the glory. I pray in Jesus' wonderful name.

AMEN

13

Hope Beyond Our Trials

"When through Fiery Trials . . ."

I am progressing along the path of life in my ordinary, contentedly fallen and godless condition, absorbed in a merry meeting with my friends for the morrow or a bit of work that tickles my vanity to-day, a holiday or a new book, when suddenly a stab of abdominal pain that threatens serious disease, or a headline in the newspapers that threatens us all with destruction, sends this whole pack of cards tumbling down. At first I am overwhelmed, and all my little happinesses look like broken toys. Then, slowly and reluctantly, bit by bit, I try to bring myself into the frame of mind that I should be in at all times. I remind myself that all these toys were never intended to possess my heart, that my true good is in another world and my only real treasure is Christ. And perhaps, by God's grace, I succeed, and for a day or two become a creature consciously dependent on God and drawing its strength from the right sources. But the moment the threat is withdrawn, my whole nature leaps back to the toys.[1]

How eloquently C. S. Lewis's words from his penetrating book, *The Problem of Pain*, describe the role of trials in our lives. Such is human nature, and such is the nature of trials and tribulations.

Remember the words from the old hymn: "When through fiery trials my pathway shall lie, Thy grace all sufficient shall be my supply"? Well, fiery trials and painful ordeals aptly describe what most of us must pass through at one time or another in life . . . some, more frequently than that.

Peter addresses Christians who are going through just such desperate circumstances.

> Beloved, do not be surprised at the fiery ordeal among you, which comes upon you for your testing, as though some strange thing were happening to you. (1 Pet. 4:12)

Ever had anything like that in your life? Not simply trials, but what Peter calls "fiery ordeals"? If so, ever heard this kind of advice on how to handle such trials?

> . . . but to the degree that you share the sufferings of Christ, keep on rejoicing; so that also at the revelation of His glory, you may rejoice with exultation. (1 Pet. 4:12–13)

Probably not!

Practical Truths about Trials

Peter was not the only apostle who wrote to Christians who were strangers and aliens in a foreign land. James addressed his letter to those who were "dispersed abroad"—another group of people far away from home, and not by choice. This also applies to those of us who are strangers in this world below and those of us forced to live in the midst of circumstances that are not our choice. To all these, James wrote:

> Consider it all joy, my brethren, when you encounter various trials, knowing that the testing of your faith produces endurance. And let

endurance have its perfect result, that you may be perfect and complete, lacking in nothing. (James 1:2–4)

From these three verses we learn a great deal about trials. Four specifics stand out.

First, trials are common for Christians to encounter.

Don't ever let anybody tell you (and don't you dare tell anybody else!) that when you become a Christian your trials are over, from then on, "you can just trust Christ and fly away like birds toward the heavens." Get real! Notice that James says *"when* you encounter," not "if."

If you're experiencing trials, you're the rule, not the exception. If you have just gotten through one, take heart; there are more around the corner! Going through a trial is one thing that pulls us together. We've got that in common.

Second, trials come in various categories.

They may be physical, emotional, financial, relational, or spiritual. They may slip in unexpectedly and knock on the door of your business, your church, or your home. They may arrive at any time or at any season. They may come suddenly, like a car accident or a natural catastrophe. They may be prolonged, like a drawn-out court case or a lingering, nagging illness. Trials can be public in nature or very private. They can be directly related to our own sin, the sin of others, or not related to sin at all.

A trial can be like a rock hitting the water. You don't cause the jolt, but you're impacted by it. You're just standing there, and suddenly the smooth lake of your life surges into giant waves and almost drowns you.

Frankly, some trials seem to blow in absolutely without reason. My brother, Orville, encountered something like that when a hurricane named Andrew blew through the community where he lived in south Florida a few years ago. It tore and ripped and screamed its way through, tearing his house apart. He had a great attitude, though. He called and said, "What an experience! It really did a lot of damage. But the good news is it tore down everyone's fences, so now we'll get to meet our neighbors."

Third, trials put our faith to the test.

No matter what its source or intensity, there's something about suffering that simplifies life and draws us back to the basics. Invariably, especially during a time of intense trial, I go back to my theological roots. I go back to what I really believe. I return to the elementals such as prayer and dependence, like getting quiet and waiting on God. I remind myself, God is sovereign . . . this is no accident. He has a plan and a purpose. Those thoughts give us hope beyond our trials.

Trials put our faith to the test as well as stretch our confidence in Him. They force us back to the bedrock of faith upon which our foundation rests, and this becomes a refining and necessary process.

Fourth, without trials, there could not be maturity.

James says we experience trials so that we may be become "perfect and complete" (verse 4), like a plant that has matured to its maximum growth and fruitfulness. That, he says, is the "perfect result" of "endurance."

Most often, because of the discomfort, the pain, or the hardship, we try to cut our trials short—to put an end to them. Before long, we're resenting them to such an extreme that we'll try anything to escape, to run from them. Instead, James says, *endure* the trial; let it come to completion. When it does, you'll be a better person for it.

Remember the words of song writer Andrae Crouch? "If I'd never had a problem, I'd never know that He could solve them. I'd never know what faith in God could do."[2]

Few feelings compare with the joy of watching God step in and solve a problem that seems impossible.

Some trials are slight, brief, and soon forgotten. Others hang on and weigh heavily upon us. They leave us exhausted and sometimes bench us on the sidelines. The latter category is what Peter is talking about when he writes of "the fiery ordeal." This is no slight struggle Peter has in mind. It's an "ordeal" . . . one from which we cannot find relief.

Biblical Strength for Fiery Ordeals

What do you do when the rug is jerked out from under you? Do you panic? Do you doubt the Lord's love? Do you trust in God to get you through the tough times? Perhaps this is a good time to go back to God's truth and read His counsel written by Christ's closest companion while He was on earth.

We can learn a lot from Peter, a man who spent over three years with Christ and who, as we have seen, both pleased Him and failed Him. In fact, most of us should be able to identify with Peter. He'd been an eager disciple, defending his Master against all comers. He'd also been a failure, denying his Lord in the pinch . . . not once, but three times, back to back. Through all this, God reshaped him into a powerfully effective man of God. The vacillating, impulsive, overly zealous Simon was changed and broken, emerging as "Peter, the rock." Now, he writes out of his maturity and seasoned wisdom, under the guidance of the Holy Spirit. These are not theoretical terms the old fisherman tosses around but words shaped in the blast furnace of his own afflictions and pain. Read them again with that in mind:

> Beloved, do not be surprised at the fiery ordeal among you, which comes upon you for your testing, as though some strange thing were happening to you; but to the degree that you share the sufferings of Christ, keep on rejoicing; so that also at the revelation of His glory, you may rejoice with exultation. (1 Pet. 4:12–13)

He begins this section by addressing his letter to the "Beloved." This is truth directed to the beloved of God . . . in other words, truth for the believer only. This is information just for the Lord's people. It's got your name on it. Think of your name here in place of unnamed folks who were "beloved" to Peter.

He then goes on to tell us how to react to this more intense form of suffering.

How to React

Interestingly, our first response to an ordeal is usually surprise—"I can't believe this is happening." But Peter says, *"Don't be surprised."* The lack of surprise will enable us to remain calm.

Life is a schoolroom. In it, we encounter pop quizzes and periodic examinations. You can't have a schoolroom without tests—at least I've never seen one. I've never seen anyone earn a high school diploma or college degree without taking exams. The same is true in graduate school. Throughout the educational process our knowledge is assessed on the basis of examinations. The curriculum of Christlikeness is much the same. Our Christian maturity is measured by our ability to withstand the tests that come our way without having them shake our foundation or throw us into an emotional or spiritual tailspin.

The wonderful thing about God's schoolroom, however, is that we get to grade our own papers. You see, He doesn't test us so He can learn how well we're doing. He tests us so *we* can discover how well we're doing. So we can put our own benchmarks on our level of maturity.

Back in 1984, when you were tested, perhaps you didn't do too well. Maybe others didn't know that, but you did. In 1989, you did better. In 1993 an even tougher test confronted you, and you did rather well. As you grade your own paper, you can see the improvement. The testing of your faith reveals your increasing level of maturity.

Many years ago a good friend of mine, Dr. Robert Lightner, who is a long-time member of the theology department faculty at Dallas Seminary, was involved in a terrible plane crash. He was in a single-engine plane that flipped over during takeoff. He was badly injured and bruised beyond recognition. His wife, Pearl, said that when she first saw him at the hospital, "I looked at this black mass of flesh, and I didn't even know who he was." Thankfully, he did recover, and today he is a living testimony of the grace of God through that ordeal. "I learned things I didn't know I needed to learn," I heard him say on one occasion. Isn't that the way it usually is? What hope this should give us!

Don't be surprised when a test comes. Even though you don't know you need to learn certain things, God knows, and He sovereignly determines, "Now's the time." God is molding you into the image of His Son, and that requires trials. So, first off, don't be surprised.

But the second reaction Peter says we are to have is even more amazing: *"Keep on rejoicing."*

I hear some of you saying right now, "What! Are you kidding me? We're talking trials, right?" Right. "We're talking fiery ordeals, correct?" Correct. "And you're telling me to keep on rejoicing?" Wrong! I am not telling you this—*God* is telling you to keep on rejoicing. "To the degree that you share the sufferings of Christ, keep on rejoicing"

James put it another way: "Consider it all joy" (1:2). Why? Because trials enable us to enter into a more intimate partnership with Christ, and if we endure them faithfully, we will receive a future reward (see Phil. 3:10 and James 1:12). Along with that, our trials here give us at least a glimpse into the magnitude of Christ's suffering for us.

Trials, therefore, become a means to a greater end: a deeper relationship with Christ on earth and a richer reward from Him in heaven.

You and I would never know such fellowship were we not put to the test. Some of you are going through trials right now that have dropped you on your knees. At the same time those trials are pulling you closer to the Lord than you've ever been in your life. That ought to bring rejoicing. You'll be more closely linked to Him. Some of the mysterious themes threaded through His Word will become clearer because you have been leveled by some unexpected affliction or enduring persecution or facing misunderstanding.

Furthermore, you can rejoice because you will receive a future reward.

As I write these words, it happens to be getting close to graduation time, those days when diplomas, honors, and special awards are granted. Each year at Dallas Seminary we have a special chapel service near spring graduation during which we distribute special awards to those who have earned them. Our "Awards Chapel" is one of the highlights in our academic year.

Did you know that in the future when we stand before Christ our Lord, there will be special awards distributed by Christ Himself? They are called crowns. And did you know that there is a unique crown given to those who endure suffering? Read James 1:12:

> Blessed is a man who perseveres under trial; for once he has been approved, he will receive the crown of life, which the Lord has promised to those who love Him.

God has a crown reserved for those who endure the fiery ordeal. My brother, Orville, will have one. Bob Lightner will have one. My wife deserves one for living with me for over forty years! And many of you will have earned that crown as well.

In case you still are not convinced that trials can bring rejoicing, I want you to look at a classic case in point, recorded at the end of Acts 5. There we find that the apostles, including Peter, had just been flogged and ordered to stop preaching about Jesus. (Pause and imagine that bloody, brutal scene.) Look at what they did while they were still bleeding from the beating.

> So they went on their way from the presence of the Council, *rejoicing* that they had been considered worthy to suffer shame for His name. And every day, in the temple, from house to house, they kept right on teaching and preaching Jesus as the Christ. (Acts 5:41–42, italics added)

These men were people just like us . . . not super saints, but real-life folks. Only difference—they refused to let their "fiery ordeal" steal their joy or deter their objective. An attitude of joyful gratitude opens our minds to glean lessons from suffering we would not otherwise learn.

So much for how to react. Now let's focus on what to remember.

What to Remember

First: *Trials provide an opportunity to draw upon maximum power.*

> If you are reviled for the name of Christ, you are blessed, because the Spirit of glory and of God rests upon you. (1 Pet. 4:14)

We must remember that we are never closer to Him, never more a recipient of His strength, than when trials come upon us. This is especially true when we are reviled for the name of Christ. One of the highest privileges on earth is to suffer for His sake. At those times the Holy Spirit draws near, administers strength, and provides an abiding presence of God's glory. If you recall the account of Stephen's martyrdom in Acts 7:54–60, which we read earlier, you'll see that's exactly what happened to him.

The second thing to remember is: *Sometimes our suffering is deserved.*

By no means let any of you suffer as a murderer, or thief, or evildoer, or a troublesome meddler. (1 Pet. 4:15)

If our "fiery ordeal" comes as a result of our own sinful behavior, then we're not suffering for the glory of God; we're merely reaping the consequences of wrongdoing we have sown. As the prophet put it, when we "sow the wind" we "reap the whirlwind" (Hos. 8:7).

Sometimes we deserve the treatment we're getting. We deserve the punishment or the loneliness, the brokenness and pain. And notice that "troublesome meddlers" are listed right along with such reprehensible sinners as murderers, thieves, and other evildoers. That ought to get our attention! The term that is translated here as "troublesome meddler" literally means "one who oversees others' affairs." In other words, a busybody. Ouch! Suffering the consequence of being a busybody brings no one applause or affirmation, only a whirlwind of anguish.

The third thing Peter wants us to remember is: *Most suffering should in no way cause us to feel shame.*

But if anyone suffers as a Christian, let him not feel ashamed, but in that name let him glorify God. (1 Pet. 4:16)

I have met folks who are ashamed that they are going through trials. Many apologize for their tears, almost as if they are embarrassed to weep. I've even known people who felt they needed to apologize because they had sought help from a professional to get through a very personal "fiery trial." Others feel ashamed because their walk of faith has caused a negative reaction. No need!

Instead of shame, we should feel honored when we suffer for our Lord. It is a privilege to bear wounds for the One who was "pierced through for our transgressions" and "crushed for our iniquities" (Isa. 53:5). That's the way Peter and the other apostles must have felt when they left the Sanhedrin, bloody but unbowed.

Self-imposed guilt and shame can be terrible taskmasters in our souls, whipping us down and keeping our spirits from soaring. Such guilt and shame have no place in our lives!

The fourth thing we need to remember is: *Suffering is usually timely and needed.*

> For it is time for judgment to begin with the household of God.
> (1 Pet. 4:17a)

One of the most difficult things to keep in mind is that we need to be purged and purified. After the fact we usually look back on the test or trial and say, "I really needed that," or, "The benefits that came from that are incredible," and we can name three or four insights we would not have gained had we not gone through the valley. Such perspective enables us to hope again.

Purging is not only needed among individuals in the household of God, but also in the church as a whole—locally, denominationally, or otherwise. Sometimes the "house of God" needs not only daily dusting but a thorough spring cleaning. Remember this the next time a scandal surfaces in the church. Don't get disillusioned. It's just God refusing to let us sweep the dirt in His house under the rug.

Sometimes we're rolling along happily, meeting our budgets, running our programs, yet there is no sense of zeal or revival among God's people. It's sort of sit, soak, and sour time for the flock. Congregations can get spoiled. With a smug shrug, they can be saved, sanctified, galvanized, and petrified. Church attendance becomes business as usual. What a miserable existence! About then God comes in and sweeps things clean as He works *through* the church in a timely and needed way.

Now look at the perspective Peter adds:

> If it begins with us first, what will be the outcome for those who do not obey the gospel of God? And if it is with difficulty that the righteous is saved, what will become of the godless man and the sinner? (1 Pet. 4:17b–18)

The latter part of that verse is a quotation from Proverbs, which the New International Version renders this way:

> If the righteous receive their due on earth,
> how much more the ungodly and the sinner! (Prov. 11:31)

In other words, if you think your testing is tough, imagine how tough it is for the person going through trials *without* the Lord. I'll be candid with you: I am absolutely at a loss to know how the lost person makes it when the bottom drops out of his or her life. This person has no Savior. No foundation. No borders. No absolutes. No reason to go on. Nothing to hold on to . . . no one to turn to . . . no way to calm his or her fears . . . no purpose for living . . . no peace in dying. Can you imagine that kind of hopelessness? If you can't, just look at what's happening in the world around you.

Imagine being without the Lord and hearing the worst kind of news from your physician or from the policeman who knocks on your door late at night. Though we, too, are rocked back on our heels by such things, as Christians we immediately turn to our sovereign absolute, our firm foundation, and we lean hard on Him. And if these earthly trials are hard for the lost to bear, imagine their having to face *eternal* judgment!

Which brings me to the fifth thing to remember: *There is no comparison between what we suffer now and what the unrighteous will suffer later.*

If we who are justified by faith have "fiery ordeals" in our walk now, imagine the inferno the lost will face in the literal fiery future that awaits them. Turn to Revelation 20:10–15 and take a few minutes to read and then imagine the horror. Talk about fiery ordeals. Talk about a reason to give your life to Christ.

Thus far, Peter has told us how to react and what to remember when we are going through fiery trials. Now he encourages us by telling us *on whom we are to rely.*

Therefore, let those also who suffer according to the will of God entrust their souls to a faithful Creator in doing what is right. (1 Pet. 4:19)

Entrust. What a wonderful word! It is a banking term in the original text, meaning "to deposit." One commentator has said, "The idea is that of depositing treasure into safe and trustworthy hands."[3] When it comes to trials, we deposit ourselves into God's safekeeping, and that deposit yields eternal dividends.

When you deposit money in the bank, there's a limit on how much the FDIC will insure under one account ownership; usually it's about $100,000. But our infinite God has no limits. Millions upon multimillions of Christians can deposit themselves in His care, and He will make every one of them good. He will hold every one of us securely. No one can declare Him bankrupt of compassion or care. God will never say to anyone, "Sorry. We're full up. That's the limit. We can't guarantee more." You can entrust your soul to this "faithful Creator."

Interestingly, the Greek word that is translated "entrust" here is the same one used by Jesus on the cross when He said, "Father, into Thy hands I *commit* My Spirit" (Luke 23:46, italics added). When we entrust our souls to God during our trials, we are following Jesus' example on the cross when He deposited His soul into the care of the Father. Again, I remind you, those without faith in Christ have no one in whom they can "entrust" their souls.

Personal Growth Through All the Heat

Tests are never wasted. God never says, "Oops, made a mistake on that one. I shouldn't have given you that. I meant that for Frank.

Sorry, Bob." It's as if the Lord has our name on specific trials. They are specifically designed for us, arranged with our weaknesses and our immaturity in mind. He bears down and doesn't let up. And we groan and we hurt and we weep and we pray and we grow and we learn. Through it all we learn to depend upon His Word. You see, there really is hope beyond our trials.

The furnace of suffering provides not only light by which to examine our lives but heat to melt away the dross. Just as famine and financial ruin brought the prodigal son to his senses, so our trials bring us to our senses and draw us into the embrace of our Father. The common response to trials is resistance, if not outright resentment. How much better that we open the doors of our hearts and welcome the God-ordained trials as honored guests for the good they do in our lives.

> Thus the terrible necessity of tribulation is only too clear. God has had me for but forty-eight hours and then only by dint of taking everything else away from me. Let Him but sheathe that sword for a moment and I behave like a puppy when the hated bath is over—I shake myself as dry as I can and race off to reacquire my comfortable dirtiness, if not in the nearest manure heap, at least in the nearest flower bed. And that is why tribulations cannot cease until God either sees us remade or sees that our remaking is now hopeless.[4]

As C. S. Lewis implies here, trials are not an elective in the Christian-life curriculum; they are a required course. Trials 101 is a prerequisite to Christlikeness. But sometimes the tests are so gruelingly comprehensive that our tendency is to drop the course entirely. Especially if we feel abandoned by God.

If that's how you're feeling in the test you are going through now, you need to consult the course syllabus for a few guiding principles. First, when trials come, it's important to remember that God is faithful and that you can rely on Him. Second, when trials stay, it's important to remember to do the right thing and to take refuge in Him. Rest in Him.

When the X-ray comes back and it doesn't look good, remember,

God is still faithful. When you read that heartbreaking note from your mate, remember, God is still faithful. When you hear the worst kind of news about one of your children, remember, God is still faithful. He has not abandoned you, though you're tempted to think He has.

At the height of one of his own personal tests, Hudson Taylor expressed his response in these words: "It doesn't matter how great the pressure is. What really matters is where the pressure lies, whether it comes between me and God or whether it presses me nearer His heart."

When we are pressed near the heart of God, He is faithful and He will hold us. He will hug us through it. We can entrust our souls "to a faithful Creator in doing what is right." But that doesn't mean things will calm down and start making better sense. Not necessarily! Our Lord's agenda for us is full of surprises, unexpected twists, and abrupt turns.

I like the way one fellow pastor put it:

> One of the most frustrating things about Jesus is that He just won't settle down. He is constantly moving us away from the places where we would prefer to stay . . . And moving us closer to . . . where we do not want to go.[5]

When you are tested, you will be tempted to resist such redirection, go your own way, fight in your own strength, and do what is wrong because it just comes naturally. It's called being streetwise (another word for *carnal*). You've fought your way thus far through life; you can fight your way through this test too.

But wait! Is that what God wants you to do? When trials linger on and you begin to wear down, the Enemy will be whispering all kinds of new carnal ideas. He'll even give you evidence that other people did those trials and got away with them. How much better to remember when trials *come* that God is faithful, still faithful. When trials *stay*, remind yourself to do what is right and take refuge in Him. Find your hiding place in Him.

"Suffering" and "glory" are twin truths that are woven into the fabric of Peter's letter. The world believes that the *absence* of suffering means glory, but a Christian's outlook is different. The trial of our faith today is the assurance of glory when Jesus returns . . . . This was the experience of our Lord . . . and it shall be our experience.

But it is necessary to understand that God is not going to *replace* suffering with glory; rather He will *transform* suffering into glory.[6]

When you and I take the long view, we should be grateful that Jesus just won't settle down. He's busy shaping us into His image . . . and for some of us, He's got a long way to go.

A Prayer for Hope Beyond Our Trials

Father, I pray today especially for those who find themselves in a dark place, who see no light on the horizon, who feel the hot blast from the fiery trials, with no relief in sight. Change this painful place into their hiding place where You are near, where You are real. Use this particular chapter to minister in a very special way to those chosen ones whom You are testing to prove their faith. Calm their fears. Quiet their spirits. Remind them that trials are essential if we hope to become Christlike.

This I pray through Jesus, who was, Himself, a Man of Sorrows, acquainted with grief . . . and who, though Your Son, learned obedience from the things which He suffered.

AMEN

Hope Beyond Religion

A Job Description for Shepherds

OF ALL THE PREACHERS who ever lived, Charles Haddon Spurgeon was among the most colorful. He was also among the most prolific . . . and among the most controversial . . . and among the most eloquent . . . and on and on I could go. Spurgeon was one of a kind—if not the greatest preacher in the history of the church, certainly among the top ten, in my opinion. Any time the subject of preaching arises either in a classroom or among a group of pastors, the name Spurgeon will soon surface.

His works are both helpful and insightful. That is all the more remarkable because he lived over one hundred years ago, from 1834 to 1892. At the age of twenty, Spurgeon was called to the New Park Street Baptist Chapel in London, where he served his Lord until he preached his last sermon on June 7, 1891. He died the following January. During his years there, it was not uncommon for his congregation to number as many as 6,000. One biographer states that people would stand in the snow in the dead of winter waiting for the doors to open to assure themselves of a seat to hear this prince of the pulpit preach. During his thirty-eight years at the Metropolitan Tabernacle (five years after Spurgeon began his ministry there, they had to build a new building, which they renamed the Metropolitan Tabernacle), he was responsible for the swelling of the membership of the church to approximately 14,500. Remarkable, remarkable man. Although a Baptist, he was an evangelical Calvinist. Most of all, he was a man made for the pulpit. As one biographer put it:

> Preeminently he was a preacher. His clear voice, his mastery of Anglo-Saxon, and his keen sense of humor, allied to a sure grasp of Scripture and a deep love for Christ, produced some of the noblest preaching of any age.[1]

Despite all his strengths and noble accomplishments, however, a great deal of criticism was leveled against Spurgeon in his day. Like Martin Luther, he seemed to thrive in the storm. He was a man I would call *unflappable*. While he was criticized for a number of things in his preaching, the two things he was criticized for in his private life are curious.

First, he loved a good cigar. One of my favorite stories goes back to an occasion when a man called on him and criticized his cigar smoking. Spurgeon's response was classic: "When I take this to an extreme, then I will stop." When the man asked, "What is an extreme?" Spurgeon replied with a twinkle in his eye, "Two cigars at one time."

The other private criticism was leveled against him and his wife because, out of their own funds, they purchased and enjoyed an extremely large home on a sizable acreage. Predictably, the American press arrived on the scene and exaggerated the report of the home. This *infuriated* Spurgeon. But he pressed on, refusing to allow petty minds and exaggerated comments to deter him from his objectives. While many around him were "religious" and tried very hard to squeeze him into their proper religious mold, Spurgeon remained a maverick at heart, fiercely independent yet Christian to the core, thoroughly committed to Christ and His Word but unmoved by the pressure in Victorian England to fall in line and blend in with his peers.

The longer I live, the greater my admiration grows for this unique vessel so mightily used of God yet so vehemently criticized by others—especially other Christians. Though dead, he still speaks. His volumes continue to stimulate and instruct those of us in vocational Christian service. Anyone who enters the ministry owes it to himself or herself to read Spurgeon and to do so at least once a month. I especially recommend his book, *Lectures to My Students*. In it he writes:

> Every workman knows the necessity of keeping his tools in a good state of repair. . . . If the workman lose the edge . . . he knows that there will be a greater draught upon his energies, or his work will be badly done. . . .
>
> . . . It will be in vain for me to stock my library, or organize societies, or project schemes, if I neglect the culture of myself; for books, and agencies, and systems, are only remotely the instruments of my holy calling; my own spirit, soul, and body are my nearest machinery for sacred service; my spiritual faculties, and my inner life, are my battle axe and weapons for war. . . .
>
> [Then, quoting from a letter of the great Scottish minister, Robert Murray McCheyne, he concludes,] "Remember, you are God's sword, His instrument—I trust a chosen vessel unto Him to bear His name. In great measure, according to the purity and perfection of the instrument, will be the success. It is not great talent God blesses so much as likeness to Jesus. A holy minister is an awful weapon in the hand of God."[2]

There is every temptation for God's people (especially God's *ministers*!) to fall in line, get in step, and follow the cadence of our times . . . and in so doing, we will become unauthentic, boring, predictable, and, well, "religious." We need to be warned against that! While we cannot be Spurgeons (one was enough), there is much we can learn much from this model of clear thinking, passionate preaching, creative writing, and unbending determination. It is nothing short of amazing that a man of his stature and gifts remained at the same church almost four decades . . . especially since he was such a lightning rod, drawing criticism for so long from so many people.

One Practical Guideline for All to Remember

Let me begin with a few practical words of exhortation about sustaining a long-term ministry. My comments here have to do with unrealistic expectations—and they occur on both sides of the pulpit. A young minister comes to a church and has expectations of the flock. On the other side, the flock contacts and calls a man to pastor the church, and they also have their expectations. Both sets of expectations are so idealistic they're usually off the graph. This has the makings of early madness in any ministry.

One of the secrets of a long-term pastorate is clear-thinking realism on the part of both the pastor and the congregation. Let's understand, most churches will never be anything like a Metropolitan Tabernacle . . . and none of us in ministry will ever be a Spurgeon. My opening illustrations in this chapter are examples of the extreme. But the fact is, most of us are far down the scale from that, and we must learn to live with that, accept it, and be content with where and who we are.

The irony is, I think if Charles Haddon Spurgeon lived today, most churches would never even consider extending a call to him. They couldn't get over his style. And if they knew in-depth the whole story behind the Tabernacle, most pastors today would not want to serve in that place. (It's amazing what a hundred years' history will do to enhance our vision of a church or a man.)

The importance of two-way tolerance is extremely significant. A pastor needs to be very tolerant of the people he is serving. And the people who are being served by the minister need to be very tolerant of him. We need to give each other a lot of wobble room. Congregations need to give each other—and their pastors—room to be themselves. Religion, by the way, resists such freedom.

Please understand, I'm not saying anyone should live a lie; nor am

I promoting an unaccountable, sinful lifestyle. I'm simply encouraging grace here . . . giving room for others to be who they really are. All of us have quirks. All of us are unique in our own way. It's important that we adapt to a broad spectrum of personality types.

I smiled when I read this little sign recently:

Welcome to the Psychiatric Hotline!

IF YOU ARE OBSESSIVE-COMPULSIVE: Please press 1 repeatedly.

IF YOU ARE CO-DEPENDENT: Please ask someone to press 2.

IF YOU HAVE MULTIPLE PERSONALITIES: Please press 3, 4, 5, and 6.

IF YOU ARE PARANOID-DELUSIONAL: We know who you are and what you want. Just stay on the line so we can trace the call.

IF YOU ARE SCHIZOPHRENIC: Listen carefully—a little voice will tell you which number to press.

IF YOU ARE MANIC-DEPRESSIVE: It doesn't matter which number you press. No one will answer.[3]

If we're going to live together comfortably over a long period of time, we have to accept one another's idiosyncrasies and styles. This is an appropriate time for me to repeat something I wrote earlier: A good sense of humor is essential, especially if you hope to survive many years in church and/or the ministry.

Two Biblical Principles Regarding Ministry

I've expressed my concern about all this because we have come to a section in Peter's letter that sort of stands on its own as it deals with the pastor and the flock among whom he ministers. It's helpful because Peter's counsel doesn't have a religious ring to it. It's refreshingly insightful. The opening lines of the chapter offer a couple of effective and important principles worth mentioning.

> Therefore, I exhort the elders among you, as your fellow elder and witness of the sufferings of Christ, and a partaker also of the glory that is to be revealed, shepherd the flock of God among you . . . . (1 Pet. 5:1–2a)

The first principle is this: *The pride of position must be absent.* Remember who wrote these words: Peter the apostle, the spokesman for the early church, the one who saw Jesus with his own eyes, who literally walked with the Messiah for more than three years. What honor had been his . . . what privileges, and yet he never hints at his own position of authority. Any sense of pride of position is absent from Peter's opening remarks. He simply calls himself, "a fellow elder, a witness of the sufferings of Christ, and a partaker of the glory that is to be revealed."

I consider these very humble words. He says nothing about his authoritative apostleship. Nothing about the importance of the recipients of his letter being obedient to his advice. He simply identifies with the elders as a "fellow elder." And if you want to make the word "partaker" a little bit more understandable, think of the word *partner.* "I'm a partner with you in the same glory that's going to be revealed hereafter." He saw himself on the same level as the other elders.

A religious ministry is an easy place to secretly construct a proud life. Unfortunately, pride can consume a person in ministry. It not only can, it *has* for some.

Stop and think about why. We speak for God. We stand before large groups of people regularly. Most ministers address more people more often (without being interrupted) than most executives of large corporations do in their work. Those in ministry can live virtually unaccountable. We are respected and trusted by most. And throughout our careers, only rarely are we questioned. When we are, our answers are seldom challenged. We do our preparation away from the public eye as we work alone in our studies. All of that is fine . . . but it's like a mine field of perils and dangers. Because before you know it, we can begin to fall into the trap of believing only what we say and seeing only what we discover. This is especially true if your ministry grows and your fame spreads. When that happens, your head can swell and your ears can become dull of hearing.

If Peter, one of the original Twelve, the earliest spokesman for the church, an anointed servant of God, would not mention his role of importance, I think we can learn a lesson about humility. Mark it down. Don't forget it. The pride of position must be absent.

There is a second principle, equally significant: *The heart of a shepherd must be present.* Remember his opening imperative? "Shepherd the flock of God which is among you." The original root word means "to act as a shepherd, to tend a flock." And don't miss the flip side of the coin: He calls the people "the flock of God."

That is why I have never cultivated the habit of referring to any congregation I serve as "my people." The flock isn't owned or controlled by the under-shepherd; they are God's people! They must ultimately answer to Him. They live their lives before Him. They are to obey *Him.* It is His Word that guides us all, shepherd and flock alike.

I like this description: "By definition, the true elder is the shepherd of the flock in which God has placed him . . . who bears them on his heart, seeks them when they stray, defends them from harm, comforts them in their pain, and feeds them with the truth."

This is a good time to add that unless you have the heart of a shepherd, you really ought not to be in a pastorate. You might wish to teach. You might choose to be involved in some other realm of ministry, and there are dozens of possibilities. But if you lack the heart of a shepherd, my advice is simple: don't go into the pastorate. It soon becomes a mismatch, frustrating both pastor and flock.

This saying used to hang in the office of my good friend and former minister of worship, Dr. Howie Stevenson. "Never try to teach a pig to sing. It wastes your time, and it annoys the pig!"

I've heard some people say, "Well, I'll just learn how to be a shepherd." Sorry. There is more to it than that. Shepherding has to be in your heart. There isn't a textbook, there isn't a course, there isn't some relationship that will turn you into a shepherd. It is a calling.

It's a matter of gifting by God, as we saw in the previous chapter. You are not educated into becoming a shepherd. Seminary may help, for during their years in seminary, most students discover whether or not they have a shepherd's heart. If they do not, I repeat, they should not pursue the pastorate.

I've seen evangelists filling pulpits, and the church is evangelized. But it isn't shepherded. I've seen teachers, bright and capable teachers, filling the pulpit, and the church is carefully instructed and biblically educated. But it isn't shepherded. A shepherd's heart certainly includes evangelism, teaching and exhortation, but it must also include love and tolerance, servant-hearted patience and understanding, and a lot of room for those lambs and sheep who don't quite measure up. Pastoring a church isn't a religious profession, not really. It isn't a business decision but rather a call of God that links certain shepherds with certain flocks.

Religion speaks in terms of hiring qualified professionals to fulfill certain responsibilities. The result is "hirelings," as Jesus called them (John 10:11–15). But in God's flock, shepherds are gifted; they are called to serve and to give themselves, to love and to encourage, to model the Savior's style. When this occurs churches are blessed and they enjoy hope beyond religion.

Three Essential Attitudes for Non-Religious Shepherds

Shepherd the flock of God among you, exercising oversight not under compulsion, but voluntarily, according to the will of God; and not for sordid gain, but with eagerness; nor yet as lording it over those allotted to your charge, but proving to be examples to the flock. (1 Pet. 5:2–3)

I find at least three vital attitudes set forth in the verses you just read. Each attitude begins with a negative, followed by the positive side.

1. Not under compulsion . . .
    but voluntarily, according to the will of God

2. Not for gain . . .
   but with eagerness
3. Nor yet as lording it over those allotted to your charge . . .
   but proving to be examples to the flock.

Attitude number one is *an attitude of willingness*. "Not under compulsion, but voluntarily." *Compulsion* means "to be compelled by force." Like getting your teenager out of bed early in the morning to go to school. That is compulsion. Peter, however, isn't referring to a teenager at school but a shepherd with his flock.

This reminds me of a story I heard several years ago. A young man was sleeping soundly one Sunday morning when his mother came in, shook him, and said, "Wake up, son. You've got to get up . . . you've got to get out of bed." He groaned and complained. "Give me three good reasons why I have to get up this morning." Without hesitation his mother said, "Well, first of all, it's Sunday morning, and it's only right that we be in church. Second, because it's only forty minutes until church starts, so we don't have much time. And third, *you're the pastor!*"

Paul writes in his swan song that God's messengers are to "be ready in season and out of season" (2 Tim. 4:2). Faithful shepherds are to be willing "in season and out of season." . . . when we feel like it, when we don't . . . when the church is growing as well as when it's not.

One of the things that intensifies burnout in ministry is a lack of willingness. And willingness depends on resting when we should so we can give it our all when we must. That's why, each time I speak to them, I encourage ministers to take a day off every week—when possible, a day and a half or two days. Why? To replenish the soul, to refresh the spirit. Furthermore, it is also imperative to take sufficient vacation time, to get away. I encourage "mini-vacations" as well—to get away with your mate, to spend time in refreshment and romance and simply the enjoyment of one another. By doing so, we are better able to do our work willingly and "not under compulsion."

I see many a frowning face and weary body when I go to pastors' conferences. Candidly, of all the groups that I minister to, few are more depressed and exhausted than a group of pastors. They are overworked, usually underpaid, and almost without exception underappreciated, though most of them are doing a remarkable piece of work.

Mild depressions can come upon us unexpectedly that erode our willingness. Often we can't explain such depressions at the time. Later, perhaps, but not when they occur.

I was reading to Cynthia the other day from the book I mentioned earlier in the chapter, Spurgeon's *Lectures to My Students*. She was in the kitchen working, and I walked over and said, "You've got to hear this." Then I read her about three pages! (Talk about a willing spirit!) Though writing more than one hundred years ago, Spurgeon described exactly some of the reasons we suffer from "burn out" in ministry today. He even admitted to depression in his own life, often before a great success, sometimes after a great success, and usually because of something he couldn't explain. He called this chapter "The Minister's Fainting Fits" (great title!). Listen to his candid remarks.

> Fits of depression come over most of us. Usually cheerful as we may be, we must at intervals be cast down. The strong are not always vigorous, the wise not always ready, the brave not always courageous, and the joyous not always happy. There may be here and there men of iron . . . but surely the rust frets even these.[4]

Let me add one final comment here . . . for the flock of God. Be tolerant with your pastor. A better word is *patient*. Try your best not to be too demanding or set your expectations too high. Multiply your own requests by however many there are in your church, and you'll have some idea of what the shepherd of the flock must live with. Be very understanding. Remember, if you write a letter that will bring his spirit down, it could wound him for weeks. Sometimes a confrontation is necessary. But even then, be kind. Be tactful. Pray for him! Encourage him! When you do, you'll find him all the more willing to serve his Lord among you.

Now, look at the second attitude: *an attitude of eagerness*. This next phrase describes not just willingness but an attitude of enthusiastic eagerness. Look how Peter expresses this: "Not for sordid gain, but with eagerness." The old King James Bible called sordid gain (money) "filthy lucre." Make certain your ministry is not motivated by the monetary, external perks. Religious circles emphasize, think about, and make a big thing of money. Guard against that.

I challenge preachers—and I have done it myself through the years—not to do a wedding just because they may get fifty dollars (or whatever) to do that wedding. Be eager to serve, not greedy! And if you're invited to participate in a week-long conference, do it because you really want to, not because you'll get an honorarium. Money is not a healthy motivation, so watch your motives.

When I was in seminary, my sister made me a small black-and-white sign that I hung on the wall in front of my desk where I studied. It read simply, *"What's your motive?"* What a searching question. I looked at it, off and on, for four years. It's a question every shepherd needs to ask on a weekly basis. Motives must forever be examined.

There is nothing quite as exciting or delightful as a shepherd who emits enthusiasm. Such zeal is *contagious!* His love for the Scriptures becomes the flock's love for the Scriptures. His zest for life becomes the congregation's zest for life. His commitment to leisure and enjoyment of life becomes their commitment to leisure and enjoyment of life. His joyful commitment to obeying God becomes theirs. No wonder Peter emphasizes eagerness. His passion for the unsaved becomes their passion. How refreshing it is to be around shepherds who are getting up in years but still eager and enthusiastic!

There's a third attitude Peter highlights: *an attitude of meekness*. I think it was with an extra boost of passion that he wrote:

. . . nor yet as lording it over those allotted to your charge, but proving to be examples to the flock. (1 Pet. 5:3)

I like the way Eugene Peterson paraphrases this:

Not bossily telling others what to do, but tenderly showing them the way. (MSG)

What concerns the old apostle here is a shepherd's exercising undue authority over others. We as shepherds must learn to hold our congregations loosely. We must watch our tendency to try and gain dominion over them, thinking of them as underlings. To avoid this, we must think of ourselves as servants, not sovereigns. Give the flock room to disagree. Assure them that they are to think on their own. But make no mistake. A shepherd who is "meek" is not weak. It takes great inner strength and security to demonstrate grace. He's willing to serve rather than demand. How beautiful, how marvelous it is, to witness one who is gifted and strong of heart, yet secure enough to let God's people grow and learn without having to fall in line with him at every point and march in lockstep to his drumbeat. The best shepherds are those who do their work unto the Lord, expecting no one to bow down before them.

While reading a recent issue of *Sports Illustrated*, I came across an article about Al Davis, owner of the Oakland Raiders football team. If you're a sports fan, you know that Davis is considered by many as one of the most greedy and proud of all owners in the business. He goes through more coaches in a decade than some owners do in a lifetime. This article reports that . . .

> Davis's abuses of power have become increasingly visible. For example, after practice it is customary for him to enter the equipment room, drop a towel on the floor and wait for an employee to clean his shoes. "I saw him make someone wipe his shoes in front of 75 people," says Denver Broncos coach Mike Shanahan, who coached the Raiders in 1988.[5]

When I read that, I thought—here's the *opposite* of servant-hearted leadership. Yet I've witnessed leaders in ministry positions who have abused their positions almost as blatantly.

I've just finished listening to a cassette tape. It's the voice of a man who has been in ministry for years, and it was as if I were listening to another Jim Jones as he preached. My heart ached for that flock who sat and endured his self-serving style. Here was a man who had gained the mastery; verbal abuse was commonly practiced. He snapped his fingers . . . they jumped. He cracked his whip . . . they bowed down. Friend, that is not "proving to be an example to the flock." That is religious abuse . . . the manipulation of a congregation . . . legalistic religion at its worst.

The pastorate brings an enormous amount of authority. Not even a board of elders or deacons, as powerful as they may be, can take the shepherd's place in the pulpit on Sunday. It is a place where he can wield incredible authority and, if he chooses to do so, pull rank. All the more reason not to abuse it. The shepherd is not a stand-in for the Lord!

What God's people need most in their minister is a model of the life of Jesus Christ. There is something convincing about a model. That's Peter's point here. The very best thing for the minister to do is live a life of authenticity, accountability, and humility. Few things win the hearts of sheep like a tender shepherd!

You may remember that Moses, toward the end of his life, was said to have been "very humble, more than any man who was on the face of the earth" (Num. 12:3). Here was a man who "pastored" millions of people, but he refused to pander to his fame. He cared nothing for the applause of the public. He would not manipulate the people. In fact, brokenhearted before God, he even said, "Just take me out of the way." This wonderful section of Scripture is a good reminder that as important as it is to be a decisive leader with strong convictions, accepting the responsibilities of the position, it is never appropriate for the shepherd to "lord it over" those in his care.

No extra charge for this little comment, but I want to underscore an earlier observation that taking control of others is a mark of insecurity. Those who must have absolute agreement from everyone are terribly insecure people. Isn't it interesting that Christ Jesus never demanded that His disciples write anything down, never once exhorted them to memorize things He said? What He told them most of all was, "Do not be afraid." That was His most frequent command. "Do not be afraid." And the other was given by implication, "Watch Me and follow My model." No one has ever had the authority over a flock like Christ, but only on the rarest of occasions did He even raise His voice . . . or rebuke His followers. Sheep do best when they are led, not driven . . . when they are released, not controlled . . . when they know they are loved, not shamed.

An Eternal Reward to Be Claimed

And when the Chief Shepherd appears, you will receive the unfading crown of glory. (1 Pet. 5:4)

I've mentioned crowns before in this book, but I've not mentioned *this* crown. Unlike the others, this is an exclusive crown. It is reserved for those who faithfully shepherd God's flock God's way. Only those who serve in this capacity will be able to receive the "unfading crown of glory." Notice, as a result of fulfilling these two principles and these three attitudes, the "crown of glory" will be awarded by "the Chief Shepherd" Himself.

Count on it, fellow shepherds. We have this to anticipate when we meet our Lord face to face.

Personal Suggestions for Both Sides of Ministry

To summarize, let me first address you who lead by saying, *keep a healthy balance.* If you teach, also be teachable. Read. Listen. Learn. Observe. Be ready to change. Then change! Admit wrong where you were wrong. Stand firm where you know you are right. You cannot win them all. And keep in mind, you're a servant of God, not a slave of the flock.

Since you are called to be a leader, when it's necessary, be a good follower—which takes us back to servanthood. When you lead, put yourself in the followers' shoes; think about what it would be like if you were sitting there listening to those things you are saying.

Neither underestimate your importance nor exaggerate your role. You are, admittedly, called of God. You represent Him, His message, His vision. You can become whipped by a congregation. (It happened to me once. It will never, by the grace of God, happen to me again.) Something tragic happens to a leader who has lost his drive and his determination. But you cannot do it all, so delegate. It's a big job to do, so invite others to help you do it. And when they do it well, give them credit.

Stay balanced. You are engaged in serious work, but (I repeat) keep a good sense of humor. Laugh often and loudly! And don't be afraid to laugh at yourself. My fellow laborers at Insight for Living make sure I do! On several occasions they have presented me with a tape containing all the "outtakes"—things they cut out of my taped messages during the year. Sort of my own private "bloopers." Some have even had the audacity to play this tape at a Christmas party for hundreds to hear and enjoy! As I listen, I cannot believe the dumb things I have said in any given year. It's enough to reduce even a strong-hearted shepherd to the size of a nit-pickin' termite!

Take God seriously, but don't take yourself too seriously.

Now, finally, to those of you being led, may I suggest that you *be a reason for rejoicing*. What a wonderful assignment!

Read the following slowly . . .

> Obey your leaders, and submit to them; for they keep watch over your souls, as those who will give an account. Let them do this with joy and not with grief, for this would be unprofitable for you. (Heb. 13:17)

Think of ways to encourage your minister or leader. Pray often for him. Model gratitude and love. Demonstrate your affection with acts of generosity. Defend the shepherd whenever possible. And when you can't, tell him face to face, and tell no one else. Do it briefly, graciously, then forgive quickly. Try to imagine being in the shoes of the one who lives with the burden of the whole flock and is never free of that. And one more thought . . . think of how it would be if everyone else in the flock were *just like you*. C'mon, have a heart! The guy's not Spurgeon . . . and even if he were, you wouldn't agree with him either.

If you will do these things for your shepherd-leader, not only will you be rewarded, you will give him and yourself new hope . . . hope to press on, hope for the second mile, and everyone in the flock will enjoy hope beyond religion.

A Prayer for Hope Beyond Religion

Father, we consider it a priceless privilege to serve You, the living God. You've made all of us with different personalities, given us different gifts and responsibilities, and yet chosen to mingle us together in the same body, over which Christ is head. There are great temptations we face as shepherds and as sheep . . . to be in charge, to force others to get in line, to make things more uniform and rigid, to get narrow and demanding, to set our expectations too high . . . to handle ministry as if it were a secular enterprise. God, we need You to keep things fresh and unpredictable and especially to keep us authentic, servant-hearted people, and easy to live with.

So give us new hope . . . hope beyond religion, hope that motivates us to press on, serving You with pure motives and eager hearts. Thank You for Your grace, our only hope, dear Savior . . . in Your name.

AMEN

15

Hope Beyond Dissatisfaction

A Formula That Brings Relief

OUR SOCIETY HAS gorged itself on the sweet taste of success. We've filled our plates from a buffet of books that range from dressing for success to investing for success. We've passed the newsstands and piled our plates higher with everything from *Gentleman's Quarterly* and *Vogue*, to the *Wall Street Journal* and *Time*. When we've devoured these, we have turned our ravenous appetites toward expensive, success-oriented seminars. We've gobbled down stacks of notebooks, cassette albums, and video tapes in our hunger for greater success.

The irony of all this is that "there is never enough success in anybody's life to make one feel completely satisfied."[1] Instead of fulfillment, we experience the bloated sensation of being full of ourselves—*our* dreams, *our* goals, *our* plans, *our* projects, *our* accomplishments. The result of this all-you-can-eat appetite is not contentment. It's nausea. How terribly dissatisfying!

"The trouble with success is that the formula is the same as the one for a nervous breakdown," says *The Executive's Digest*. If you find yourself a little queasy after just such a steady diet, you don't need a second helping of success. You need a healthy dose of relief.

Interestingly, very few address that which most folks want but seldom find in their pursuit of success, and that is contentment, fulfillment, satisfaction. Rarely, if ever, are we offered boundaries and encouraged to say, "Enough is enough." And so we work harder and harder, make more and more, yet enjoy all of it less and less.

If we're hung up on any one subject in America today, we are hung up on the pursuit of success. Yet I don't know of another pursuit that is more deceptive—filled with fantasy dreams, phantoms, mirages, empty promises, and depressing disappointments.

Johnny Cash wasn't far off when he groaned, "If you don't have any time for yourself, any time to hunt or fish—that's success."

Today's Major Messages, Promising "Success"

The ad campaigns that come out of Madison Avenue promise much more than they can deliver. Their titillating messages fall into four categories: fortune and fame, power and pleasure.

Fortune says that to be successful you need to make the big bucks. Why else would the Fortune 500 list make such headlines every year? Anyone who is held up as successful must have more money than the average person.

Understand, there is nothing wrong with money earned honestly. Certainly there is nothing wrong in investing or giving or even spending money if the motive is right, if the heart is pure. But I have yet to discover anyone who has found true happiness simply in the gathering of more money. Although money is not sinful or suspect in itself, it is not what brings lasting contentment, fulfillment, or satisfaction.

Fame says that to be successful you need to be known in the public arena. You need to be a celebrity, a social somebody. Fame equates popularity with significance.

Power says that to be successful you need to wield a lot of authority, flex your muscles, take charge, be in control, carry a lot of weight. Push yourself to the front. Expect and demand respect.

Pleasure implies that to be successful you need to be able to do whatever feels good. This philosophy operates on the principle: "If it feels good, do it." It's just a modern version of the ancient epicurean philosophy, "Eat, drink, and be merry, for tomorrow you may die."

Fortune. Fame. Power. Pleasure. The messages bombard us from every direction. But what's missing in all this? Stop and ask yourself that question. Isn't something very significant absent here?

You bet. A *vertical* dimension. There's not even a hint of God's will or what pleases Him in the hard-core pursuit of success. Note also that nothing in that horizontal list guarantees satisfaction or brings relief deep within the heart. And in the final analysis, what most people really want in life is contentment, fulfillment, and satisfaction.

My sister, Luci, told me about the time she visited with a famous opera singer in Italy. This woman owned a substantial amount of Italian real estate, a lovely home, and a yacht floating on the beautiful Mediterranean in a harbor below her villa. At one point, Luci asked the singer if she considered all this the epitome of success.

"Why, no!" said the woman, sounding a bit shocked.

"What is success then?" asked Luci.

"When I stand to perform, to sing my music, and I look out upon a public that draws a sense of fulfillment, satisfaction, and pleasure from my expression of this art, at that moment I know I have contributed to someone else's need. That to me describes success."

Not a gathering of expensive possessions but a deliberate investment in the lives of others seems to be a crucial factor in finding fulfillment and contentment. Service. Help. Assistance. Compassion for others. Therein lies so much of what brings a sense of peace and true success.

In light of that, it seems, success is not a pursuit as much as it is a surprising discovery in an individual's life. All this brings us back to Peter's letter—old, but as we're discovering, ever relevant.

God's Ancient Plan: The Three A's

You younger men, likewise, be subject to your elders; and all of you, clothe yourselves with humility toward one another, for God is opposed to the proud, but gives grace to the humble.

Humble yourselves, therefore, under the mighty hand of God, that He may exalt you at the proper time, casting all your anxiety upon Him, because He cares for you. (1 Pet. 5:5–7)

The world's strategy to climb the ladder of success is simple: Work hard, get ahead, then climb higher—even if you have to claw and step on and climb over the next guy; don't let anything get in your way as you promote yourself. The goal is to make it to the top. It doesn't matter how many or who you push aside along the way, and it doesn't matter who you leave behind, even if it's your family or your friends or your conscience. It's a dog-eat-dog world, friends and neighbors, and the weak puppies don't make it. To survive, you have to hold on to the ladder for dear life. To succeed, you have to fight your way to the top . . . and never stop climbing.

I shook my head in disappointment when I read of Jimmy Johnson's decision to walk away from his wife and family several years ago when he became head coach of the Dallas Cowboys. He didn't deny it or hide it or apologize for his decision. He saw this major career promotion from the University of Miami to the Cowboys organization as his opportunity to make it to the top, big time. There was no way he would let anyone or anything get in his way; this was his moment to succeed, to move into big money. And things like home and family and kids (and grandkids!) were not going to stop him. He dropped all those responsibilities like a bad habit and split for Dallas like a hungry leopard searching for food.

In the world's eyes, he's now reached the pinnacle. A winning record, two Super Bowl rings, enormous amounts of money, fame, a yacht, several private enterprises, and now the Miami Dolphins with even greater hopes for more and more and more. As the public watches and reads of Johnson's accomplishments, most salivate. "The man's got it made!" would be the general opinion of athletes and sports fans and entrepreneurs and executives around the country. That, to them, represents success at its best.

God's plan, His ancient plan, is much different. We see it spelled out for us here in Peter's strategy for the right kind of success. In the three verses above, we see a series of contrasts to the kind of thinking I just illustrated. To keep everything simple, I call them the three A's: authority, attitude, and anxiety.

Authority

Peter's first piece of counsel advises us to submit ourselves to those who are wise and to "clothe" ourselves with humility.

> You younger men, likewise, be subject to your elders; and all of you, clothe yourselves with humility toward one another, for God is opposed to the proud, but gives grace to the humble. (1 Pet. 5:5)

The "clothe yourself" metaphor comes from a rare word that pictures a servant putting on an apron before serving those in the house. Perhaps Peter was recalling that meal in the upper room when Jesus wrapped Himself with a towel and washed the disciples' dirty feet (see John 13). Reclining at the table for their last meal with the Master, Peter and the other disciples had come to the table with dirty feet. The Savior, humbling Himself to the role of a servant, "clothed Himself" with a towel and, carrying a basin of water, washed their feet. I really believe the old fisherman was remembering that act of humility as he wrote these words in verse 5.

"Be subject to," he says—it's in the present tense here, "Keep on being subject to . . ." In other words, submission is to be an ongoing way of life, a lifestyle. We are to listen to the counsel of our elders in the faith, to be open to their reproofs, watch their lives, follow the examples they set, respect their decisions, and honor their years of seasoned wisdom. We must always remember that we need others. Their advice and model, their warnings and wisdom, are of inestimable value, no matter how far along in life we are.

I remember Dr. Howard Hendricks telling me years ago, "Experience is not the best teacher. *Guided* experience is the best teacher." The secret lies in the "guide"!

Bricklaying is a good illustration of this. As a novice, you can lay brick from morning to night, day in and day out, gaining several weeks of experience on your own, and you'll probably have a miserable-looking wall when you're finished. But if you work from the start with a journeyman bricklayer who knows how to lay a course of brick, one after the other, your guided experience can create a wall that is an object of beauty.

Proud independence results in a backlash of consequences, the main one being the opposition of God (see James 4:6). The original idea of God's opposing the proud is found in Proverbs 3.

> Do not envy a man of violence,
> And do not choose any of his ways.
> For the crooked man is an abomination to the LORD;
> But He is intimate with the upright.
> The curse of the LORD is on the house of the wicked,
> But He blesses the dwelling of the righteous.
> Though He scoffs at the scoffers,
> Yet He gives grace to the afflicted.
> The wise will inherit honor,
> But fools display dishonor. (Prov. 3:31–35)

In contrast to the humble, those who are proud in their hearts *scoff* at the Lord. This term expresses scorn and contempt. But God, not the proud, has the last scoff! As Solomon put it, "He scoffs at the scoffers."

When you submit yourself to those who are wise, instead of flaunting your own authority, you will have a greater measure of grace.

> But He gives a greater grace. Therefore it says, "God is opposed to the proud, but gives grace to the humble." (James 4:6)

And that is certainly what today's models of success could use a lot more of—a greater measure of grace. Isn't it noteworthy how rarely those who are on an aggressive, self-promoting fast track to the top even use the word *grace*. Grace, says Peter, is given by God to the humble, not to the proud.

Attitude

Peter's second strategy for success has to do with attitude. We must, he says, humble ourselves under God's mighty hand.

> Humble yourselves, therefore, under the mighty hand of God, that He may exalt you at the proper time. (1 Pet. 5:6)

In the Old Testament, God's hand symbolizes two things. The first is discipline (see Exod. 3:20, Job 30:21, and Ps. 32:4). The second is deliverance (see Deut. 9:26 and Ezek. 20:34). When we humble ourselves under the mighty hand of God, we willingly accept His discipline as being for our good and for His glory. Then we gratefully acknowledge His deliverance, which always comes in His time and in His way.

In other words, as we saw in the previous chapter, we don't manipulate people or events. We refuse to hurry His timing. We let Him set the pace. And we humbly place ourselves under His firm, steadying hand. As a result of this attitude—don't miss it!—"He may exalt you at the proper time."

I must confess there are times when God's timing seems awfully slow. I find myself impatiently praying, "Lord, hurry up!" Is that true for you too?

In today's dog-eat-dog society, if something isn't happening as quickly as we want it to, there are ways to get the ball rolling, and I mean *fast*. There are people to call, strings to pull, and strong-arm strategies that make things happen. They are usually effective and always impressive . . . but in the long run, when we adopt these methods, we regret it. We find ourselves feeling dissatisfied and guilty. God didn't do it—we did!

When I was led by God to step away from almost twenty-three marvelous years at the First Evangelical Free Church in Fullerton, California, and step into the presidency of Dallas Theological Seminary, Cynthia and I immediately faced a challenge . . . in many ways, the greatest challenge of our lives and ministry. What about our radio ministry, Insight for Living?

The seminary is in Dallas, Texas; IFL is in Anaheim, California. In order for Cynthia to remain in leadership at IFL and provide the vision that ministry needs, she has to be in touch with and available to our radio ministry, and she and I, both, need to be engaged in some of the day-to-day operations of IFL. Meanwhile my work at the seminary requires my presence and availability on many occasions. If I hope to be more than a figurehead, and I certainly do, then my presence on and around that campus is vital. But it's hard to be two places at once. I tried that several years ago, and it hurt!

Obviously, then, it makes sense for IFL to move to Dallas. But moving an organization that size (with around 140 employees) is a costly and complicated process. We have a continuing lease on our building in Anaheim, no property or building as of yet in Dallas . . . but she and I cannot continue to commute indefinitely. We have been doing that for well over two years—long enough to know we don't want to do that much longer! On top of all that, there's no money to move us.

So . . . we have two options, humanly speaking. We can run ahead, make things happen, manipulate the money needs, and get the move behind us . . . or we can "humble ourselves under the mighty hand of God" and pray and wait and watch Him work, counting on Him to "exalt us at the proper time" (answer our prayers, provide the funds, help us find a place in Dallas for relocating IFL, and end our commuting). And so we wait. We make the need known . . . and we wait.

We're still waiting. We're still praying. We *refuse* to rush ahead and "make things happen." Admittedly, we get a little impatient and anxious at times, but we're convinced He is able to meet our needs and He will make it happen! Meanwhile we must be content to humble ourselves under God's mighty hand.

What does it mean to humble *yourself* under the mighty hand of God in *your* job, vocation, or profession? What if you're not getting the raise or the promotion you deserve? What if you are in a situation where you could make things happen . . . but you really want God to do that?

Think of David, the young musician, tending his father's sheep back on the hills of Judea many centuries ago. He was a self-taught, gifted musician. He didn't go on tour, trying to make a name for himself. Instead, he sang to the sheep. He had no idea that someday his lyrics would find their way into the psalter or would be the very songs that have inspired and comforted millions of people through long and dark nights.

David didn't seek success; he simply humbled himself under the mighty hand of God, staying close to the Lord and submitting himself to Him. And God exalted David to the highest position in the land. He became the shepherd of the entire nation!

You don't have to promote yourself if you've got the stuff. If you're good, if you are to be used of Him, they'll find you. God will promote you. I don't care what the world system says. I urge you to let *God* do the promoting! Let *God* do the exalting! In the meantime, sit quietly under His hand. That's not popular counsel, I realize, but it sure works. Furthermore, you will never have to wonder in the future if it was you or the Lord who made things happen. And if He chooses to use you in a mighty way, really "exalt" you, you won't have any reason to get conceited. He did it all!

How refreshing it is to come across a few extremely gifted and talented individuals who do not promote themselves . . . who genuinely let God lead . . . who refuse to get slick and make a name for themselves! May their tribe increase.

Anxiety

Peter's third strategy for success tells us to cast all our anxiety upon God.

> Humble yourselves . . . casting all your anxiety upon Him, because He cares for you. (1 Pet. 5:6–7)

The original meaning of the term *cast* literally is "to throw upon." We throw ourselves fully and completely on the mercy and care of God. This requires a decisive action on our part. There is nothing passive or partial about it.

When those anxieties that accompany growth and true success emerge and begin to weigh you down (and they will), throw yourself on the mercy and care of God. Sometimes the anxiety comes in the form of people, sometimes it comes in the form of the media, sometimes it comes in the form of money and possessions, or a dozen other sources I could mention. The worries multiply, the anxieties intensify. Just heave those things upon the Lord. Throw them back on the One who gave them.

I love David's advice:

> Cast your burden upon the LORD, and He will sustain you;
> He will never allow the righteous to be shaken. (Ps. 55:22)

I have a feeling David wrote that one after he'd "made it," don't you?

If you've ever carried a heavily loaded pack while hiking, mountain climbing, or marching in the military, you know there is nothing quite like the wonderful words from the leader, "Let's stop here for a while." Everybody lets out a sign of relief and *thump, thump, thump, thump,* all those packs start hitting the ground. That's the word picture here. Release your burden. Just drop it. Let it fall off your back. Reminds me of John Bunyan's pilgrim when he came to the place of the sepulcher and the cross; the burden of sin fell off his back.

So here's the simple formula that will enable you to handle whatever success God may bring your way and will provide you with the relief you need while waiting:

SUBMISSION + HUMILITY − WORRY = RELIEF

Submission to others plus humility before God minus the worries of the world equals genuine relief. It will also provide hope and contentment without the pain of dissatisfaction.

Our Great Need: Effecting Change

Now I wish all this were as simple as just reading it and saying, "That's it. I'm changed. It's gonna happen." Believe me, it doesn't work that way. So let me suggest some things we need in our lives to effect these changes.

To grasp what true success really is and how to obtain it, we need to tune out the seductive messages from the world and tune in to the instructive messages from the Word. How? It occurs to me we need at least three things to make this happen.

First, we need direction so we can know to whom we should submit.

Let's understand . . . start trying to please everybody, and you're assured of instant failure and long-term frustration. We need God to direct us to those to whom we should submit.

Who are the people I should follow? Who are the folks I should watch? Whose writings should I read? Whose songs should I sing? Whose ministry should I support financially? Whose model should I emulate?

We need direction from God. So begin to pray, "Lord, direct me to the right ones to whom I should submit." Count on Him for direction.

Second, we need discipline to restrain our hellish pride.

Pride will keep rearing its ugly head. The more successful we get, the stronger the temptation to rely on the flesh. We've thought about that already in previous chapters. I use the words "hellish pride" because it is just that. Pride will whisper ways to promote ourselves (but look very humble and pious). Pride will tell us how and when to manipulate or intimidate others. We need discipline to keep ourselves from being our own deliverers. We need discipline to stay *under* the hand of God. Remember that—*under* His mighty hand. But pride hates being *under* anything or anyone. So ask God for discipline here.

Third, we need discernment so we can detect the beginning of anxiety.

Ever have something begin to kind of nag you? You can't put your finger on it. It's fuzzy. Sort of a slimy ooze. It's just growing in the corners, nagging you, getting you down. That is the beginning of a heavy anxiety. We need discernment to detect it, identify it, and get to its root so we can deal with it. When we see the beginning of anxiety for what it is, that's the precise moment to cast it on God, to roll that pack on Him. At that moment we say, "I can't handle it, Lord. You take over."

And how are these needs met? Through the Word of God. The principles and precepts of Scripture give us direction, discipline, and discernment.

Do you find yourself caught up in the success syndrome? Are you still convinced that the world's formula is best? Do you find yourself manipulating people and pulling strings to get ahead? Are you, at this moment, in the midst of a success syndrome you started, not God? No wonder you feel dissatisfied! That type of success *never* satisfies. Only God-directed success offers the formula that brings contentment, fulfillment, satisfaction, and relief.

God's success is never contrived. It is never forced. It is never the working of human flesh. It is usually unexpected—and its benefits are always surprising.

The hand of God holds you firmly in His control. The hand of God casts a shadow of the cross across your life. Sit down at the foot of that cross and deliberately submit your soul to His mighty hand. Accept His discipline. Acknowledge His deliverance. Ask for His discernment.

Then be quiet. Be still. Wait. And move over so I can sit beside you. I'm waiting too.

A Prayer for Hope Beyond Dissatisfaction

We are so grateful, Father, for the truth of Your Word—for the Old and New Testaments alike . . . the teachings of Jesus, the

writings of Peter, the profound songs of David, the law of Moses. All of it blends together in a harmony, a symphony of theological and practical significance. You have us under Your hand, and in our more lucid moments we really want to be there. In times of impatience and wildness we want to squirm free and run ahead. Thank You for holding us, for forgiving us, for cleaning us up, for accepting us, for reshaping us, for not giving up on us. And at this moment, we give You the full right to discipline, to direct, to deliver in Your way and in Your time. Give us great patience as we wait. Humbly, I pray and submit to You in Jesus' name.

AMEN

16

Hope Beyond the Battle

Standing
Nose-to-Nose
with the Adversary

"AS YOU LOOK back over your life, at what places did you grow the most?"

Whenever I ask this question, almost without exception the person will mention a time of pain, a time of loss, a time of deep and unexplained suffering in his or her life. Yet when suffering rains down upon us, our tendency is to think that God has withdrawn His umbrella of protection and abandoned us in the storm. Our confusion during those inclement times stems from our lack of understanding about the role of pain in our lives. Philip Yancey is correct in his analysis.

> Christians don't really know how to interpret pain. If you pinned them against the wall, in a dark, secret moment, many Christians would probably admit that pain was God's one mistake. He really should have worked a little harder and invented a better way of coping with the world's dangers.[1]

Nevertheless, the pain rages on. With relentless regularity, we encounter hardship and heartache. We give ourselves to a friendship, only to lose that person in death. We grieve the loss and determine not to give ourselves so completely again . . . so loneliness comes to haunt us. Is there no hope beyond this? We find the answer to that age-old question, according to Peter, is a resounding YES!

Interestingly, the apostle never once laments the fact that the people he was writing to were suffering pain and persecution, nor does he offer advice on how to escape it. Instead, he faces suffering squarely, tells them (and us) not to be surprised by it, and promises that God provides benefits for enduring life's hurts. Even when life is dreary and overcast, rays of hope pierce through the clouds to stimulate our growth. In fact, without pain there would be little growth at all, for we would remain sheltered, delicate, naive, irresponsible, and immature.

Let's get something straight. Our real enemy is not our suffering itself. The real culprit is our adversary the Devil, the one responsible for much of the world's pain and danger. Although God is at work in the trials of life, so is Satan. While God uses our trials to draw us closer to Him, Satan tries to use them as levers to pry us away from Him. That tug-o'-war only intensifies the battle! Not surprisingly, Peter gives us some crucial advice on how to do battle with the Devil and how to keep him from gaining victory over our lives.

Battle Tactics

In his book *Your Adversary the Devil*, Dwight Pentecost compares the tactics of a physical battle to those of the spiritual one.

> No military commander could expect to be victorious in battle un-less he understood his enemy. Should he prepare for an attack by land and ignore the possibility that the enemy might approach by air or by sea, he would open the way to defeat. Or should he prepare for a land and sea attack and ignore the possibility of an attack through the air, he would certainly jeopardize the campaign.
>
> No individual can be victorious against the adversary of our souls unless he understands that adversary; unless he understands

his philosophy, his methods of operation, his methods of temptation.[2]

This being the case, it should not surprise us that Peter begins by identifying the enemy and his general modus operandi. Whoever denies the fact that there is a literal enemy of our souls chooses to live in a dream world, revealing not only a lack of understanding but also a lack of reality. Throughout the Old Testament and the New we find ample evidence of a literal Devil, an actual Satan—a very real "adversary," to use Peter's word.

His Identity, Style, and Purpose

> Be of sober spirit, be on the alert. Your adversary, the devil, prowls about like a roaring lion, seeking someone to devour. But resist him, firm in your faith, knowing that the same experiences of suffering are being accompanied by your brethren who are in the world. (1 Pet. 5:8–9)

The original term translated *adversary* refers to an opponent in a lawsuit. This individual is a person on the other side. An adversary is neither a friend nor a playmate. An adversary is no one to mess around with—and no one to joke about.

Satan's constant relationship with the child of God is an adversarial relationship. Make no mistake about it; he despises us. He hates what we represent. He is our unconscionable and relentless adversary, our opponent in the battle between good and evil, between truth and falsehood, between the light of God and the darkness of sin.

"Your adversary, the devil," puts it well. That's the way Peter identifies the Enemy—boldly, without equivocation. "The devil" comes from the word *diabolos*, which means "slanderer" or "accuser." Revelation 12:10 states that the enemy of our souls is "the accuser of our brethren." He accuses us "day and night," according to that verse. Not only does he accuse us to God, he also accuses us to ourselves. Many of our self-defeating thoughts come from the demonic realm. He is constantly accusing, constantly building guilt, constantly prompting shame, constantly coming against us with hopes of destroying us.

Did you notice his style? "He prowls about." The Devil is a prowler. Think about that. He comes by stealth, and he works in secret. His plans are shadowy. He never calls attention to his approach or to his attack. Furthermore, he is "like a roaring lion." He is a beast, howling and growling with hunger, "seeking someone to devour"! To personalize this, substitute your name for "someone." When you do, it makes that verse all the more powerful. "Your adversary, the devil, prowls about like a roaring lion, seeking to devour _____ ." I find that has a chilling effect on my nervous system.

He isn't simply out to tantalize or to tease us. He's not playing around. He has a devouring, voracious appetite. And he dances with glee when he destroys lives, especially the lives of Christians.

A. T. Robertson wrote, "The devil's purpose is the ruin of mankind. Satan wants all of us." It's wise for us to remember that when we travel. It's wise for us to remember that when we don't gather for worship on a Sunday and we're really out on our own. It's wise to remember that when we find ourselves alone for extended periods of time, especially during our more vulnerable moments. He prowls about, stalking our every step, waiting for a strategic moment to catch us off guard. His goal? To devour us . . . to consume us . . . to eat us alive.

I hope you've gotten a true picture of your enemy. He's no sly-looking imp with horns, a red epidermis, and a pitchfork. He is the godless, relentless, brutal, yet brilliant adversary of our souls who lives to bring us down . . . to watch us fall.

Our Response

Peter's opening command alerts us to our necessary response: "Be of sober spirit, be on the alert."

Satan doesn't like chapters like this. He hates exposure. He hates being talked about. He certainly hates it when truth replaces fantasy and people are correctly informed. He especially hates having all of his ugly and filthy plans and destructive ways identified.

> *Be Alert.* As his possible prey, however, our primary response should be to keep on the lookout for the predator.

Satan is a dangerous enemy. He is a serpent who can bite us when we least expect it. He is a destroyer . . . and an accuser . . . . He has great power and intelligence, and a host of demons who assist him in his attacks against God's people . . . . He is a formidable enemy; we must never joke about him, ignore him, or underestimate his ability. We must "be sober" and have our minds under control when it comes to our conflict with Satan.[3]

The Devil's great hope is that he will be ignored, written off as a childhood fairy tale, or dismissed from the mind of the educated adult. Like a prowler breaking into a home, Satan doesn't want to call attention to himself. He wants to work incognito, undetected, in the shadows. The thing he fears most is the searchlight of the Scriptures turned in his direction, revealing precisely who he really is and what comprises his battle plan.

> *Respect Him.* To defeat the Devil we must first be alert to his presence . . . respect him—not fear or revere him, but respect him, like an electrician respects the killing power of electricity.

One caution here, however.

> A part of this soberness includes not blaming everything on the devil. Some people see a demon behind every bush and blame Satan for their headaches, flat tires, and high rent. While it is true that Satan can inflict physical sickness and pain (see Luke 13:16 and the Book of Job), we have no biblical authority for casting out demons of headache or demons of backache. One lady phoned me long-distance to inform me that Satan had caused her to shrink seven and a half inches. While I have great respect for the wiles and powers of the devil, I still feel we must get our information about him from the Bible and not from our own interpretation of experiences.[4]

Please be careful that you don't identify every ache and pain or every significant problem you encounter as being satanic in origin. My brother mentioned to me that he once counseled a woman who said she had "the demon of nail-biting." I've met a few who said they fought against "the demon of gluttony." (From their appearance, they were losing the war.) That is not a sign of maturity. I get real concerned about folks who blame the Devil every time something happens that makes life a little bit difficult for them. In fact, it can even become an excuse for not taking responsibility for your own life and your own decisions and choices.

So be alert and be sober. Be calm and watchful. Or, as Moffatt renders it, "Keep cool. Keep awake." We use that word *cool* very lightly today, but here it means a calm coolness. Like professionals in an athletic contest. The best in the game stay cool, calm, collected, and clear-headed, even in the last two minutes as they drive hard for the win, the ultimate prize. So be calm, but be on the alert. Satan's prowling around. This is no time for a snooze in the backyard hammock. He's silently maneuvering a brilliant strategy with plans to destroy us. This is serious stuff!

By the way, I've never seen a prowler who wore a beeper. I've never heard of a prowler who came honking his way down the street with a loudspeaker, saying, "I'm gonna slip in through the sliding door of that home at 7147 Elm at two o'clock in the morning." No, you know a prowler doesn't do that. He comes with stealth. He silently slides his way in. And you never even know he's in your house until he's robbed you blind.

Last fall Cynthia and I had the scare of our lives—literally. I was ministering at a hotel in Cancun—a nice, safe, well-equipped hotel. We turned in for the night around 11:30 or so and were soon in Dreamland. Shortly before 1:00 A.M. Cynthia's loud, shrill scream startled me awake. "There's a man in our room!!"

I looked toward the sliding-glass door that opened onto the patio . . . and there he stood, silent and staring into our room. A chill raced down my spine. The door had been slid open, and the curtains were blowing like sails into the room from the wind off the gulf waters. In fact, it was the surge of the surf that had awakened Cynthia, not the intruder. He had not made a sound . . . nor was he easily visible, since he was dressed in dark clothing.

I jumped out of bed and stood nose-to-nose with him . . . and yelled at the top of my lungs, hoping to frighten him away. For all I knew he had a gun or a knife, but this was no time to close my eyes and pray and lie there like a wimp. Slowly, he backed out of the room, jumped off the seawall, and quickly escaped. Hotel security never found a trace of him, except for a few footprints in the sand. He was a prowler who came, most likely, to steal from our room. Talk about a lasting memory!

Our adversary is a prowler. He comes without announcement, and to make matters worse, he comes in counterfeit garb. He is brilliant, and you and I had better *respect* that brilliance.

I've heard young Christians say things like, "This Christian life is thrilling. I'm ready to take on the Devil." When I can, I pull them aside and say, "Don't say that. It's a stupid comment! You're dealing with the invisible realm. You're dealing with a power you cannot withstand in yourself and a presence you have no knowledge of when you say something like that. Get serious. Be on the alert." Usually that's enough to wake 'em up. Every once in a while it's helpful to be knocked down a notch or two, especially when we're starting to feel a little big for our britches.

I heard a funny but true story recently about Muhammad Ali. It took place in the heyday of his reign as heavyweight champion of the world. He had taken his seat on a plane and the giant 747 was starting to taxi toward the runway when the flight attendant walked by and noticed Ali had not fastened his seat belt.

"Please fasten your seat belt, sir," she requested.

He looked up proudly and snapped, "Superman don't need no seat belt, lady!"

Without hesitation she stared at him and said, "Superman don't need no plane . . . so buckle up."

Don't be fooled by your own pride or softened by some medieval caricature of an "impish" little devil. Our adversary is a murderer, and except for the Lord Himself, he's never met his match. We may hate him . . . but, like any deadly enemy, we had better respect him and keep our distance. There's a war on!

Resist Him. After we are alert to him and respect him, we must resist him. Don't run scared of the enemy. Don't invite him in; don't play with him. But don't be afraid of him either. Resist him. Through the power of the Lord Jesus Christ, firmly resist him.

"But resist him, firm in your faith," writes Peter. Kenneth Wuest has a wise word of counsel on this.

> The Greek word translated "resist" means "to withstand, to be firm against someone else's onset" rather than "to strive against that one." The Christian would do well to remember that he cannot fight the devil. The latter was originally the most powerful and wise angel God created. He still retains much of that power and wisdom as a glance down the pages of history and a look about one today will easily show. While the Christian cannot take the offensive against Satan, yet he can stand his ground in the face of his attacks. Cowardice never wins against Satan, only courage.[5]

I like that closing line.

Once we have enough respect for Satan's insidious ways to stay alert and ready for his attacks, the best method for handling him is strong resistance. That resistance is not done in our own strength, however, but comes from being "firm in faith." An example of this can be seen in the wilderness temptations of Christ when He resisted Satan with the Word of God (see Matt. 4:1–11).

You know what helps me when I sense I'm in the presence of the enemy? Nothing works better for me in resisting the Devil than the actual quoting of Scripture. I usually quote God's Word in such situations. One of the most important reasons for maintaining the discipline of Scripture memory is to have it ready on our lips when the enemy comes near and attacks. And you'll know it when he does. I don't know how to describe it, but the longer you walk with God, the more you will be able to sense the enemy's presence.

And when you do, you need those verses of victory ready to come to the rescue. The Word of God is marvelously strong. It is alive and active and "sharper than a two-edged sword." And its truths can slice their way into the invisible, insidious ranks of the demonic hosts.

Although our own strength is insufficient to fend him off, when we draw on the limitless resources of faith, we can stand against him nose-to-nose, much like I did with that intruder at Cancun. And such faith is nurtured and strengthened by a steady intake of the Scriptures.

Furthermore, the strength that comes from faith is supplemented by the knowledge of that company of saints stretching down through history, as well as present-day believers joining hands in prayer across the globe. There is something wonderfully comforting about knowing that we are not alone in the battle against the adversary.

In spite of faith and in spite of friends, however, the battle is *exhausting*. I don't know of anything that leaves you more wrung out, more weary. Nothing is more demanding, nothing more emotionally draining, nothing more personally painful than encountering and resisting our archenemy.

The devil always has a strategy, and he is an excellent strategist. He's been at it since he deceived Eve in the Garden. He knows our every weakness. He knows our hardest times in life. He knows our besetting sins. He knows the areas where we tend to give in the quickest. He also knows the moment to attack. He is a master of timing . . . and he knows the ideal place.

But I have good news for you. Better still, Scripture has good news for you. When you resist through the power and in the name of the Lord Jesus Christ, the Devil will ultimately retreat. He will back down. He won't stay away; he'll back away. He will retreat as you resist him, firm in your faith.

Remember Ephesians 6:10–11: "Be strong in the Lord, and in the strength of His might. Put on the full armor of God, that you may be able to stand firm against the schemes of the devil."

This is where the Christian has the jump on every unbeliever who tries to do battle against the enemy. Those without the Lord Jesus have no power to combat or withstand those supernatural forces. No chance! They are facing the enemy without weapons to defend themselves. But when the Christian is fully armed with the armor God provides, he or she is invincible. Isn't that a great word? Invincible! That gives us hope beyond the battle.

It's a mockery to say to those who are not Christians, "Just stand strong against the enemy." They can't. They have no equipment. They have no weapons. A person must have the Lord Jesus reigning within to be able to stand strong in His might.

Our Rewards

Will there be suffering in resisting Satan? Yes. Will it be painful? Without a doubt. I have found that there are times we emerge from the battle a little shell-shocked. But after the dust settles, our Commander-in-Chief will pin medals of honor on our lapels. And what are they? Peter tells us.

> And after you have suffered for a little while, the God of all grace, who called you to His eternal glory in Christ, will Himself perfect, confirm, strengthen and establish you. (1 Pet. 5:10)

He will "perfect, confirm, strengthen and establish" us. Talk about hope beyond the battle! Here is the biblical portrait of a decorated war hero, a seasoned veteran from the ranks of the righteous whose muscles of faith have been hardened by battle. It is the portrait of a well-grounded, stable, mature Christian. Christ will make sure the portrait of our lives looks like that, for He himself will hold the brush. And His hand is vastly more powerful than our enemy's.

I remember one night when I was taking care of a couple of our grandchildren. It was late in the evening, but since grandfathers usually let their grandchildren stay up longer than they should, they were still awake. We were laughing, messing around, and having a great time together when we suddenly heard a knock at the door. Not the doorbell, but a mysterious knocking. Immediately one of my grandsons grabbed hold of my arm. "It's OK," I said. The knock came again, and I started to the door. My grandson followed me, but he hung onto my left leg and hid behind me as I opened the door. It was one of my son's friends who had dropped by unexpectedly. After the person had left and I'd closed the door, my grandson, still holding on to my leg, said in a strong voice. "Bubba, we don't have anything to worry about, do we?" And I said, "No, we don't have anything to worry about. Everything's fine." You know why he was strong? Because he was hanging on to protection. As long as he was clinging to his grandfather's leg, he didn't have to worry about a thing.

That happens to us when we face the enemy. When he knocks at the door or when he prowls around back or when he looks for the chink in your armor, you hang on to Christ. You stand firm in faith. You put on the "armor of God" (Eph. 6:11–20—please read it!). You have nothing to worry about. *Nothing.* For, as Peter reminds us, our Lord has "dominion forever and ever. Amen" (1 Pet. 5:11). He is the one *ultimately* in control, and that is something in which every believer can find strength to hope again.

Necessary Reminders

Now, I want to tie a couple of strings around your finger as reminders as we bring these thoughts to a close. This advice has helped me throughout my Christian life, and I think you may find it useful.

First, never confuse confidence in Christ with cockiness in the flesh.

Confidence and cockiness are two different things. When you're facing the enemy, there's no place for cockiness. There is a place for confidence, however, and it's all confidence in Christ. You tell Him your weakness. You tell Him your fears. You ask Him to assist you as you equip yourself with His armor. You ask Him to think through you and to act beyond your own strength and to give you assurance. He'll do it. I repeat, it's all confidence in Christ. It's not some sense of cockiness in the flesh. You're a Christian, remember, not Superman or Wonder Woman.

Second, always remember that suffering is temporal but its rewards are eternal. Paul's wonderful words come to mind:

> Therefore we do not lose heart, but though our outer man is decaying, yet our inner man is being renewed day by day. For momentary, light affliction is producing for us an eternal weight of glory far beyond all comparison, while we look not at the things which are seen, but at the things which are not seen; for the things which are seen are temporal, but the things which are not seen are eternal. (2 Cor. 4:16–18)

Our Lord set the example for us, "who for the joy set before Him endured the cross" (Heb. 12:2). We have all read the Gospel accounts that chronicle Christ's suffering on the cross. We have all heard the Good Friday sermons that recount the horrors of crucifixion. As we look up at Him there on the cross, we can sense His shame and feel the anguish of His heart as we stand at arm's length from His torn and feverish flesh. What we can't see is the joy that awaited Him when He surrendered His spirit to His Father. But He saw it. He knew.

Imagine for a minute how horrible that nightmare of the cross really was. Then imagine, if you can, how wonderful the joy awaiting Jesus must have been for Him to have willingly endured that degree of suffering and injustice. That same joy awaits us. But we have to stoop through the low archway of suffering to enter into it. And part of that suffering includes doing battle with the adversary.

There is probably no book, other than the Bible, that is as insightful or creatively written concerning the strategies of Satan than C. S. Lewis's *The Screwtape Letters.* Here is a sampling of Satan's strategy as articulated by the imaginary Screwtape, a senior devil, who corresponds with his eager nephew to educate the fledgling devil for warfare against the forces of "the Enemy"—that is, God.

> Like all young tempters, you are anxious to be able to report spectacular wickedness. But do remember, the only thing that matters is

the extent to which you separate the man from the Enemy. It does not matter how small the sins are, provided that their cumulative effect is to edge the man away from the Light and out into the Nothing. Murder is no better than cards if cards can do the trick. Indeed, the safest road to Hell is the gradual one—the gentle slope, soft underfoot, without sudden turnings, without milestones, without signposts.[6]

A Prayer for Hope Beyond the Battle

Almighty God, You are our all-powerful and invincible Lord. How we need You, especially when the battle rages! Thank You for standing by our side, for being our strong shield and defender. We have no strength in ourselves. We are facing an adversary far more powerful, more brilliant, and more experienced than we. And so, with confidence, we want to put on and wear the whole armor of God . . . and, in Your strength alone, resist the wicked forces that are designed to bring us down.

Give new hope, Lord—hope beyond the battle. Encourage us with the thought that, in Christ, we triumph! In His great name I pray.

AMEN

17

Hope Beyond Misery

Lasting
Lessons

I HAVE BEEN encouraged by the fact that in his writings Peter gets us beyond the misery part of suffering.

You have noticed, haven't you, how we all throw pity parties for ourselves when suffering comes? It's almost as though we capitalize on the downside rather than focus on the benefits that come from the hard times. How easily we forget that growth occurs when life is hard, not when it's easy. However, it is not until we move beyond the misery stage that we're able to find the magnificent lessons to be learned. The problem is, we almost delight in our own misery.

In keeping with that, Dan Greenburg has written a very funny book, *How to Make Yourself Miserable*, in which he says:

Too long have you . . . gone about the important task of punishing yourself . . . by devious or ineffective means. Too long have you had to settle for poorly formulated anxieties . . . simply because this vital field has always been shrouded in ignorance—a folk art rather than a science. Here at last is the frank report you have been waiting for. . . . It is our humble but earnest desire that through these pages you will be able to find for yourself the inspiration and the tools for a truly painful, meaningless, miserable life.[1]

The truth is, of course, that we don't need any help in this area. We have perfected the art of misery all by ourselves. We know very well how to capitalize on misery, how to multiply our troubles rather than learn—through the sometimes torturous and yes, humiliating experiences of life—the vital lessons that bring about true joy, true meaning, and true significance in life.

I think it was Charlie "Tremendous" Jones who said, "There is something wrong with everything." Have you found that true? No matter where you go or what you do, is there something wrong with it? Murphy's Law says, "If something can go wrong, it will." Another of Murphy's Laws says, "That's not a light at the end of the tunnel. That's an oncoming train." And then one wag adds, "Murphy was an optimist."

The problem is, when we're all alone, when we are feeling the brunt of the experience, when we are in the midst of the swirl, when we can't see any light at the end of any tunnel, it isn't funny.

As the apostle Peter so masterfully presents in his letter, however, suffering is not the end; it's a means to the end. Best of all, God's end for us is maturity. It is growth. It is a reason for living and going on.

Five Observations and a Set of Bookends

As we look back at the things we've seen in this book, a few broad-stroked observations stand out in sharp relief. Perhaps by reviewing where we've been, we'll be able to sharpen our perspective to an even keener edge.

First, Peter wrote the letter. Though it may seem simplistically obvious, this fact offers us a unique encouragement. Along with James and John, Peter was one of the inner circle of three confidants to whom Jesus revealed himself most fully. Of the twelve disciples, Peter was regarded as the spokesman. Never one to teeter on the fence of indecision, Peter was impulsive, impetuous, and outspoken. He often put his foot in his mouth. He knew the heights of ecstasy on the Mount of Transfiguration and the depths of misery and shame on the night of his denials. And yet, in spite of his flaws and his failures, he is called an apostle of Jesus Christ. What grace!

This is tremendous encouragement for all who fear that their flaws are too numerous or their failures too enormous to be given another chance.

I'm sure Peter looked back on many occasions and thought, *I wish I hadn't said that.* (Haven't we all?) But I'll tell you something else about Peter; he wasn't afraid to step forward—to put it all on the line.

Are you one of those people who never goes anywhere without a thermometer, a raincoat, an aspirin, or a parachute? Not Peter. He went full-bore into whatever he believed in. No lack of passion in Peter! What he lacked in forethought he made up for in zeal and enthusiasm.

Admittedly, that kind of lifestyle is a bit risky and unpredictable.

Do you ever envy some of the experiences of Peter kind of people—folks who are willing to say what they think or admit how they feel, even though they may be wrong? How much more fun it is to be around people like that than around those who are so careful and so closed-in and so protected you never know what they really feel or where they really stand. They're very, very cautious, ultra-conservative thinkers who wouldn't even consider taking a risk. And they get very little done for the kingdom because they are so busy guarding everything they do and say.

Not Peter. Peter says, in effect, "I wrote this. Yes, I'm the Disciple who blew it. I failed Him when He was under arrest. I spoke when I shouldn't have. But I write now as one who has learned many things the hard way, things about pain and suffering. I don't write out of theory; I write from experience."

Second, hurting people received the letter. They are not named, but their locations are stated in the first verse of the letter. Peter wrote "to those who reside as aliens, scattered throughout Pontus, Galatia, Cappadocia, Asia, and Bithynia."

These hurting people, scattered outside their homeland, were lonely and frightened aliens, unsure of their future. But though they were homeless, they were not abandoned; though they were frightened, they were not forgotten. Peter reminds them of that. They were chosen by God and sanctified by His Spirit, and His grace and peace would be with them "in fullest measure."

Whenever you find yourself away from home, whenever you find yourself feeling abandoned and frightened, overlooked and forgotten, Peter's first letter is magnificent therapy. I suggest you read it in several versions. The Living Bible, the New International Version, J. B. Phillips's paraphrase, and Eugene Peterson's paraphrase, *The Message*, will give you a good start. Read through without a break, if possible. Read it through sitting there in that hotel room or alone in your cell or apartment or home. It is excellent counsel for those who are hurting. It will assure you of your calling and reassure you that grace and peace are yours to claim in fullest measure.

Third, this letter came through Silas. The person to whom Peter dictated his words was Silas, one of the leaders in the early church (referred to in 1 Peter 5:12 as Silvanus).

Silas was a cultured Roman citizen, well educated and well traveled. Peter was a rugged fisherman, a blue-collar Galilean with little or no schooling, but apparently (beginning with 5:12) he took the pen in his own hand and wrote the final lines of the letter. We know that, not only because of the substance of verses 12–14, but because of the style. The grammar, syntax, and vocabulary become simpler in the Greek text.

The rest of the letter, however, came *through* Silas. If you're like most people, you don't know enough about Silas to fill a three-by-five card. Some people know him only as the guy who carried Paul's bags on long trips. Paul gets all the attention, yet it was Paul *and* Silas who carried the gospel. Silas was Barnabas's replacement on Paul's missionary journeys. Paul *and* Silas were the ones who sang in the jail there in Philippi at midnight. And Silas was the one alongside Paul when the man was stoned. Silas was one who really understood the hearts of Paul and Peter.

Look at Acts 15:22 in case your respect for Silas needs a little bolstering.

> Then it seemed good to the apostles and the elders, with the whole church, to choose men from among them to send to Antioch with Paul and Barnabas—Judas called Barsabbas, and Silas, leading men among the brethren.

Here is a man who was one of the "leading men" of the church in the first century, and at the writing of this letter, he remained alongside Peter. In fact, Peter calls him "our faithful brother (for so I regard him)" (1 Pet. 5:12).

God gives Peter the message, Silas writes it down, and the Spirit of God ignites it. There may have been times when Silas was the wind beneath Peter's wings. We all need a Silas . . . someone willing to stand alongside us.

Fourth, the letter concludes with a greeting from a woman.

> She who is in Babylon, chosen together with you, sends you greetings, and so does my son, Mark. (1 Pet. 5:13)

Now, obviously, everybody wonders who "she" is; who is the woman "who is in Babylon"? Most interpretations fall into two categories: Peter could either be referring to "woman" in the figurative sense, as the bride of Christ, or he could be using the word literally. If the latter is correct, the woman referred to may possibly be Peter's wife. We know Peter had a wife because Jesus healed Peter's mother-in-law. Then, in 1 Corinthians 9:5, Paul makes note of the other apostles' wives, which likely included Peter's wife. Clement of Alexandria states that she died as a martyr for the faith, so she may have been well-known among the early Christians. No doubt those who first received this letter knew who the woman was whether or not we do.

Fifth, the letter's final command is one of intimate affection. This old fisherman still has a lot of love left in him. He has not become jaded. Look how he expresses himself.

Greet one another with a kiss of love.
Peace [*Shalom*] be to you all who are in Christ. (1 Pet. 5:14)

The kiss of the Christian was called "the shalom," or "the peace." With the passing of time, the practice of the kiss of peace has disappeared from the church. It is fascinating to trace through church history how the kiss shared between people of the faith became less and less intimate. In fact, if you are a romantic-type person given to warm affection, it's enough to completely deplete all wind from your sails! In the first century, a kiss was placed on the cheek of believers as they arrived and as they left the fellowship of the saints. As time passed, people began kissing the precious documents rather than each other. And before long, a wooden board was passed among the people and everyone kissed that plank of wood. (That sounds exciting, doesn't it? "Let's go to church tonight. We'll get to kiss the board.") Anyway, through it all, the church lost the sense of affection and intimacy along with the embrace of peace.

Originally, as they kissed each other's cheeks, they would say to one another, "Peace be with you," or simply *Shalom*. And that's exactly what Peter does here. "Greet one another with the kiss of peace."

Augustine said that when Christians were about to communicate, "they demonstrated their inward peace by the outward kiss."

The formal kiss was the sign of peace among early Christians, demonstrating their love and unity. This outward sign reflected an inward peace between believers, a sign that all injuries and wrongdoing were forgiven and forgotten. Some traditions should be reinstated!

Personal Applications

Well, so much for the bookends that open and close Peter's letter. Now let's take a last look at the contents and how they can speak to us in our personal situations.

Three times in the letter Peter refers to the reader, which gives us a clue to the letter's structure. In fact, the letter falls neatly into three distinct sections, each one detailing the "how" of an important truth: a living hope and how to claim it (1:1–2:10), a pilgrim life and how to live it (2:11–4:11), and a fiery trial and how to endure it (4:12–5:11). An application of these three major messages should give us hope beyond our misery.

A Living Hope and How to Claim It

> Blessed be the God and Father of our Lord Jesus Christ, who according to His great mercy has caused us to be born again to a living hope through the resurrection of Jesus Christ from the dead. (1 Pet. 1:3)

The idea of "living hope" occupies Peter's mind throughout this section of the letter. And how do we claim that living hope? By focusing on the Lord Jesus Christ and by trusting in "the living and abiding word of God." Living hope requires faith in the living Lord and His Word.

The grass withers and dies, flowers bloom and die, but the Word of God "abides forever."

That's a great image, isn't it? Especially in a culture like ours where people are so grass conscious. Just look at the commercials that start appearing on television in late winter, and the countless "garden centers" devoted to our yards and gardens that you can find across the country. We know what happens when we neglect our grass or our gardens—but the truth is, they will eventually wither and die anyway.

There is nothing tangible on this earth that is inspired but the Word of God, this book that holds God's counsel. It doesn't tell us about the truth; it *is* truth. It doesn't merely contain words about God; it *is* the Word of God. We don't have to try real hard to make it relevant; it *is* relevant. Don't neglect it. You can neglect your grass. You can neglect your garden. But you dare not neglect the Word of God! It is the foundation of a stable life. It feeds faith. It's like fuel in the tank. Don't wait till Sunday to see what the Scripture teaches.

We have a living hope, and Peter's words in this section tell us how to claim it—by faith in our Lord Himself and by faith in what He has written, His Word.

The Pilgrim Life and How to Live It

As Christians we live in a world that is not our home. We looked at this, in depth, in chapter 11. We live as pilgrims on a journey in another land. If you want to know how to live the life of an alien, a stranger, a pilgrim, Peter's letter will help.

We claim our living hope through faith, and we live the pilgrim life by submission. In fact, if there is one theme that stretches through this central section of Peter's letter, it is submission. We need to be reminded of it again and again and again because we are an independent lot. Especially here in America, we are so ornery and stubborn. It's come to be known as "the American way." It's the reason many sailed the Atlantic and later came west. It's built into our independent spirit to make it on our own, to decide for ourselves, to prove, if only to ourselves, we can do it! That may be the explorer's life or the pioneer's life . . . but it's not the pilgrim life. The pilgrim life is a life of submission, which works directly against our nature.

But where? When? To whom do we submit? As we saw earlier, Peter spells it out.

In government and civilian affairs. "Submit yourselves for the Lord's sake to every human institution, whether to a king . . . or to governors . . ." (1 Pet. 2:13–14). If you have a president, submit to the president. In Peter's case, they had an emperor. And what a monster he was. Nero. Yet Peter said, "Don't fight the system. Submit."

At work. "Servants, be submissive to your masters" (1 Pet. 2:18). My, that cuts cross-grain in our day of unions and strikes and lawsuits and stubborn determination to have it our own way. Peter says, in effect, "Submit to your boss or quit!"

Submit! Make the thing work or get out. Submit.

At home. "In the same way, you wives, be submissive to your own husbands." And in order for that to work, "You husbands likewise, live with your wives in an understanding way" (1 Pet. 3:1, 7). "Likewise" is a rope-like word that wraps itself around this chapter and part of the previous one, sustaining the thought of submission.

I remember talking with a young couple a few years ago when I observed a sterling example of this. He was a dentist in his mid- to late thirties, and he and his wife had come to a meeting where they found themselves rethinking their life plans for the future. Afterward, he said to me, "I'm thinking seriously about going into the ministry."

I said, "Really? Have you had any training at all?"

He said, "No, not formally. I'd have to go back to school. I'd like to have your suggestion about seminary and what you think would be best for me."

So we talked for a few minutes, and I concluded with this counsel. "If you are happy doing what you're doing, don't just jump into ministry because it seems fascinating or appealing to you."

The next day he came to me and said, "Your words really made me think throughout the night. To tell you the truth, I am very fulfilled in dentistry, and I find a lot of satisfaction in it."

His wife was standing beside him, and I turned to her and said, "And how do you feel about this?" She had a terrific answer. She said, "You know, Chuck, when I married this man I really gave myself to this marriage. And I determined that this man who is walking with God was worth working alongside of, no matter what and no matter where. However God leads him, I'm a part of that plan."

"How do you feel about going into ministry?" I asked.

"If he's convinced, I'm convinced," she said.

Now I know this woman. She's no dummy. She's no vanilla shadow, standing there sighing, "Whatever he wants is fine with me." She's not a beaten-down, doormat kind of wife. That's not the kind of woman she is, and that's not the kind of woman Peter is talking about here. There's vitality and zeal and strength of soul in her life. And she can say, "I am confident God is working in my husband. I wouldn't think of going some other direction." A harmonious blend of give and take is what Peter has in mind here.

In the church. "To sum up, let all be harmonious, sympathetic, brotherly, kindhearted, and humble in spirit; not returning evil for evil, or insult for insult, but giving a blessing instead; for you were called for the very purpose that you might inherit a blessing" (1 Pet. 3:8–9). Now isn't there a lot of submission at work there?

And a few verses later (3:22) we see that even the angels, the authorities, and the powers are subjected to Him. Just picture those magnificent angelic creatures bowing in submission to the risen Christ.

My suggestion on the heels of all this? Work on a submissive spirit. Don't wait for the media to encourage you to do this . . . it'll never happen. Ask God, if necessary, to break the sinews of your will so that you become a person who is cooperative, submissive, harmonious, sympathetic, brotherly or sisterly, kindhearted in every area of this pilgrim life.

Remember, ultimately we are not submitting to human authority but to divine authority. God will never mistreat us. Bowing before Him is the best position to take when we want to communicate obedience.

The Fiery Trial and How to Endure It

No matter how fiery the trial, the main thing is that you and I remember the temperature is ultimately regulated by God's sovereignty (see 1 Pet. 4:12–19). It's also important to understand that we don't suffer our trials in isolation; we are part of a flock that is lovingly tended by faithful shepherds (see 1 Pet. 5:1–5). Finally, we need to know that no matter how formidable our adversary, the power of God is available to help us endure (see 5:6–11).

And how do we endure the fiery trials that engulf us? By cooperation. We need to cooperate with God by trusting Him—with the leaders of the church by submitting to them, and with faith by standing firm and resisting the assault of the devil.

As you struggle with fiery trials, call to mind the sovereignty of God. Nothing touches you that hasn't come through the sovereign hand and the wise plan of God. It must all pass through His fingers before it reaches you. Ultimately He is in control.

As you endure the fiery trial, be in touch with and faithful to the flock of God.

And through it all, rely on the power of God. As we learned in the previous chapter, we must rely on that.

Four Lasting Lessons/Secrets of Life

We have finished his letter . . . but the ink from Peter's pen leaves an indelible impression on our lives. Along with everything else he tells and teaches us, I want to mention four lasting lessons, four secrets of life, that stand out in bold relief. All of these give us hope beyond our misery.

First, when our faith is weak, joy strengthens us.

> In this you greatly rejoice, even though now for a little while, if necessary, you have been distressed by various trials, that the proof of your faith, being more precious than gold which is perishable, even though tested by fire, may be found to result in praise and glory and honor at the revelation of Jesus Christ; and though you have not seen Him, you love Him, and though you do not see Him now, but believe in Him, you greatly rejoice with joy inexpressible and full of glory. (1 Pet. 1:6–8)

> Beloved, do not be surprised at the fiery ordeal among you, which comes upon you for your testing, as though some strange thing were happening to you; but to the degree that you share the sufferings of Christ, keep on rejoicing; so that also at the revelation of His glory, you may rejoice with exultation. (1 Pet. 4:12–13)

No matter how dark the clouds, the sun will eventually pierce the darkness and dispel it; no matter how heavy the rain, the sun will ultimately prevail to hang a rainbow in the sky. Joy will chase away the clouds hovering over our faith and prevail over the disheartening trials that drench our lives. In this regard I am often reminded of the promise from the Psalms.

> Weeping may last for the night,
> But a shout of joy comes in the morning. (Ps. 30:5)

Second, when our good is mistreated, endurance stabilizes us.

For this finds favor, if for the sake of conscience toward God a man bears up under sorrows when suffering unjustly. For what credit is there if, when you sin and are harshly treated, you endure it with patience? But if when you do what is right and suffer for it you patiently endure it, this finds favor with God. (1 Pet. 2:19–20)

The word *endure* in verse 20 means "to bear up under a load," as a donkey bears up under the load its owner has stacked high on its back. This patient bearing of life's cumbersome loads is made possible by love, made steadfast by hope, and made easier by example.

When we suffer, even though we have done what is right, there is something about endurance that stabilizes us. When our good is mistreated, endurance stabilizes us.

My hope for every one who reads these pages is that you will learn how to endure. Picture yourself as that little burro, abiding under the heavy load piled upon its back. Such quiet and confident endurance stabilizes us.

Third, when our confidence is shaken, love supports us.

Above all, keep fervent in your love for one another, because love covers a multitude of sins. (1 Pet. 4:8)

Love is the pillar of support when our world comes crumbling down around us. That's why, when warning about the end times, Peter puts love on the top of the survival checklist.

Fourth, when our adversary attacks, resistance shields us.

Be of sober spirit, be on the alert. Your adversary, the devil, prowls about like a roaring lion, seeking someone to devour. But resist him, firm in your faith, knowing that the same experiences of suffering are being accomplished by your brethren who are in the world. (1 Pet. 5:8–9)

When Satan stalks us like a roaring lion, we're not instructed to freeze, to hide, or to tuck tail and run. We're told to resist. And that resistance forms a shield to protect us from our adversary's predatory claws.

What Really Counts

And so we reach the end of Peter's letter that has endured the centuries . . . and the end of my book that may not endure to the end of this century, less than five years from now. But that is as it should be. God's Word will never fade away, though human works are quickly erased by the sands of time.

My concern is not about how long these pages remain in print but how soon you will put these principles to use in your life. That's what really counts in the long run. That's the important issue. Frankly, that's why the old fisherman wrote his letter in the first place. To help us hope again.

Hope to go on, even though we're scattered aliens.

Hope to grow up, even though we, like Peter, have failed and fallen.

Hope to endure, even though life hurts.

Hope to believe, even though dreams fade.

A Prayer for Hope Beyond Misery

Our Father, we thank You for sustaining us in Your grace through times that absolutely defy explanation, times of suffering and misery, times of mistreatment and disappointment.

Thank You for being a Friend who is closer than a brother, for meaning more to us than a mother or a father. Thank You for Your mercy that takes us from week to week through a life that isn't easy, dealing with people who aren't always loving and encountering battles that leave us exhausted. Thank You for strength that has come from a little letter written by an old fisherman who understood life in all its dimensions: failure and disappointment and victory and joy and intimacy. We commit to You, our Father, the truth of what we have read. Help us to find hope again as a result of putting these truths into practice. In the lovely and gracious name of Jesus Christ I pray.

AMEN

Notes

CHAPTER 1 HOPE BEYOND FAILURE

1 Eugene H. Peterson, *The Message: The New Testament in Contemporary English* (Colorado Springs, Colo.: Navpress, 1993), 486.

CHAPTER 2 HOPE BEYOND SUFFERING

1 Warren W. Wiersbe, *Be Hopeful* (Wheaton, Ill.: SP Publications, Victor Books, 1982), 11.
2 Julie Ackerman Link, "Fully Involved in the Flame," *Seasons: A Journal for the Women of Calvary Church*, Spring 1996, 1. Copyright Calvary Church, Grand Rapids, Michigan. Used by permission.

CHAPTER 3 HOPE BEYOND TEMPTATION

1 Kenneth S. Wuest, *In These Last Days*, vol. 4 in *Wuest's Word Studies from the Greek New Testament* (Grand Rapids, Mich.: Eerdmans, 1966), 125–26.
2 Randy Alcorn, "Consequences of a Moral Tumble," *Leadership* magazine, Winter 1988, 46.
3 Stuart Briscoe, *Spiritual Stamina* (Portland, Oreg.: Multnomah Press, 1988), 133.

CHAPTER 4 HOPE BEYOND DIVISION

1 Kenneth S. Wuest, *First Peter: In the Greek New Testament* (Grand Rapids, Mich.: Eerdmans, 1956), 48.
2 Edward Gordon Selwyn, *The First Epistle of St. Peter*, 2d ed. (London, England: Macmillan Press, 1974), 153.

CHAPTER 5   HOPE BEYOND GUILT

1. Quoted in *Dear Lord*, comp. Bill Adler (Nashville: Thomas Nelson, 1982).
2. Quoted in *More Children's Letters to God*, comp. Eric Marshall and Stuart Hample (New York: Simon and Schuster, 1967).
3. Quoted in William Barclay, *The Letters of James and Peter*, rev. ed., The Daily Study Bible Series (Philadelphia, Pa.: Westminster Press, 1976), 203.
4. Wiersbe, *Be Hopeful*, 57.

CHAPTER 6   HOPE BEYOND UNFAIRNESS

1. Barclay, *The Letters of James and Peter*, 210–11.
2. J. H. Jowett, *The Epistles of St. Peter*, 2d ed. (London: Hodder and Stoughton, n.d.), 92.

CHAPTER 7   HOPE BEYOND "I DO"

1. Joseph C. Aldrich, *Secrets to Inner Beauty* (Santa Ana, Calif.: Vision House, 1977), 87–88.
2. Philip Yancey, *I Was Just Wondering* (Grand Rapids, Mich.: Eerdmans, 1989), 174–75.
3. Barclay, *The Letters of James and Peter*, 218.
4. Edwin A. Blum, "1 Peter" in *The Expositor's Bible Commentary*, vol. 12, ed. Frank E. Gaebelein (Grand Rapids, Mich.: Zondervan, 1981), 237.
5. *Los Angeles Times*, 23 June 1988.
6. Gary Smalley and John Trent, *The Gift of Honor* (Nashville: Thomas Nelson, 1987), 23, 25–26.

CHAPTER 8   HOPE BEYOND IMMATURITY

1. Robert A. Wilson, ed., *Character Above All* (New York: Simon and Schuster, 1995), 219–21.
2. Oswald Chambers, *My Utmost for His Highest*, special updated

edition, ed. James Reimann (Grand Rapids, Mich.: Discovery House, 1995), November 16, n.p.

3   Alvin Goeser quoted in *Quote-Unquote*, comp. Lloyd Cory (Wheaton, Ill.: SP Publications, Victor Books, 1977), 200.

4   Cited in Jon Johnston, "Growing Me-ism and Materialism," *Christianity Today*, 17 January 1986, 16-I.

CHAPTER 9   HOPE BEYOND BITTERNESS

1   Retold from "Toads and Diamonds," *The Riverside Anthology of Children's Literature*, 6th ed. Boston: Houghton Miffiin, 1985), 291–93.]

2   Malcolm Muggeridge, *Twentieth-Century Testimony*, (Nashville: Thomas Nelson, 1988), 18–19.

3   Barclay, *The Letters of James and Peter*, 230–31.

CHAPTER 11   HOPE BEYOND THE CULTURE

1   J.R. Baxter, Jr., "This World Is Not My Home," © copyright 1946. Stamps-Baxter Music. All rights reserved. Used by permission of Benson Music Group, Inc..

2   Quotes from Georgia Harbison, "Lower East Side Story," *Time*, 4 March 1996, 71.

3   Wuest, *First Peter: In the Greek New Testament*, 110.

4   D. Martyn Lloyd-Jones, *The Christian Warfare* (Grand Rapids, Mich.: Baker, 1976), 41.

5   John Hus, quoted in John Moffatt, *The General Epistles: James, Peter, and Judas* (London: Hodder and Stoughton, 1928), 147.

CHAPTER 12   HOPE BEYOND EXTREMISM

1   Wiersbe, *Be Hopeful*, 107.

2   Mahatma Gandhi quoted in Brennan Manning, *Lion and Lamb* (Old Tappan, N.J.: Revell, Chosen Books, 1986), 49.

3   Jowett, *The Epistles of St. Peter*, 166–67.

4   Ibid., 167.

5   Anne Ross Cousin, "The Sands of Time Are Sinking."

CHAPTER 13   HOPE BEYOND OUR TRIALS

1   C. S. Lewis, *The Problem of Pain* (New York: Macmillan, 1962), 106.
2   R. C. H. Lenski, *The Interpretation of the Epistles of St. Peter, St. John and St. Jude* (Columbus, Ohio: Wartburg Press, 1945), 213.
3   Andre Crouch, "Through It All," © 1971, by Manna Music Inc., 35255 Brooten Road, Pacific OR. 97135. International copyright secured. All rights reserved. Used by permission.
4   Lewis, *The Problem of Pain*, 107.
5   M. Craig Barnes, *When God Interrupts* (Downers Grove, Ill.: InterVarsity, 1996), 54.
6   Wiersbe, *Be Hopeful*, 115–16.

CHAPTER 14   HOPE BEYOND RELIGION

1   J. G. G. Norman, "Charles Haddon Spurgeon," in *The New International Dictionary of the Christian Church*, rev. ed., ed. J. D. Douglas (Grand Rapids, Mich.: Zondervan, 1978), 928.
2   C. H. Spurgeon, *Lectures to My Students* (Grand Rapids, Mich.: Zondervan, 1962), 7–8.
3   Source unknown.
4   Spurgeon, *Lectures*, 154.
5   Michael Silver, "White Tornado," *Sports Illustrated*, 3 June 1996, 71.

CHAPTER 15   HOPE BEYOND DISSATISFACTION

1   Jean Rosenbaum, quoted in *Quote-Unquote*, 315.

CHAPTER 16   HOPE BEYOND THE BATTLE

1   Philip Yancey, *Where Is God When It Hurts?* (Grand Rapids, Mich.: Zondervan, 1977), 22–23.
2   J. Dwight Pentecost, *Your Adversary the Devil* (Grand Rapids, Mich.: Zondervan, 1969), Introduction.
3   Wiersbe, *Be Hopeful*, 138.
4   Ibid.
5   Wuest, *First Peter: In the Greek New Testament*, 130.
6   C. S. Lewis, *The Screwtape Letters* (New York, N.Y.: Macmillan, 1961), 3.

CHAPTER 17   HOPE BEYOND MISERY

1   Dan Greenburg, *How to Make Yourself Miserable*, (New York:
    Random House, 1966), 1–2.

ABOUT THE AUTHOR

CHARLES R. SWINDOLL serves as president of Dallas Theological Seminary. He is also president of Insight for Living, a radio broadcast ministry aired daily worldwide. He was senior pastor at the First Evangelical Free Church in Fullerton, California for almost twenty-three years and has authored numerous books on Christian living, including the best-selling *Grace Awakening, Laugh Again,* and *Flying Closer to the Flame.*

WOMEN CAN WAIT

Also by Terri Schultz

Bittersweet: Surviving and Growing from Loneliness

WOMEN CAN WAIT
THE PLEASURES OF MOTHERHOOD AFTER 30

TERRI SCHULTZ

A DOLPHIN BOOK

Doubleday & Company, Inc.
Garden City, New York 1979

Dolphin Books
Doubleday & Company, Inc.
ISBN: 0-385-14040-1
Library of Congress Catalog Card Number 77-11394
Foreword copyright © 1979 by Don Sloan, M.D.
Copyright © 1979 by Terri Schultz
All Rights Reserved
Printed in the United States of America
First Edition

TO THE WOMEN IN THIS BOOK,
WHO IN SHARING THEIR LIVES CHANGED MINE—
TO MY FRIENDS
MICHAEL, EILEEN, ROBIN, AND MARY ALICE,
WHO ARE WAITING—
AND TO NORMAN.

Foreword

by Don Sloan, M.D.

I guess the first time I ever heard the term "elderly primi-gravida" was when I was a medical student, and an expression that made someone "elderly" at thirty-five made sense then. It was not until years later that I realized that I, too, had become trapped into looking at age from a relative view, like the proverbial blind man who felt the elephant on its tail and decided the animal was small. Or like our own teen-age children who consider people "over the hill" at twenty-five.

These myths, as with others, can be amusing and often do us no harm. But sometimes they do. Sometimes myths serve to keep a people down, deny people a right, or deprive people of education and awareness. The result is the perpetuation of information that condemns a person to accept something in life that might be detrimental to his or her well being or emotional growth. Such a myth is that of the "elderly primigravida." I hope that as you read through *Women Can Wait* you will come to realize, as I did in my awakening, that this myth—that a woman is dangerously "old" to have her first child in her thirties—must be put to rest. This book should do it.

One myth is tied into another. In the myth of the "population explosion," for example, it apparently serves someone's purposes to have us believe that there are too many people to feed, clothe, and house—as though our world can get used up. The fact is that the world is a big place with plenty of resources. True, they must be cultivated and preserved so that they serve the needs of the many rather than the few, but there's plenty to go round. Among the greatest sufferers from this myth have been those who yearn for motherhood and can accept its demands, and yet who during their twenties resisted because of a burden of guilt and now, during their thirties, feel they are too old. Thank you, Ms. Schultz, for pointing out the fallacy of that myth also.

As I read through *Women Can Wait* I could not help but realize that so many will be able to identify with the women who describe their own histories. As I progressed through my years of medical practice I watched my patients become older as I became older and heard more and more concerns about starting families at 30 . . . 32 . . . 35 . . . 38 . . . 40 . . . 42.

And many of my patients who wanted a "later" pregnancy were concerned about the judgment of the people in their lives—their friends, parents, ministers, neighbors, doctors. Each needed support in her efforts to undertake the pregnancy that she sincerely wanted but was sometimes ashamed or even afraid to begin. So, much of my job as her doctor was to provide her with valid and accurate infor-

mation—education so that she could dispel the untruths—
those myths—and then could face the emotional decision
backed up by strength and factual knowledge.

Why is it that for so many women pregnancy is viewed
as a task? A stress? A period of anxiety? It's mainly because
of the ambivalences that are built into it. If you look at
pregnancy objectively, it appears as a negative in many ways
—the weight gain, the loss of body form, the digestive up-
sets, all are part of the physiology of pregnancy. For some
women at any age, there are medical risks during pregnancy,
which are discussed in this book.

Then there are the financial factors. It is expensive to
have a baby in our modern world. It takes a new wardrobe
and new furniture or a larger apartment, not to mention
hospital and medical fees. And maybe you'll not feel energetic enough or have enough "love" left over to carry out
a full working and social schedule.

Have I painted a picture of gloom? I did so to make my
point. If all the above is true—and it is—then why do so
many women become pregnant, and why do even more
women want to but hesitate?

It's because pregnancy cannot and should not be looked
upon simply as an objective biological fact. It is as subjective
a phenomena as can be found in all of the human experience. Today, more than ever, it is elective—no one *has* to
be pregnant, objectively, that is. That subjective drive, that
positive thinking obviously outweighs all the negative
aspects I have just mentioned.

There are also traditional external forces that encourage
pregnancy. One of these is religion. Perhaps based on a time
when the world needed people to propagate the faith, religion urged pregnancy—and the more orthodox the faith,

the stronger the urging. There is also a social pressure to be a parent, to fulfill a role, to perpetuate our races. In some countries, there are actual financial rewards for pregnancies because of the values governments and societies place on children. Some even have laws that permit a man to discard a wife if she is infertile.

And inwardly, there is the desire in most women at some point to act out her uniquely female role, to have a sense of completeness and maturity through childbirth, to produce something of herself that no one else, no other organism, can produce. It has been described as a "mark of immortality." For more and more women, this desire manifests itself not in the teens or twenties, as in previous generations, but a decade later—in the thirties.

Any woman who has had the experience of pregnancy, or will have it, could do a better job than I in describing the fulfillment of gestation. Suffice it to say that those positive feelings must outweigh by far the negative ones. Millions and millions of women continue to have millions and millions of babies. When they get pregnant, however, they all too often become victimized by anxieties, by ambivalence. Now that I am pregnant, they must ask, can I handle it? Am I healthy enough? Am I stable enough? Am I good enough? Can I love enough? Am I patient enough? When a woman is older, despite her maturity, the anxieties can be even more marked because of old myths.

The modern social attitude about "elderly primigravidas" is probably the continuum of ancient times when women and men were categorized by "climacterics." Climacteric, a modern word to describe reproductive capability and the beginning of the geriatric age, actually means "rung of ladder." As the story goes, the woman's life was divided in seven-sevenths. (By tradition, seven was always an important number—seven gods, seven seas, seven days of the week, the seven continents, etc.) The first seventh was infancy and youth; the second, the age to puberty; the third, the age to majority (twenty-one); the fourth, the age of reproduction; the fifth, the declining years; the sixth, the menopause; and, finally, the seven-seventh, or forty-nine, the end of life.

Women Can Wait will marvelously take you through your "sevenths." It will help you realize that to be over thirty and pregnant is often to confront and overcome the prejudices against women who take on families at that time. How many times I have heard a patient exclaim to me, "But doctor, everyone thinks I'm crazy to give up my independence at this age. Won't I feel frustrated and tied down?" Or, "Aren't I too old to start with a baby? Won't I feel like a grandmother when my child is a teen-ager?" Or, "Won't my husband and I be more distant from each other if a newborn enters our household?"

The only answer I have is to ask rhetorically, "Do you want those things to happen?" Couples over thirty who debate the issues of parenting too often do so based on a lack of information, and ignorance of other people's experiences. Ms. Schultz evidently sensed that. She gives you here enough to put those doubts to rest and, more importantly, gives you enough to raise your consciousness and deal with the problem straight on.

I am a physician. I am an obstetrician. I am trained to heal and obey the tenet: "Do No Harm." What is my role? What is the role of the physician, the healer? As a group, we represent a tremendous force of power and authority. If we fail, you the patient have been failed by an important source of confidence and projection. Today, when you wish to take advantage of the medical breakthroughs and the enlightened attitudes that can allow you to experience the most that your era can offer, the obstetrician and the part of the world that s(he) controls is vital to you. Because of that, I hope my colleagues read *Women Can Wait*. We can all learn.

For it is the physician community that must respond to the needs of our patients in a way that allows the medical establishment to display not only its technological skills but also its emotional awareness and sensitivity to the patient. I guess it all boils down to attitude. Our judgment must be one of description, not prescription. We must adapt to the way "it is" or has become, rather than to what it "should be" or how it was. To some, motherhood is an oversold myth, an imposition designed to meet a society's demand, or a family's pressure, or a religion's influence. But for many, motherhood is now a choice. Women are saying, "No, you don't have to have a baby if you don't want to." Ms. Schultz is saying here that your decision to have a baby should be based on fact, not myth. On knowing, not guessing. On understanding, not wondering.

Lastly, there is you, the reader, and your responsibilities. You and your doctor are a team. S(he) is a human being subject to the prejudices of culture just as anyone is. No education or training process is above it. If he or she fails you, remember that, in part, you have permitted him/her to do so. Hopefully, you will be able to share the experience of pregnancy and parenting with *all* those involved. That means all, including your physician, must be comfortable with what is going on.

If you are a woman who waited, read and wait no more.

DON SLOAN, M.D.

Contents

Introduction

Putting It in Perspective

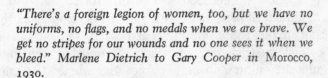

> *"There's a foreign legion of women, too, but we have no uniforms, no flags, and no medals when we are brave. We get no stripes for our wounds and no one sees it when we bleed." Marlene Dietrich to Gary Cooper in Morocco, 1930.*

For the first time in America, large numbers of women are breaking ranks with history and choosing to delay motherhood. Last year alone, about 80,000 women between the ages of thirty and forty-nine gave birth for the first time. They joined almost half a million women who in recent years have also waited until their thirties or forties to have their first child.

Obstetricians and gynecologists in urban areas are noticing that more of their patients are giving birth to first babies after the age of thirty, thirty-five, or even forty. Now their informal observations are buttressed by recent government statistics: In 1978, the National Center for Health Statistics reported that 76,782 women over the age of thirty gave birth for the first time in 1976 (the most recent exact figures available). While birth rates for women in younger age groups continue to decline, the birth rates for women ages thirty to thirty-nine *increased* 5–10 per cent that year, and the Center noted that this increase of older mothers is caused by the fact that, for the first time, women are *choosing* to postpone pregnancy and motherhood. When looking at the overall perspective, statistics also show that today more than 5 per cent of the women in this country had their first child at or beyond the age of thirty-five—a figure that climbs as high as 20 per cent in urban areas. All signs indicate that this trend will grow in future years.

Postponed motherhood is occurring for several reasons. It is, at least in part, a response to social developments that began in the 1960s. During that decade, women became the first beneficiaries of what is probably the most significant cultural invention since the wheel: the mass-production of the birth-control pill. Although the Pill has become a mixed blessing because of its potentially dangerous side effects, it nevertheless gave women more control over their reproductive lives. Biology, so it seemed, was no longer destiny; women did not *have* to be mothers until and unless they wanted to. The Pill paved the way for yet another major cultural transition: the re-emergence in the late 1960s of a lively feminist movement. It is no coincidence that Gloria Steinam and Ortho-Novum 21 were sweeping the country at the same time. Women were getting the same message from the pharmacists and the feminists: They *could* control their own lives, they *could* choose to live the way they wanted—and the implications of this message spanned the bedroom to the board room.

When the Pill and, later, feminism arrived on the scene, many welcomed it, but others feared it might threaten tra-

ditional American values—those values including the prop-
osition not only that all men are created equal, but also
that a woman's place is in the home. Some believed that
if women no longer were destined to procreate, they might
perhaps refuse to procreate. For a while, the dire predic-
tions seemed true. The birth rate began to decline. Only in
the last few years has it become apparent that the cause of
this decline is not because fewer women are having children, but because women are having fewer children. Now
it is also apparent that they are having those fewer children
later in life.

These women find that it is not only personally desirable, but it is now also considered medically safe to have
their first baby later. Most doctors know that a woman in
good health can count on having a normal pregnancy and
delivering a healthy first baby when she is in her mid-thirties or even in her early forties. This more relaxed attitude
among doctors derives in part from the fact that women
are taking better care of their bodies and are living longer
than women of earlier generations. It is also due to the development of amniocentesis—a safe and effective medical
test that detects genetic abnormalities in the fetus.

With amniocentesis, the most common fear among
older women—the fear of bearing a child with Down's
Syndrome, or mongolism—is alleviated. The incidence of
Down's Syndrome in the fetus does increase slightly with
age, although not to nearly the proportions women have
been led to believe. Women ages 30 to 34, for example,
have about one chance in 850 of carrying a fetus with
Down's Syndrome; women aged 40 have one chance in one
hundred. Amniocentesis does not reduce these statistical
possibilities, but it does confirm that the fetus is normal in

the great majority of older women. In doing so, it also curbs needless "panic" abortions in older women.

Until now almost nothing has been known about the private lives of these thousands of women who are waiting until they are older to have their first child. We know only that they tend to be primarily white, middle-class, and urban—for these are the women who have the education, the money, and the freedom to opt for delayed pregnancy. Most of these women share a common social history: They grew up in the conventional fifties, survived and absorbed the culture shock of the sixties, and then dispersed during the introspective seventies into very separate and private lives.

Because they are diverse in their beliefs and scattered in their geography, many of them feel alone. Joan Murray, a television producer who waited until forty to have her first baby, remarks, "I felt very isolated—and very brave—when I decided to have my baby. I was wondering how I was going to hang out in the park with a bunch of twenty-year-old mothers. I hadn't realized how much things have changed. When I walked into my first Lamaze class, every pregnant woman in the room was over thirty." Two months before giving birth, she testified before a house subcommittee on communication in Washington, D.C. "When the women lawyers on the staff saw I was pregnant, they all came up to me and said, 'How old are you?' When I told them, they would say, 'Thank God! It's so great to see someone like you. I'm in my thirties and I've been thinking I should start having children soon, but I didn't know anybody else out there was doing the same thing at my age!'"

This is a book to reassure women who wait that they are

not alone, and to describe the quality of women's lives both before and after postponed childbirth. I am thirty-two and childless, and want some day to have children of my own, so I have a personal as well as a sociological interest in finding out how motherhood at the age of thirty-five or forty affects the day-to-day life-styles of women. I took my own ambivalences, my doubts, my hopes, and my tape recorder into the homes and offices of eighty women in major cities around the country. As my tape recorder whirred, these women described:

—why they waited.
—what factors entered into their decision to give birth.
—how a baby affects their career.
—how it affects their marriage.
—how they manage their time.
—whether they had any regrets about waiting.
—how they integrate personal plans and dreams with the needs of a growing child.

As these women talked to me they also nursed, answered phones, put children to bed, fixed and served dinner, worked at drawing boards, signed expense vouchers, kissed husbands hello and good-by. They talked while eating tuna fish on rye in their plush corner offices; they talked while janitors emptied garbage cans around their feet; they talked while dogs barked and clocks chimed and fireplaces crackled and babies sucked, cried, cooed, and jabbered. Their words were punctuated by the frequent laughter of women enjoying their hectic lives. When I left them, I always felt exhilarated and touched by what they had shared.

This book is divided into four sections: the first is "Waiting," in which women discuss their relationships,

their careers, their quest to find themselves, and their am-
biguities toward motherhood.

In the second section, "Deciding," women describe the
specific events, the emotional catharses, the turning points
that lead them to decide—often quite suddenly—that *now*
in their thirties or forties is the time for a baby.

The third section, "Birthing," includes the most up-to-
date medical information on older pregnant women, as
well as the personal experiences of women on the delivery
table, including those growing numbers of women who are
delivering by Cesarean section.

In the fourth section, "Mothering," women describe
how the presence of a baby changes their feelings about
work, about their husbands and friends, about their own
mothers, and most of all about themselves and their lives.

Following these four sections, I present five of the interviews intact. These women represent a cross-section of
women who wait.

Whenever possible, I quote the women directly. Their
own descriptions of their most personal hopes, fears,
conflicts, resolutions, and ambivalences are always vivid—
sometimes funny, sometimes poignant, often surprising.
They tell the story of a generation of women who are coming to terms with themselves. Their story is the story of
women struggling to integrate complex lives—and suc-
ceeding.

As thousands of women delay childbirth in the next few
years, it will become even more clear to what extent these
women are the front line of a major social transition. They
are unique, determined, often very brave, and their experiences of motherhood are important for women of all ages,
now and in the future. They serve as beacons for other

women who are waiting. They serve as reassuring guides for older women who, right now, are giving birth to their first babies.

Most of all, they confirm the benefits of delayed motherhood. Their words are anchored by a maturity, a sense of self-fulfillment, and a joy that they sought to achieve early in life, before they gave birth, and that they feel is enhanced and enriched by their decision to have children later—when those children are most deeply appreciated, are least threatening, and become, in all ways, a final celebration of oneself.

WOMEN CAN WAIT

Chapter One

Waiting—The Reasons

————◆————

"If a young girl asks my advice about having a child, I would say—wait until you're at least thirty. Thirty-five is even better. Youth is wasted on the young. Even if you just sat home for thirty years, you ought to have some kind of experience, a little bit of life, under your belt."
Hilda A., who had her child at thirty-five.

FREEDOM

Who exactly are the women who wait to have children? What are the major factors in their decision? How do they differ from women who have children young, or who have none at all? Many of the women I interviewed say they simply want to be free. For them, the desire to have a baby is balanced against the fear that the restraints and obligations of motherhood will undermine the professional and personal freedoms they have struggled so hard to win. This fear of lost freedoms is experienced by almost all women who choose to delay motherhood. In the last decade, women have fought hard to break out of traditional roles.

They have entered new job areas—women now climb telephone poles, trade stocks on the floor of the New York
Stock Exchange, pilot commercial airplanes, weld, drive
semi-trucks, and sit on judicial benches. Women who have
put their energies into proving they can do a job "as well as
a man" are understandably hesitant to risk throwing away
those hard-won gains.

By becoming pregnant and a mother, women naturally
wonder whether the stamp of those traditional roles might
once again be upon them and might overwhelm them,
overshadowing their other accomplishments. The vice-
president of a large Chicago corporation told me that,
when she was pregnant, "grown men in my office whom I
have dealt with professionally for eight years began calling
me 'ma.' It was as if I had spent a decade of my life trying
to be taken seriously as a functioning adult woman and
then, in a second, all I was, was pregnant." She found that
when she made her feelings known, however, the male employees changed their tone. Instead of patronizing her,
they began to tell her how much they really admired her.
"I began to realize," she says, "that in a way, they were
jealous. They were as stifled in their male roles as women
have been in female ones. They have, for the most part,
sacrificed their personal lives for their professional ambitions—while I was managing to combine both."

This ambivalence toward relinquishing hard-won gains is
a natural, realistic, and healthy feeling, and it encompasses
women's personal lives as well as their professional ones.
Before the 1960s, not much had changed substantially in
terms of women's roles from Emma Bovary's day, a hundred years earlier, when, feeling strangled by her dull life,
Emma hoped she would give birth to a boy. "The thought

of having a male child was an anticipatory revenge for all her earlier helplessness. A man, at least, is free. He can explore passions and countries, surmount obstacles, taste the most exotic pleasures. But a woman is continually held back," Flaubert wrote in 1857.

Rather than feel this kind of constraint, many women choose to delay or eschew engagement rings, postpone matrimony, and vacillate over motherhood long beyond the point their mothers or grandmothers once did. And today there is no reason to rush into marriage or pregnancy: In Madame Bovary's day, American women could expect to live only to the age of forty; today, their average life expectancy is seventy. Since the care and feeding of children takes up only about one third of this life expectancy, many women are increasingly aware that, for them, motherhood is better late than ever.

They can be free to travel, to work—they can, while still young, exorcise their wanderlust, nurse their ambitions, nurture their emotional and spiritual needs, without feeling stifled. As a corporate executive who had her son at the age of thirty-five explains, "I wanted to investigate myself, to feel more settled in my career, to stop feeling erratic bouts of craziness—as though I could chuck everything and take off for Rio tomorrow."

When women say they are postponing motherhood because they want to be free, they each have different definitions of freedom in mind. For some, freedom means affirming themselves—they want to live in new cities and foreign countries, to party, to travel, to explore different life-styles, to experiment with different men and living arrangements. Having done all this, they *then* feel much more positive about going ahead and having children. As one thirty-six-year-old mother of two told me, "My friends who had children young went through years of frustration. They would look at my life and tell me, 'You're so lucky. You travel. You eat out. You work. We're stuck in the house.' Now that I'm older my attitude (toward full-time mothering) is that I don't mind not going to a restaurant —I've been. I don't mind not traveling—I've gone there. It doesn't mean I'm never going to do it again. It's a temporary pause, a refocusing of my energy."

For others, freedom means rebellion—they have felt driven from an early age to escape from the constraints of a small town or suburb, or a conservative or unloving home environment. Often, they believe their emotional survival is at stake. They wish primarily to have a chance to be by themselves, to enjoy themselves without parental constraints, to explore themselves without guilt, before seeking new commitments. For many women, this rebellion is quiet and personal—it involves a rejection of the past, a running away from the old in order to find themselves through something new.

For some, however, the rebellion is also a political and social statement—they hope to overhaul certain parts of society as well as their lives. These women tend to explore popular movements and participate in social causes. Some of them were involved in the marches and movements of the 1960s, and found that only after the Vietnam War could they refocus their energies. This is one reason why women like Jane Fonda waited to have children.

Some women retreated from public protest when they felt bored or tired, or felt they had achieved their goals. Many others simply gave up, disappointed by society's failure to listen and change. One New York woman who was active in civil rights until the age of thirty explains what happened to her, "After the Harlem riots, my Core chapter fell apart. People got discouraged and depressed. We realized we couldn't make any significant changes. We were doing grass roots work in Harlem, organizing rent strikes— we weren't out to change the world, we were out to change a building, and we weren't getting anywhere. After the riots a lot of us went to jail, and it seemed futile. Most of the women I knew became apolitical and moved away." One year later she got married, and when she was thirty-five she had her first child.

An older father caught up in the activism of the 1960s explained most succinctly the sentiment I heard from many older mothers as well, "All of us were brainwashed in high school about zero population growth. I used to have nightmares that we would be shoulder-to-shoulder on this planet. I wanted to be a good citizen and not have any children. Then there was the ban-the-bomb movement. I didn't want to bring a child into a society where he's going to die of radiation. Then there was the Vietnam War. Why should I rear a child so he can get hauled off by his government to die in a rice paddy?"

And others, caught up in the early feminist movement, went through a metamorphosis. After beginning their feminist involvement in the 1960s, with a deep and often vocal anger that exploded in venomous rhetoric against men, scorn for their own mothers' lives, and disdain for all housewives in general, they progressed to a new level: They began to implement changes in the courts and in Congress, and they emerged, after a decade, mellower, wiser, more forgiving. One early feminist who had her first child at the age of thirty-nine explains, "Ingrid Bengis' book, *Combat in the Erogenous Zone*, epitomized all my hatred toward men and my frustration at being female. For the next five years after reading that book, I worked for the Equal Rights Amendment, for gay rights, for black rights—and then it began to dawn on me that I still wasn't taking care of myself. It had become too easy for me to blame everyone else for what I began to see were my own particular personality problems and my self-destructive relationships with men. Once I realized that, I got some therapy and found out how to be happy with myself. As a result, I am a more effective feminist because I am no longer anti-male; I'm just pro-woman."

The one thing all these women have in common is that they feared jeopardizing their independence. They were wary of submerging themselves in traditional female roles. And they were pleased to find that those fears were *not* realized once they did finally give birth. Because they waited for motherhood, they did not feel stifled by children. In fact, they discovered that their children enhanced rather than diminished the richness of their lives. As one woman psychologist who waited told me, "When women patients come to me and lament, 'I'm over the hill. I'm thirty years old and I have to have a baby,' I make a point of saying, 'Why? I waited until I was forty-two, and now I am the fifty-seven-year-old mother of a teen-ager, and it's fabulous!' "

Affirmation

Diana R. is a classic example of a woman who chose to affirm herself. Like most women today, she felt she wanted to "make something" of her life. But Diana's case is particularly interesting because she took such bold and yet at the same time careful steps to insure that her independence would not be stifled. She affirmed herself in a way that was acceptable to the society in which she was reared. She followed the "right" career, and she married young. Yet, having taken all the proper steps, she then weaned herself from her work and her husband and went on to pursue everything she really wanted from life. As an explorer, she is constantly expanding her horizons, adding new experiences and new friends to her repertoire of life.

Diana grew up in a small town near Tacoma, Washington, where, she says, most young women were engaged to be married before the end of high school. During her tenth high school reunion, she found that out of a graduating class of six hundred women, only twelve had pursued any career outside the home. Those who did had become nurses or teachers, and "did it part time, in conjunction with being the mother of three or four kids."

Diana had always envisioned a different kind of life for herself. "I was always an independent sort—like my mother," she says. "My mother worked as a butcher and a meat wrapper, and she always prodded me to make something of myself. My parents gave me a good, solid background—they must have loved me very much, because I'm a very secure person. I always felt restless, but I always got support for doing what I wanted for myself."

While other girls were winning diamond rings, Diana won a teaching scholarship and, when she was seventeen, moved to Seattle to become an elementary school teacher. However, she was much more interested in the city lights than in her studies. "The teaching scholarship was the only acceptable way I knew how to get out of town," she says. While in school, she met her future husband, a local university student who was planning to set up his orthodontic practice in Massachusetts after graduation. She married him, and as soon as they moved East she left him. "I was twenty-one years old and wanted to be free," she says. "I wasn't callous, I was just confused, and eager for more from life." She studied at Hunter College in New York, where she received a master's degree in business. Then she started her own advertising agency, and later founded one of the first women's artist co-operatives in the country.

"I just wasn't interested in settling down," she says. "My relationships with men didn't last very long. If we had a disagreement, I would say, 'Well, I'm not interested anymore'—and leave. I did the things I feel most women should be able to do—but I also realize a lot of people didn't like me for being so independent. My mother shuddered when I hitchhiked through Europe, rode a motorcycle through Russia, and learned how to fly a single-engine plane. My boy friend objected when I took karate, or when I flew to Nashville to meet Robert Altman when he was filming there, just because he intrigues me.

"When women's liberation came along, I thought a lot of it was fairly silly, but it has strengthened the ideas I have always held. It has made me feel more secure in some of the things I wanted to do—secure enough to feel I could be married and be a mother and still be myself."

Diana gave birth when she was thirty-nine years old, and married the father—who is ten years younger than she—after the baby was born. Through all this, she received her parents' love and support. "When I told my mother I was pregnant, she didn't ask me when I was going to get married—she just held my hand, kissed me, and said she thought it was wonderful. Then we went upstairs to tell my father, who is from a very proper English background, and my mother said, very calmly, 'We're going to tell you something and we want you to be excited, but if you're not —fake it.' He was actually very good about it, although I had to put up with nine months of, 'Where-is-the-son-in-law-who-goes-with-this-story?' "

Today, Diana takes full-time care of her baby, and is teaching herself piano and French—two things she has always wanted to learn. She can do both with the baby on her lap, and is delighted with her role of mother. "I resent being labeled anything. I *love* being female. I'm very opinionated. I'm very giving. I like cooking for somebody, taking care of somebody, and I like the same in return. I don't feel being a mother is my 'role' in life, anymore than being a teacher or a businesswoman was. I don't want to be the 'little wife at home' where somebody else is taking care of me. I still have $4,000 saved. When that runs out, I will go back to work. Meanwhile, I am delighted about my child, my husband, myself, my life in general—I feel I have it all, and I've compromised almost nothing."

Women who are like Diana, who seek out new experiences and stay open to life, are able to make of life a celebration. Because she has a deep faith in herself, because

she has a sense of humor, good instincts, insatiable curiosity, and a lot of love—she has not felt intimidated by people
who disapprove of her. For women like her, delayed motherhood is like a bonus for being female. It is one more
experience—natural, fulfilling, and completely unthreat-
ening.

Survival

Other women postpone childbirth because they feel it
might jeopardize their very survival. They feel a need to
question, and often to reject, the assumptions with which
they were reared. Some felt misunderstood and unloved.
Some felt their parents were old-fashioned, hypocritical, or
themselves trapped in unhappy lives. Whatever the reasons, they wanted to smash the old patterns and create new
ones for themselves. One such woman is Ava S.

Ava, like Diana, also left home at the age of seventeen.
She sought both adventure and escape. Ava was the daughter of Indianapolis schoolteachers who believed in discipline and punishment. "I had to ask permission to do
everything," she recalls. "When I was twelve, I still had to
be in bed by 7:30. Even on New Year's Eve, I had a 10
P.M. curfew. They expected high grades and total obedience. In a way it was terrific because it gave me a lot to
rebel against."

After several experiences that left Ava with the feeling
there was no one at home she could confide in or seek sympathy from, she ran away—first to Chicago and then to
New York. She had been taking ballet lessons in Indianapolis, and she had brought her toe shoes with her to

the city. "I was good, I knew how to dance, and I got work right away," she says. "I took three ballet classes a day, and my whole life revolved around what I ate, the shape of my toe shoes, and each evening's performance. I was incredibly dedicated, but very self-centered. When you dance, *you* are what you're selling. Your body is a machine, and you have to keep that machine in order."

She joined the Ballet Russe, which toured dozens of cities around the world each year. During that time she married and divorced. Then, at the age of thirty-two, she remarried and had her daughter, Tracy, who is now fourteen. The second marriage lasted eleven years before it, too, ended in divorce.

Now, at the age of forty-six, Ava looks back on her life—her struggles to be free of her rigid upbringing, her successful career as a dancer, and her belated role as a mother—with pride, and she hopes her daughter's life will be as fulfilled as hers has been. "If she doesn't want to have a career, and just wants to marry young, have children, and be someone's wife, I would be frightened for her," Ava says. "Marriage is in such a terrible state today that to depend on a man to support you is foolhardy."

Ava feels she has made the right decisions for her life—including her delayed motherhood—and she hopes that, by her example, she has given her daughter the strength and wisdom to do the same.

Both Diana and Ava had a private vision of how life should be lived, and each pursued quite single-mindedly the personal goals they had established for themselves. Once they achieved those goals, they felt free to bear children and able to integrate those children into their lives without threatening their hard-won accomplishments.

Social Rebellion

Many other women who also seek self-fulfillment have no clear-cut personal goals to aim for. Instead of relying on themselves, they find someone or something to whom/which they can attach themselves—an escape hatch through which they can channel their frustration. Unlike Diana and Ava, who built their own paths to freedom in a careful way, who were self-sufficient and self-reliant, many of these women search for a Yellow Brick Road—a path laid down by someone else, a path they can follow in the hope that someone wiser might be found along the way to help them map out their own particular routes to happiness.

Many of these women were involved in the upheavals of the 1960s—the civil-rights movement, the anti-war movement, the guru movement—and were sometimes tossed about during their twenties like ships floundering at sea. It was not until they reached the calmer waters of their thirties that they could feel ready to have children.

For many women like these, the road through the 1960s, and through their twenties, was a tortuous one. Here is a story of one woman who went through great transformations during that decade, upheavals that kept her so busy she had no desires, or opportunity, to settle down.

Eileen M. followed a route that took her around the world—from Philadelphia to Nepal and back again. It was a path that also took her through different worlds—from working with rock festivals to working with corporate executives. She is now thirty-two, and pregnant with her first child.

Eileen was born in San Diego. Her father was a doctor, her mother a housewife—and from an early age Eileen was programmed to follow their approved life plan. After graduating from high school, she went to secretarial school and then to nursing school. Her mother was pleased that Eileen had chosen traditional female occupations, but Eileen felt increasingly discontent and finally left nursing school and worked her way through college.

While she was in college, she started using her nursing skills to set up free medical clinics at rock festivals. After college she found a job counseling heroin addicts in the San Diego area, and then later became an abortion counselor.

During this time, she became increasingly critical of her parents, particularly her mother. She saw her mother as a "trapped" woman who had wasted her life—and decided she would not let herself be lured into that same position. "She always gave me a double message," Eileen recalls today. "One was, 'Do as I have done, get married and have children.' When I was twenty-three, she announced that when she was *my* age, she had already had me. The other message was, 'Do not do as I have done. I am frustrated with my life. You should have a career.' Neither of my parents recognize even now that I have a college degree and am no longer a nurse. They had role-played me into being a nurse, and that was as far as they could go with me."

Then, when she was twenty-five she found out she was pregnant, and she flew to New York to have an abortion. Although she had no qualms about counseling other women who sought abortions, she found that her own abortion disturbed her deeply. "I flew back to San Diego, went out on a date that night—and went into a crying jag that lasted for weeks," she says. She was plagued by depression, and it took her several years to recover from the emotional devastation of that abortion. "It was not a child I wanted, the father was not a person I was really involved with—and yet something in me snapped. I couldn't allow myself to think, 'Hey, there's a child, a living thing inside of me, and I killed it.' But I *felt* that way. I felt I had killed a part of myself."

On the rebound, feeling needy, she followed a new boy friend to Los Angeles, where he was hoping to become an actor. "It was time for me to move. In some way I was running—I was always running in those days," she says. Then she found a job as an administrator with the city of Los Angeles.

After a year, she became interested in meditation, so she quit her job and followed a guru to India, Nepal, and Pakistan. For three months, she lived in an ashram on the banks of the Ganges. "I did learn how to turn inside and find some of the internal peace I was looking for," she says. "But in retrospect, I was really looking for someone, some group, to take care of me without my having to work for it."

Eileen returned to Los Angeles, tried living in another ashram, and found she could not tolerate the collective life-style. She moved into an apartment with a friend, and found a job as a campaign planner for a Los Angeles politician. Although she felt more at ease with herself—she kept soul-searching. She worked with a gestalt therapist, and then tried transactional analysis.

"My basic problem," she says, "was a lack of self-esteem

and a tendency to fall in love with bastards who gave me a hard time. I grew to have a stronger sense of who I am, of my strengths and weaknesses. Once I had greater respect for myself and a greater faith in my own ability to do certain things, I was ready for marriage and children."

Finally, at the age of thirty-two, she married her husband after turning him down three times. Although she still has a tendency to run from responsibility and commitment, she feels for the first time in her life secure enough to welcome a child into her life. She became pregnant eight weeks after the wedding, and is anticipating the arrival of her child with joy.

Feminism

While feminism was yet another "cause" that swept the country in the 1960s, it must be distinguished from other social movements—such as the civil-rights or anti-war movements—when talking about why women delay childbirth. Nothing has had as great an impact on this new trend toward postponed parenthood as feminism. Women who are feminists often consider their stance as both an affirmation *and* a rebellion: It affirms women's rights to take a full and equal place in society; it rebels against the traditional attitudes that have prevented women from reaching that full and equal place. Similarly, feminism is both a political *and* a personal statement. The personal issues of feminism cannot be segregated from the political and social issues. Abortion, methods of childbirth, number of children, day care, attitudes toward mothering, career choice, and success, all affect each woman, and all are inherent in the cause of feminism.

For these reasons, it is important to take a separate look at the odyssey of a feminist—a woman who came of age during the rebirth of feminism in the 1960s, and whose feminist beliefs transformed her entire life. It wasn't until the age of thirty-four that she had the first of her three children.

Miriam C.'s story is familiar to many women who married young, felt stifled and unhappy in their marriage, and were then exposed to the newly emerging feminist literature and rhetoric. Miriam found she had to re-evaluate her previous beliefs and restructure her entire life. Feminism consumed several years and all her energy. Today, at the age of forty-two, Miriam is a housewife and a mother. Although on the surface it appears that her life has turned out to be the domestic one she longed for when she was young, and later rejected, she has, in reality, emerged at the other end of a complex emotional maze—a maze that totally altered her perceptions of herself, men, marriage, and children.

When she was sixteen, Miriam was sent to St. Louis to attend a special school for bright children. She majored in boys, and hoped to graduate by marrying a man who would make the cover of *Time* magazine. Ever since she was small, she had wanted children—her favorite high school job was baby-sitting, and she had no doubt that the production of babies would be one of her first adult functions.

For a while, her life went according to traditional plan. When she was eighteen she married a medical student she had met on her college campus, and slipped into the comfortable life that was expected of the wife of a doctor-to-be.

She was going to become a grade school teacher, and after his graduation she and her husband were planning to move to Hales Corners, a comfortable suburb of Milwaukee, where his father, also a doctor, had his practice.

Then a crack appeared in the smooth surface of their marriage. Miriam was invited and expected to join the Wives and Fiancées Club at the medical school—and she refused to do it. At the time, she could not explain why. "There just seemed to me something terribly wrong with all that business," she says today. "I just didn't like the idea of it. In the college lunchroom, my classmates were showing off their engagement rings and playing bridge. I thought it was appalling. The men liked their women that way, and when I started to criticize, they would say to me, 'Why are you being so castrating?' They would say, 'You're acting too aggressive. Why can't you be more feminine, like the other girls?' It hurt me terribly. Gradually, I began to feel suffocated by the life I was leading. I began to feel as if I were living in a pillowcase."

Her ambition bothered her—and at the same time she felt guilty about feeling guilty. "I was a child of the times, who was afraid to be herself," she says. Over her husband's protests, she changed majors and began to work for a doctorate in psychology. Then, four days after she received her degree, she walked out on her husband. It was 1959 and she was twenty-two years old. She knew she was supposed to feel guilty again, but she felt only relief. "I knew I could work and take care of myself. And I knew I no longer loved my husband. I could finally admit that I had married him partly because I had wanted to get out of my parents' house and partly because I thought no one else would marry me."

During the next few years, she began to hear and read about a newly emerging "woman's movement." "I remember, in the early beginning of the movement, I was having dinner with my mother and she said, 'Oh my God! A bunch of Lesbians—that's all they are!' And I thought, 'I know that's not true. That's an antediluvian statement to make. Why would she say a peculiar thing like that?' Then I realized that she was threatened, that those women with the engagement rings were threatened, that my ex-husband was threatened, by the idea of women being free and equal —an idea that I had been fighting for before it even had a name. I can date my first serious attraction to the movement from that moment."

The more she read about feminism, the better she started to feel about herself. "It was a tremendous relief, because in the years I had been married and in school, I had been in situations where, if I had been a man, people would have rewarded me. Instead, I had been told to keep my place. It always bothered me, and it never seemed to bother anybody else. Now I had some support for my own experiences."

During her late twenties and early thirties, she deflected her desire to have children through her work: first as a psychologist in a children's home, and then as a family therapist. She lived alone for a few years, then with a man, and then at the age of thirty-four she married a man who respected her work, her feminism, and her spunk. She began having children almost immediately. "I had a large dose of drive-to-have-kids. While I was pregnant with each of my three children, I felt high, and the first delivery was probably the most exhilirating experience I have ever had or will ever have in my life," she says.

"As a feminist, I feel a little funny admitting it, but I like filling the role of mother and housewife. I like society to see me this way. I get a kick out of it. And since having my three kids, I feel more confident, more energetic, more . . . oatsy, than ever before. The confidence comes from doing what *I* have wanted to do for myself all these years, and having kids has been only a part of it.

"One of the problems with the women's movement is that it hasn't addressed itself enough to this issue of motherhood. For so long, having kids was the only thing women were allowed to do, supposed to do, and I think there was a reactionary response to that. We feminists said, 'Anybody who wants to have kids or be with kids must be a ninny. We're all supposed to go out and have careers.' Well, I *had* my career, and having kids is absolutely fantastic after that.

"I am forty-one years old, and yet I have this surge of energy now that I've never had before. I am running a house with three kids without outside help. I have started a neighborhood newspaper. I work several days a month as a family counselor. I've been involved in the school and confronted almost single-handedly an agency of the state to force the school to make needed structural changes in the building.

"And the kids are a continuing miracle to me. Sometimes I look at them and think, Those are *my* kids? Those people came out of *me*? It feels wonderful."

In the last few years, feminism has been attacked for being anti-children and anti-male. A division has been drawn in some people's minds, with the Total Woman on one side pitted against the Bra-burning Lesbian on the other. Clearly, women are more complex than either of these characterizations allows room for.

Most feminists are like Miriam—average women from middle-class homes who have experienced the social frustrations of being female and decided to do something about it. Because they delay childbirth does not mean they abhore children. Because they live alone or divorce, does not mean they dislike men. On the contrary—it often means they like children and men enough to not want to end up resenting them. It simply means, as Miriam so aptly demonstrates in her own life, that they are seeking to affirm themselves—and having children is, for many, a final and delightful product of that affirmation.

FEELING DIFFERENT

In all times and through all ages, certain people feel from an early age that they are in some ways "different" from the other people around them. In the past, women who felt this way often struck out on their own. Some became noted for accomplishments in a man's world—such as Madame Curie, Margaret Mead, Golda Meir, George Sand —and they were often treated as men, or as "nonwomen"— exceptions to the rules of acceptable female behavior. They excelled in areas usually reserved for men. But then there were few directions in which women could channel those feelings of uniqueness. As a result, those who felt different simply became known as eccentrics, the oddballs of a community.

All children and adolescents, female and male, are at certain times aware of a uniqueness that sets them apart from other people. But in some children it becomes a strong un-

dercurrent that carries them along even into adulthood;
they feel displaced and would like to find a niche where
they fit in. As adolescents they begin to attach labels to
themselves that will explain and perhaps justify their sense
of being separate and out of the mainstream. They call
themselves intellectuals, late-bloomers, tomboys, or loners.

The quest to "belong" often entails a move from small
towns or suburbs to urban areas where the greater variety
of people offers almost every woman a chance to form a circle of friends or co-workers or neighbors who share common interests and attitudes. "From the age of ten on, I
couldn't wait to get out," says one woman who grew up in
a tiny Kansas town (population: 133). "I longed to hear
Schubert instead of the country and western music I grew
up with. I hungered for Chinese food instead of ribs. I
liked reading Sartre instead of movie magazines, maybe because I identified so much with his fictional characters. I always felt like odd-man-out, I always felt lonely—even
though I had three sisters—and I *knew* there must be other
women out there who felt the same." When she was eighteen she left home to work in Los Angeles. She later went
to college, became a music historian, and had a baby at the
age of thirty-eight.

Another woman recalls, "I loved to work with machines,
to overhaul engines, and it caused a minor scandal in Rock
Springs, Wisconsin. While other girls were necking in cars,
I was fixing them. I spent a lot of time in overalls, and I
thought of myself the way other people did—as a kind of
freak." She later studied engineering in Milwaukee and had
a child at the age of forty.

Many of these women had active fantasy lives as children, spurred on by books that, in their empty hours alone,

projected them among new people and into new places
where they would feel comfortable. These women were
often popular, but described themselves as *feeling* un-
popular—they worked to belong to the right group of girls,
the cheerleader squad, the forensics team, to date the right
men. But it was with a sense of relief that they left their
parents' homes and their childhood schools to begin another life.

Individualists

Emily B., from Parkers Prairie, Minnesota (population:
882), is a beautiful woman with long blond hair, who bears
a striking resemblance to folk singer Mary Travers. But despite her beauty, she remembers being the ugly duckling of
her town. In some ways, she seemed to be the local Wonder Woman—president of her class, star of most of the
school plays, soloist in the glee club, declamation champion, science fair winner, math winner—everything she
did, she did well. In other ways, she seemed to be a loser.
She was never invited out on a date, and she never had a
boy friend during her high school years.

"I thought I was an untouchable," she says. "It never occurred to me that I might have been intimidating to the
boys, although in retrospect I think maybe that's what happened. At the time, however, I just felt unhappy, felt I
wasn't making it in small-town society. I always felt I
didn't belong there, and I was always interested in getting
out. I read *The New Yorker* whenever I could get my
hands on it. I was reading John Barth and Donald Bar-

thelme when I was fifteen. I was very interested in experimental American fiction and theater."

Emily left Parkers Prairie to attend college in New York, where she now lives and works as a fiction writer. "My mother would like to see me teaching school in a little town, with a husband who is 'in cement' as they say out there, leading a 'normal' life. I think it's what all mothers want for their children, and I'll probably want it for mine: BE NORMAL. But I haven't led a very safe life. I am an intellectual, although that is not as esoteric as my mother thinks. Being a free-lance writer is a little like being a dirt farmer: You plant a crop and try your best to make sure you're growing it properly, and you never know when a storm is going to come through and wipe out your best efforts. If a storm *does* come through, you put away your plow and pack up your pride and go to work in town in the factory until the next growing season. Then you try again."

Emily is now preparing for yet another "different" lifestyle—she has decided to have her baby alone, without a father around.* "My mother has reacted to my pregnancy by being concerned that I am once again setting myself apart from 'normal' people. There is that wonderful Robert Frost line, 'Home is the place where, when you have to go there, they have to take you in'—and that is true of my family. They may not approve of what I do, of my going against convention, but they have always accepted whatever I did with love and concern."

For the last five years, Emily has been building a house on property she owns in upstate New York. Always the individualist, she plans to live there when she gets old. "I call

* The factors that she considered while making her decision will be discussed further in Chapter Two, "Deciding."

it Random House, because that's how it's being built—randomly," she says. "It is a pipe dream. Still, it's a dream I hope to make come true. I see myself thirty years from now, an eccentric gray-haired old lady driving a broken-down forty-year-old car and living in a house with fifteen spiral staircases, twenty-two towers, and not a single working bathroom."

Linnea D. also felt "different" growing up, but unlike Emily she felt her family—especially her father—understood and spurred her on to do exactly what she wanted to do, when she wanted to do it. Linnea has been married three times; she had her first and only child, a daughter, at the age of forty-two. Her daughter is now fifteen years old.

"I have always held attitudes that were not typical of the times," Linnea says. "When I was eighteen, in 1938, I had premarital sex—unusual for that day. And I certainly wasn't your basic 1940s girl. I had been married twice by then, both times because I was too dumb to say no. I couldn't bring myself to say I didn't love the men, which is the only reason that counts, so I gave every other kind of excuse imaginable until I had used them all up—and then I went to the altar. I would have been quite happy to live with both of those men, but they didn't want it—the social stigma bothered them. I left both men because I just didn't feel like the marrying kind. I was really a loner—and I just preferred to stay that way."

Linnea's main interest was singing, and after she graduated from college she went into show business. She formed a singing trio, traveled around the country on tour, and made records with Capitol. She then moved to Los Angeles, where she became friends with people in "progressive politics," people whose beliefs led eventually to the Un-American Activities Committee inquisitions. Linnea stayed with her singing career until her early thirties, when she returned to college to earn a degree in psychology, and at the age of thirty-seven she started her own private practice. She had no interest in motherhood until she met her third husband. That marriage lasted fourteen years, and she has recently separated from him, too.

"I feel like I've been a liberated woman all my life, and I attribute my attitude to my family," she says. "I was always considered the oddball, but I always got rewards for it. My father was an Orthodox rabbi who loved his work, and my mother was a successful business person who earned almost as much as he did. My whole family was very nonchauvinistic toward women. My mother's mother was the most admired person in the entire clan. She had ten children and was almost illiterate, and yet she was smart and logical and practical. She spoke three languages and understood the whole Talmud.

"When I was five years old, in 1925, my father told me he thought I should become a doctor. Can you imagine how many women doctors there were in 1925? It was a radical idea. Later, he told me he thought I had such a remarkable mind it should be used for something unusual.

"Their attitude imbued me with the feeling that I could do anything I wanted—and so I did. Now, when women patients come to me and lament, 'I'm over the hill. I'm thirty years old and I have to have a baby,' I make a point of saying, 'Why? I waited until I was forty-two, and now I am the fifty-seven-year-old mother of a teen-ager, and it's fabulous!' "

Until now, most women who felt differently did not

have the option of postponing motherhood until their mid-thirties or even early forties. They did not have the biological time, the education, or the family support that would have given them the opportunity to pursue their identities. As a result, many resigned themselves to an early marriage and children, and to a lifetime of feeling misunderstood and unfulfilled—often with unhappy results for parents and children. Today, for the first time, women can explore all facets of themselves without fear of losing the chance for motherhood.

Minorities

Some women feel out of place for obvious cultural and racial reasons. Theresa V. is a Japanese-American who married late and had her first child at the age of forty. When she was eleven years old, she and her family were placed in a detention camp on the East Coast. "Growing up Japanese-American during World War II, I had other things on my mind besides boys," she says. "I was automatically somewhat ostracized. I was the kid who was always the smartest in school, who was the class president—but I never had a boy friend. My girl friends had to fix me up for the senior prom. I just got my A's and headed my nose for Bryn Mawr, which is where I ended up going.

"From an early age, I knew that I would always work, that coming from a racial minority I had to rely on myself to survive. I never saw how I would fit in a baby—and there was no one around to be the father. And, if you look at my choices—why would I put all my heart and all my aspirations into something that had eluded me? I put my energies where I knew they would pay off—into my career in films."

Like Theresa, Toni P. deferred motherhood for pragmatic reasons. Toni is a thirty-seven-year-old black woman who grew up in Woodlawn on Chicago's South Side. Toni married when she was thirty-two and had her first child last year at the age of thirty-six.

"College was the only road out, and my mother started telling me as far back as I can remember to take it," she says. "There is an ad for the United Negro College Fund of a black woman scrubbing floors to put her kid through school—that's how it was in our house. I got out on scholarships and whatever money my mother could give me."

After graduating from the University of Pennsylvania with a law degree, Toni worked for the Office of Economic Opportunity in Washington. "I had a lot of energy, and no particular interest in settling down. There was a whole new white world out there, and I wanted to find out how it worked, to infiltrate it so I could make it work for me." Toni returned to Chicago in 1970, joined a private practice, and bought her mother a house in the Chicago suburb of Melrose Park. When she did finally marry, it was to a man she had known since childhood, who had also worked his way from the black ghetto to the white corporate world. Now that she is firmly entrenched in the middle class, Toni plans to have several children "who will never know poverty."

CAREERS

The women we've met so far do have careers, but those careers are not the major reason they give for waiting to have children. It is true, however, that more women *are* waiting for that reason alone. Some want a chance for success, fame, and fortune; others just want time to save money—to buy furniture, to travel—before giving birth. The U. S. Department of Labor reports that in the late 1960s, more young married women began for the first time to work outside the home. Today, a record-breaking 35 million women hold jobs.

The number of career women has increased in the last decade for several reasons. First, feminism has begun to exert psychological pressure on all women by advocating that women as well as men validate themselves through the paid work they do. Next, continuing inflation often dictates that all adults in the household bring in an income. Third, rising divorce rates have made it clear that a woman can no longer rely on her husband to provide financial security for the rest of her life. Fourth, new government affirmative-action programs have expanded job opportunities for women, encouraging more women to learn some sort of paid skill outside the house. Added to these social phenomena is one other simple, basic fact: More and more women feel that their lives will be happier and more fulfilled if they work outside their homes.

This attitude, and the social support women now receive for working, is a reversal of the attitudes faced by working women twenty years ago. By 1940, 14 million women were in the labor force, but many of them worked only because their husbands had gone off to war. After World War II, men retrieved most of those jobs, and Rosie the Riveter returned to the kitchen. In the 1950s, the Department of Labor statistics show that most of the women entering the labor force were older married women whose children had grown. Only in the late sixties did young women begin to keep their jobs even after they married and had children. For some of these women, working was a matter of economic necessity, not of choice. But even they no longer had to feel embarrassed or apologetic, feel ashamed or like a "bad mother" because they left home to go to an office or a factory five days a week.

For many women, the right to work was long overdue. "I've watched my mother struggle with this problem, all her life," says one psychologist who had her child at thirty-seven. "She wanted to be a doctor, but her brother was the one who was sent to medical school. He flunked out, and went to work for the post office; she was sent to teacher's college. She has always resented not only the fact that she couldn't become a doctor, but also that she married a man who could not support her, and so she had to work at a job she never liked. As a feminist, I feel sad about it. I see how it's eaten away at her. Today she is seventy years old and has deteriorated not physically but emotionally. Her whole life is cooking for my father. For her, feminism came too late."

Doctor

Gay L. is a doctor for whom the change in attitudes came just in time. Gay, who lives in a large brownstone in the Park Slope neighborhood of Brooklyn, was a medical student until the age of twenty-four, then an intern, then a resident. Not until her early thirties, when her career was well underway, did she think it was time to "participate in the growth and development of a couple of human beings." She had a son at the age of thirty-five, and a daughter at the age of thirty-seven.

Gay has never married, and is rearing her children alone, without the father. Instead, she has formed a co-operative with two couples and their two children. They all live in her house and share equally in the household work. She has also reduced her office hours to seventeen hours a week to allow her to spend as much time as possible with her children. "I would not have considered having children had I not known I could live reasonably comfortably with a part-time job," she says. "Many women end up rearing children alone these days, and it is difficult to do when you have to work full time or live on welfare. Because I have a well-paying career I can afford to live as I want, and I haven't been in any way trapped by my children. With group living, I think children can lead well-rounded, stimulating, exciting lives even with a single parent. And they see their mother leading a well-rounded, stimulating exciting life as well."

As with all the women we've met, in the undercurrents of Gay's life are several channels of interest beyond a ca-

reer, which contributed to her decision to delay motherhood. She used her medical knowledge to direct the southern wing of the Medical Committee for Human Rights
during the civil rights drive of the mid-1960s, and she also
worked with the committee to provide medical aid in Chicago during the Weathermen's "Days of Rage." It is a
time she recalls with nostalgia and pride. "My career has
involved me in many areas of life that aren't merely self-
serving," she says. "And it has taught me how to be more
compassionate, more patient, more understanding with
other people as well as with my own children."

Judge

A similar attitude is shared by Paula C., a judge sitting
on the Supreme Court of a Midwestern state. She waited
until she had finished law school and established her practice before she had her son, Daniel, at the age of thirty-one.
Daniel is now thirteen years old; Paula has been married
for twenty-four years.

"I have always been career-oriented," she says, "and before I had a child, I wanted to be sure I could afford a
housekeeper to help with childrearing and cleaning, so I
could continue my work. I have always wanted to work,
and have always been aware of the role women have played
in the development and economy of this country.

"In the Midwest, women settlers were very active in running family businesses, in setting up churches and schools.
Clara Barton, who founded the Red Cross, was fired by the
President because he felt it was immoral to have men and
women working together—yet women have persisted.

Today, the Red Cross is considered a conservative, respectable organization, but Clara Barton was a radical—way ahead of her time—when she sent women to work on the battlefield. Yesterday, men were wondering whether women were strong enough to pound typewriters—today, they wonder whether women are strong enough to drive trucks. Women's liberation is an evolution, not just a product of the 1970s.

"I don't believe in stereotyping any individual. That is why I now find it so exciting to view the world through the eyes of my thirteen-year-old son. I love watching how he learns and explores all possibilities. I love watching his mind open like a flower. This weekend he wrote an essay for school on whether it was right for the American colonies to object to taxation by the British crown—and I enjoyed immensely reading it. I call the time I spend with my son 'quality time,' as opposed to 'quantity time.' I'm not with him because I *have* to be. I'm with him because I enjoy him, and I pack in everything I can."

Potter

Not all women who delay child rearing in order to pursue a career are attracted to high-powered and well-paying jobs. Greta D. was deeply involved with pottery, and until the age of thirty-five she didn't feel ready to deflect any of her creativity from the molding of clay to the molding of children. She married at the age of twenty-three, and for the first eight years of marriage both she and her husband were firmly against ever having children. Then, slowly, they changed their minds.

But before she agreed to get pregnant, Greta made sure her art would not be threatened by motherhood. "I set specific goals for myself," she says. "I didn't reach *the* goal I really wanted, which was to become rich and famous in my field. But I set other more realistic goals—to have a certain number of shows, which would give me satisfaction. I had two shows, six months apart. It was very very hard to do, but I wanted to push myself, to prove I could handle it. In addition to those shows, I continued to work for my private customers, too."

Her daughter, Clara, is now twelve months old, and Greta is ready to return to her pottery. "I made the right decision to accomplish something in my art before taking time out to have a child," she says. "Having Clara was like an interlude, and now I am ready to get back to my work. I could only allow myself this interlude because my work had gathered enough momentum, and I had gained enough experience, to be able to set it aside for a while.

"And my confidence in my own artistic abilities has permitted me to enjoy rearing her. In a way, watching the evolution of a child is even more creative than potting. A lump of clay just turns into a pot. Clara is this lump of flesh that was born and is turning into something much more complex—a human being."

Secretary

For Glenda A. a career meant travel rather than riches or prestige. She spent ten years working and living in the major cities of Europe. Glenda began work as a high school teacher in her home town of Atlanta, Georgia, and then decided to take less-exciting jobs in more exciting places. For the next few years she worked as a secretary in Geneva, Madrid, London, Paris, Rome, and Munich. Finally she came to New York and found a job as secretary to the president of a national woman's magazine. While there, she was promoted to assistant to the president.

"I certainly didn't want to settle down and get married right out of college," she says. "I had zero interest in falling in love. There was a lot I wanted to get out of my system. I just had the feeling I would be a much better mother later on, and I was right. My values have solidified. A lot of things that seemed important to me in my twenties appear superficial now. I think added wisdom and maturity go very well with parenting," she says.

Glenda married when she was thirty, had her first child at thirty-three, and her second at thirty-four. She has not worked since the birth of her first baby. Today, she is a housewife and a feminist. "I am absolutely opposed to job discrimination against women," she says, "and I fight it whenever I can. I worked so long in secretarial jobs that sometimes I would just get into a *rage* at the attitude held by many people that my job was a 'woman's job' and therefore second-rate. Working in Manhattan, it quickly became clear to me that it is the women who are really running the offices—the women who come in by subway and bus from Brooklyn and Queens and New Jersey every day because they don't get paid enough to live in Manhattan. They are the ones who organize their bosses' schedules and field his telephone calls and proofread his letters and find his lost correspondence and offer day-to-day business advice.

"Working on a national woman's magazine, I also saw

that many of the supposed job 'opportunities' for women are just tokenism. While I was there, the federal government finally came into the magazine to stop job discrimination, and one of my big projects was to develop an affirmative-action program for women. You wouldn't think you would need one when 75 per cent of the staff is female. But on the management level, there was hardly a female face to be seen."

Today, however, Glenda has mixed feelings about returning to work while her children are young. "Although I am a feminist, I disagree strongly with feminists on their push toward day care. I am deeply opposed to institutionalizing young children. On the other hand, I am sometimes restless at home. It is a shock to be suddenly isolated from the adult world, to feel the whole world is going on around you as before and you are no longer part of it. You begin to talk like a two-year-old; you stop thinking like an adult. But I am not going to go back to work and sit at a typewriter again. There's no job I can do that would pay me enough to make it worth the sacrifice I would have to make to not stay home during my babies' early years."

The Mid-career Switch

More and more women are finding that, in their late twenties or early thirties, they are dissatisfied with their chosen occupations. They decide to pull a mid-career switch—which further postpones parenthood. They spend ten years as an editor, and then become a lawyer. They begin a career in social work, and then go on to become a buyer at a big department store.

When this happens, what sometimes appears on the surface to be a random career change is, in fact, a slow evolution toward maturity, and the apparently arbitrary switch in career interests is really a weaning from childhood fantasies and parental expectations.

Dorothy's Delayed Adulthood

This change never occurs overnight, and many women remain unaware of what is happening to them: They simply know they are dissatisfied with their job, bored, restless, eager for "something else." They may at first deflect this restlessness into other outside activities—they may learn to play tennis, take some college courses, go on a diet, move to a new location. Eventually, they begin to recognize that they have changed, and the career of their choice no longer brings them satisfaction. It takes courage to change careers, and for many women the evolution is slow and painful. For many, it implies not just a change of office, but an entirely new outlook on life.

Let us follow Dorothy L. as she switches careers. Dorothy's example is very interesting, for her life reflects clearly the elements of change and the nature of the struggles faced by many women today. Only after her career change, which took years to accomplish, did she feel ready to have children.

Dorothy is a bright thirty-six-year-old who is now production manager for an industrial film company. But she thought, when she left her home town of Hagerstown, Maryland, for Boston, that she would spend the rest of her life as a registered nurse. She went to nursing school and for thirteen years worked in several Boston hospitals. Then when she was thirty-three she decided to launch a totally new career—and returned to college to learn about the film business. Only now, with success in this new endeavor, does she feel ready to have children.

What made Dorothy change her mind about nursing? "A few years ago I was in a woman's group with five other nurses, and we talked about why we all went into nursing. It seemed to many of us that there was something very neurotic about needing to take care of people to that extent. While nursing can be very satisfying, it is also draining emotionally because it involves giving and giving and giving. A lot of us nurses seemed to need to rescue, to be the nurturer. There came a time for me when I couldn't do it anymore. And I realized that this drive to nurture other people was connected with my not having children of my own yet."

Dorothy recalls that from the time she was two years old her mother gave her nursing kits and lectures telling her that *she* had always wanted to be a nurse. Dorothy also recalls that as a child she had always wanted to have children of her own. "As a child, I was always the little mother. I had a room full of dolls, and I mothered my dolls to death. I dressed and undressed them a dozen times a day, and I had a dozen doll carriages, cribs, and doll houses set up in my playroom. When I was twelve, I was heartbroken when my mother wouldn't give me another doll for Christmas. She said I was too old, that my doll years were over."

Today, Dorothy has a fairly clear picture of the tug-of-war that made her wait to have children. As long as she tried to remain a child—by living a life of trying to please her mother and fulfill her mother's deferred fantasies of being a nurse—she was unable to picture herself as the mother of a child of her own. As long as she nursed other adults—as her mother wanted—she couldn't feel adult enough to nurse her own baby. Yet, she did not realize these conflicted motivations behind her career until she had talked with other women who were also nurses.

Once Dorothy could admit her ambivalence toward her mother's message to be a paid nurturer, she began to notice other mixed feelings toward her mother as well. She remembers that her mother was the ideal wife and mother, a loving woman whose total energy was focused on her family. While Dorothy enjoyed *having* a mother like that, she began to realize that she didn't necessarily want to *be* a mother like that. But before she could tackle that larger issue, she spent much of her twenties hiding safely inside her nurse's uniform, and protecting herself against any further life decisions by avoiding assiduously any men who might lure her into long-range commitments.

LEARNING TO LOVE WELL

For women like Dorothy, children are delayed not only because of career preoccupations, but also because they cannot, for various reasons, maintain a comfortable long-term relationship with a man.

Many women say they retain strong symbiotic emotional ties with their own parents, ties they want to break before they feel free to marry or have children. This idea of wanting to separate from parents came up repeatedly as a theme among the women I interviewed, perhaps because of our increased sophistication about the dynamics of mental health. Many women want to understand the nature of these bonds, before having children of their own.

Some feel they over-identify with mother, and are afraid of being "trapped" by children and husband in the ways they feel she was trapped. These women describe many of their mothers as controlling and manipulating women who resented their children and their husbands.

Some women also say they chose unstable or unavailable men as a reaction against father. Rather than take the risk of marrying someone like Dad—who they see as passive, uninvolved, weak, and unable to show certain emotions —they avoid marriage altogether.

After a few years of repeated disappointments in their love life, women realize they are following patterns that lead to failed relationships.

Break-Away: Shattering Symbiotic Patterns

Let's follow Dorothy again, since her delayed mother-hood revolves around many of these issues. Dorothy married when she was twenty-four and still a nurse, and the marriage lasted two years. It began with husband and wife playing the traditional marital roles. She did what she calls the "slave work"—the cooking, cleaning, shopping. She felt compelled to come home from work and cook fancy dinners every night. Even though her husband didn't ask her to do it, it was what her mother had always done. Then the young couple moved to the East Village, and the marriage began to fragment under the new hippy life-style.

"Instead of cooking dinners, we had tuna fish sandwiches. He began to stay up half the night painting. There

were no arguments, but we were both frightened by the
changes. We finally just got a divorce, and remained
friends. We never understood what the marriage was all
about," she recalls. From then on, she chose to be with
men who weren't "available"—who were married, or Don
Juans, or who didn't want to settle down.

Although she seemed to be passively drifting, she was
also managing to actively avoid what she saw as the trap of
being a traditional housewife. As the years passed and she
matured, Dorothy became aware that her ambivalence
over her nursing career and her ambivalence over commitment to a man were connected.

Here is how she describes her gradual evolution and
growing awareness:

"My parents had the ideal marriage for the 1940s and
1950s. They were very close, dependent, and symbiotic. I
admired it, and yet I also felt confused about my role as a
woman. On the one hand, my mother's role was very attractive to me. She was the *real* mother you see in the ads.
She took wonderful care of us three children, of my father,
and she was very warm and loving. She didn't work outside
the house—she was always there for us. She baked fresh
pies almost every day. She was very nurturing, which is the
part of her I liked. On the other hand, her emotions were
cramped, bound up—like Chinese girls used to have their
feet bound physically. I would come home from school and
occasionally find her in tears, and that was the only visible
sign that she wasn't absolutely happy.

"I have always made it a point to be with men who are
not like my father. My father is a very strong, demanding,
autocratic man, who is always home with mother. I am
sure he was never involved with other women. He has a

very structured, compulsive kind of behavior. He got a job as a pharmacist with a company the day after he finished college, stayed at the same job twenty-five years, got the watch, retired, went to Florida, and has been there ever since and loves it.

"It left my mother feeling as though she hadn't done all the things she had wanted to do. After rearing three children, she had hoped to travel for a few years, and that didn't happen because he retired with very little money. Instead, they are eking it out, waiting for pension and Social Security checks.

"To avoid being with men like my father, I have always sought out men who need a lot of freedom, who have affairs with other women, who keep me in a state of constant turmoil. Now that I am for the first time finding out what I want to do for myself, I no longer feel that need to be with unavailable men. I no longer have to drive myself to avoid marriage and children, because I have been able to break away from my parents' roles and construct my own life. Now that I feel like an adult, I am ready to settle down and have children. For the first time in my life, I am with a man who feels the same way."

The Romantic: *Clinging to the Impossible Dream*

Dorothy found herself grappling with very real conflicts in her life. Other women, however, nurture yet another dilemma: They harbor romantic visions of love and marriage that act like acid on a relationship, and wind up dissolving it. They claim to be looking for the perfect man and the ideal love—a search that is often a thin disguise for running away from involvement and commitment. For various reasons, men fail to live up to these women's high standards. The women feel discontent, disappointment, or anger—and each relationship ends, only to be followed by another, similar one. This pattern inevitably delays marriage and childbirth.

Robin M., who is thinking of getting pregnant for the first time at the age of thirty-seven, says she spent the first thirty years of her life programming her broken hearts. She tried to live her life as if it were a film in which she played the starring role. She finally went into therapy to find out why she avoided so diligently any kind of permanent relationship.

"*Roman Holiday* was my favorite movie," she recalls. In many ways, the film embodied the fantasies she held onto through her early adult years. Although she first saw it when she was thirteen, she was still acting it out when she was thirty. The film starred Audrey Hepburn, who played a beautiful young princess who was attending school in Rome. The princess had never done anything "ordinary" people did; had, in fact, never lived like a "normal" teenager. One day she decided to run away, and she hid in the back of a laundry truck as it was leaving the palace.

Robin describes what happens. "Lo and behold! She winds up meeting Gregory Peck. He is a poor reporter, assigned to cover Rome. She spends the night with him—sleeping in the far corner of his bed, of course. When she wakes up in the morning, she doesn't know where she is at first—and she is s-o-o-o-o beautiful! They spend the whole day doing the things she has always wanted to do: she sits in a cafe drinking wine, she gets her hair cut.

"But in the end, she has to leave him. She has to go back

to the palace to meet her obligations to her country and her family. She tells him, 'When I leave, I am going to turn the corner and not look back, and I would ask you to do the same.'

"The next day, she gives an interview to the press—she has supposedly been ill for two days. Gregory Peck is there. A reporter asks, 'Princess, of all the cities you have been to in Europe, which city did you like best?' She says, 'Well, it's very difficult to say. I love each one in its own way.' Then she looks at Gregory Peck and she says, 'No—most of all—Rome.' He is crying. She turns around and walks away.

"That film was always very symbolic to me, and at first I didn't know why, but now I think it was because I programmed *myself* as a princess for tragedy. With the help of these kinds of movies and the Catholic Church and the example of my parents' unhappy marriage—all those things grabbed hold of me."

Robin's best friend, Shirley V., is another woman who at the age of thirty-one is also still trying to outgrow a heavy dose of self-inflicted romanticism. When she was twenty-two, Shirley got married in the courthouse in Seattle, Washington, and she and her husband spent the next five years farming in the Cascades. "I know that I married Sam in order to be able to divorce him," she says. "I needed to go out West and live in the mountains and be married—I was living out a childhood fantasy, and I lived it out to the very end. We were like desperate kids. A lot of it was good, but a lot of it was crazy.

"I think what I did was sad, but we didn't destroy each other—if anything, we helped each other grow up. I didn't do it maliciously. I didn't know at the time what I was doing. After the divorce, I had a lot of trouble separating from him, and we continued sleeping together a lot. It was a very passionate five years, very unrealistic but very exciting, and I never want to be involved in anything like that again. It was right from the movies—a romantic, dependent, distorted kind of love. It was too needy, too desperate. We wanted so much for the other one to do for us what we couldn't do for ourselves.

"Both of us knew, deep down, that we were living in a Disneyland. I really wanted a child but somehow we kept putting it off. When Sam said, 'Okay, let's do it,' I would say, 'Let's wait until spring.' Then spring would come and I would say, 'I'm ready now,' and Sam would say, 'Let's wait until fall.' "

But now, four years later, she still finds herself afraid of real intimacy. She, like Robin, hopes that through therapy she can explore the roots that have nourished these exciting but abbreviated and unrealistic relationships with men. Once she understands herself better, then she wants to have a child.

Each of us develops certain personality patterns in order to get along in the world. In the past, those patterns were usually passed along from generation to generation. Today, it is different. Today, we are aware that some of these patterns are self-defeating while others are growth-promoting. Their existence does not necessarily indicate a neurosis, but it does indicate that we are complex beings who are only now becoming aware of our complexities.

For most of us, our ties to our parents are offset by our drive to be independent adults; our romanticism is balanced by our realism; our fears of intimacy are offset by our drive to be close to someone. But once a woman becomes aware of and uncomfortable with certain traits that she feels may be unhealthy or may stifle her own maturity, there is no turning back. Often, these women choose to work toward a resolution of these conflicts, and they decide to postpone motherhood until they have done so.

Chapter Two

Deciding—The Triggers

....•——◄——◆——►——•....

"All I really know for sure is that I want a child, I want a child, I want a child. The thought of it warms me from top to toe. I don't want to be on my deathbed saying that the only thing in my life I regret is never having had a child." Jane E., who is pregnant at thirty-four.

When a woman who is in her thirties or forties does at last decide to have a child, her decision is often a rapid one. She doesn't vacillate—she just *does* it. She knows the time is right. The measured and logical reasons she gave for waiting no longer seem valid. She feels she is moving into a new life cycle. Time and again, women told me they began to notice infants in restaurants, on the buses, in the parks.

One woman told me that after vowing for thirty years never to have children, she found herself thinking about being pregnant all the time. "If I saw a pregnant woman, my eyes would follow her across the street, into a shop—I felt curiosity, interest, maybe envy. I kept saying, 'I'm too busy,' but the thought just wouldn't go away. I hate the idea of there being a biological imperative, but I finally began to accept that on some level I did want to have children, and if I wanted to do it, then it was time to get started."

Women who had avoided the subject of babies brought it up suddenly over dinner. "My husband looked at me as if I were insane," one woman recalls. "I was thirty-seven years old, and he had given up on me. Every time he had broached the subject in the past nine years, I got defensive and uptight. I always felt cornered. Now, I didn't feel that way anymore. Something shifted inside of me, and I felt there was now room in my life, in our lives, for a child. He was ecstatic."

Rarely do these "triggers" that prompt pregnancy seem to be the logical end of their reasoned, measured wait for motherhood. For example, women who waited in order to carve their careers suddenly change their minds about the importance of being successful. Women who were waiting until their marriage stabilized suddenly decided they wanted to get pregnant even knowing it might cause divorce—having a baby simply became more important than winning the promotion or losing the man.

This is not always true. Sometimes the timing coincides with planned events or transitions. Some women wait until that final trip to Europe, that next promotion, or that special romantic night when she and her husband hold each other close. One woman traveled to the Baja Peninsula, so she could get pregnant while the whales spawned. Another couple, Jean and Ken L., waited six years until the last payment on their $60,000 Yonkers, New York, home was in the mail. "We were very bad at saving money, so we decided to buy this house, borrow most of the downpayment, and then force ourselves to work hard to pay it off as quickly as possible," says Jean. "We made the last payment in December, I took out my IUD, and in two weeks I was pregnant."

But for the majority, it seems that at some point in mid-life women begin to evaluate their first thirty years and reorder priorities for the next thirty. Miriam C., the feminist we met in the previous chapter, compares her mid-thirties' drive to have children with the experience of listening to a distant orchestra playing Mozart. "You hear the music of, say, the 'Piano Concerto in F Major,' and it is faint but poignant, intriguing, and it lures you. You strain to hear a particular instrument in the background—you *know* it's there, know just how it sounds. All your attention becomes focused on that distant, unseen magic—" She stops suddenly and laughs at her own allegory. "I mean, how else can you explain it? You have to be *crazy* to do what I did and have three kids," she says. "Who knows? Maybe it's just some chemical ingredient in the blood that triggers that drive to have kids."

THE SIX M'S OF MOTHERHOOD

The most common "triggers" mentioned by the women I interviewed are the Big Six M's of Motherhood:

Mysterious Metamorphosis—an unexplainable yet insistent sudden longing for a child.

Menace of Menopause—a fear that time is running out.

Mortality—a reaction to the death of a parent, close friend, or husband.

Money—the improvement or readjustment of personal finances.

Maturity—the awareness of having matured and developed a stronger sense of self.

Misplaced Mothering—a determination to stop investing their "nurturing" instincts in men.

MYSTERIOUS METAMORPHOSIS: MOTHER NATURE CALLS

This sudden envy of other women with children, this longing for a child of one's own, creates a metamorphosis in women—an abrupt change of heart, mind, and plans. It comes as a special surprise to women who have disliked children all their lives. One woman who, during her teens and twenties, had such an aversion to children that she even avoided sitting next to pregnant women on buses, told me after the birth of her baby in her mid-thirties, "I began to feel I wanted to do the thing I was most afraid of, the thing I had always avoided—get pregnant. Also, my body wanted to do it, to have a child and find out what it was like and test myself. And it turned out to be a successful test."

The crystallization of this decision is explained in many different ways, depending on the inclination and temperament of the woman it strikes. Some call it "biological imperative"; others call it "mystical"; still others insist it is only "delayed social conditioning." But whatever the cause, they all feel in common that, suddenly

—a career is not enough.
—travel is not enough.
—money and security are not enough.
—a husband is not enough.

They want a baby. The result is predictable: Another woman in her thirties or early forties, another woman who foreswore maternity and pregnancy, contributes to the already rising birth rate for her age group and gets pregnant.

Milly A., a successful advertising executive who became pregnant at the age of thirty-six, recalls, "Almost overnight I went from years of saying, 'I don't want a child, it's not for me, I want a career' to wanting a child badly, obsessively, day and night. I don't know if it was a physiological imperative, or an emotional one. But by the time I decided I wanted to have a child, I was walking around the city staring at pregnant women, going into maternity shops, seeking out babies in parks. It was an idea whose time had most definitely come."

Rikki L. is a particularly clear-cut example of a woman who had a rapid change of mind about having children. During her thirties, she had three abortions. Babies were a trap and something to be avoided at all costs, she felt. Then, at the age of forty-four, she got pregnant for a fourth time. Unlike the previous three times, her reaction this time around was positive. She realized she was rather old to be delivering a first child, but she had an amniocentesis and all the other precautionary tests now available to older mothers. When all the results were favorable, she decided to proceed.

Rikki explains why she postponed motherhood for so long: "From the age of sixteen, I had said, 'I am not going to have any babies.' My mother claims I never wanted to touch the dishes or clean the house. I liked to race motor-cycles as a teen-ager. I didn't want anybody to think I was going to be a housewife—I was going to be different, an in-teresting person. I felt I would rather be forty years old and not have a child and say, 'Well, I would have liked to have had one,' than have a baby when I was young and then sit around for twenty years resenting it. I knew instinctively it wouldn't be good for me."

Rikki, like most older mothers I met, does not seem to fear being the "old" mother of a teen-ager, or running out of energy, or of dying while her child is still young. On the contrary, she feels that having children later in life will keep her younger longer. "I realize I am going to be an 'old' mother, that kids will be coming over and will say—'Oh, is that your grandmother?' But I've always been a youngish woman—in looks and attitude. I come from a family that grows old gracefully and dies graciously, usually in their sleep, of coronaries. My great-grandmother lived to be one hundred and five. I may not be so fortunate, but I guess I'll muddle through it all right—and it helps to know that there are a lot of other older mothers out there. Even though I may not meet them, I know they're there."

She also feels her added maturity is a blessing, for herself and her child. "A friend who is my age, and who had had four children by the time she was twenty, told me the other day, 'Watching you, I see what a gift a child can be. When I had mine, they seemed to be a nuisance. You have a totally different attitude about it. Perhaps I really *will* appreciate my grandchildren.' She knows that because I waited my son's presence is like a miracle to me, not an imposition. I feel as if he's on loan, and I'm just supervising his growth until he's on his own."

In some women, this drive to have a child is so strong that they decide to go ahead even if they are not married. For Jane E., thirty-four, who comes from a conservative family and lives in a conservative town, the decision was not made lightly. She may marry the father after her child is born, but it is a marriage about which she still has hesitations. "I finally decided I couldn't just sit and wait for my knight in shining armor to come along and grab me up and say, 'Do you want a kid? Here's a kid.' I couldn't wait for somebody else to decide what I was going to do with my life. When I was pregnant, my gynecologist asked me if I realized the ramifications and responsibilities of being a single parent. My reaction was, 'Yes, I understand them.' But not until I have had the experience will I know what it all means.

"All I really know for sure is that I want a child, I want a child, I want a child. The thought of it warms me from top to toe. I don't want to be on my deathbed saying that the only thing in my life I regret is never having had a child."

THE MENACE OF MENOPAUSE:
FATHER TIME THREATENS

Other women decide to have a baby when they suddenly feel they are running out of time. The years tick by, but they are involved in their careers, their hobbies, their relationships. Then, often following a "crisis" birthday—when a woman turns thirty or thirty-five or forty—she decides it is now or never.

These women lay claim to no special urge to get pregnant. Instead, they often feel that their years of indecision, their continued postponement of a definite commitment to motherhood, may close the door forever on the possibility of having a child. And so they decide to go ahead. "I examined and investigated the possibility of motherhood for years with my analyst," says one woman. "When I turned forty, she said to me, 'You can put that decision on hold as long as you like, but you have to recognize the reality of a biological time clock for women.' I had been ducking that issue, and I finally had to confront the fact that no action was *an* action. If I waited too long, the decision would be out of my hands and the choice would be gone forever. I ran down all my excuses: I have to travel, I can't afford it, my career comes first. Finally I realized that I was copping out. Yes, I wanted a baby; no, I couldn't wait much longer. It seemed that the 'some day' I kept talking about was today. So I had one." She gave birth when she was forty-one.

Many women who vacillate about motherhood have been deeply involved in their careers. For years time seemed on their side—they knew that they would earn more money, win more prestige, be more successful as they grew older, just as men did. But suddenly, as with men, time seemed to turn against them. While men begin to worry about coronaries, these women begin to muse over their ovaries. They begin to weigh the rewards of their career against the possible loss of a chance for motherhood— and they decide to opt for pregnancy.

Ann S. is a typical example of a woman caught in this dilemma. All her life she had been an achiever, a woman determined to accomplish something in the world. When, at the age of thirty-eight, she was appointed curator of a major museum in the Midwest—a goal she had coveted for ten years—she began to suffer an attack of age anxiety. She began to doubt the wisdom of her driving ambition.

"Suddenly, my work seemed like a poor excuse for not having children. I got depressed. I couldn't work well anymore or go anywhere. I didn't want to see friends, go on trips, do anything," she recalls. "I had always assumed my work would be my life. But if you work very hard, sometimes you miss things—you're preoccupied and aren't aware of other needs. That's what happened to me. Suddenly work just didn't seem rewarding enough, fulfilling enough.

"I realized I didn't have all the time in the world. I realized I had a million excuses not to have a child, and all the excuses were very good, very smart, very intelligent, very practical, they all made sense. In fact, I looked like an idiot *wanting* a child. But if you really do want a baby, then none of those very good excuses matter. The women in my family tend to have early menopause, and I decided not to tempt fate."

Once Ann had made up her mind, she told her husband about her decision. He objected. He had two teen-age children by a previous marriage, and did not want the responsibility of a young child at his age. But Ann persisted. "Once I realized it was an important issue for me, I couldn't say, 'Okay, if you don't want to have a child, I won't.' After several months, he finally agreed. If he had continued to say no, I would have left him, even though we'd known each other for ten years. I know other women whose husbands don't want children, and whose love for the man seems to be so complete that a child isn't necessary. That wasn't my case."

Ann's son is now seventeen months old, and she feels more fulfilled than ever before. Her husband, too, seems to genuinely enjoy his son, and he helps with some of the child care. But Ann smiles and says, "My husband is not your split-it-down-the-middle kind of man. He is more your let's-go-back-to-the-macho-male-superiority kind of man."

As with many career women who have children later in life, her employer offered her a flexible working arrangement. She now works part time at the museum, where they have hired an acting curator until she returns to work full time next year. She seems to accept the bulk of child care with equanimity, perhaps because she got what she wanted. And she received an unexpected bonus as well: For most of her life, she was plagued with migraine headaches, but now they have disappeared. A few years earlier, when they had become unbearable, she had gone to see a headache specialist. "He said, 'If you don't want to get headaches anymore, get married and have children.' I said to myself, 'What a creep. He has some nerve sitting there and telling me to marry and have children as a cure for my headaches.'

"I got married, and my headaches did let up. Then I had the baby, and I haven't had a headache since." She laughs and bounces her baby on her lap. "The answer was simple," she says. "I no longer get the headaches because I no longer worry about myself so much—between work and the baby, I can't afford the time!"

Ann feels her career success has made her a more contented mother. "Before, I could never have appreciated that deep sense of joy I find in my child. Now looking at him, I remember what it's like to feel carefree, to run a distance just for the fun of running, the way little children do. He jumps up, runs twenty feet, stops, turns around, stands there and starts to coo and laugh—and it makes no sense to me, because I've used my brain for so long for work instead of for fun. Then he'll run back, stop again, wiggle his toes—and I know that I did it once, too, and it seems very familiar again. It makes me feel more spontaneous, more childlike—something I appreciate even more now that I'm almost forty."

MORTALITY: IN DEATH, NEW LIFE

For women who choose to give birth late, the choice is always a celebration of life. For many, it is also a coming to terms with their own mortality, a reflection of their growing awareness of death. In their thirties and forties, women find that friends and acquaintances their own age are beginning to die—of heart attacks, of cancer, in accidents. Their parents begin to die of old age. Youth and health are no longer taken for granted. "I understand," said one woman whose mother had died, "that you really can get left without somebody you want to see tomorrow, but you're not going to get to them in time."

Some women, shaken deeply by the unexpected death of a husband, friend, or lover, reassess their priorities and find, for the first time, that giving birth comes out on top of the list of things to do, of goals to fulfill. This reaction is one way to affirm life, and can also alleviate the empty feeling left by the death of someone close. As one woman said after her husband's death, "I felt that I would be permanently lonely if I didn't have a child, that a child would provide a special connection with life and living, that otherwise I would just keep getting older."

Other women want to have a child following the death of a parent or grandparent. The death of a parent not only saddens us, it frightens us as well. Our parents have always been our hedge against mortality; they stand between us and our death in a symbolic and significant way. Once they die, that buffer zone is gone. We become the next in line to go; now it is our generation's turn. We realize in a way we never realized before that we are not immortal after all.

A woman also realizes, following her parent's death, that the only living testament remaining from her parent's life is *her* and any siblings she may have. Suddenly, the idea of providing an heir for posterity, of perpetuating the species, takes on new significance. "There are certain qualities my mother gave to me that I want to pass on," one woman told me, explaining why she was pregnant five months after her mother had died. "My sense of humor, my love of music, my independence—I thank my mother for all of these, and I feel it would be a great waste if they ended with me, with my death in twenty years."

The process of childbirth itself often imbues women with the sense that they are confronting their own death while creating new life. The blood and pain and the presence of doctors undoubtedly contributes to this feeling, even though, in fact, childbirth is very safe today—as safe for older women as for younger ones. Author Rainer Maria Rilke described this life-death duality when he wrote in *The Notebooks of Malte Laurids Brigge*, "And what a melancholy beauty it gave to women when they were pregnant and stood there, and in their bodies, upon which their slender hands instinctively rested, were two fruits: a child and death. Did not the dense, almost nourishing smile . . . come from their sometimes thinking that both were growing?"

Glenda A., the secretary we met in the last chapter, went through successful natural childbirth that, nonetheless, she describes as an "out of body" experience similar to those found in Dr. Elisabeth Kubler-Ross's book, *Life After Life*. "I felt like I was going into a twilight zone," she recalls. "I could hear the voices of the nurses, but I felt I was somewhere else listening to them talk about me. I didn't feel pain so much as disembodiment, as if I were going through a primal, even supernatural, experience. It was like hallucinating without drugs."

Why exactly does the death of a loved one trigger this desire to give birth? For Elizabeth L., the longing for a child was clearly her way of confronting her mortality, and of alleviating the loneliness she felt after her husband's unexpected death. Elizabeth married when she was twenty-nine years old—a first step toward domesticity she had avoided until then.

When she graduated from her South Dakota high school, she told herself that she was certainly never going to marry—she was going to college. After college, she told herself she was never going to marry—she wanted a career. She spent the first five years of her successful career as a corporate financial advisor telling herself she would never marry, and the next five years discovering that all the men who interested her were already married to somebody else.

Then, when she was twenty-nine, she met and married Frank, a Chicago real estate broker.

For three years, Elizabeth and Frank had a busy happy life together. Neither of them considered having children—at least, not for a few more years. Then Elizabeth arrived home from work one evening to find the police waiting for her. Frank had been injured seriously in a collision on the Kennedy Expressway. He died en route to the hospital.

Elizabeth recalls what happened next: "I was thirty-two, on my own again, and I found myself in a very uncomfortable position. Frank and I had been building a relationship that would lead into our having children, and suddenly all that had been taken away from me. In a way, my position wasn't too different from that of a woman who gets divorced at that age. But the big difference was the impact death had on me. I had never been close to anyone who had died before, and suddenly I was the principal griever.

"Frank's death caught me up short in terms of what was important in life. It made me feel life is just a little cycle we go through, that we live and we die and we have children after us. One of my major reactions to Frank's death was to want a child very much.

"Loneliness was a part of that desire, too. I felt that I would be permanently lonely if I didn't have a child, that a child would provide a special connection with life and living, that otherwise I would just keep getting older. I wasn't sure that anything else would alleviate that loneliness, no matter what kinds of rewards I had in work or anywhere else. My loneliness was like a free-floating anxiety, that doesn't attach itself to anything, doesn't have any dimension to it. I envisioned my whole future all the way to my death as lonely, with nobody to come to my funeral."

After Frank's death, Elizabeth lived alone and tried to readjust to her new life. She disliked living alone again. Yet she also disliked the thought of dating again—of starting over. She wanted to meet someone, to have a child, and yet she balked at trying to be "social." "I felt that every other liaison in my life would be temporary," she says. "In all the obvious ways, having a child is also temporary. They grow up and go away, and you can't attach yourself to them. Yet, I felt it would root me in life in some way, and that everything else was abstract."

Finally, Elizabeth met an older man who "knew from the beginning that the next thing I wanted in my life was a child. As things moved along and we started to address that question seriously, it turned out he didn't want a child. He had already raised one family, and didn't want to do it again. So we parted ways and I started dating other people. But we would speak on the telephone, and each time I told him I had a date he would get upset. I would say, 'What do you expect? I can't get married and have a child unless I first go out with someone.' He would say, 'Well, yes, but you can do that next year.' We do love each other very much, but we are both determined people and we wanted different things in our lives. But finally there was a meeting of minds."

Their compromise was that she would have the baby but —like Ann in the previous chapter—she would handle most of the child care. As she talks, Elizabeth is nursing her three-month-old baby under the harsh light of a bare bulb in her husband's art studio. Her soft beauty survives its scrutiny as she bends tenderly over her child. "I feel very at ease being a mother. And the baby *has* eased my loneliness, because I have produced something to fill some of the void in this world—something that will go on after me. I have been through a lot, been tested in the extreme. I know now what my limits are. I know I won't break down, I know I'm a lot tougher than I thought. At a younger age, I was uncertain about who I was and what I wanted—even with Frank, I couldn't have handled motherhood. Now, it's been the luckiest, loveliest thing I've ever done in my life. I no longer feel incomplete."

This need to ward off emptiness, to forestall existential anxiety, by giving birth after the death of someone close, is a normal and common reaction. It is a life-preserving mechanism. And there is yet another common reaction triggered by death, particularly the death of a parent: It is a sudden feeling of being free for the first time. Women who feel this way *do* mourn the passing of a parent, *do* feel a genuine sadness and loss, but at the same time they also feel as if a burden has been lifted from their shoulders. If they have been unable to separate from their parents before, this final biological act can separate them suddenly and irrevocably. They face not only the recognition of their mortality, of their essential aloneness, but also of their new freedom from parental authority, disapproval, judgment, guilt, and criticism. The loosening of this last physical bond often enables them for the first time to consider children with eagerness instead of apprehension.

This is what happened to Candice P. Candice always wanted children, but waited until the age of thirty-five, after the death of both her parents, before going ahead with motherhood. In fact, it was no coincidence that she also waited to marry until after her father died. "He was extremely dictatorial," she says. "That was the kind of man I was drawn to—a dictator—and at the same time I couldn't tolerate that kind of man. Even as an adult, my father had a great hold over me. I was afraid of him and admired him at the same time. I didn't feel free to find a man *I* would like—a gentle, quiet man—until after he died." She married that kind of man, a high school philosophy teacher, eight months after her father's funeral.

She felt similarly bound to her mother, and waited until after her mother's death to get pregnant. It was not a conscious decision—rather, she kept telling herself the time "wasn't right." Then six months after her mother's death, she felt an overwhelming urge to have a child. "My mother's attitude was that children are oppressive. When she was pregnant with me, she wore a great big coat and didn't tell anyone about it. She made it clear her children brought her no pleasure."

Candice feels that, while her mother was alive, she would have been vulnerable to her criticism, and would have adopted many of her negative attitudes. "I would have been a terrible mother," she says. "I would have complained about my child, and been worried about the quality of her behavior—especially in front of Mother. Now I can be less of a perfectionist, and I am less likely to see the baby as a reflection of myself.

"I am especially happy to have a girl, because in a way it gives me a chance to rectify the past. Now that *I* feel free, *she* can be free. She won't be burdened with 'have to's' from the past, and she can develop a strong sense of pleasure and enjoyment of herself. For instance, when I am feeding her at the table, the important thing is the pleasure she gets from the food and not whether I'm getting it all

down her throat. When I bathe her, I want her to feel it is
a loving thing. When I wash her hair and she goes 'ahhh!'
and smiles, then I feel good about the kind of mother I
am."

MONEY: EMILY COUNTS HER PENNIES

For some women, money is the major factor in deciding
when to give birth. This is particularly true for women who
grew up in poor families, or women who saw their mothers'
freedoms limited by their pocketbooks. "My father walked
out when I was eight, and my mother was totally unprepared for it," one woman says, explaining her decision to
wait. "For ten years she worked as a bookkeeper to feed
and clothe my two brothers and me. She would come
home at six, fix dinner, pack our next day's lunches, clean
or iron, and fall into bed at eleven. Her whole life revolved
around the lack of money. I swore I would never get myself
in that situation."

Two of the women I interviewed had each saved $10,000
as a cushion before having their babies, and were glad they
did. The money carried them through those first months,
when they wanted to spend more time with their children
and less time at work. Another woman, accustomed to her
financial independence, found it difficult to adjust to a
new and more dependent status. "When the bill for the
baby's first checkup came, it created a crisis," she says. "It
was addressed to me, but John was paying. Even though
we had agreed to this arrangement, I found it very hard to
give him the bill. It's not as if I was asking him to pay my

Saks bill, but still, it seemed like some sort of ethical vi-
olation."

The money issue is a sticky one for these women. On the
one hand, most of them do not manage to save thousands
of dollars, and they come to the realization that they will
probably *never* feel they have enough money to afford a
baby. On the other hand, they find it hard, during those
early months of a baby's life, to reconcile themselves to living on someone else's money.

Emily B., the woman who always had felt different and
who left her Minnesota town to move to New York and
write, resolved this dilemma in an interesting way. For
years, she had geared her plans for motherhood around her
bank account. While working as an editor in a publishing
house, she wanted a child but her salary was too low to
cover the day care she would need in order to continue
working.

When she was thirty-one, she left her office job and
began to work as a fiction writer. For a while, she made a
meager living. Then her agent sold her idea for a novel to
a major New York publisher for $10,000. For the first time,
it occurred to Emily that she might be able to be a writer
and a mother at the same time. She dreamed of instant
fame and fortune.

"I wrote the novel to be a best-seller, and everybody who
saw it said, 'This will make you a fortune,'" she says. "So I
hinged the idea of having the baby on the paperback sale: I
was planning to get $50,000 to $100,000 for my share,
which would give me enough to relax and have the baby in
peace.

"The month I finished the book, I took out my IUD. I
had read it takes about six months to normalize the ovula-

tory cycle after the IUD is removed, and I figured it would take six months to negotiate the paperback sale." She and the father-to-be went away on a romantic holiday to make a baby. The week she returned, her publisher sold the paperback rights for $5,000—of which she would get half.

She was devastated. "I may have lost the baby over the shock, or perhaps I wasn't pregnant—I was never really sure, but that baby didn't work out. It took me a month to recover from the disappointment."

Then, for the first time, Emily began to view her money in a new light. "At this point I realized something. Most people, when they decide to have a baby, don't have the comfort of knowing they have $50,000 in the bank. Even without a windfall, I was still making a living. I was supporting myself as a writer. So I made a leap of faith—I had just signed a contract for two more novels, all prospects looked good—and I decided to go ahead and do it anyhow."

She quickly worked out the logistics. She could work at home and have a baby-sitter come in part time while she was writing. "I figured if I wanted to spend time at home with the baby, it would be better for me to have it now, while I had a couple of books to write. It means I have two years of writing ahead of me, during which time I could have the baby, an income, and be home at the same time. If I don't make any money from the books, then perhaps I will have to go back to a nine-to-five job."

Emily's financial situation is especially important because she can depend on little or no other income. She is completely self-supporting. She is having her baby alone. The man she has loved for five years is an American living in Tokyo, and they seldom see one another.

"All my reasons for having a baby alone are as practical as my timing," she says. "First, during twelve years as an adult in the world, including the two years I was married, I haven't run across any man I could see myself settling into a life with. I've met some men I think are wonderful, impressive, who I've loved in different ways and, in some cases, in all ways, but there has never been a circumstance where it would have worked out, where we could have made a life together. I think I am drawn to people who are very independent, who have exciting lives, and my life has been exciting in its own way—I do what I want, I meet interesting people, I work on my house in the country, I make myself fairly happy.

"So I like the way my life is right now. I'm satisfied with it. And the father's attitude is that he respects my ability to handle my life. Instead of being threatened by the idea, the way some men might be, he took it at face value for what it was, which is: I care about him very much, but we don't have much chance to see each other. He is one of the most intelligent, sensitive, lovely people I have ever met. And we will always have a relationship—at least a friendship, even if the romance goes away."

She is as pragmatic about her relationships as she is about her bank book. "It would be nice to think I might meet someone whose life complements mine, who would add to my life and not stop me from doing the things I want to do—but that's a pretty tall order. And I certainly wouldn't want to put off motherhood while I waited for that to happen. If it ever *does* happen, it would be wonderful. If it does happen, I can't imagine any man who would have that relationship with me would be disturbed by the fact that I have a baby, or babies, and had them out of wedlock. If he *were* disturbed, I wouldn't be interested in him."

For those majority of mothers with husbands, the timing of children often remains as income-oriented as Emily's. Money is a staple of life. It has long been axiomatic that career women have it, while mothers and housewives do not. Instead, mothers and housewives pay another kind of price. As one mother explained, "When you are living on someone else's income, there are always strings attached. My husband would say, 'I work for most of the money and therefore I deserve—' and then you fill in the rest of the line. Usually it's—'I deserve to rest when I get home.'"

Now, these have and have-not barriers are breaking down, however, and each woman who wants to be a mother can usually find a way of doing so without sacrificing her autonomy. Some, like Emily, work at home and hire a baby-sitter. One woman swapped "work years" with her husband: She worked as a management consultant for two years and supported him while he finished law school; then he supported her for two years while she had a baby and enjoyed motherhood. At the end of the two years, she found a housekeeper and returned to work.

Each person's solution is as individual as her finances. Luckily, women today have it better than ever before— especially those women already established in careers. Flexible employers, the availability of day care (especially in urban areas), sympathetic parents and in-laws, and a supportive husband all combine to make late motherhood much easier on the pocketbook as well as on the psyche.

MATURITY: THE WISE OLD WOMAN OF 31

Other women begin to feel it is time for a baby not because of any unexpected prompting from Mother Nature, or because of menopausal panic, or because of a catalyst like death, an inheritance, or a balanced budget—but simply because they feel they have matured into motherhood. The decision is, for them, an acknowledgment of their own emotional growth, and often coincides with the comfortable evolution of their marriage and their career.

"Before now, I just felt I wasn't ready yet," says a thirty-eight-year-old mother. "I believe Erik Erikson talks about a 'generative phase' that people go through. I simply wasn't generative yet. I think I reached a point when I wanted to have a baby because I was happy with my life, I felt fulfilled, full of life, and ready to share it. I felt strong enough to take on the responsibility."

During this maturation process, some women find they grow apart from their husbands, and divorce. Others find they draw closer to their husbands, and decide to get pregnant. Holly R. found it took her marriage ten years to mature to the point of pregnancy. "The first ten years, we knew we wanted a baby, but we were still growing up ourselves," she says. "Today, our marriage is better than it ever was, but first we had to go through real growing pains in our relationship brought on by the changes in each of us."

The story of Tina H. is particularly revealing in this context, for she had to disengage herself from many adolescent hesitations that involved her parents, her fear of emotional dependence, and her distrust of her own good instincts about men. For Tina, no single catharsis changed her life. To an outsider, in fact, her life seemed very stable—she held the same job and lived with the same man for eight years. But underneath this stable exterior, she was changing.

For Tina, the idea of having a baby blossomed after her period was late, and she found herself feeling deeply disappointed that she *wasn't* pregnant. It was then she realized that she was ready. "Before, I had been extremely careful about birth control. But once I realized I might want a child I became more careless. I became willing to accept that it could happen," she says.

But it had been a slow, step-by-step evolution for her to reach that point. She left her home town of Cincinnati for Washington, D.C., at the age of twenty to pursue a career in conservation. She did not want to get married. "I was very opposed to the idea of marriage, probably because of my mother's marriage—she was divorced when I was a teen-ager, and then she really had to struggle to bring us up. Also, while growing up I didn't know of any happily married people at all. It seemed that marriage was a curse, really, and people who might otherwise have been happy were miserable instead. I couldn't see myself getting tied into a relationship I didn't like, and I knew that disengaging yourself from marriage was a messy and unpleasant business."

At the age of twenty-three, Tina began living with a man who, eight years later and five months into her pregnancy, would become her husband. "Even though it looked like we were having a permanent relationship, it took me a long time to even consider that we could stay together. I liked to think I could leave any time . . . could disengage myself easily. The truth is, if you are involved in a live-in relationship, you never do disengage yourself easily. But you do have fewer legal complications to worry about.

"And Leonard, my husband, is so different from the kind of man I had thought I wanted—a man like my father. My father was always a kind, nice man, but as I matured I realized he was a *man* in the negative sense of the word. He did not feel it was manly to play with his children. He never helped around the house. He liked to go hunting with his dogs. Although I doubt he was an unemotional man, he certainly seemed that way to his children—at least that is the way I perceived him. I always thought his relationship with my mother was distant but fine, and we were all shocked when there was a divorce."

All of this influenced Tina, some in healthy ways and some in less-than-healthy ways. She had learned to be independent, but she had yet to learn how to overcome her fears of commitment. She had learned not to rely on a man for emotional or financial support, but she had yet to learn how to nurture the delicate and shifting balance of a mutually healthy dependency. Until she realized her own strength, she would remain afraid of imitating her parents' weaknesses.

She was fortunate to find herself drawn to a stable, loving man who was willing to wait for her to grow through her fears and hesitations. "I began, as I grew older, to appreciate Leonard, and I became aware that my relationship with him is totally different from my parents' relationship with each other. They had almost nothing in common, and we have a lot in common. Leonard is an artist and interested in nature; I am a conservationist and love art. We are alike in the way we think, in the way we respond to joy, to anger, to sadness. We do have a *real* communion with each other.

"For years Leonard tried to talk me into marriage, to 'solidify the relationship.' I didn't really agree with him, until I got pregnant. Then he felt quite upset that I was still saying 'no.' And I began to think about what my single status might mean for the child. Even though we live in a more enlightened era, there is still a lot that a child must cope with if his parents are not married. I began to feel I was holding onto an ideal that was no longer realistic. I knew we would stay together, so it seemed irrational to keep saying 'no.'"

With her career established, backed by the support of a long and reliable relationship, it seemed natural to get pregnant and to marry at the age of thirty-one. She had overcome, through her work, through her trust in Leonard, through the day-to-day process of growing up, her adolescent fears of sacrificing her happiness for security. She came to see that the two were not mutually exclusive. "I feel very solid," she says. "I feel that having a child will not change my perception of myself, that I am not going to invest my whole being in my child, which I think would be a bad mistake. Also, I am mature enough to raise a child intelligently. I would have made a lot of emotional mistakes if I had had a child before now."

MISPLACED MOTHERING:
LUCILLE'S LAMENT

Some women decide to have children after they begin to realize that all their lives they have been mothering men instead of babies. In the past, it was believed that the "mothering" instinct was an intrinsic part of female behavior, and that even childless women diverted this natural instinct into other areas: They planted flowers and tended gardens; they created patchwork quilts; they baked cookies for the neighbor's children; they "oohed and aahed" over other people's infants. In short, they satisfied their nesting instincts as best they could.

Now, psychologists are unsure whether that nurturing instinct is, in fact, unique to the female of the species. They feel that men, too, have a strong nurturing instinct. In the past, this was generally restricted to the disciplinary and educational aspects of child rearing. Now, many men are delighted to feel free to cuddle, coo, and burp their babies. "I have a powerful nurturing instinct in me," one older father told me with pride. "Unless I keep telling myself it's 'parental' and not 'maternal' I could get hung up on the idea that the way I feel toward my child is too feminine, and my macho might feel threatened." He laughs, and shrugs his shoulders, obviously not too worried about these new feelings.

For women, unlike men, this maternal instinct has been the only traditionally accepted way they could express and release many of their creative energies; and for this reason, women have often clucked over their husbands as well as their children. Today, women have many more creative outlets. Yet even the most successful career women can still slide into a pattern of mothering men—because it is familiar, comfortable, and often appreciated. These women are often attracted again and again to men who are immature, who need a lot of support and attention. Once they realize this, it is often the first step toward learning to be with more mature men, to develop more realistic and longer-lasting relationships that evolve into motherhood.

Regina M. is one woman who unlearned a lifetime of misplaced mothering and taught herself how to redirect her nurturing instincts—first, toward taking care of herself, then toward caring for a real infant.

When she was twenty-one, Regina married a man ten years her senior. Although he was older, she soon learned that she was more mature, that he needed mothering—and so she quickly became a mother to him. She devoted her time to taking care of him and, most important, to administering to his emotional wounds. He was a free-lance writer, and when he failed again and again to sell his stories, he began drinking heavily. As he slid into alcoholism, she became even more of a rock. "I was," she says, "the best thing that ever happened to him."

It was easy for Regina to play the role of competent efficient helpmeet. She had been playing that role all her life. Regina's mother, a professional pianist, had always preferred her work to child care. When her husband insisted she stay home with her children, she obeyed—but not enthusiastically. She treated her children as if they were a burden, and Regina soon learned to take care of herself. She became independent and self-sufficient. "I looked like a strong take-care-of-everything kid," she says. "Emotionally I wasn't, of course. But I had a clever facade of being so okay that I never had to ask anyone for anything."

Regina's marriage lasted three years, and after it broke up, she did what she had long wanted to do—she went to art school and then taught art. For the first time, she began to baby herself instead of other people. She spent much of her time alone painting. In her late twenties, she decided to start her own business, and opened a shop in Greenwich Village that sold books and the paintings done by herself and her friends. "My business was my baby," she says. "It was full time—demanding and draining—but it was the first time I was doing something to please myself rather than someone else." Once she had established herself professionally, she found she began to be interested in a new kind of man—men who were her equal, who knew how to take care of themselves, how to live on their own.

She took a cruise alone to the Caribbean and met a man who felt as she did. Two years later they married and when she was thirty-six she had her first baby, who is now three months old. "Joseph, my husband, claims he has a powerful maternal instinct—and, in fact, right after the baby was born he even stayed home from work to help me. In the past, I could never let anyone mother me. My attitude was —I'll do it myself, thank you! Now sometimes I am his little girl and sometimes I am his mother, and sometimes I am his lover and sometimes I'm his friend—and sometimes with the baby we're just three little kids, and the dog takes care of all of us," she laughs.

"The last ten years of my life have been like a journey. It's like walking outside your door and you just keep on walking through strange lands—you feel wonderment, exhaustion, fear, exhilaration, great joy. You feel lost and you also feel you are finding yourself, you feel alone and anxious and yet you also feel—especially when pregnant—a great animal connection with the world. It's been hard work, and it's also been miraculous. I never thought I deserved anything so good."

Other women fail to realize their patterns of misplaced mothering until it is too late. Then, with a real baby in hand, they find the big baby, the husband, gets jealous and walks out the door. Lucille B., at the age of thirty-seven, is one of New York's most successful businesswomen, a vice-president of one of the country's largest corporations, overseer of the lives of a dozen middle-level executives. She has a model's figure, a cover-girl face, a computer brain, and an artist's instinct. She is, in sum, a super-woman. Yet, every man she has ever been drawn to, including the man she married, has needed to be taken care of. We met in her white-carpeted corner office overlooking Central Park. Under the impatiens banked against her window are piles of children's books she is reviewing before reading them aloud to her two-year-old son, Jason. ("Grimm's is out— too gruesome. *Ms.* magazine's stories for liberated children —out, too humorless. I think we'll stick to fire engines, trucks, and animals for now," she says when we meet.)

"I delayed my maternal instincts for so long that I rerouted them—I lavished them on the men I knew, and gravitated toward men who were childlike," she says. "My husband is an inventor, a lovely person, and an absolute child. All my men, including my husband, have always expected dinner on the table every night, hot food in their stomachs, and clean socks. And they always look so bereft when they don't get these things that it touches my heart and makes me *want* to do it for them. In return, I get a childlike devotion. And the closer it borders on admiration, the better I like it."

Lucille postponed motherhood, feeling that even though she wanted children, she wasn't yet ready to have them. "There were too many other things to do. Not that I thought those other things were more exciting. I just felt I had too many pulls in my life, and I wouldn't be a fit enough mother until I could feel the time was very right for me. I wanted to investigate myself, to feel more settled in my career, to stop feeling erratic bouts of craziness—as though I could chuck everything and take off for Rio tomorrow. In fact, I have a very stable job record, and I didn't do those things—but I wanted that feeling that I *might* do them to subside."

For Lucille, the trigger was a gradual recognition and growing resentment that she was babying her husband, accompanied by the realization that she was ready to baby a real baby. All other systems were also go—her career and her emotions were stable, and the time seemed "absolutely ripe." Her only qualm was how the presence of a real baby would affect her five-year marriage.

Her husband welcomed the child in theory, but had a different reaction when confronted with reality—a reaction Lucille had half-expected, yet dreaded. "Some husbands do, in fact, bring babies who are nursing to the mother in the middle of the night," she recalls. "Mine wanted to know what the trampoline act was on the bed. After a period of time, he moved into another room to sleep because he didn't want to be disturbed in the morning when I would get up with the baby. It seemed to me that since I was willing to work and deal with the baby and manage a household, I needed every ounce of support he could give me. I had a housekeeper during the day, and asked him if he could be with the baby from 5 to 6 P.M.—between the time she left and the time I got home. He said he simply did not want to do it—that he hated watching the baby. He felt more and more oppressed. We weren't having any fun. He didn't enjoy the baby, and it dampened a lot of my enjoyment.

"I guess all those homilies about jealous fathers applied to him. I became terribly aware of the inequities in our relationship. There was a real infant, not an adult infant, in the family, and the needs were very immediate. I expected those needs would be met without any kind of excuses from either of us. I felt we had had our place in the sun and should move over a bit and make room in our lives for this new person. I guess I had expected some mirage of maturity. I thought all of a sudden the baby would grow us both up. I had been preparing for it—but he hadn't."

For now, she and her husband live separately, although he sees the baby every day. "Now I am rearing Jason alone, with a full-time housekeeper but no real father around. I'm not particularly proud of that—it's just the way it is. My husband and I have a clearer understanding of each other. And now he spends that hour with Jason each day that I would have died to have him spend before—between five and six—and he does it willingly. He seems rather proud of the child, and yet is simply not capable of giving me the kind of reassurance and support I need. It's terribly important that a woman who is not planning to stay home and do full-time child care have a willing partner. If you have a good relationship with your husband, chances are it will continue. But if you have an immature relationship, it's going to exacerbate everything."

Despite this rupture, Lucille remains very glad she became a mother during this time of her life. "I thought when the time was right lights would be flashing in the sky saying, 'This is the time.' That didn't happen. I just felt ready to put my mothering instincts in the right place for once. Some of these realities about the nature of my relationships with men would have been good for me to see earlier in life. But then I probably couldn't have handled them. Now I'm ready to get it right—to be a mother to my child, and an equal partner to a man."

Chapter Three

Birthing—The Experience

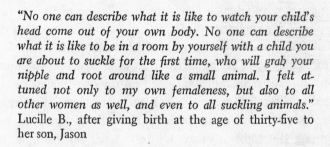

"No one can describe what it is like to watch your child's head come out of your own body. No one can describe what it is like to be in a room by yourself with a child you are about to suckle for the first time, who will grab your nipple and root around like a small animal. I felt attuned not only to my own femaleness, but also to all other women as well, and even to all suckling animals."
Lucille B., after giving birth at the age of thirty-five to her son, Jason

Every woman has heard rumors about the dangers of pregnancy and delivery for women over thirty-five. The most common among them are:

—they have longer labors.
—they are more likely to have complications.
—they are more likely to have a child with birth defects.

I have taken a hard and serious look at the validity of these rumors, and find that they have been exaggerated and greatly overstated. The old wives' tales surrounding older pregnancies do not reflect modern reality. Almost 80,000 women over the age of thirty gave birth for the first time during 1976, and the great majority of them had normal pregnancies and deliveries.

THE MEDICAL FACTS

This gap between myth and reality exists in part because statistics have not yet caught up with this sudden surge of births for older women. The National Center for Health Statistics reported on this recent trend for the first time last year, when it found that while the birth rate had declined for younger women, it had actually risen 5–10 per cent for women ages thirty to thirty-nine. This is the first time women are giving birth at an older age in great numbers, and all signs indicate, based on my own review of the medical literature from the last ten years, that future studies will be even more positive than those done so far. Among the eighty women I interviewed, for example, all reported healthy pregnancies, the majority reported short four- to six-hour labors, and all except one delivered a healthy child. In that one exception, a thirty-year-old woman had a stillbirth.

But most pregnancies and deliveries are perfectly normal, and the informal comments of doctors support this more positive view. "We now have evidence that if a woman has no chronic diseases—diabetes, hypertension, and the like—having a first baby after thirty-five can be as safe and uneventful as giving birth in your twenties," Dr. David Sherman, a New York obstetrician/gynecologist, reported recently.* Dr. Sherman estimates that 20 per cent of his deliveries of first babies in 1977 were from women over thirty-five.

The single most important development contributing to this more relaxed attitude toward delayed childbirth is the routine use of amniocentesis for women over thirty-five. Amniocentesis is virtually 100 per cent effective in determining all major chromosomal abnormalities in the fetus, including the most common one, Down's Syndrome, or mongolism. It is a relatively simple procedure, which usually takes about an hour and is performed in an outpatient hospital room. The effectiveness of this procedure is one reason why so many women are now waiting until the age of thirty or older to have their first child. And 95 per cent of the amniocentesis results do come back favorable—showing a normal, healthy fetus without any signs of defect.

During amniocentesis, the mother receives a local anesthetic. The doctor then inserts a hollow needle into the fluid that forms a protective amniotic sack around the fetus, and extracts one ounce of amniotic fluid. The fluid is sent to a laboratory, where it incubates for about three weeks, and is then examined. Most doctors also use ultrasound to determine the exact location of the fetus before performing amniocentesis, in order to avoid any slight possibility of disturbing the fetus. When ultrasound—sound waves of high frequency—is beamed at the fetus inside the mother's uterus, it produces a hazy picture, called a sonogram, on an oscilloscope. With the aid of the sonogram, the physician can determine precisely where to insert the needle.

* *Family Circle*, September 1978.

It is generally agreed that the risk of bearing a child with Down's Syndrome increases with age. But although the risk does increase, it is important to keep it in perspective: The odds of carrying a fetus with Down's Syndrome are generally agreed to be 1 in 850 for women ages thirty to thirty-four; 1 in 280 for women ages thirty-five to thirty-nine; and 1 in 100 for women ages forty to forty-four. This means that a woman aged thirty-six who is bearing her first child has about a $\frac{3}{10}$ of 1 per cent chance of carrying a fetus with the syndrome; a woman aged forty-three has a 1 per cent chance. The overwhelming majority of women deliver normal, healthy babies. And for the minority, the chances of delivering a child with birth defects is reduced to near-zero with amniocentesis.

By relieving this fear, amniocentesis also reduces "panic" abortions sought by older women in the past. "Contrary to early expectations, amniocentesis doesn't create more abortions, but actually prevents unneeded abortions," says Dr. Hans Lehfeldt, a New York obstetrician who has delivered almost three thousand babies—many of them to older mothers—during his fifty years of practice. Dr. Lehfeldt's own wife was forty-two when she had her first child. "Older women have always known they have greater chances of chromosomal abnormalities, and this anxiety in the past often drove women into illegal abortions. Today, they can receive amniocentesis, and in a great majority of cases, we can reassure them that there is no problem, that they can go ahead and safely have the child."

Both ultrasound and amniocentesis can be used for other medical purposes as well. With ultrasound, the doctor can measure the size of the fetal head for an accurate "due date," watch for intrauterine growth retardation, check for twins, diagnose whether the pregnancy is in the uterus. Later in pregnancy, amniocentesis can be used to check for Rh blood disease, diabetes, and toxemia. Toxemia is a metabolic disorder found in some pregnant women with hypertension or diabetes. It is characterized by high blood pressure, fluid retention in the tissues, and protein in the urine. The presence of toxemia can prevent the placenta from functioning properly.

Doctors also monitor older mothers for the presence of fibroid tumors—benign growths of fibrous tissue located in or attached to the uterus. Small fibroids are usually harmless, but larger ones can cause miscarriages.

It must be kept in mind, however, that there is no reason why a healthy woman who takes good care of herself cannot deliver, in her thirties or forties, a healthy and normal child. When an older woman is thinking of getting pregnant, she should have a complete physical checkup before doing so. When pregnant, she should abstain from caffeine, cigarettes, drugs (including aspirin and novacain), avoid overeating, and develop a regular program of balanced exercise that will keep her muscles relaxed and in shape.

Women are aging more slowly today because they *are* taking better care of themselves. The medical definition of an "elderly primigravida"—a woman having her first child over the age of thirty-five—does not yet reflect this prolonged youthfulness of today's woman. The definition was adopted twenty years ago by the Council of the International Federation of Obstetricians and Gynecologists, when women were having children younger and dying earlier. She was then considered a "high risk" patient during

pregnancy—a label that many doctors now feel lacks validity.

"More recently," Dr. Ian Morrison wrote in the Febru-
ary 15, 1975, *American Journal of Obstetrics and Gynecology*, "It has been recognized that, granted careful prenatal
care, maternal mortality rates in the elderly primigravida
group compare favorably with the figures for the younger
age groups . . ."

At that time, Dr. Morrison had completed a five-year review of 127 women who delivered their first children over
the age of thirty-five in the Health Sciences Center in
Winnipeg, Canada. Twenty-six per cent of the patients
were over forty, and the eldest was forty-six. Here is what
he found:

—3 per cent of the infants had some form of congenital
  abnormality.
—11 per cent of the infants delivered were smaller than
  average.
—14 per cent of the infants were premature.
—the perinatal (around birth) mortality rate for the
  fetus (usually associated with a prolonged pregnancy
  of more than forty weeks or a prolonged labor of more
  than twenty hours) was 4.7 per cent.

However, these figures are pessimistic in the light of
more recent studies. In January 1978, Dr. Pauli Kajanoja
and Dr. Olof Widholm of the Department of Obstetrics
and Gynecology at Helsinki University Central Hospital in
Finland published in the journal of *Obstetrics and Gynecology* the results of a seven-year study of 558 women who
delivered their first babies at the age of forty and over. They
found that "today, an elderly woman has a good chance of

giving birth *to a healthy child* after a safe pregnancy." (Italics are mine.) The major difference between this study and the previous one is that this study reported a perinatal mortality rate of only 2.8 per cent—about the same as that in younger women. They feel that "the drop in perinatal mortality among infants (of older women) . . . is probably a result of more effective antenatal care, even though premature births have become more numerous as the percentage of elderly primigravidas has increased."

The doctors conclude that if a woman over forty has good obstetrical care and a carefully monitored delivery, she and her child will both fare well. In other words, the healthy older woman who wants a baby will in all likelihood have no trouble delivering one successfully. Today, Drs. Kajanoja and Widholm say the physician can assure older women that they have a "good chance of achieving a favorable result from the point of view of both mother and child."

THE JOY OF BIRTH

A healthy woman who gives birth later in life can rest assured that not only will her pregnancy in all likelihood be normal, but she also has the added bonus of a strong psychological motivation: For women who wait, even the less-than-pleasant aspects of any normal pregnancy, such as morning sickness, are often experienced with joy and a sense of humor.

Lucille B., the corporate vice-president we met in the previous chapter, describes her experience: "I wanted a child so much that every twinge of nausea was, for me, a cause for rejoicing. I remember the first time I felt like vomiting from morning sickness, a wave of nausea washed over me and I backed up against a wall—then I caught sight of myself in the mirror and I was actually grinning. The first time I felt life in me, I was so excited I couldn't sleep all night."

In many ways, Lucille's attitude toward birth was typical of the women I met. She took natural childbirth classes, and she also took a prenatal dance class with Dr. Elizabeth Bing, who pioneered the Lamaze method of prepared childbirth in this country. "It did my morale wonders to see other women with whale bellies lying on the floor in leotards," she says, smiling. Lucille also stopped smoking, drinking, and taking aspirin and she cut coffee and tea from her diet. And, like most women I interviewed, Lucille stayed active through pregnancy and up to the last few hours before delivery.

"I was working in my office until 9:30 the night I had the baby, trying to get things cleaned up," she says. "I had apparently been having twinges and had not really paid a lot of attention because I was so involved with people in the office. I got home at 10:30, ate an enormous dinner—which you're not supposed to do after 9 since most women give birth in the middle of the night—and I even drank my first scotch in nine months because I couldn't sleep.

"I got up at 1:20 in the morning, vomited all that dinner, and barely made it to the hospital. My doctor didn't make it. Two interns delivered me—one of them, a woman who had been in obstetrics two weeks, had hands like a truck driver. They were like the witches in Macbeth, hovering around my birth canal. They were horrible, but the delivery was wonderful. I had not a lick of anesthetic. When I saw my child emerge, I felt as if I were undergoing mitosis—suddenly I had become two. No one can describe what it is like to watch your child's head come out of your own body. No one can describe what it is like to be in a room by yourself with a child you are about to suckle for the first time, who will grab your nipple and root around like a small animal. I felt attuned not only to my own femaleness, but also to all other women as well, and even to all suckling animals. My response was that primitive, that intense."

"No one told me," another woman says, "that wanting to deliver a child is just like wanting to hunker down and go to the bathroom. I felt a tremendous pressure, but no pain, and my husband—who was with me in the delivery room—said I was making a face that made me look like a wolf. The doctor said, 'One more push and we'll have this baby.' I didn't believe him. I closed my eyes and pushed, and when I opened them I was looking into the bright blue eyes of my newborn child—I can still see her expression of total wonderment. I held her right away, although I didn't feel that overwhelming attachment to her, that bonding, that some women describe. The attachment grew as I got to know her. Then, right after the birth, the nurse took us to a private room and left the three of us alone."

A flight attendant who had her first child at thirty-three says, "Jeff and I were the first in our group of friends to have children, and everyone thought it was funny. They celebrated my baby's impending birth by throwing a birthday party in advance, and I was drinking wine and dancing until 3 A.M. The next morning I woke up with what I thought was a terrible hangover. As the hours went by, the hangover did not get better—anyway, my baby was born at 6 P.M.

"The delivery was simple and was over quickly. I was rather amused with myself because all along I had been asking my doctor, 'Can't we have dim lights instead of bright? Can't we have daffodils? Can't we have Bach instead of Muzak?' Then, when the time came, I didn't really care! I was only interested in watching her being born. The nurses held my shoulders to help me sit up, and I could tell the instant she came out because I fell over backwards from the sudden release of pressure. Jeff, meanwhile, was taking pictures of the baby coming out; afterwards, he just sat there holding the baby and saying, 'I expected to like her, but I didn't know I would like her so much so soon.' Then he telephoned everybody and said, 'Two pushes and she popped right out! It was so terrific—I can't wait to have another one.' I still wasn't feeling on top of the world, and I said, 'Hummm. Okay. You have the next one.'"

THE PAIN OF BIRTH

Not all women, however, breeze through labor and delivery with unalloyed joy. Most of the women I interviewed had taken prepared childbirth courses, and as a result, many felt disappointed and deceived when the pain of childbirth prevented them from living up to the image of the controlled, quietly breathing woman reclining Madonna-like on the delivery table.

"I remember screaming and then, as soon as the contraction was over, saying, 'Oh God, I'm sorry.' The pain just takes off beyond you," says Marilyn C., the feminist with three daughters (Chapter One). "My first child—who weighed nine pounds, three ounces—was born at 11:11 on a Sunday morning, and for two months after that, if I happened to look at a clock around that hour I would begin to shake.

"I always heard from other feminists that childbirth would be hard, laborious, but manageable—I had never expected that excruciating sense of being torn apart. Each time I gave birth, I felt a lot of guilt about losing control. But the odd thing is, except for that first birth, I always forgot about the pain after about four hours. It was like trying to remember how it felt to be violently sick to your stomach—once it's over, you can't bring it back. Each time I was going through it, I swore I would never do it again; and each time it was over, I couldn't wait to do it again. It was the most exhilarating experience in my life. I only stopped because my husband didn't want any more children."

A few women—especially those who have never before been hospitalized—also fear that the intense pain they associate with childbirth might even drive them crazy. Linnea D., who had her daughter at the age of forty-two (Chapter One), recalls that as she left her house for the hospital, she found herself touching the walls, trying to control her panic. "I had this feeling that I wasn't going to come back. I didn't think I was going to die—I thought I might end up in the psychiatric ward of Bellevue," she says. "Only later did I remember that my mother had traumatic births, with very long labors, which she had told me about when I was small.

"In fact, I did have long labor—thirteen hours—and the worst part was that I wasn't making any progress. I wasn't dilating enough, and finally my obstetrician came in and said, 'I think we should do a cesarean, don't you?' I said, 'I don't care if you take it out of my ankle, my armpit, my nose—just get it out!' I was very upset, but when I saw her born it was all worth it. She was spectacular. I remember a nurse asking, 'Well, doctor, what is it? A Napoleon or a Josephine?' There was silence and then the doctor said, 'Wow! That's some Josephine!' She weighed almost ten pounds, and had a full head of hair. The moment I saw her, I knew the pain no longer mattered."

CESAREAN SECTIONS

The one medical practice that causes concern to some physicians and has brought deep disappointment to many of the women who have undergone the experience is the growing use of the cesarean section—a rate that has risen to 31 per cent among older mothers.†

In a cesarean section, the baby is extracted through an incision made into the uterus. During a medical emergency, where the life of the fetus or the mother is endangered, cesareans are a crucial and positive operation. But many women who took prepared childbirth courses and entered the hospital expecting to deliver a baby naturally often feel bitter when, with little prior warning, the doctor

† This percentage was cited in both of the Winnipeg, Canada, and Helsinki, Finland, studies mentioned in this chapter. It is from three to ten times higher than the rate of cesareans performed on younger women.

decides to perform a cesarean, or C-section, sometimes because it is more convenient as well as safer.

"My mother had big healthy babies the natural way, and it never occurred to me that I wouldn't be a good deliverer of babies, too," says Peg M., a social worker who delivered her baby at age thirty-five. "But after ten hours of labor, my doctor decided I was dilating too slowly and he was going to do a cesarean. I wanted to continue with the labor, but I was in a lot of pain just then, and in no position to argue, so I agreed. It was midnight, and I think he really just got tired of waiting and wanted to get home.

"I was totally unprepared for what happened next. First, they wouldn't allow my husband in the delivery room, as we had planned. Then, when I got onto the operating table, while I was drained and dead tired and very vulnerable, the anesthesiologist said, 'Now, when you wake up . . .' I said, 'But I don't want to be put to sleep,' and he said, 'If you're not put to sleep you are going to have to stay perfectly still for two hours in this uncomfortable position.' They were taping down my arms and legs. He really scared me because he made me feel if I didn't co-operate I could do something harmful to the baby. My obstetrician leaned over and said, 'He's really right.'

"I couldn't go out and get a book, couldn't talk to anyone—I was stuck, and so I said, 'Okay.' Only later did I find out that the general anesthetic wasn't at all necessary, that I *could* have watched my baby being born with just a local anesthetic. It was just more convenient for them. I still, after eight months, have a lot of anger about that—toward the hospital and my doctor, of course, but most of all toward myself—for failing, for not being able to do what the 'total woman' is supposed to do."

Many cesareans like Peg's are considered borderline—done officially because it is "safe" but done, in fact, because it is more efficient for medical personnel, and keeps the operating room on a tighter schedule. In an interesting study done by Dr. Berkeley Merrill and Dr. C. E. Gibbs, of the Department of Obstetrics and Gynecology at the University of Texas Health Science Center-Medical School in San Antonio,†† it was found that half of 634 women who would have routinely received cesarean sections in a San Antonio hospital had safe vaginal deliveries when allowed to go into labor. All the women had previously given birth by cesarean section, and until now doctors had assumed "once a C-section, always a C-section"—an assumption that saved them time and cost the patient more money. Merrill and Gibbs point out that the vaginal deliveries saved the women 35 per cent to 40 per cent of the cost of a cesarean section.

However, a cesarean need not always be traumatic, especially if a woman has prepared herself for even the remote possibility of undergoing surgery. Regina M., whom we met at the end of Chapter Two, told her doctor during one of her office visits, "I want to talk about what's going to happen if I have a cesarean." He reassured her, "No, no, don't worry. Everything is fine. You aren't going to need a cesarean." She persisted, "I hope not, but this is what I want in the event I *do* have to have one." She then detailed her demands: She wanted her husband, Joseph, in the room with her, she wanted to be awake, she wanted a horizontal incision.

She went into labor a few weeks later, entered the hospi-

†† The study, reported in *Obstetrics and Gynecology*, July 1978 was conducted from 1970–74 at the Robert B. Green Hospital in San Antonio.

tal and, after fifteen hours of labor, the baby turned in her uterus and she had to have a cesarean. "I got everything I wanted, because I have an honest doctor," Regina says. "He waited to the last minute to do the cesarean, because he knew how much we wanted natural birth, and he wanted it to be the kind of experience we had hoped for. Finally, when he said, 'Well, I'm afraid you're never going to get there without a cesarean,' we agreed on the operation. I felt a little let down, but not devastated."

She was wheeled into surgery, where both the assisting doctor and the anesthesiologist ordered her husband out of the operating room. "My doctor told them, 'He's going to keep her company. He's going to stay. I made a promise and intend to keep it.' They had a fight right there in the operating room, but my husband got to stay. Then the anesthesiologist tried to talk me into a general, and I insisted on a spinal.* He tried to intimidate me, but it didn't work because I had done my homework and I knew my options. I got my spinal.

"I was awake, with my husband beside me, when I saw them lifting the baby out of me. Then they put his cheek next to my cheek and I felt such *love*—it astounded me! I mean, I wondered how I could feel such love for this—bloody creature? Here I was, my stomach still open, laughing and crying at the same time. But before I had a chance to hold my baby, they took him away to the nursery, and they took me to the recovery room. My husband and I be-

---

* A spinal is a pain-killing drug injected into the fluid surrounding the spinal cord, and can be administered right before delivery or a C-section to eliminate pain in the lower part of the body. A spinal will probably prolong the delivery, since it interferes with muscle contraction. It can also cause severe headaches afterward, as well as a sharp drop in blood pressure during delivery.

lieve in maternal-infant bonding, so Joseph went into the
nursery to retrieve the baby. The nurses said, 'Oh no, she
can't hold the baby yet.' My husband can be a very determined person, and he stood his ground and said, 'My wife
is supposed to get Demerol, and she's not taking any Demerol until you let her hold her baby.' By using blackmail,
he finally got the baby back and brought him to me. The
baby looked at me with big wide eyes and then went for
my breast and started nursing—like a puppy. So the birth
turned into a positive experience, even though it wasn't the
way we had dreamed and planned."

Regina does still retain some lingering disappointment,
but no sense of bitterness or failure, about her cesarean.
"When I look at my child now, it's hard for me to envision
him ever having been inside of me. My only point of
conflict is that I wonder—if I had felt him coming down
the birth canal, felt him coming out of me—whether I
would feel more connected to him. I feel mildly deprived
about not having had natural childbirth. But on the scale
of things to feel deprived about, it's hardly a big thing.
More importantly, I feel wonderful that my husband and I
didn't submit out of fright or fatigue or ignorance to petty
hospital rules, that we stuck up for what we wanted, and
we got it."

HOSPITALS AND DOCTORS

The only aspect of childbirth about which the women I
interviewed complained repeatedly is their vexed relationships with the hospitals, doctors, and nurses involved in the

delivery of their babies. The wonder of giving birth always prevails, but that wonder is dimmed by what these women perceive as a constant skirmish with regulations in order to have prepared childbirth in a congenial atmosphere.

Janet L., who gave birth at age thirty-nine and is married to a doctor, told me a story similar to many I heard. "Because of my husband's connections, I found a group of medical people who were particularly excellent, who had world-wide reputations, and who were very efficient," she says. "They didn't seem a bit worried about my age, and gave me all the tests I needed, including amniocentesis. I assumed they would also do a good job when it came to natural childbirth. But they were funny about that—they didn't discourage me when I told them I was taking the Lamaze classes. They just said, 'Oh yes, we'll talk about that later'—but they never did.

"When it came time to deliver, I went to the hospital as planned and while I was having the real tough labor pains, my doctor appeared and said, 'Now would you like us to give you an epidural?'† He had never discussed this with me before—I didn't even know what an epidural was. I think he was hoping I would say, 'Anything, an axe, do something so I can't feel the pain.' But I was still aware enough of my own long-term desires to say, 'No, I don't need it.' I knew if I took it, I would regret it later.

"My doctor let me go through with the natural childbirth, but his attitude was not exactly enthusiastic, and I could tell he was getting impatient with me. I realized that

† During labor, doctors can administer an epidural, a painkiller similar to the spinal, except that it is injected just outside the membrane covering the spinal cord, and is held in place by a fine threadlike catheter. It, like the spinal, is often associated with prolonged labor, because it interferes with contractions.

hospital personnel go along with natural childbirth only because if they don't do it, the hospital will lose half its pregnant patients—it's what *women* want. The whole attitude is that you, the woman giving birth, are there to accommodate the doctor who is delivering the baby. You become the secondary figure. The doctor is central.

"The large hospital I went to was not really geared for natural childbirth patients. They did what I asked, but it was like a waiter bringing me something I requested that was not on the menu—no involvement, no enthusiasm, no encouragement, or emotional support."

While it is not recommended to have a child alone at home whether you are young or older, more women are choosing to give birth with the help of a midwife rather than a doctor. Usually the midwives work in a medical center (sometimes hospital-affiliated) where a doctor and surgical equipment is available if there is an emergency. And home births are also on the rise—a sign that women are demanding more humanized childbirth and will take the risks necessary to get it.

Theresa W., who had her first child at age thirty-three in a hospital and her second at age thirty-five in a medical center with a midwife, describes the difference, "The first time, my doctor was marvelous. He handled everything with real professionalism. But I didn't want that. I'm not a back-to-the-earth fanatic, and I do appreciate the medical efficiency, but I just wanted a more pleasant, more caring attitude, instead of having all those machines stuck on me, and doctors and students coming in to visit, and my filling out forms in triplicate.

"I feel that giving birth is a woman's business. And when it's over, I want to feel *I* gave birth to my child, not that someone yanked it out of me and then sent me a bill. I had that pleasant, caring feeling the second time, when I went to a maternity center with midwives on the staff.†† I loved it. My labor was very long—seventeen hours—and a midwife stayed with me the whole time. Towards the end, the doctor came in, said hello, asked if everything was okay, and then left. The baby was born shortly afterward.

"The hospital had, right after the first birth, sent my baby to the nursery and my husband back home. The medical center had a completely different attitude—they brought in a crib for the baby, and a cot for my husband, and we all stayed together in my room that night. In the hospital, I had to wait three days to be discharged; in the center, I went home after twelve hours. There is nothing in this world that compares to the high of having a baby under these circumstances—nothing! Nothing! I was in pain, yes, but afterward I could have done cartwheels off the table. I was so proud of me and the way I went through it. I was a real trooper. We did it the way we wanted to, and I'll always treasure that."

Those women like Regina and Theresa who were aware of their options, who knew their rights as patients, who knew what they wanted during the delivery of their babies, and had made their wishes clear to the doctors and the hospitals beforehand—and who were flexible and realistic enough to readjust their expectations if need be, without a sense of failure or guilt—were the women who retained the most pleasant, joyful, and richest memories of childbirth.

†† Theresa delivered her second child at Metropolitan Medical Associates, P.A., in Engelwood, New Jersey.

Chapter Four

Mothering–The Life-style

"I feel a tangible physical link with her that is different from any other love I've known—it comes from holding her . . . from feeling her tiny arms and legs. The first time she differentiated me from everybody else, the first time she hugged me back, the first time she said, 'I love you'—I practically fell on the floor!" Ginny May, who gave birth to her daughter at age thirty-four.

In the past, motherhood was considered an exalted state of being. It merited songs, tattoos, prayers embroidered on pillowcases. As men became soldiers, so women became mothers—guardians of morality at the hearthside. Each sex was destined, it seemed, to emulate, protect, and defend those qualities thought to be unique unto itself. The very words Mother Earth, Mother Nature, Mother Mary symbolized the voluptuousness, the ubiquitousness, the sacrifice, the eternal sacrament of motherhood.

In the past, a woman who was not a mother by the age of thirty was considered an aberration. She was equated with the barren soil, the fading blossom. She was a figure of ridicule, and of pity. Careers and mothering were considered mutually exclusive. Schoolteachers and librarians became symbols of "old maids" because they were the positions commonly sought by those women who wanted, or were obligated, to work rather than become mothers.

Today, "motherhood" has been removed from its pedestal. For a while demographers even feared a spiraling population decline. Women's oppression in her husband's bed, depression in her kitchen, suppression by her very own mother, have been psychoanalyzed and the results—generally unfavorable—have been published in even the most traditional women's magazines.

We know today that mothering can make us feel anxious, frustrated, conflicted, angry—but what about the good parts? And there *are* many good parts to being a mother—especially an older mother—as I learned from the women I interviewed. "When I come home feeling depressed, feeling out of focus, my child's perceptions can turn my outlook around completely," says Jane P., who gave birth to her now-four-year-old daughter when she was thirty-three. "I see things in her that bring back feelings in me that had been lost. When it snowed last week I went out walking through the park with her, and she began jumping in the snow drifts instead of walking on the little paths. Suddenly, I remembered feeling that pure excitement and pleasure again. Sometimes I sit and rock her. There was a thing my mother always used to do when I was sitting on her lap—she would always tuck my hair behind my ear—and now I find myself doing that with my baby. That action triggers a wave of wonderful memories.

"And what a treat it is to watch a child grow. As much as you give, you get back in equal amounts—she gives me love, affection, companionship, whimsey, laughter, and real joy. Do you realize how rare it is to feel *real* joy? I know she will grow up and leave. I know my career, my friends, will be here long after she has gone. But to have a child, *my* child, for even a little while—I could not imagine life without her."

THE JUGGLING ACT:
HANDLING WORK AND BABIES

Those working mothers I met are all, without exception, three-ring-circus busy. Many of them feel torn between two conflicting desires: one, to return to work full time—for the independence, the money, the stimulation; the other, to remain home and watch their child grow. This ambivalence has no predictable or easy resolution. Avid career women find themselves giving up their jobs and staying home content to be housewives; women who plan to stay home change their minds and find they can't return to work fast enough. "At first, I was happy to stay home," says a forty-two-year-old singer who had her first child at thirty. "I would just smile at my baby all day. I had a wonderful time with him. Then one day he reached for my hair, grabbed it, and pulled. I said, 'Okay. It's time to go back.' I got a nurse and a part in *Hello Dolly*, and I've been working ever since."

Ginny May: Full-time Work

Today, the guilt over the mother-career conflict is modulated, especially for a woman who has children after her career is already established. Then husband, parents, friends, employers will often rally to help her return to work.

Ginny May S., a children's book editor with a three-year-old daughter, has support from all these quarters. "Growing up in the nineteen fifties, I always assumed I would stop working when I had children," she says. "Most of the people I went to school with had children when they were twenty-two or twenty-three, and did stop working. I saw no reason why I should be different. But I went to Paris after college, where I worked as an *au pair* girl. For several years, that experience doused my desire to be a mother and housewife. I married Tom when I was twenty-seven, and we just kept waiting until 'the time was right' to have a child. Finally when I was thirty-three we realized that the point would never come where we felt we really had enough money—so we just went ahead. Neither of us felt totally ready, but we felt if we were going to do it, we should do it soon—especially if we wanted more, which is something you don't know until you've tried *one*."

Getting Employer Support

Ginny May continues. "I had never planned on a career. I took this job when I was thirty and only then did my ideas about working mothers begin to change. My boss was a woman who had a young son and who was also very successful in her career. The woman I replaced was leaving because she had just had her second child—but she had continued working after her first. So I had in front of me examples of these people who did it—who were mothers *and* career women.

"As the months of my own pregnancy went by, I became more and more reluctant to even consider giving up my job. If my boss had been less supportive, had said, 'Well, I guess you'll be leaving us now that you're pregnant,' then I might have left. Instead, I was encouraged by everyone to stay.

"And during my two months' pregnancy leave, I found I was bored at home. I'm just not that crazy about infants, even when they're mine. I really missed books, the people I see during the day, the excitement of my job. I like publishing because I can be around people, but I can also close the door and dig into a manuscript. I suppose it's escaping—and I couldn't escape at home, where I was faced with the reality of a hungry, wet child and housework and laundry and cooking and all the things I really hate to do.

"At 9:30 the morning I came back to work from maternity leave, I found a note on my desk from my boss. It said, 'In the spring we are starting our new paperback line. You are in charge. I am going on vacation next week. Before then we have to choose a name, a format, and the initial titles. The first meeting is at 10 A.M. today.' Ginny May laughs when she remembers the turmoil she felt. "I was literally thrown back into work with a splash. I have always wondered if she did that on purpose—but, in any case, there was certainly no looking back. And that year turned out to be my most rewarding professionally. I ended up editing the best book of my career. Everything seemed to happen to reinforce my decision to keep working."

Having a Husband's Encouragement

Ginny May's husband, a film producer, also supported her return to her job. "I do feel Tom is more 'maternal' than I am," Ginny May says. "He has a lot of tenderness and patience, and there have been times when he handled our baby better than I did. I remember once when she was choking, and while I was panicking Tom just picked her up and took care of it. Someone there said, 'Well, he's so terrific, it makes you wonder which one is the mother.' I felt half-insulted and half-pleased. Tom was so good with her that sometimes I even resented it—he adores the baby, and I wasn't used to sharing him. But then I would remind myself that he has come a long way from the days when he wanted nothing to do with housework.

"I remember, right after we were married, the first time it became clear I was supposed to do all the cooking and cleaning. I had just come home from the office and Tom was waiting in his armchair. I wondered, why is he just *sitting* there? He kissed me hello, I fixed dinner, did the dishes—and he just sat there! That lasted a few weeks. Then we started talking about it, and he had to admit that it wasn't too terrific. It began to change gradually—by the slow-drip method. We didn't have a confrontation where he said, 'Okay, from now on we'll share the work.' It just evolved. We still come home and fight about who's going to cook dinner—but at least now it's an open question. Usually, whoever feels weaker that day does it."

Winning Family Approval

Ginny May's own mother is dead, but she has found in her in-laws a new family to attach herself to—a family that, at first, frowned on her career. "Tom comes from an old Yankee family. Their real pleasure in life is their children, and their grandchildren. They made me aware of the satisfaction of a family network. But Tom's mother has always been a housewife, and she was very disapproving about my job. She used to make comments like, 'I always say you have to make a choice—a career or a baby,' or, 'There's a limit to how many things you can do well.' She is one of those super-organized women. She makes her own clothes, is a marvelous cook, plays golf. She always says, 'I could never have gone into business' which is bullshit because she could have run General Motors. Now she has changed her mind about my working. In fact, she has been totally converted, and I think she may have some doubts about the wisdom of her own early choices. She sees how well my daughter has done, and she can't say my working has hurt her in any way, because it obviously hasn't. She keeps saying that my daughter is the best-adjusted, friendliest, smartest of all her grandchildren."

Coming to Terms with Herself

How does she feel about her job today, three years after her daughter's birth? "I stay at my job not for the money—after paying the housekeeper and other child-care expenses, I clear forty-five dollars a week—but because I know I would be a burden for my child if I felt that I had no life of my own, that I'm living through her. I don't want to give up work that satisfies me. My work is so stimulating that, in a way, I go home refreshed."

Yet Ginny May retains some guilt about her decision. "My feeling about the importance of my work was crystallized by my decision to have a child. I told myself, 'If you're going to continue working, you had better be seriously committed to what you're doing to justify leaving your child with someone else.' I do feel my attachment to my daughter grows as she gets older and responds more to me. I feel a tangible physical link with her that is different from any other love I've known—it comes from holding her, from her warmth, from feeling her tiny arms and legs.

"I feel if anyone tried to harm her, I would murder them. The pain I feel through her amazes me. I took her to play with some other children, and when one of the children shoved her I suffered a thousand times more than she did from the rejection. And the joy she gives me is just as strong. The first time she differentiated me from everybody else, the first time she hugged me back, the first time she said, 'I love you'—I practically fell on the floor! I miss her during the day."

This guilt among working mothers is shored up by the real desire to share in and help mold their children's lives during those first formative months and years. Those mothers who have sympathetic employers can often work out a compromise in their working schedule and still retain a full-time job. When Lucille B., the successful business executive we met in Chapter Two (who liked to mother her men) balked at leaving her baby behind on business trips, her employer paid to have a nurse and the baby travel with her.

"I am not going to leave that child alone until he's at least three years old," she says. "I didn't have him so someone else could bring him up." The first month after he was born, Lucille worked at home and her secretary joined her there each day. "I've been with this company long enough so they trust me and let me make my own decisions. As long as the work gets done, they don't care where I do it." Now she spends three mornings a week with her son's play group. "It's time I deliberately take off from work, and it means I have to work later and take work home. I have a tremendously responsible job, and I have to work very hard at it. But my working life comes a close second to my child. I never go out on a date at night until I have put him to sleep. My child is absolutely paramount."

Andrea C., who gave birth at the age of thirty-two, often brings her six-month-old daughter to her Chicago office with her. "When the weather is good and I have extra work to do, I pick her up from day care at 5 P.M. and bring her back to the office with me. I have a collapsible crib in the office, and sometimes when she is a little sick, I bring her to work so I can watch her.

"My employers love having her in the office. She was the first baby to actually hang around, and she has become the in-house infant. She feels comfortable there, and gets to be around a lot more adults, male and female, than she would be if I isolated her in the house with a baby-sitter. She has made a successful debut: No one seems to do less work, and she has humanized the whole environment."

Other women decide after giving birth to pursue a part-time career. Some invent new jobs—a Manhattan woman left her work in the theater, which involves unpredictable and often late hours, and started a successful catering business by making quiches in her kitchen. "I had never made a pastry shell in my life," she says, "but once I decided to do it, it had to be perfect. I threw away hundreds of pounds of butter, and I became obsessed with rolling out the perfect dough." Once she had perfected the art, she called *New York* magazine's "Best Bets" section and said, "Hi! I'm an actress and I make quiches." They said, "Great, bring one down." She did, they wrote about it, and the phone never stopped ringing. "I am not a trained cook, but I have a feeling for food and I'm very organized," she says. "I get tremendous satisfaction out of being my own boss. My biggest frustration in show business was working for people who didn't know business. I love making the financial decisions. I hire people, handle the bills, rent the equipment—everything."

Elizabeth: Part-time Work

And some women try to convert what was once a demanding full-time job into a half-day part-time job. Elizabeth L., the corporate financial adviser we met in Chapter Two, who wanted a child following the death of her first husband, is trying to squeeze two jobs into each day: child care and high finance. Rather than take the three-month maternity leave offered by her company, she returned to work immediately on a six-month half-day basis. She spends mornings at home with her child, and afternoons scrutinizing portfolios. Both jobs demand more attention than she feels she can give to either of them.

Shifting Priorities

"With a baby this age, I can't really *manage* my time— it's all hers. She's the one in charge of my time. In a way, you become the property of your child. My entire weekend is spent on *her* laundry, doing things for *her* room—it's a shock at first to realize how consuming a baby's needs are.

"I stay with her each morning, which means I can sleep a little later if she's kept me up during the night, can play with her a little, can nurse her. It is true that at some point every day, I walk out and someone else comes in to take care of her—but I don't feel I'm *managing* time at all right now. I'm simply consuming it.

"A lot of my delivery at work has been poor. It has been quite an adjustment to find that when I promise somebody I'll do something right away—I don't always get it done right away. There was a point right after she was born when I was trying to work from home, and I began to get overly apologetic on the phone to people for her. I found myself saying that I *had* to do this and *had* to do that for her, found myself blaming her, using her as a scapegoat— even though I wanted to do it and was going to do it for that reason. The psychology of it turned around on me.

"I also discovered that I didn't feel it was an adequate excuse to tell somebody I was very sorry, I hadn't been able to do it because my baby was keeping me busy. I have for years held a low opinion of marriage and motherhood. I had fortified myself with the idea that it was the 'right thing' for me to be out there working. Yet I want her, I love her, and I enjoy her tremendously. So I had to acknowledge that some of my past ideas were screwed up. I had to sit down and talk to myself about blaming her for my own feelings of inadequacy."

Re-evaluating Feminism

Elizabeth feels that feminist attitudes have contributed to her mixed feelings toward mothering. "I am a feminist," she says, "and I started at a very young age assuming I would do only the things boys are supposed to do. I was a terrible tomboy: I always ran around trying to be the first girl allowed in boys' clubs. I wound up doing weird things like running movie projectors, which bored me to death, but I wanted to be the first girl in the projectionist room." She pauses, and sighs.

"Actually, I consider myself more of a humanist than a feminist. I believe in people liberation—there are valuable differences between men and women, which I value. That's where I part company with strict feminists, who I feel try too often to imitate the male world. I think that's the wrong tack. And I think some feminists may have absorbed that traditional male scorn of motherhood: They believe that breast-feeding a baby doesn't have as much value as feeding a client in a banquette of an overpriced French restaurant.

Learning to Compromise

"I just hadn't realized how tempting my child would be," Elizabeth says. "I can spend an hour just cooing with her, and I feel it's 'lost' time, it's nonproductive and wasted time, even though it brings me great pleasure and it is exactly what I want to do."

Despite these tensions in her life, Elizabeth doesn't foresee how she could ever give up her work. "I want to be a working mother, because I feel it is the best for everybody —it's best for me, my husband, my child. If I stay home and do child care day after day, I find it's hard, tiring work, and not very interesting or refreshing. I start to drag and take it out on the baby or my husband or the cats. If I go out and do other work, I can forget a bit about my mothering responsibilities—and I believe it's not good to take mothering too seriously, because you lose your sense of humor. I come home with new ideas, with a 'cleared space' inside my head, and enjoy my baby that much more."

FULL-TIME MOTHERING: MELODY

Because a child *is* so tempting, a few women with good careers decide to abandon those careers. The decision often comes as a surprise to them and to everyone around them. "I loved my work, and I never saw myself as a housewife," says Melody V., a thirty-six-year-old mother who left her well-paying position as personnel manager of a Boston department store. "My work was, in many ways, my life, and

I couldn't imagine staying home. But when I was seven
months pregnant, I was called for jury duty, and when I
went to the court house I found all these people riding
the subways during working hours. I realized how out of
touch I had been with the world. It gave me a taste of what
it was like not being at a job from nine to five every day."

Despite her glimpse of a more flexible life-style, Melody
didn't yet think seriously about leaving her job. She arranged for a three-month maternity leave, and worked up
until the day her baby was born. But then, during her stay
at home, she began to dread returning to her office. "I used
to ask my friends who stayed home with children, 'What
do you *do* all day?' I couldn't figure out how you could
spend your entire day at home. Now I know. You just
spend it, that's all. In some nice ways, in some not-so-nice
ways, the day gets filled. You look at the baby and she
smiles and you melt with joy. It's something I never
wanted when I was twenty or twenty-five or thirty—but I
want it now."

Changing Her Mind

On the day she was to return to work, she called her boss
and told him, "I just can't leave my baby." She explains
her decision to me now, two years later, with her husband,
Mark, beside her. She now has two children, and doesn't
plan to return to work for at least two more years. By then,
she realizes, she will probably have to start at the bottom
of the career ladder again.

"It scares the hell out of me. I don't like the feeling of
losing my independence, of not earning my own money.

Even though I had saved some money, it is hard living on one salary. But I made the choice. It was not inflicted on me. Mark was open to either my getting a housekeeper and working, or my staying home. But when the first baby reached twelve weeks, when she stopped being a lump and began to have an alert, active and responsive personality, I was hooked. There was no way I could leave her."

Confirming Her Choice

Melody has had two years to reflect on her decision. "If I had had my child ten years earlier, I know I would have made this decision to stay home because I would have thought it was better for the baby. I would have felt I was sacrificing a career for a child, and I don't think anybody should ever do that. Later, I would have felt like saying, 'Look what I could have. been if it hadn't been for you.' Now I feel I made a well-thought-out decision, based on *my* own needs. We wanted both these children, we wanted them badly, and if I gave up my career—at least temporarily—it was because I chose to. It had nothing to do with self-sacrifice. I want to be with them. I don't want to miss out. My mother worked outside the home for a while when I was a baby, and I know she felt left out. My aunt was taking care of me, and one night my mother came home from work and I said something in baby talk. My aunt understood, and my mother didn't. She said, 'Okay. That's it. If I don't know what my own child is saying, then I'm not going to work anymore.' She never had an outside job after that, and I don't think she regretted it for a minute.

"If we need money badly, I will go back. But I've had my career in business—now it's time for me to have a career in mothering. This is my time for children, and it makes me feel good. My friends who had children young went through years of frustration. They would look at my life and tell me, 'You're so lucky. You travel. You eat out. You work. We're stuck in the house.' Now that I'm older my attitude is, 'I don't mind not going to a restaurant—I've been. I don't mind not traveling—I've gone there.' It doesn't mean I'm never going to do it again. But I no longer have that lust for getting away, for getting out. It's a temporary pause, a refocusing of my energy. I am loving every minute of it—no, not every minute—but I'm learning all the time about my children, about myself. It's an incredible experience."

EFFECTS ON MARRIAGE

Children can enrich a marriage and at the same time highlight problems. Just as women cannot always predict how a child will affect their thinking about careers, in a similar way they find the presence of a child provokes unexpected changes in their relationships with their husbands. Some couples find they become more interdependent, and a child strengthens their bonds with one another. Just as often, however, a child can bring new tension.

If the marital relationship is stable, chances are it will not be damaged and can even be enhanced by the presence of a third person who will, for a while, demand all the nurturing a couple once lavished on each other. If the relationship is unequal or dishonest, if there are unresolved tensions and problems, then a child can seem like an unforgivable intrusion, and can destroy the tenuous emotional harmony a couple has struggled to achieve over the years. In these cases, it is easy for the child to become the focal point of blame, with each person accusing the other of acting toward the child in a way that is destructive to the relationship.

Losing Autonomy

After giving birth, a woman faces inevitable changes in her life-style. She often becomes more dependent on outside help—usually on her husband, but sometimes on a parent, a lover, or a paid housekeeper as well. She finds more is demanded of her physically and emotionally. She has less time for herself, she gets less sleep, and her attention is more divided. Despite women's liberation, the women I interviewed did most of the child care: The father rarely handles the bulk of it, although sometimes the couple will split it 50–50.

Still, despite these added pressures, all the women I met cope very well with their lives, and all feel they are more mature, happier, and more content than they had been when they had only themselves to worry about. "It is actually a relief to be less narcissistic," says Paula A.* "After the baby was born, my single friends couldn't understand why I couldn't stay on the telephone with them anymore listening to their stories about he-said-and-she-said-and-they-said. My single friends stopped talking to me. They didn't un-

* Paula A.'s experience of motherhood begins on page 161.

derstand I had a new life that was making demands on me
every minute, and I couldn't afford to live vicariously anymore, to spend my time in gossip. Also, they were jealous
of the time taken away from them. Instead of sharing my
child with me, and participating—they got mad. When you
don't have a child of your own, you can afford to indulge
the childlike parts of your friends' personalities. When you
do have a child, you have to operate with a new maturity
all around."

Many women are proud of themselves for tightening up
their lives, for paring down their wasted time, for making
every moment count. When there is tension in their marriage, they learn how to defuse it, to compromise, to me-
diate. They find that a child's presence breaks down many
romantic fantasies that still linger, and clears the way for a
new, straightforward relationship with their husbands,
friends, and parents. As one new mother, who is thirty-
two, explains, "When you have the pressures and responsibilities of a child, it's almost impossible to stay 'romanti-
cally involved with' a man—the romance leaves the picture
and what you get is 'involved with.' Your relationship becomes—very honest. There's no running away from an unpleasant situation, and when you fight you can't walk out
on each other the way you might before. Not when there's
an infant at stake."

The older mother is usually more mature, more aware of
the origins of potential conflicts. Often, she works out in advance the time schedules and budget allocations that will
allow her to feel comfortable caring for a newborn baby.
With her husband and employer, she agrees on a reasonable
maternity leave—usually two to three months. She braces
herself for a certain loss of freedom and flexibility—a loss

that often does not bother her now, in her thirties or early forties, as much as it would have when she was younger. She has matured to the point where the insistent and immediate demands of a child no longer cause resentment, where she feels she can give to a child without taking too much away from herself.

A Check List for Successful Mothering

There are common potential trouble spots faced by women who are older mothers, accustomed to independence and involved in their careers. Women who resolve these conflicts before a child is born can look forward to a smoother transition into motherhood:

—*Child Care*. Make as specific plans as possible for child care *before* the baby arrives.

—If you and your husband plan to share child care, specify how the day will be divided and who will do which chores.

—If you plan to hire outside help, begin to look early, before the baby is born, for housekeepers, baby-sitters, or nurses with whom you will feel comfortable. Begin by checking local newspaper ads and asking for advice from other working mothers.

—Check out local day-care facilities to see which, if any, are acceptable to you.

—*Money Management*. Decide how you are going to handle the expenses incurred by a third person. Itemize those expenses as closely as possible. They will vary depending on where you live. New York City is most expensive, and a mother who plans to continue working full time should allocate as much as $10,000 a year for child care, including the cost of a housekeeper. If one parent plans to reduce work from full to part time, or to quit entirely, budget accordingly. If there is money saved, decide how much of it you are willing to divert for child rearing before one parent returns to full-time work. If you agree specifically on who pays for what, as changes occur you can negotiate accordingly.

—*Free Time*. Allow time for each parent to get away from the house and their jobs—both together, without the baby, and alone without each other or the baby. Consider all child-care options for this free time, including the use of parents for baby-sitters, or child-swapping with friends—they take your child for a weekend, and you take theirs another time. Be sure you agree on how much travel, entertaining, and going out you would feel comfortable with after the baby is born. Never assume your husband feels as you do. Always talk it out.

The Ties that Bind

Vicky P. of La Jolla, California, is a case in point: She has handled each of these tensions as they appeared. As a result, her marriage is strengthened, and she is happier. Vicky and her husband, John, were married for eleven and a half years before she gave birth to her first child at the age of thirty-three. Vicky, an interior designer, worked full time for a large and well-known interior design firm until she gave birth; now she works part time, usually from home. When we meet it is 8 P.M., and she has just put her three-year-old, Jason, to bed. Vicky is slim and sophisticated, soft-spoken yet self-confident. Her husband, John, forty, is an advertising executive and has a child by a previous marriage. He helps only minimally with child care.

"A child is the most selfish thing in the world—that's the way it survives," she says. "And when you're tired or upset or mad and want to have a good fight with your husband, you can't do it if the child needs attention. We have a beautiful baby. He is exactly what we wanted, and we both adore him. I feel this incredible warmth toward John, knowing that the two of us produced this beautiful child. But it doesn't change how we basically feel about each other. It doesn't make me more forgiving. In fact, I find the presence of an infant has created tension in several ways.

"First, there was tension when John felt excluded. After Jason was born, John would call me several times a day from his office, as he always had. But I couldn't talk to him anymore. I would always be busy with the baby and would have to say, 'Honey, I'll call you back.' I wouldn't call back, and he would call again and would feel hurt. Finally I said, 'Darling, you know you are my first love. But the baby needs me. He's totally helpless. You're not.'

"This must happen to every couple that has a child—suddenly you just don't have time together anymore. There's a whole level of your adult being that is taken away from you, that ongoing friendship and intimacy is slighted because you're tending to the child or you're tired. When John comes home from work, instead of handing him his slippers I hand him the baby. In the early days, especially, each time we tried to have a quiet candlelit dinner, it was interrupted by cries. And sex—there are no more sensual mornings in bed. Now we wait until the baby is asleep. It's hard not to get drawn into a cocoon with the baby, so that your whole life is spinning around his needs.

"Also, I was getting uptight about being confined to the house. It was hard for us to go anywhere together. The three of us went to see a photography exhibit at the museum, and I'm sure John remembers the pictures, but I remember Jason whining. One of the pleasures of my life was being able to walk out the door when I wanted, to go shopping or to the beach—a pleasure I took for granted until I couldn't do it anymore."

She sighs, and looks around her comfortable living room. "I began to feel my identity was being displaced. For the last three years I have bought clothing only for the child and not for me. I felt I needed only blue jeans because that was my new image. It didn't seem appropriate to wear sexy dresses if I was a mother." She laughs, and draws her angora shawl more tightly around her shoulders. "I used to spend a lot of money on clothes. Now when my copy of Vogue comes it lies around unopened. When I do open it my reaction is, 'My God! Mothers don't wear that!'"

Vicky and John also began to argue about child care. "John loves to play with him, but he has problems changing a diaper. He loves feeding him from time to time, and carrying him around if he's fussy. But his participation is limited. He had a child by a previous marriage, and he made it clear he felt his child-rearing days were done. When he does help, it's always volunteerism on his part. In the beginning, this made it very difficult because John would come home tired and I would have been home all day handling the baby and making telephone appointments with clients. John just wanted to sit down and relax. I was ready to throw the baby at him and leave the house.

"A lot of times, that made me very angry because it reflected my new financial dependence—when you are living on someone else's income, there are always strings attached. John would say, 'I work for most of the money and therefore I deserve—' and then you fill in the rest of the line. Usually it's—'I deserve to rest when I get home.'"

All of Vicky's feelings—her total involvement with the baby, her restlessness at home, her loss of identity, her resentment over the division of child care—are problems commonly faced by new mothers. Vicky feels that if she had had her child when she was younger, she would have been ill-equipped to handle them, and her marriage might have suffered. Instead, she found a new and stronger bond began to develop with her husband.

"We had a great advantage being married for so long, knowing each other so well, having a very verbal relationship where we always sit down and talk about problems we're having with one another. That is very important because there are so many fears and anxieties with a new child, and it requires a lot of talking. In the beginning, I wasn't sure how to handle a baby—when he cries, do I go get him or do I let him cry? We would have arguments over it: I would want to pick him up, John would want to leave him alone. But we always resolved it because we have a deep commitment to each other.

"I began to see ways in which I was trying to control John —if he didn't do what I wanted him to do, I would act as if he didn't love me. In fact, he just had his own very separate ideas about certain things. And he began to appreciate my needs more and became much more sensitive to them.

He saw that he had always held macho ideas about parenting—and about me. We began to break down some of our assumptions about each other that develop when you live together every day for twelve years. We had been too busy for 'philosophical' conversations about our lives—but the baby's presence triggered those kinds of discussions; the baby brought us together.

"But it takes such emotional maturity to have a child. It's very easy to lash out at the child because you're angry or tired or upset about your husband. Unless you have a strong sense of your own self-worth, unless you have a good solid marriage, you're sunk."

Vicky could hire a housekeeper and return to work full time, but she feels torn about leaving the baby. "I tell myself, 'The baby needs me. The baby doesn't know he needs me and I don't know if the baby really needs me, but I *think* the baby needs me. Maybe I need the baby more than the baby needs me!'" She shakes her head and laughs. "There's that sense of not wanting to miss what's happening. I've always believed that having a child is very narcissistic. What you love in that child—that enamored feeling—is so closely tied with loving yourself. I guess that's why parents are so crazy about their own kids. We really do keep focusing on ourselves, and when we see something in our child that is not so hot, then we turn it into somebody else's quality—your husband's quality!"

Finding Yourself

Not all women feel their identities are compromised by motherhood, and for some, the experience can even lead to a new sense of self-respect and independence that revitalizes a dull marriage. Christina S., for example, was docile during the eight married years before, at the age of thirty-two, she gave birth to her daughter, Cheryl.

"Before she was born, I didn't do anything by myself. I didn't go to the movies by myself, parties—if I wasn't with my husband, I wouldn't go. Then, when Cheryl was born, my husband and I had a choice of baby-sitting for each other or hiring baby-sitters. We found that hiring baby-sitters was an awful task because we could never be sure who was going to show up. The only chance he had to see Cheryl was on the weekends, and one weekend he said, 'Look, go out, go away, go to the museum. I don't care, just get out of the house. Go." Obediently, Christina left. She went alone to the movies for the first time in eight years.

On her next Saturday off, she went to the Museum of Modern Art for the afternoon. "It felt very strange," she recalls. "I realized I had been using my husband and then my child as a protection against the world. In the museum I felt closed in on myself, as if I couldn't let anyone else in, as if I wanted to pretend I were invisible." Every weekend during the first year of her child's life, she trekked off on some new adventure—a concert, dinner with friends, a walk through Central Park, a day trip canoeing or skiing.

As an extension of this metamorphosis, Christina took a job with a weekly newspaper, and her husband began to participate even more actively in child care. "I had a hard time letting go of that role as mother," Christina says, "but it did become clear to me very quickly that there is no such thing as 'maternal' instinct. Maternal instinct is simply experience—the experience of the person who is there most of the time with the child, figuring out what to do. Babies change so much from day to day that the person who spends the most time with them knows what the baby's cry means."

Like Vicky, Christina and her husband began to see each other in a new light—and at first they both felt threatened by the changes. Her husband started to object to her weekend hours away from home. "Suddenly, I could make decisions about my life that had nothing to do with him," she recalls. "Suddenly, he felt, I might be deciding that I could leave him one day." Christina started to object to her husband's style of "mothering." "I had to make a conscious effort not to interfere when he was with the baby. I would think to myself, 'If I were caring for her now, I would not be doing what he is doing.' I would force myself to walk out of the room to keep from sounding like an expert.

"Sometimes, when I couldn't control myself, we would have fights. I would say, 'I don't do it like that,' and he would get furious and say, '*I'm* taking care of her at this moment'—and he was right. It's easy to want to be the 'expert' if you're the one who's home, and if you are not doing anything else. It becomes hard to give up that little bit of expertise you have developed. But I finally realized that if he is doing something different, so what? The baby will survive. If he makes a mistake, the baby won't break.

"Now our relationship is much better, because we're on a more equal level. It's conceivable that I would have gone through this metamorphosis without having had Cheryl, but who knows? The fact is that having her was a catalyst to what happened. My husband and I are closer than we ever were, but in a more grown-up way. I used to have this romantic view of the two of us against the world—I don't feel that way anymore. Now we are two separate people—each of us enjoying the world, enjoying one another, enjoying our child."

FATHERING

More men are taking an active part in child care. Sometimes the reasons are practical: Both parents work days, and they agree it is only fair to share the child care at night. But some men, like Christina's husband, seek out the opportunity to be involved in child care as much as possible. Like older mothers, older fathers also feel more prepared to enjoy their children. "My husband likes the mothering even more than I do," says Deborah M. of Chicago.† "He could hold the baby endlessly whereas after a while I just want to be free."

In the Chicago suburb of Des Plaines, Bill McC., an Irish thirty-six-year-old schoolteacher, is bouncing his seven-month, twenty-pound son on his lap. He is more than just a proud papa: He took a one-year leave of absence for child care. "I took advantage of the inability of the city to discriminate based on sex—if mothers can get child-care leave, why can't fathers?" He laughs, and his son coos and drools down his father's shirt. Bill carefully wipes himself with the clean diaper he holds, an automatic gesture he has performed hundreds of times before.

Bill married for the first time when he was thirty-four. "I was having too good a time in my twenties to settle down," he says. "I was a drummer in a rock band, which didn't

† Deborah's story begins on page 143.

lend itself to marriage. I wasn't prepared to come home every night to the same face, the same house. I wanted to be free to pack up and leave, to say, 'I'm going, and I'll see you whenever I get back.' I just wasn't prepared to come home every single night and do the middle-class suburban two-cats-and-a-dog-and-a-baby-and-two-cars-in-the-garage routine—which is what I'm doing now, in spades." He does not, however, look the least bit discontent as he hefts the family cat onto his chair to join father and son.

Bill and his wife, Sandra, who works part time as a nurse, share child care almost equally, although Bill does slightly more. It is often he who gets up in the middle of the night to walk the baby, he who changes diapers, he who spends hours dangling toys in front of his child. "Of course," he says, "in an Irish family the number one son is everything—it's the rule of the first-born, the king's first son becomes king. I feel that way about my child, but I also feel a man misses out on a lot when he doesn't help rear his babies. At first I had a hard time explaining this to my father, who is a rough-and-tough Irish cop, but I think now he sees I won't turn soft.

"Part of the reason I have felt so close to my son from the beginning is because I saw him born. Delivery is an experience that any man who can tolerate the blood and gore should witness. It's not just the physical experience, and it's not just emotional either—it's on a higher level. It made me appreciate my wife's true beauty and her strength. It's like a binding together of all your experiences in life—obviously, I can't find the words to describe it.

"And I feel delighted that I have a chance to rear my son differently than I was reared. My father has two emotional stages. One is calm, and the other is explosive. He will be delighted, and then suddenly he will blow his top. Also, my father rarely took the time to explain anything to me. I'd say, 'Why?' and he would shout, 'Because I said so!' My father did give his children good values—we are all educated, we are all basically decent people. But he didn't give us his time and attention, he didn't show us his vulnerabilities. He never seemed real to me.

"Now I have a chance to give that to my son—to give him understanding when he feels frustrated, to give him my help when he is helpless, to show him I love him and respect him—and I think both he and I will be better people because of it. For the first time in my life, I am content doing something. I am content being a father. Content is not the word—I'm happy as a crock of shit," he says, and beams from ear to ear.

Richard F. is another father who is happy to take care of his baby. "I have a powerful nurturing instinct," says the thirty-three-year-old New York psychiatric social worker. "Unless I keep telling myself it's 'parental' and not 'maternal,' I could get hung up on the idea that the way I feel toward my child is too feminine, and my macho might feel threatened." He laughs at the idea, and surveys his living room, where his wife, Margie, is nursing their two-month-old son.

"When Margie got pregnant, I looked around at our environment with a new eye, as if I wanted to make sure there were no predators around, and that my child would be brought home to a safe space," he says. "I knew that the doctor next door to us had a zoo of a practice, and was treating junkies—so that became my first priority. I gathered together a group of people on the block and we formed the Christopher Street East Block Association—in

New York, you always need a group behind you to have any clout—and got the junkies out of our front yard. I started making a safe place inside the house as well. We got rid of all our furniture with sharp edges. Now there's not a sharp edge in our living room—and everything is carpeted. The living room is like a big play room for all of us."

When Margie had a cesarean delivery, Richard was by her side in the operating room. Then he took three weeks off from work, and took care of his wife and child. "I wanted to do it. It gave me pleasure. Even in the hospital, when the nurse came around to change the baby's diaper, since Margie was flat on her back, I said, 'Let me.' I remember dropping his drawers and taking off his diaper and saying to Margie, 'Have you seen his bottom yet?' The nurses thought we were crazy—but we both wanted to see every inch of our newborn baby. Then as I was changing his diaper I tickled his behind and he took a dump on my arm—changing diapers is a very complicated procedure—and Margie and I got hysterical. All the nurses laughed about the funny father in 309."

During his three weeks off, Richard cooked, shopped, laundered, "the things you do if you live alone, but you let the woman do when you're a couple. Somebody had to manage the household, to be sure there are clothes to wear, that Margie's eating well, that the food is attractive and well-presented. I drew up menus the way they did at the hospital, she would circle the choices at breakfast, and I would go buy what she wanted for lunch and dinner, and prepare it.

"I really didn't mind. We know a lot of other couples who are similar to us, where the husband is actively involved. So I know it's okay to be interested in my baby and nurturing to my wife sometimes. We went to a friend's house on Sunday—they just had twins—and he and I didn't go off to watch football. We sat there and talked about whether to use Pampers or diapers, about how it feels to be a father."

Richard waited until his thirties for fatherhood, in part because of his response to the social movements of the 1960s, and also because he feared copying his own father. "All of us were brainwashed in high school about zero population growth. I used to have nightmares that we would be shoulder-to-shoulder on this planet: I wanted to be a good citizen and not have any children. Then there was the ban-the-bomb movement: I didn't want to bring a child into a society where he's going to die of radiation. Then there was the Vietnam War: Why should I rear a child so he can get hauled off by his government to die in a rice paddy?

"I felt very adamant against having children, but it all went out the window when I met Margie. We started to face the fact that you miss a tremendous part of living if you go through life without having reproduced.

"From the beginning, I decided I didn't want to be excluded from any part of child rearing. My father always stepped back and let my mother take over the chores that involved babies. My mother wasn't methodically excluding him—she just took charge and he let it happen. He simply did not want to be bothered. His attitude was that he had worked hard all week and he wanted to be left alone. My friends' fathers would take them to Saturday matinee— mine would tell me to get lost. I feel that my son is absolutely entitled to my time. He's not *ours*—we're just here to help him along in whatever ways we can."

MAKING PEACE WITH THE CHILD IN YOU

The act of becoming a mother alters forever the relationship between a woman and her own mother. It tends
to be a watershed—a woman either moves closer to her
mother, or establishes more distance. Most of the women I
interviewed felt that they had begun to mellow toward
their mothers.

Ann S., the museum curator who had her baby at the
age of thirty-nine†† didn't even speak to her mother for five
years before the baby was born. "She's a very possessive,
domineering woman, and we just didn't get along," Ann
says. "But since my baby, we have a line of communication. Now I can listen to the idiotic stories she used
to tell me about my childhood. I used to be very intolerant
and say, 'I've heard that before, Mother. Yes, I know you
nursed me until I was eleven months old. Yes, I know I
could recite "'Twas the night before Christmas . . ." when
I was five.' Now I listen and, in fact, ask her questions.

"She has also been more kind and less judgmental toward me. When you give your parents a grandchild, something does come over them. It's like giving them a precious
gift, and they're grateful, and suddenly you're a very nice
person. If you did anything wrong earlier, you are forgiven.

"It's funny—when you have children, you completely
lose center-stage, and in a way it's a great relief. When we
go to visit my family, nobody even asks how I am—all the
attention is focused on the grandchild. I said to my hus-

†† See Chapter Two, "Menace of Menopause."

band, 'No wonder I didn't talk to my mother before—I had nothing to say. Now we have some neutral territory.' And maybe it's part of my generational function. I feel my mother likes me better because I've done what was expected and produced a grandchild."

Often, the newly acquired role of motherhood enables women to act with more compassion, to forgive their mothers for what they thought were unforgivable faults. "Until I had my own child, I saw my mother as an uptight lady, a super-mom personified, with an overwhelming need to control everybody," says Christina S.* "I never realized what her life must have been like. She had three kids within four years, and now I wonder how she did it and survived. Kids don't understand rules and regulations—especially two-year-olds, who have all the mobility of a child and no common sense. My mother was in her early twenties—still a child herself. The only way she knew how to handle her situation was to impose rigid controls. If I had had children when I was her age, I would have done the same. And if I was failing at that, as she was, I would have become depressed about failing, as she did." Christina sighs. "Even though she had a college degree, and felt more comfortable working outside the home, she did what she thought you were supposed to do if you were a woman: She got married and had kids. Now I see she did the best she could."

Sometimes the arrival of a grandchild precipitates a mother-daughter crisis that results in new closeness. Naomi M., who had her child at the age of forty-two, recalls what happened when her mother flew to San Francisco to be

* See page 125.

with her during her delivery. "My baby was born prematurely in a hospital that strongly emphasizes the mother's role in these cases because many mothers abandon their babies if they're in the incubator for long. So nurses and my husband and friends kept saying to me, 'Hold the baby, cuddle the baby'—they ignored my mother, and since I was so preoccupied with the baby I pretty much ignored her too.

"My mother stayed two weeks and when she was leaving she started to cry, saying that she felt rejected. It turned out that not only was she upset by the way I treated her, but also that she was reliving the whole experience of a baby *she* had had prematurely, who had died. So we formed quite a close bond that strengthened our relationship. And my just having the baby, nursing it, holding it, has let me know something of what her experience as my mother must have been . . ." Naomi stops suddenly, and wipes a tear from her cheek. "My relationship with my mother has always been very powerful and disturbing. She gets very anxious with me. She wants things to happen between us, in her own way. She is not the kind of person who can just *be* there and let things happen and go along with it. Now I understand more her possessiveness, and her guilt, and her need to feel loved by me."

Sometimes these confrontations with mothers, like those with husbands, are a necessary stage of maturation, a prerequisite for a woman's own ability to be a separate and mature adult, a wise and loving parent. This was true for Linnea D.,† the New York therapist who had her first child, a daughter, at the age of forty-two. Like Naomi's

† See "Individualists" in Chapter One.

mother, Linnea's mother flew to her daughter's side for the birthing. "At first I didn't realize her intentions. After the baby was born, she kept hanging around, and I kept waiting for her to fly home. Then I realized she was making long-range plans to stay. She had just decided she was going to live with us and raise my baby. She's a very willful woman," Linnea says.

"It led to a fundamental confrontation. I knew that for the first time in my life I was going to have to say 'no' to my mother. I had often rebelled against her before, but they were secret rebellions, which I handled by moving away from her, by not taking her into my confidence. I had never really said, 'no.'

"It killed me to have to tell her to leave. I kept hoping something would happen and she would leave on her own. Finally one day in the kitchen I said to her, 'Mom, all of us can't live together in the same house.' She said, 'Oh, if I had realized that, I wouldn't have come all the way from California to be with you.' I said, 'If you want to live near us, I'll get you an apartment nearby. But we just can't be here together.' Then she said, 'How can I tell my friends I live in the same city as my daughter and don't live with her? I never thought it would work out like this.'

"I said, 'But *nobody* wants to live with their children unless they can't afford to live on their own. You're very lucky. You're financially independent. You have lots of friends. You have children who love you.' She said, 'I have children who love me, but I don't have a home.' Then I felt just awful. But I wasn't going to budge. It took me forty-two years to do this. I just knew it would be like a suicide if I gave in. I held my ground, and two days later she left.

"And because I could break from my mother, I was also able to be wiser with my own daughter. One day, shortly after my mother left, I was combing my hair, preparing to feed my daughter, and as I was looking in the mirror it suddenly occurred to me—maybe my child won't like me! Maybe my daughter is one of those kids who's not going to like having a mother who's older than her girl friends' mothers, who's not going to like having a mother who's a professional person—you know, kids like different things. I realized that my daughter didn't have to like me just because I was her mother, and that I was going to have to work for her to like me as much as she would work for me to like her—that it wasn't just built in. The only thing built in was that we were going to be together."

Fifteen years later, Linnea asked her teen-age daughter whether it did, in fact, bother her that her mother was now a ripe old fifty-seven. "She said no, it didn't bother her at all, and in fact, I looked as young as some of her girl friends' mothers," Linnea says with a smile. "She said all her girl friends envied her—not for my age, but for my attitudes, which I guess are more flexible. She said the only thing she minded was that sometimes she would like me to do certain athletic things with her—like swimming. She's a very good athlete, very well co-ordinated.

"And I said, 'I wouldn't have done those things with you at any age. I don't like sports, I've never been good at them, and I'm especially afraid of water.'

"And as for me, I like being the older mother of a teen-age girl. I don't really feel my age—she keeps me young. Half the time I have to look in the mirror to realize I have wrinkles on my face. What should fifty-seven feel like? I don't know. I do know that if she had been born earlier, it wouldn't have worked out nearly as well. Because I waited, there has not been one second since her birth that I ever resented her or anything I had to do for her, any accommodation I had to make because she was in my life.

"If you are a person for whom age or chronology matters, then perhaps it matters when you have your children. But someplace along the line, I realized that age was only a number. It's true that at some point you are physically too old, past menopause, and you can't make babies anymore. But other than that, age really doesn't make any difference."

Every woman wants to be a *good* mother. Until now, every woman did not have the option of waiting until she was ready to try. As we judge our parents, so our daughters will judge us by our regrets as well as our successes. Our daughters and sons will mark, by their imitation or their rejection of us, the kind of mothers that we were. Will we be any better than those mothers who have children young? If age does bring maturity, then we just might have a chance.

"My daughter is a legacy," says thirty-three-year-old Ruby K., a small, blonde, energetic woman, who teaches sociology at Northwestern University. We meet late at night, in her office. "My mother was an exceptional parent, and I wanted to become a mother—not to be immortal or to pass on good genes—but just to have the experience of mothering, to be able to give a child the kind of love my mother gave me. My mother always took me seriously, even though she knew it would all pass. She was my friend, always able to say, 'I understand that this is really important now, even though I can tell you in six months it won't be. But that doesn't mean I denigrate it or think it's ridiculous.' She was fun, good com-

pany. She had a great sense of humor. Only later did I realize that humor was how she let out the pain.

Ruby's mother had married when she was twenty-one.
She had wanted to go to law school, but her husband for-
bade it—and she soon had two children to keep her busy.
"As her marriage got worse, her relationship with my
brother and me got better because it became the focus of her
achievement in life. When I was eighteen my father divorced her. She said she felt she had been fired from the only
job she had known for twenty-five years. She just did not
know how she was going to go back out in the world, get
work, and function at forty-five—begin again. It was 1965.
Betty Friedan's book *The Feminine Mystique* had just
come out, and she had read that. She had sought it out, and
found it extremely interesting, but it was too late for her.
She didn't have the strength to say, 'I'm going to live at
least another twenty-five years, and now I'm going to do all
those things that I didn't think of before.' There was no support in the culture for her to do that. One year after the
divorce, she killed herself.

"She was a very independent woman who had grown accustomed to a dependent state, and she couldn't switch
back. She couldn't handle the conflict. She couldn't go to a
psychiatrist—in our family you didn't take your problems
to other people. So she tried to solve them on her own.
After she died, I found twenty-five pages of legal paper on
which she had written, on both sides, the story of her life,
trying to figure out where her culpability lay.

"Despite what happened, she was a good influence on
me in a lot of ways. The qualities she instilled in me, I
would like to be able to instill in my daughter—independence and a sense of humor, a good laugh every day. Loy-

alty. Friendship—friends can get you through times no other things can get you through. Times of no money, no sex.

"But, I want my daughter, unlike my mother, to be free to choose the kind of life she wants. She can be a Rockette or a doctor or a suburban housewife. I don't care—as long as it's what *she* wants to do. And I know, as my mother didn't, that I cannot protect my child from everything. I know that to will happiness as a goal is a crock of shit, a piece of middle-class stupidity. You end up when you're seventeen or eighteen walking around wondering why, if all they want for you is happiness, happiness isn't showing up? Where is this happiness? Happiness is something you learn to make for yourself, as you mature and learn about love.

"In return, I would hope that my daughter can give to somebody else what I hope I give to her. I hope that, when she is able to look at my life, whether she emulates it or rejects it, that she will not deprive herself of sharing herself with somebody else. I don't expect her to do what I want. I expect trouble and sorrow and pleasure and joy. I certainly don't expect it to be simple, just because I have her life scenario worked out—what mother doesn't? I like to make plans, but I don't need to follow them—whether it's a life plan or a plan for the evening. If it gets screwed up in the middle and another plan shows up, that's okay too. I certainly take raising her seriously, but I don't want to spoil the fun and spontaneity by taking it too seriously. I think an awful lot of people don't have much fun with their children because it's all bound up in duty and morality and pleasing your husband and pleasing your grandparents."

Ruby sighs and looks thoughtfully at the framed picture of her daughter on her desk. "The most fascinating thing about this motherhood bit is that I find I despise maintaining my daughter's life support system, and yet I love being a mother. I hate doing three laundries a week. I hate schlepping my brains out on public transportation. I've turned into a packhorse. I hate all of that stuff. And yet, it has nothing to do with how I feel about her—I am a very impatient person, a short-tempered person, a very hyper person, and yet I leave all that behind when I deal with her. Then I have patience, and am always in a good mood—whether it's 6 A.M. or midnight. That's why I loved breast feeding so much. It was a way of slowing me down, of stopping the nervous energy I live on. It gave me periods every day to get used to the baby, to get to know her, times when I didn't have to be Miss Efficiency because I could not do anything except hold and feed the baby.

"Because my mother died young, I do understand death is not just an abstract piece of business. I understand that you really can get left without somebody you want to see tomorrow, but you're not going to get to them in time. I hope I live to see my daughter grow up. But I don't spend a lot of time thinking about it. I only think about mortality in airplanes. I took my first vacation without Rebecca when she was eighteen months old. When I flew to New York, I thought, 'Suppose I get into the air and . . .' I told my friend Patricia, who is taking care of her, 'Please, if I die in the air, let Rebecca know how much I wanted her.' It's a way of spitting into the wind."

Chapter Five

Celebrating Yourself—Five Women Speak in Praise of Motherhood

----- ◆ -----

"A pride came out in myself that I had never experienced in my whole life."

Paula A.

I realized in the course of my interviews that, while these women's experiences can be dissected into convenient and helpful patterns with which we can all identify, the pacing of their lives is more random and trickier to analyze. The timing of critical events, of conscious decisions, of subconscious turning points is equally important for a woman's option of motherhood, and yet cannot be dissembled to fit the chapters of a book.

The ebb and flow of each woman's life is different—some women marry young, divorce, then remarry and have children; some women wait to marry; some women stay married to the same man for a decade before beginning a family; some women never marry. And because each of our lives is in flux, I saw many of these women's attitudes and experiences change even during the year I was in touch with them while preparing my manuscript. While transcribing the tapes of our conversations, I became aware that in many cases the celluloid was already relaying history rather than current events.

And I also realized, listening again and again to these tapes, that a woman who says she waited to have children because of her career, for example, is usually shortchanging other underlying factors of her decision. On the surface, it may be true that her career came first. But below the surface there are additional social and psychological factors that prompted her to wait. The order in which and the reasons for which women change jobs, change locations, change men, and change their minds about motherhood, are as important as the major patterns they represent.

Let us take a look, then, at five of these women, who can serve as role models for many of the rest of us. Some are married, some are divorced, and some are single (reflecting a small but growing number of women who have children alone); some always wanted children and some thought they never did; some enjoyed childbirth as the peak experience of their lives, and others recall it with fear; some feel the presence of a child has weakened their relationships with their husbands, others feel new vigor and strength in the relationship; some enjoy staying home after working in an office for so many years, others find that their careers are enhanced and enriched by motherhood. Some of these women feel guilty about over-identification with their careers; others feel guilty about enjoying motherhood so much.

All feel the presence of a child has changed their image of themselves for the better and has enriched their lives. All are intelligent, articulate, and open about their feelings.

But their major common denominator is that they are women in their thirties who chose to wait to give birth, who are glad they waited, and who are willing to share their most personal thoughts about their work, their children, and the fathers of their children with other women who also wait.

DEBORAH

"The experience of mothering has made me kinder. It stretches you: Whatever you are to start with, you become more, you absorb more, you learn more, you share more . . . All your capacities are tested."

Deborah M., a native of Chicago, is thirty-seven years old. She had her first child at the age of thirty-four, and is now four months pregnant with her second child. When we meet, Deborah is in her kitchen fixing dinner. She is wearing a gingham dress and has a bow in her hair. She is both barefoot and pregnant, a state she never thought she would find herself in, much less let herself enjoy. After settling her son in front of the television set, she escorts me to the bedroom and closes the door so we can be undisturbed. As she talks, she rocks slowly back and forth in a white wicker chair.

Deborah married when she was twenty, and then waited fourteen years to have a baby. One of the reasons she waited was because she switched careers in her twenties—from teaching to writing. She began reaching her new career goals before making the decision to have a baby. Deborah found that having a child later in life is an exhilarating experience, so much so that she eagerly awaits the arrival of her second child.

"My husband and I have known each other for nineteen years, and we love each other dearly. But neither of us really wanted children during our twenties. Both of us need a lot of privacy. We enjoy being by ourselves, not in groups. When we take a vacation, we usually don't spend all our time with each other. We like to be alone as well as together. The idea of throwing a baby into this terrified me. I was protecting that little piece of myself that hadn't been encroached upon already by family, friends, husband. I also felt I couldn't do everything. I had to make a choice between doing something for myself or having a baby. I felt I could get what I wanted, or I could just get old.

"To take care of a very young child, you must give yourself up for periods of time. Their demands come first, and it is only because they are children and you're an adult— that's what it means to mother someone. I knew that, and I didn't want it, at least not in my twenties. Having a child was something my husband and I envisioned for the future —there always seemed to be a lot of time. I was also waiting to be smitten by this overpowering desire to give birth, and that feeling never came. It turned out that I decided to have a baby only when I was finally doing what I really wanted to do, which was to write a novel. For years I had been saying, 'I want to write, I want to write,' and I finally arranged it so I could. I quit my teaching job, I had a typewriter, paper, solitude—and as I was finishing the novel and feeling very good about it I knew that this would be a good time for me to get pregnant.

"It was no accident, and it was not serendipity. We had money, and money helps oil things, but even without money the advantage of having a child later is that you can set up your life first. I was very conscious of wanting to earn my master's degree first, which I did. Of getting teaching experience first, which I did. Of writing a novel first, which I did. And then I made the decision: I am going to work it out so I can fit in a baby, too. I felt: I *can* do it!

"It was an exhilarating feeling, after being afraid to have children all those years. At last I had enough confidence in myself to go ahead, to create a child, to open up my life to someone new. And it helped to know my husband was making enough money to supplement mine so that I didn't have to be a full-time mother. I could write, even though my writing might not earn much money at first. That made an enormous difference to me. I know I would not be a good full-time mother. But I also know I am an excellent part-time mother. I think the super-mother image demanded of women in this country is awful, and just impossible to live up to if you want to retain your own identity too.

"Ironically, there is also social pressure put on you to separate from your child. I nursed Joshua for six months, and people who should have known better were saying, 'He's going to be too dependent.' I thought, 'Dependent! This child is hot out of the womb, where he was totally dependent!' In fact, he is now almost four, and is mature for his age. Last night I received a report on him from his school, and one of the things the report said was, 'He is a child who is very comfortable with himself and with other people.' That made me feel great. I feel very good about what I've done for my child.

"If I had had him ten years earlier, I know he would have been different, because I would have treated him

badly and with less patience. I know I would have resented
him. Instead, my husband and I used our twenties to learn
about life, to travel around the world. Before I got pregnant we went on a big trip to Africa—we sort of knew we
were getting closer to the baby thing, and this was a last
fling for us—and I thought it would cure my appetite for
traveling. It didn't, of course. After Joshua was born, I
couldn't bear my itchy feet, and when he was one year old
we went to the Yucatan. We took Joshua with us because
until he understood the concept of "tomorrow," we never
even left him overnight at my mother's. Just because he
was small doesn't mean he can't feel as much as a big person. I have this theory that people think that just because
children are short, they have short emotions. If my husband didn't come home for a day or a week without telling
me where he was, it would terrify me, and I'm an adult.

"So we took Joshua with us to the Yucatan, and on the
trip he got an earache and a fever and I thought to myself,
'You bitch. You want to go see some barren empty land,
where there is no doctor or medical aid, and because of you
the kid is going to go deaf.' That was the last time we took
him to an exotic place. But I do love to travel. I postponed
this decision to have a second baby because I wanted one
more dynamite trip. I dragged my husband and child off to
France for a month and we rented a house on the Riviera—
it was a big blow-out, a fantasy that finally came true. It
was our first real family vacation. Then I came home and
got pregnant in a week. When I hear people talking about
China and Cuba, I am raring to go. I can't do it now,
of course, but I will do it eventually. None of that has
changed; my life hasn't stopped. In fact, it has expanded.

"Having a baby changes your perspective so much—so

very much. Sure, I still get bored being around children for great lengths of time. It's often a pleasure to be with Joshua, but on the other hand I would often rather be reading than sitting on the floor playing with blocks. But I am much more tolerant of people now. Joshua has made me see there are other people in the world besides adults, and their lives are very important and valuable and beautiful. I never used to look at little children on the street; they were meaningless. After Joshua was born, I couldn't believe I had overlooked such an interesting, exciting world. The experience of mothering has made me kinder. It stretches you: Whatever you are to start with, you become more, you absorb more, you learn more, you share more, you do more, you love more. All your capacities are tested.

"I used to feel that my giving birth would be my death. I'm overdramatizing it, but that's how strong the feeling was. Now I realize that mature and sophisticated people can switch roles in their lives. They are many things—children, parents, wives, lovers, teachers, writers—they can handle complex situations, and that is what is meant by maturity. Now it amazes me to remember that until I had Joshua I was never even comfortable around babies. They were foreign, threatening, and I stayed away from people who had them. I would get angry when children interrupted my conversations. If somebody said, 'Here's the baby. Do you want to hold the baby?' I would get very embarrassed. I wouldn't know how to hold it, and when the baby started to cry I would think, 'Something is wrong with me.'

"I always assumed there was a certified *way* to be with a baby, and I always assumed other people knew about it because I certainly didn't. The first time I took Joshua out in the carriage I was blushing and giggling all the way down the street because I thought it was such an archetypical image, and I felt like an imposter. *Me* pushing a carriage! It was so weird. I thought, 'Now I'm going to reach Lincoln Park and all the other mothers are going to know how dumb I am. Then I began to realize that no one knew—every woman was doing what was comfortable for her and the baby, and every baby's different! I learned to love other women as a result of that experience. There are some frightening, isolating moments when you have a new baby, and there's no one else in the world besides another mother who wants to listen to your fears.

"When Joshua was four days old, for instance, his toes started to turn yellow. When babies are born, they sometimes get a little jaundice, it's nothing serious, but I had never heard of yellow toes. I was leafing through Dr. Spock under Y for Yellow and T for Toes—I never thought of looking under J for Jaundice. And as I am leafing through the book I am thinking, 'My baby is turning yellow.' I called my doctor, who was out of the office, and then I called a friend. I said, 'Help. His feet are yellowing.' She explained what was happening, and finally we did get it all straightened out. But in the beginning it seemed I could never get it all together. In the morning I would be bumping around in my terry-cloth robe with the flaps down—I was nursing—and I would be tired from interrupted sleep, and I never seemed to be able to get to the park with Joshua until about 3 P.M. The good mothers came in the morning. I would see them strolling up State Street, going home, and I would be struggling down the block with this child with his bonnet askew and the good mothers would say, 'Gee, the sun's setting.' There was a whole crew of us inefficient mothers gathered in Lincoln Park at night. We called ourselves the night owls, and our children just sort of got used to the dark. I'm still not the world's most confident mother, but now it doesn't bother me because I know my heart is in the right place even if I sometimes feel like a klutz.

"But as much as I enjoy Joshua, at my core I feel my main identity is as a writer. I am, of course, neither just a writer, nor a mother, nor a wife—I am none of those things without the other. I identify totally with my work. I think men, too, identify entirely with work—and I have some of that same syndrome. I think of it as a flaw; I have trouble just relaxing and indulging. I tend to drive myself. I'm very uncomfortable just *being*. I have to think: 'What have I achieved today?' In fact, when I was pregnant, I had to finish my novel before I gave birth. I thought, 'God only knows what's going to happen afterward, I must finish this' —and I did finish it. I was in my ninth month and in labor when I staggered red-eyed into my agent's office and threw the manuscript at her—and then I went to the hospital.

"I had this fantasy—that if only I could prove to the world that I was a writer, that I was someone, then I could relax and be a mother. Otherwise I was shit. Of course, it didn't work out that way. The novel was rejected, I was a mother, and I wasn't shit. I rewrote the novel four times and never did sell it. I spent four-and-a-half years on it. After I had the baby, I took six months off, and then started writing again. I worked five days a week all day in my house. A housekeeper came in at 9 A.M. and I went to my desk. But when Joshua got to be two, he started to run in and out of my room. If I locked the door he would bang on it and cry, and it made me so nervous I got nothing done.

"I finally rented the mimeograph room of a political candidate's office for fifty dollars a month, and that was very significant because it meant that for the first time I was really treating myself as a serious writer. I had always feared I would be considered a dilettante, that people would say, 'Oh yes, everyone is writing feminist novels this year,' or, 'Yes, I often sit down and write when the weather is nice.' My writing is going much better, and I am actually beginning to sell some of my short stories. But my mother still says, 'Let's have lunch since you're not working.'

"I'm very unpleasant when I'm not working well, and my husband will do anything to be supportive. I don't know how much has to do with his feminism, and how much with his sense of survival. If I'm unhappy, I do a good job of making him unhappy as well. And with a child it is especially important to keep your problems in perspective. My husband and I have a very solid relationship, but we still have our problems. Having a baby put a strain on us: we can't cuddle and baby each other—the baby comes first. My husband was also jealous at first of the baby. It *is* a real love affair between mother and child, especially if you're nursing. I felt a strong poignant yearning for my child. The second my milk came in, the baby would start to cry, even if we had both been asleep. How can anyone, including my husband, compete with that?

"We worked that out, and in the last two months we've also been in therapy together to try and sort out our own personal problems from our basic day-to-day problems of living together. I wanted to go into therapy because I thought, 'I'd better figure out how I am going to have a

child and be comfortable with myself at the same time—
otherwise it's not going to work.' The therapy has been a
great success, and I am a proponent of good serious therapy if you have the money and the time. In fact, I don't
understand how people stay married without going into
therapy at some point. By the age of eighteen months, each
of us has really been formed. Then we go through life with
this veil over our eyes, often shadow-boxing with our past
through the person we're living with. It is sometimes hard
to distinguish what makes us angry from the past, and
what makes us angry in the present.

"I have a feeling psychotherapy is like the germ theory
when it first came out: Very few people believed in the
germ theory, and it took years to gain recognition. The idea
that there were invisible things called germs must have
seemed ridiculous, and it took a long time to get people to
wash their hands. In the same way, most people have no
idea of the ripples that affect your life because of problems
you had long ago. And these problems become cyclical
through your children if you don't deal with them.
Through therapy I now understand what motivates me,
why I feel certain things—even why I chose my husband. I
understand my husband better, and we are closer than ever
because of it. I am also more free to rear Joshua in the way
that is healthiest, instead of ways that are just a result of
my own habit and training.

"I have some very negative things to say about my parents, but I try not to lay them on my child. Everyone goes
through that. My aim is to let him be who he is, let him experience his whole range of emotions. I was reared to be a
very good girl—I am still biting my nails because of it. It
takes a lot of energy to be good. I'm trying now to be bad,

but it's very hard to undo being good—because that was
the only kind of child my parents could cope with. I have
seen Joshua get angry with my mother and punch her, and
my mother would laugh and hug him and say, 'He's just
playing'—which would frustrate him all the more because
she was completely denying his right to be angry. Unlike
my mother, my reaction is, 'You can't hit me because that
makes *me* angry. I know you're angry but go hit the pillow
or something'—at least I acknowledge his feelings.

Now I am both excited by and anxious about this new
baby. When we first had Joshua, my husband wanted six
more. He was ecstatic. I feel so great about Joshua, I am getting such an ego boost from him that I am certainly willing
to invest in a child one more time—although six seems a
bit much. This pregnancy is different from the first one.
The first time I was pregnant, I never focused on the baby,
just on my body. I was very blasé. In my eighth month of
pregnancy we went off to the empty side of Crete, riding
around in a jeep in the middle of nowhere—because I felt
terrific. Now I realize there's really a person inside, and that
person's life is being affected by everything I do, and I didn't
know that before. I don't know how I will juggle two children and work. But I didn't know how I would juggle *one*
child and work. I just did it, that's all. All I do know is
that once I had a child, I felt a deeper ability to love. I felt
enlarged by it, and I want that to happen again.

FRAN

*"By the age of thirty-one I was lucky enough to get on
top of things—to establish my priorities and begin to*

reach my goals—and then I had my child. By waiting, I
alleviated a lot of anxiety and eliminated a lot of regret."

Fran T. lives in a large plant-filled house in Woodstock, New York. She is a lawyer and a photographer, and was thirty-two years old when she gave birth to her daughter, Felicia, who is now five. One year after giving birth, Fran presented and won her first argument before the United States Supreme Court. When I arrive at Fran's home, she and her daughter are in the kitchen baking cookies. Her husband, Bill, is in the basement building a wall unit for the stereo. He takes over the cookie project while Fran invites me upstairs to her den. Hanging on the stairwell wall are photos of her mother arranged in sequence from birth to death. It is part of a one-woman show that Fran exhibited recently in a New York gallery. As we sit down on the cushion-strewn floor, Fran tells me she is two months pregnant with her second child. She is now thirty-seven years old.

Unlike Deborah, who switched careers in her twenties, Fran has nurtured a profitable law career. While Deborah married young and then waited fourteen years to have a baby, Fran married late and had her first child only two years after the wedding. But both women shared one thing in common: an anxiety about whether they could be good mothers.

"I had never been alone in a house with a child until I suddenly had Felicia. I had no experience of children. I had no siblings. I never baby-sat. Because of that, I never romanticized what might happen. I never thought it would be easier than it was. If anything, I had a clear intellectual understanding of what would be *hard* about it, and no sense of the ways in which it would be wonderful. My ignorance was a nice protection because motherhood turned out to be a pleasant surprise instead of a disappointment.

"When Bill and I were first married, I made a lot of speeches about how I wasn't the least bit interested in children. We talked about it intermittently, but I was incredibly pressed for time—I was a lawyer three days a week and a photographer four days a week—and I had no intention of having a baby. I didn't see how I could add children to an already complicated life.

"But after two years of marriage, I turned thirty, and I found myself thinking about being pregnant. In fact, I thought about it all the time. If I saw a pregnant woman, my eyes would follow her across the street, into a shop—I felt curiosity, interest, maybe envy. I kept saying, 'I'm too busy,' but the thought just wouldn't go away. I hate the idea of there being a biological imperative, but I finally began to accept that on some level I did want to have children, and if I wanted to do it, then it was time to get started. And, in the back of my head, I also felt that if I decided I *never* wanted children it would become a real problem between my husband and me.

"Also, our lives were pretty much in order for the first time. Bill had a teaching job he really liked; he felt settled and satisfied. I had worked out a good balance between law and photography. Then I watched a television series on Leonardo da Vinci, and I was impressed by Da Vinci's insatiable curiosity, his desire to know everything and experience everything possible. I wanted to taste life too, and I began to think it would be foolish for me to miss the fundamental female experience of giving birth, and motherhood. The idea of having a baby became more attractive than ever. I finally decided I wanted to do it because I couldn't decide not to do it. I decided to become ambivalent with children instead of without them.

"But I kept asking myself, 'Why am I doing this?' And it occurred to me that my mother had always given me the impression that I was a great source of pleasure to her on some inarticulate level. She had always acted as if I had been an enriching addition to her life, rather than a handicap. My mother was also a lawyer and a judge, and in her day was a very powerful and successful politician. She was thirty-five when she married, and forty when I was born. She had several miscarriages before she had me, and she gave birth to me at the height of her professional power. I didn't threaten her success—I augmented it.

"She was a fantastic role model. She taught me that I can do anything in the entire universe. Because of her, I have none of those traditional doubts about whether you can have a career and children. She did it. She hired a housekeeper and a full-time baby-sitter. She could afford it, it's what she wanted to do, and she did it. Yet, even though both my parents were 'out' all the time—they worked days, and went to political dinners most nights—I felt incredibly loved, very sheltered, very protected, very desired. My mother and I were very close. We had a wonderful relationship. She was very open-minded and patient, very good at explaining things to me, very generous in showing that she loved me.

"My husband and I can't afford and didn't really want full-time child care. We wanted to be with our daughter as much as possible while she was small, and we both have flexible careers that allow us to spend time at home during some weekdays. So we worked out the following schedule:

From the time Felicia was born until she was two-and-a-half, we both worked three days a week. During those three days, I went to my law office and he went to school, and a baby-sitter came to the house. The other four days a week we stayed home and split up the child-care time between us. We would get up in the morning, have breakfast together, and then count the number of hours between breakfast and dinner. We would then divide the hours in half: half of them, I could use to do my photography or anything else I wanted, while Bill took care of Felicia—and then vice versa. It worked out very well.

"Then, after two-and-a-half years, Bill got a full-time job for the first time since she was born. So we had the baby-sitter come four days a week. I continued to work in my law office three days a week as before, and then I spent the fourth day at home doing photography while the baby-sitter was there. On the fifth day, I took care of Felicia, and then on weekends Bill and I split the child care as before.

"Now that she is older we don't need such a formal split. But when she was tiny, the person taking care of her couldn't really do any work for long concentrated periods of time, so it was more important to divide responsibility. Dividing up the time like that involved real mental discipline, because it means you can't just do whatever you would instinctively want to do at any given moment, but it was effective.

Obviously, having a child has made Bill and me much more interdependent. Now each of us always knows where the other one is, and when the other one is coming home. I invited a friend who has no children to dinner the other day, and she said, 'I would love to come if I can find out where my husband is, and if he'll be home on time to come.' That kind of independence would drive us both crazy at this stage. And logistics is also a factor in sex now. With a child in the house you have less spontaneous sex because you can't do it in the middle of the morning when the child's around. It doesn't mean our sex life has decreased; it just means we have to time it more deliberately. Our lives are more home-centered now, and we rarely go out. But we have always stayed home a lot, even before we had a child.

"Partially as a result of our clear understanding about child care, our marriage has been a happy and successful one. Having a child didn't strain it in any basic way because each of our lives changed in equal proportion. We still have a lot of hassles about the nitty-gritty details of life, but we're good at coping with them as they come up. We never go to bed angry with each other, and we've never had a fight that extended past that immediate hour. The nitty-gritty problems of today are the same problems we were having seven years ago. Bill is usually accusing me of not cleaning the kitchen well enough when it was my turn to clean the kitchen—an accusation that is usually justified. And we still take turns putting Felicia to bed—the one not putting her to bed clears the table. Because my mother was a professional woman, I grew up thinking those domestic things were beneath me. I entered my marriage acting very much like a spoiled man—and you can see the evidence of it here. I'm still not the world's greatest housekeeper. But I don't think clean sinks are always a true and valid sign of mother love.

"I have the feeling that one of the reasons I feel so happy being a mother is because I have a lot of basic gut-level ego strength. I may have doubts about whether I can be the best lawyer or the best photographer or the best mother, but I never have any doubts about whether I am a worthwhile person. I know that may sound silly, but I have a basic self-pride that I find lacking in a lot of women. It comes from having parents who feel that same kind of pride in themselves, and if I can instill that in my children, that is the most important way I can affirm myself. It isn't something you *do* for your child, it's something you are. My parents had no doubts, no anxiety about their own ability to cope with the world, and they passed that attitude on to me. That is a virtue of having older parents, and of being an older mother.

"To be a mother and a career woman takes a tremendous amount of energy and discipline and flexibility. You have to be young enough to have that energy, but mature enough to have that discipline and flexibility. I think it is very important for a woman to be established in her career —if she wants a career—before she has children. Otherwise, it is too tempting to fall into that trap where the woman stays home because she is earning less or her position is lower than her husband's. If you already have an ongoing career, then there isn't any reason to think about giving it up completely.

"The only mothers I know who have regrets about timing and organization are those who did stop what they were doing and subsequently regretted it. And they tend to be the women who had children young. When you're twenty-one, how can you not have doubts about your priorities? Everyone has doubts at twenty-one. But by the age of thirty-one I was lucky enough to get on top of things —to establish my priorities and begin to reach my goals— and *then* I had my child. By waiting, I alleviated a lot of anxiety and eliminated a lot of regret. I didn't, at twenty-one, feel I was going to wait to have children until I was on top of things—it wasn't until I was on top of things that I *wanted* to have children.

"Sure, there are still days when I sit in my photography studio and think, 'What is all this crap I produce and call art?' and I think maybe I should go downstairs and wash the dishes instead. In looking back at the last five years, I know that I have spent less time on my work than I would have spent if I hadn't had a child. Yet I am more disciplined than I was before. I have less free time, so I use all my time very well. I am very ambitious, and my photography career, which interests me more than law, is progressing. So I have no bad feelings about children slowing me down. I would like to be a financially successful and well-received photographer, and obviously, I'm not there yet. But I'm still young enough to hope for that, and there's no reason to think that someday I can't have it.

"I had expected a child to deflect me from my work, but I hadn't expected a child to be such an enormous amount of fun. That's one reason why I've decided to do it again. For the first three years after Felicia was born, I swore I would never have another baby. I had natural childbirth by the skin of my teeth—she was a breech baby, and it was very hard. I was glad to have done it naturally, but I was in labor fourteen hours. When I finished giving birth, I thought only with pity—real gut pity—of women who were still pregnant and were going to have to deliver their babies. It was the most painful, the most intense, as well as the most exciting experience of my life. But then an extraordinary biological phenomenon occurred: Within four hours after delivery, the visceral memory of that pain was

gone. It is truly a marvelous invention of nature, like a biological erasing mechanism for the perpetuation of the species.

"Then, when Felicia was three, and suddenly much easier to take care of, I started to feel popcorny again—like I
wanted more. Every once in a while the idea of another
child would creep into my head unbidden, and I would
slap myself and proceed with what I had been doing
and say, 'Hey, pull yourself together.' I was amazed and
stupefied that the idea attracted me again. When she was
first born, I didn't feel that automatic overwhelming
mother love for her that I hear some women talk about. It
grew as I got to know her. She just got more seductive as
she got older. Once she could do things with me, she
seemed like more fun. The idea of never having another
four-year-old was depressing!

"And my decision was spurred by a medical consid-
eration. My doctor told me I had fibroid tumors, and while
he said it was nothing to worry about, he also said I
couldn't use the IUD because of it, or take the pill. I
started using a diaphragm again, and Bill kept feeling it,
and it interfered with sex. So I went back to the doctor
and he said, 'Well, you can either have a baby or have your
tubes tied.' I certainly didn't want to shut off my option of
having more children, so Bill and I talked about it and decided it might be fun to have another kid, and if we're
going to do it, we might as well do it now. I have done everything I wanted to do despite having one child, so I
didn't agonize over the decision to have another. I went
home from the doctor, talked with Bill, and got pregnant
that night.

"I have no illusions about how difficult it will be, but

now I also realize how wonderful it will be. My decision to have children has brought me closer to realizing Da Vinci's dreams of experiencing all of life to the fullest. It takes work to do that, it takes lots of love, it takes courage, it takes the ability to absorb frustration and set-backs, it takes openness to receive the boundless, total love a child can give you, it takes a strong ego and a sense of humor. My child brought out all of that in me, and for that alone I will always cherish her presence in my life."

PAULA

"It's very difficult to live in a society that's so self-centered, so empty. Everything you do is for yourself. With a child, it's different—you're still doing it for yourself, but it bears a different kind of fruit. I watch a person growing —growing up. She gives me back something that nothing else, no one else, can give me."

Paula A., a fashion designer, lives in an elegant Soho loft in Manhattan. She is thirty-seven years old, and she had her child when she was thirty-three. In many ways, Paula is very different from Fran: Fran waited until she was twenty-eight to marry, Paula married young and divorced quickly; Fran was wary of small children, Paula has always loved them; Fran has a thoughtful loving husband, Paula is rearing her child alone. Yet they have this in common: Although their life-styles have been very different, neither of them felt ready until their mid-thirties to have a child. They have traveled very separate routes, yet today both are happy they waited for motherhood.

As with Deborah, I visit Paula at dinner time—her only free hour of the day. She answers the door, a bubbly cheerful woman dressed in blue jeans and a black turtleneck sweater. Her boy friend and her new live-in maid, a student from France, are in the kitchen preparing the meal. Paula brings cheese and crackers to the living room, and curls up on the couch. Her daughter is playing a quiet card game at the far end of the room with her cousin, who is visiting for the day.

"I moved into this loft, had interior walls built, had it decorated, while I was pregnant. I lived in a mess of saw-dust, but I wanted it ready for my baby, so I could have her and stay home and work—so that I could have it all. It has worked out fantastically well. I knew when I got pregnant that it could be difficult having and rearing a child by myself. I would have preferred to be with a man, and I was living with her father at the time she was conceived. I loved him, but we had a very stormy relationship. I knew it might not last, so when I found out I was pregnant, I had to make a choice: Get an abortion, or have the child.

"I thought it over. I figure that when you break up with someone it takes you a year before you really recover from it enough to allow yourself to get involved seriously again. Then it takes another year of being with somebody before you're in a position to decide whether you want to have a child together. Then it takes about another year to get pregnant and deliver a baby. That was three years. I was thirty-two at the time, and I didn't want to wait three more years. So I said, 'Now or never.' Her father was very bright, attractive, healthy—and those were considerations. I knew the genes were good. And during the first few months of pregnancy I had a fantasy that he and I could work it out. He was very ambivalent about me, about the baby—one weekend he would be nice, and then I wouldn't hear from him for weeks. He would be inconsiderate, rude —and then kind. I felt like a yo-yo.

"Then something happened that was a turning point in my life. One day it hit me: I would have to explain my behavior to this child I was creating, and if I allowed somebody to treat me in a disrespectful manner, how could I justify myself to this unborn child? How could I say, 'Well, I let myself be abused.' A pride came out in myself that I had never experienced in my whole life. It was an incredible change, and I became in many ways a new person —my own person. I realized I could live according to the precepts I had established over the years for myself. I realized that I wanted to be for my child what I felt I *should* be for myself. And that day, when I had that insight, was the last time I ever spoke to her father.

"Of course, when you decide to have a child on your own, the questions you ask yourself are a hundred times more intense than the questions a married couple would ask. As a single woman I had to question myself again and again: 'Do I want this child? Can I face this? Am I willing to give up my life-style, my freedom? Am I willing to face criticism from my family and friends?' I was soul-searching constantly. And each time a friend challenged me, I would start at square one and go through every question again. The answer always came up, 'Yes.' I felt that I shouldn't have to go through life without experiencing such a primitive part of myself, such a wonderful part, simply because I wasn't married—because society might frown on me. It's not the first time I've felt frowned upon. I was married at the age of seventeen and divorced at the ripe old age of twenty-two. I was the only divorced person I knew in the whole world—that was 1958. I was so mortified about it that I used to lie and say I was unmarried, because I thought if people knew I was a divorcée they would think I was a whore—everyone knew that divorced girls screwed, and in those days no girls were supposed to screw.

"Despite my unmarried status, I am so delighted I decided to go ahead. The moment of her delivery was the greatest moment of my life. I had natural childbirth and saw her born, and the minute I saw her, I loved her. Right now I am going through some crises in my business, and it convinces me more and more that having her was the best thing I ever did in my life, that she is my greatest accomplishment. She has given me staying power. There are things I put up with in business that I wouldn't have put up with before. She gives me a reason to go on with things. In our society, a lot of people have a low tolerance level for stress: When the situation becomes difficult, they leave. They walk away. I am a fighter, and having a child makes it that much more important for me to fight for something. It's very difficult to live in a society that is so self-centered, so empty. Everything you do is for yourself. With a child, it's different—you're still doing it for yourself, but it bears a different kind of fruit. I watch a person growing—growing up. She gives me back something that nothing else, no one else, can give me.

"Sure, there are compromises and sacrifices. There is no parent in the world who doesn't give up something for his or her child. If you go out to eat with a friend, you will give up your favorite restaurant to eat in her favorite restaurant. How can you not give up things for someone you care about? But that doesn't mean it's negative. Sometimes on a Sunday I would like to sleep, or just be quiet, and I can't do that anymore. Then I remember all the Sundays of despair, when I was alone. Sundays for single people can be awful. Sundays now are such fun. We stay in bed and read the paper together, or we bake something, or we go to a puppet show. I have a family now. I gave up, and I received.

"If I had had a child at twenty—how would I have known this? I look at young mothers, and they must be so bitter sometimes. There is a whole world out there, and they haven't been in it, and here is this child clinging to them, pulling on them—they must resent it. An older mother resents it a lot less. There has not been one single occasion where I have sat in my house and wanted to go out—to a party, to an opening, to a romance. I have already been through all that. So what if I go to a party and meet Prince Charming? I've met my Prince Charming, several times. I've been with the Beautiful People. I've worn the finest clothes. I've dined in the best places and danced until dawn. I loved doing it, and now I love doing this.

"The only magic thing you need is money. She is already taking horseback riding lessons at the age of four. And when she was eighteen months old I put her in a nursery school. If somebody had told me before she was born that I would do that, I would have said, 'How dare you even imply that I would do such an awful thing?' But she was with her nurse in this big house with all her toys, and I suddenly realized that if I didn't get her near other kids she would grow up to be a zombie. She was living in a vacuum. She never saw anybody her own size. Now she is with ten other kids, and the change in her is unbelievable. She does need other children around; she is much happier.

"It makes me feel very proud to give her what other couples don't give their kids. And it makes me frightened if I feel that what I give her is in jeopardy. One day recently I thought I was going to lose my business, and I took a walk through Central Park to calm down. I was severely depressed and in a panic. There in the park I saw all these families who were not well off—they were probably making $8,000 a year, and they had four or five kids and the kids had on shoes and clean clothes. And I realized no matter what happens, I can make it.

"The only difficult part of having her alone, without a man around, was during the pregnancy. The changes in my body astonished me and frightened me and disarmed me. I couldn't see my feet, and I thought I would never be thin again. Pregnancy heightens sexuality and asexuality at the same time. You're involved completely with creation, and yet you feel as sexy as an elephant. Without someone around who could reinforce my concept of myself as a sexually desirable person, I found it difficult.

"I needed some outside support, so I joined a group for pregnant women. But I soon learned that all the others in the group were welfare mothers. Their life-style was so far removed from mine, I wondered how I would feel. I went to the first meeting and I said, 'The great fantasy of my life was to get married and go through pregnancy with a husband at my side. And every evening he would pat my stomach and smile with pleasure about 'us having this baby.' Then we would go to the delivery room together and he would hold my hand and stroke my forehead and tell me how beautiful I am during the entire delivery.

"The women listened to me and then said, 'What? Are you kidding?' One woman said, 'When I had my first baby, my husband went through all the Lamaze classes, and then he got to the hospital and saw all those pregnant women in labor, and he left.' Another one said, 'My husband won't even go to the Lamaze classes with me, and he hates the way I look.' They were telling me that even married women are not assured of the kind of support I wanted. I thought I had this problem just because I was alone. It never dawned on me how difficult it can be for a man to deal with pregnancy.

"Even my doctor, who is a very renowned and prestigious gynecologist, had trouble treating my pregnancy in an emotionally healthy way. I said to him when we first met, 'I plan to have this child alone, and I'm going to need a lot of support.' He said, 'Don't worry. We'll love you and take care of you.' When I was married my ex-husband was going through medical school, and a lot of his courses were on tape, so I have a little background in medicine and I ask a lot of questions. It turned out my doctor was interested in being paternal, but not in answering my technical questions. We got into a few fights about that. And then he made his patients wait for hours for their appointments. Finally I said to him, 'I'm a businesswoman. I can't come in for a 10 A.M. appointment and sit here until noon. Would you ask a man who was the head of a corporation to do that?' I became considered the office crank, and he began to resent me.

"Then, when I was five months pregnant, I decided to go on vacation. I said, 'Doctor, I want to go away for Christmas. Is there anywhere you *don't* want me to go?' He said, 'Why don't you go to Grossingers?' After I got up from the floor laughing, I said, 'Excuse me. If you're going to deliver my baby, I think we ought to get acquainted. I'm not the kind of person who goes to Grossingers. What I had in mind was Lima, Peru.' He got very upset. He said, 'Peru! You can't go there—the altitude is too high.' So we worked on a compromise, and I wound up going to Puerto Vallarta in Mexico. There I was on the beach all alone and five months pregnant in my bathing suit. I had a wonderful time.

"But from then on, it was a war between my doctor and me. At one point, he was treating me like I was the oldest mother who had ever crossed the threshold of his office. I had to take a lot of precautionary tests, and one of them involved getting a gallon jar and collecting urine in it all day long. At that time, my home was a pile of dust and I was spending nights at a friend's house. I was carrying my clothes around in a shopping bag, and I just couldn't walk around with this gallon jar of urine. I called my doctor and said, 'I don't know what this test is for, but I can't do it. It's aggravating me more than whatever good it might be doing diagnostically. You're going to have to survive without it. I won't do it anymore.'

"I was not his easiest patient. But I wanted to keep using him because he has an excellent medical reputation. Then we had one last showdown over allowing a woman friend to be with me in the delivery room. She had gone to all the Lamaze classes with me, but he said, 'It's against policy to have her in the delivery room.' I spoke with the head of the hospital, who told me, 'The only person who can come into the delivery room is somebody who is involved with you and loves you.' I said, 'Look, doctor, if somebody comes to my house every single day to lie on the floor and go through these exercises with me, and goes twice a week to Lamaze class with me, then they are damn well involved, and how dare you say that I have to be deprived of that person because it's not a male.' So I called a friend of mine, who is a very wealthy woman and contributes to the hospital. I told her the story, she called the hospital, and they finally agreed to my request. But I hadn't envisioned fighting so hard for such a simple thing.

"I also fought a battle in paternity court to get the father's name on her birth certificate. It was important to me because—for years I lived the life of a hippy. Now for the first time I became worried about things like insurance, security, doing the right things for my baby. I didn't want the father's money—I don't need it. I just didn't want my child to have a birth certificate that says: Father Unknown. I'm not a hippy anymore. I'm a middle-class lady, and I can't just throw it all away. I felt "Father Unknown" was a lie, because I *knew* who the father was, and she had the right to know it on paper. Now she's like any kid of divorced parents, she has a father and a mother, and she can decide how to handle it when she's older.

"When she was three, she began asking me where her father was. She came home from a weekend in the country with other children who live with their fathers, and she said, 'Mommy, some little girls have mommies and some little girls have daddies and some little girls have mommies *and* daddies, and I only have a mommy—right, Mommy?' My mouth dropped. There was silence. I thought about it and I said, 'Well, that's true, but you do have a daddy except he doesn't live with us.' She said, 'Where is he?' I said, 'Well, we didn't get along, so he went away, but he never saw you, and if he did see you, I'm sure he would love you, and you know Mommy loves you more than anything in the world.' That seemed to satisfy her. Then my father, to whom she had been very close, died in June. After his death, I overheard her saying, 'I have two daddies. One is in heaven and one got mad at Mommy and ran away.' So I tried to bring it up again and clarify it for her a bit more. I'm sure as she grows older I will have to keep elaborating the explanation, and she will have to deal with it. But she's pretty tough; she'll cope all right. I think in another ten years the problem of having only one parent will not be as enormous for my child as it would have been a generation ago. Divorce is more common, more families are breaking up, and even people in their fifties and sixties suddenly find themselves going to singles bars.

"I have a lot of confidence that it will all turn out okay, because I have a lot of confidence in myself, and it's in large part due to my experience of nurturing and loving a child. I spent a large part of my life, especially during my twenties, apologizing because I was born smart, feeling I had to hide my talent. If only for my daughter's sake, I could never do that again. I want my child, because she is a girl, to never have to decide whether she *should* succeed. I want every alternative to be open to her, every single one. If she wants to be a full-time housewife, that's fine, but it should be because it's her *choice*. My hope is that my daughter won't feel she has to do the opposite of what I've done, that she will like me as much as I like her, that she won't have to put energy into resenting me but instead will be a free person, a free woman who is able to do exactly what she wants with her own life. I wouldn't have had that wish for her ten years ago, because ten years ago I wasn't capable of wishing such lovely things even for myself."

MARILYN

". . . having this child was a positive sign of strong self-confidence. I finally believed I had the ability to do it without destroying the rest of my life—without diluting my creative energies. . . . I feel it's a kind of resurrection, a rebirth, a renewal . . ."

Marilyn T. is a well-educated, articulate woman who was born in Boston and has lived in the San Francisco Bay area since 1966. She and her husband, Tom, have been married fourteen years—she is an anthropologist and a painter; her husband is vice-president of a large San Francisco clothing store. Both are Quakers. By choice, they waited thirteen years—until she was thirty-four years old—to have their first child, James.

Unlike Paula, whose pregnancy wrenched apart her relationship with the father, Marilyn found that her pregnancy cemented her marriage. And while Paula attributes her decision to wait to her desire to find the right man for a father, Marilyn feels her decision to wait was based largely on her symbiotic link with her own mother, and her ambivalence toward her own femaleness—toward being a woman in a man's world. Until she was able to break that link with her mother, and until she was able to overcome her aversion to pregnancy and motherhood, Marilyn felt threatened and unable to cope with the intrusion of a baby. Marilyn, like Fran and Deborah, also wrestled with the fundamental problem of how to balance a career and a baby. And, like Deborah, she switched careers in her mid-twenties—an im-

portant transition that made her even more glad she postponed until her thirties her decision to have a baby.

When Marilyn and I meet, it is a rainy Sunday afternoon,
and she is sitting on the kitchen floor playing with her
baby, who is eighteen months old. He has just awakened
from his nap and during the interview he begins to play
with the tape recorder, fascinated by the soft swishing
sounds of the tape. Then Marilyn cradles him against her
breast, and he becomes quiet.

"I think many women who wait, like me, prefer to postpone the decision indefinitely because it threatens them a
great deal. During my twenties, I didn't think I ever
wanted to have a child. After college, I did graduate work
in anthropology for five years on a fellowship. And then,
when I was twenty-seven, I began painting full time without ever having gone to art school. I came to painting late
because of the old association of painting being woman's
work. Where I grew up in Boston, painting is what a number of married women did after their children had grown.
They just sort of daubed away, and it wasn't a serious occu-
pation. As a child, I had a very strong sense of masculine
protest—or whatever you want to call it—that made me reject all the feminine occupations. It wasn't until I moved to
San Francisco that I put my painting in perspective, and
saw it as a life's work.

"Then I began feeling my art was my life. When I
would go on so-called vacations, I wouldn't feel alive unless
I brought my paints with me. If I couldn't paint, I would
feel I had disintegrated. I feel that if I don't work, then I
practically don't exist. I think that's what life should be:
pleasurable work. If you can find the kind of work that's
pleasurable, that's fantastic. And if you've done that, as I

did, you don't want to sabotage it with the presence of a child.

"Of course, during my twenties I didn't ignore totally the issue of motherhood. I spent years debating my hesitations, my questions surrounding it. Half the time, while I was reading Henry James, I would be meditating inwardly on these questions: Why did I feel so hostile toward motherhood? Why did I feel a strong sense of treachery when a friend would have a child? Today it is already a pattern to not have children until you're older, and yet I always felt the force of this kind of social identification—motherhood goes with marriage. I just felt, since the age of five or six, a great sense of revulsion against the biological facts of pregnancy. A generation ago, those feelings would have been my downfall. I would have been considered a barren woman, an anomalie, a social misfit, if I were married and chose to not have children. I would have been a disappointment to my parents and my husband. As it was, there was no daily pressure on me, just a subtle psychological pressure. An aunt did once ask me why I wasn't having children yet, and I gave her a morose look and said, 'Well, we're trying.' I made her feel so embarrassed about intruding in our private affairs that neither she nor anyone else in the family ever asked again. Of course, I didn't say *what* we were trying to do—which was, in fact, to *not* have children.

"When we moved into this house, we really began nesting. We were both in our early thirties. My new career as a painter was going well, and I began to feel I wanted to do the thing I was most afraid of, the thing I had always avoided: get pregnant and have a child. I had always harbored a fear of having children, and it even made me sever connections with my friends who had children. I had really shut myself off from a whole part of my past out of fear, and finally I felt it was important to face that. Also, my body wanted to do it, to have a child and find out what it was like and test myself. And it turned out to be a successful test. I did it well—I had the amount of courage necessary.

"When I stopped using birth control, it was like a dare, like Russian roulette. For three years, I didn't get pregnant and I began to think I might be sterile. Then when I found out I *was* pregnant my first reaction was, 'Oh no, I am going to get an abortion.' I had never had an abortion, but in my mind I had always considered it as the only alternative to burdening my life with a baby. I told my husband I was pregnant and wanted an abortion. He has always liked and wanted children, but he also feels I have the right to do with my body as I wish. I could tell he was upset, but he said, 'Think about it. Don't make an instant decision. Talk with a few people about it, and then decide.' Instead of talking to people, I went upstairs into my studio and thought for two hours, and I decided that it was okay, that I would have this baby.

"When I think now that I even considered an abortion, it chills me. I sat in the hospital after my child was born, looking at the children in the park across the street, and a funny, teary, sentimental feeling came over me—some call it postpartum depression—and one of the things I felt most strongly was that all my upbringing had brought me to the point where I would have *killed* this particular kid who I really think is *the* kid I wanted. He is exactly the kind of person I like; he has all the qualities I wish I had myself. And I thought, 'There must have been something wrong with my education and my ideas that would lead me to the point where I wanted to kill this child.'

"While I was in the hospital after giving birth, I had the strange feeling that this was a much nicer thing that had happened to me than I had ever expected it to be, and that people had somehow misled me. Everything I had ever read warned me that having a child was the end of your life. My mother had two children, and she was the kind of woman who was not very interested in cooking and hanging around the house. She wanted a full-time career, so had to sacrifice it to a certain extent for her children. She could have been a big business executive and instead she lowered her sights, although she did keep on working. But I always felt she didn't take to child care. She was well-educated—she had a master's degree—and she really did determine my sense that child care is something a woman would never want to do full time. A lot of women in the 1950s who did take care of their children full time talked about it as if it were a sort of—hell. And I think possibly it can be hell, unless that's what you really choose to do. Women who have children young sometimes do so simply because they don't know what else to do, and then they chafe under the restraints a child imposes.

"Because I waited to have my baby, my reaction has not been negative at all. For me, having this child was a positive sign of strong self-confidence. I finally believed I had the ability to do it without destroying the rest of my life—without diluting my creative energies in work or in my relationships with other people. In the back of my mind I always thought that giving birth was like going to war—facing death, life and death both—and that it takes a certain amount of courage. And if you go through the birth well, and you're pleased about the way you did it, then it only builds your confidence further. It did that for me: I went through it well, I didn't feel pain the way some people do, the Lamaze method worked for me, and I held on okay. My success with childbirth has had a wonderful effect on me. And having a child in my life has organized my life in a most remarkable way. I feel it's a kind of resurrection, a rebirth, a renewal—I have created something unique, I am recreating my own childhood through my child, and I am reaffirming my entrance into womanhood—adulthood. I have been painting more and better. My life is much nicer than it was before.

"James's birth has also made my marriage a happier and richer one. My husband is a businessman who thinks of himself as a poet and who has at times written beautiful poetry. But for many years, perhaps because we have been married for so long, we have been like two people who lived in the same place but were not really married. We would both come home from our day jobs and work on our night jobs—me on painting, him on poetry. We liked each other, we had similar tastes, and there seemed to be reasons to stay together, so we just sort of trotted around in the strange way people do, not really together, yet not thinking of moving apart.

"Our marriage had developed a bad case of inertia, and having the baby was a wonderful thing for us. It gave us a very clear common interest. He is a wonderful father, and James absolutely adores him. He takes care of James a great deal for me so I can paint every day. Fathering has been painful for him because he had a very bad childhood, and he sees, through James, all the things he didn't get for himself as a child. But he's been able to overcome the bad fathering he had in order to be a good father himself. Yet, there is a price to be paid: He feels jealous that this child is getting what he never got. He feels jealous that this child is a happy child. He remembers that when he was a child, nobody helped him at all. He was very bright, and taught himself the alphabet when he was three. Yet his parents thwarted him constantly. Now his son is growing up with a totally different experience.

"My own childhood was not very warm and loving, and I too am now aware of that. I grew up with governesses, and the baby nurse doesn't love you—you're just a job. Few baby nurses have that same absolute adoration for a child that the mother has. And I am convinced that the first six months of a child's life are extraordinarily important. I spent as much time as I could in those early months just plain smiling at James. I would look at him and grin. Really! I just smiled at him a lot. I took him around my studio and he looked at the paintings—the amaryllis and the wine goblets and the flowered dresses—anything that would be fun or make him feel joyful and very much wanted.

"He's a kid who amuses himself easily. He is very intelligent, very easy-going—and I think temperament and character are largely a matter of luck in a child. I had a strong feeling from the moment he was born that he was a very reasonable child. Whenever he cries, there is a reason, and that's very reassuring. He has never fussed about things like a wet diaper. He'll go all through the night and have a damp and dirty diaper, and play for two hours in the morning with it on and never complain.

"Child rearing was usually handled very differently in the days when I was brought up. Not only did people not breast feed—which I did, and loved—but they also fed babies 'on schedule.' It had to have a short-range effect, and maybe even a long-range effect, of totally frustrating the child. When you are a baby, your strongest needs are physical. When you are hungry, you must be fed—and right away, not in half an hour. If you are cold, you must be covered. You have only the power to beg people to fulfill your physical needs. And if your world is full of people who say, 'No—I'm not going to feed you now. When you've fallen asleep out of hunger, then I'm going to wake you and feed you,' it has to create a basic anxiety in a child.

"In the past, when children would cry and cry and cry and nobody could figure out what was wrong, the mother would feel her baby was this perverse young child who was trying to annoy her. His spirit had to be broken. He had to learn discipline. So she would shut the door and leave the poor baby crying for hours at a time. We're all victims of that kind of treatment, and because of it a lot of us never felt mothered. I never felt mothered, and it's very hard to explain this to someone like your mother. Of course my mother loves me in her fashion, but she just didn't happen to do the right things at the right time.

"I also have the feeling that while she loved me, she also resented me. Certainly that message came across very clearly. A lot of people are very good with tiny babies, and I can tell by the sweet way she handles James that there is a lot of natural loving in my mother. But with older children she is very controlling and dominating—and that sort of domination always makes you feel you're not wanted. She was very critical of me, so I always tried to do what would get her love. Because of that, I always felt like a little automaton—the kind of small wind-up figure they made in the seventeenth century that would start playing a little piano. She was the person who wound up the toy, and I was the toy that performed. I did well in school and in my anthropology career—and yet somehow it was not real, not authentic, because it was all on her energy. It took me twenty-seven years before I could unwind.

"A lot of friends who waited to have children have also told me they had similar feelings, and that they waited to outgrow their lingering resentments and build up self-confidence to cope with something as complicated as having both a career and a baby. And it *is* complicated. You have to have tremendous problem-solving capabilities, the same kind of capabilities you need in just about any other kind of managerial job, and a lot of people feel they don't have those capabilities. Just the strategic and physical skills needed to change a dirty diaper is fantastic. It's really a two-person job, even a three-person job! I still remember that first moment of panic that first week: how do I bathe him and keep the excrement from getting all over everything? It's really spectacular, and it involves much-underrated skills.

"Now that he is older, I am painting again seven hours a day. Two New York galleries are interested in my work, which thrills me. My mother is a very good grandmother, and gives me a hundred dollars a month to help pay for baby-sitters while I paint. So it is all working out. It does seem that James's birth has freed me in some way that shows in my work. Before, I was fighting against myself to do better. Now I am flowing with myself. And a lot of the change in me has to do with my overcoming this basic fear of letting my own body do what it does naturally: give birth. I remember once getting on a bus in Boston with my best friend from high school, and there was a pregnant woman on the bus and I whispered, 'Let's not sit next to her'—as if her condition were contagious. It was truly childish of me, but that's how basic my fear was.

"Norman O. Brown in *Life Against Death** talks about there being a certain age in which boys and girls feel a violent revulsion for the mother, feel she must have been castrated because there is no other explanation for her body, and feel a horror for all she seems to represent. They react by inventing worlds that ignore, or deny, her existence. That phenomenon may be, in fact, a root of anti-feminism, and explain why it is found in women as well as in men. That sense of revulsion is much more easily resolved if you're a man because you don't have to identify with that person. If you're a woman, then you can end up spending a lot of time denying the identification. Those attitudes affect all women to some extent, I'm sure, and they probably affected me.

"And women also tend to project to their children, particularly to their sons, their own sense of contempt for themselves by exaggerating the accomplishments of the son and making everything he does seem magnificent and everything she does seem unimportant. When she passes on those attitudes about herself, they become tradition. In line with that insight, both my husband and I thought, quite irrationally, that we were having a daughter. We felt that if we weren't sterile—I had used no birth control for three years, so it had been a possibility—then we were at least semi-sterile. Producing a daughter meant semi-sterility to us—I even went out and bought a bonnet with strawberries on it. I felt I couldn't have the kind of pregnancy

* *Life Against Death: The Psychoanalytical Meaning of History*, Wesleyan Univ. Press, 1959.

that would produce a boy—that is, a *real* pregnancy. Isn't that incredible? Especially coming from someone who has been called a suffragette. It was foolish, as were many of my older attitudes toward mothers and children.

"Now it is through my art that you can see the kind of mother I am and can become. I define the style of my art as mannerism. You get a painting where the whole point of the painting is not the picture of the Madonna but that the Madonna should be as tall as possible and the child should be as long as possible—a tremendous distortion while playing with the traditional motifs. If I can do really good painting, then that is the most important way I can reflect my success as a mother as well. I want to be as good as Georgia O'Keefe—she is the greatest living painter, yet she's not mentioned the way deKooning and Pollock are. Perhaps that deep deep revulsion against the biological, that anti-feminism, somehow weighs against all the accomplishments that all women make.

"All the accomplishments, that is, except one: giving birth, nursing, and nurturing. And that one accomplishment is for me a release, a new lease on life. By learning that giving birth to a baby was not giving death to myself, I have become a more courageous person. It's as if someone had, on my invitation, shoved me gently off a cliff, and instead of meeting the end of myself, I floated down to a whole new world within myself."

JOY

"The older you are, the better you feel about yourself. And the better you feel about yourself, the more com-

fortable you are with other people's personalities and
differences. With maturity, you learn to be flexible, to be
tolerant—you have a wisdom that creates a good setting
for kids."

Joy L. is among the most financially successful of the
women I interviewed: She is a vice-president of one of the
country's largest banks. She graduated from Radcliffe and
from Harvard Business School, and six years ago married
an equally successful Los Angeles attorney.

Joy waited until she was thirty years old to marry, and
then waited three more years to have her first baby, a boy
named Daniel. When she was thirty-six, she had her second child, a girl named Chloe, who is now three months
old. She hopes to have two more children before she turns
forty.

Unlike Marilyn, Joy has never felt threatened by the idea
of having children. She has never been ambivalent about
her femininity, or resentful toward her own mother, with
whom she feels close. While Marilyn is analytical and introspective about her reasons for postponing motherhood,
Joy tends to be more pragmatic: During her twenties, she
says, she was simply too busy to marry or to be a mother.

Like Marilyn, however, Joy too has found that the presence of children has enriched her marriage. And, like Marilyn, she knows she is a much better mother now than she
would have been ten years earlier.

Joy greets me at the door to her plush office. After telling
her secretary to hold her calls, she closes the office door and
settles comfortably behind a wide antique rosewood desk.
She is a pert, attractive woman who, despite the disheveled
papers on her desk, exudes an aura of efficiency.

"I had half a dozen opportunities to marry, going all the way back to my college days, and somehow or other I didn't do it. By putting off marriage, I was also putting off having children. At the time, it just seemed to 'happen' that way, but now I think I subconsciously orchestrated the whole thing. I think a lot of women don't get married and get pregnant today until their lives are somewhat in order, until they have some sense of self. And I think that's very healthy.

"In my case, I went out with a guy for two years in college and he expected me to marry him. The weekend his father was coming to meet me, I backed down. I said, 'Look, I'm not going through with this. It was a big mistake.' It was all very unpleasant, although since I was going on to graduate school it made it easier for me. I had something specific in front of me, an alternative to marriage.

"From then on, I usually picked men to go with who were clearly unavailable. They were interesting and glamorous, but never quite at that stage where they were ready to marry. Or I would go out with men who were in the middle of divorce, which I think is almost a guarantee that it won't work out, since they still feel upset and angry and in turmoil about their ex-wives.

"By the time I met my husband, Frank, on a blind date, I was thirty years old, and I was ready. I wasn't desperate nor was I uncomfortable about not being married. I had worked nine years. I had learned to live by myself, and had a support structure of family and friends. I had gotten to the point where I was used to going to things—parties, movies, openings—by myself if I chose to—a silly marker, I suppose, but an accurate one. But I also felt I would probably be happier getting married, and I think that was true.

"Frank and I were immediately attracted to one another. He had a combination of qualities that meshed with mine, and he also had a sympathy for and acceptance of working women. We match well. I am a relatively strong personality, and so is he—no one is going to run over the other. And our marriage has improved. I think if a marriage works well, you can become more independent—I don't mean independent of each other, but comfortable as separate individual people. That's what has happened to us.

"For us, there was never a question of whether we would have children, only of when. I am not a child-oriented person—I do not have any particular interest in small babies. It's just that my parents, who waited to have children, seemed to enjoy them, and everybody else I know who had kids in their thirties seemed to enjoy them, and I thought we would enjoy them too. I always felt I would miss out on something if I didn't have children. I thought they would add something to our lives, and I was right. And once we had one, we just assumed that with two we would double the pleasure—which is just what happened.

"But for me having children was like taking a Kierke-gaardian leap of faith. Suddenly I was in my ninth month of pregnancy and I thought, 'Oh, my God. What are we doing? How is it going to work out?' When you are pregnant, you are often irrational anyway—it just throws you off, your hormones alter. In my case, that doesn't matter too much, because I tend to be very self-controlled. But while I was pregnant, things that previously didn't bother me at all would *almost* make me cry.

"As it turned out, both my pregnancies were very easy. I had no morning sickness—everytime I thought I might feel nauseous, I ate a few crackers and it went away. I think morning sickness is part psychological, but it's also part physiological. If you're busy and have to keep going, it helps. But my secretary and I were pregnant at the same time—she was four months behind me—and it was very sad because every morning she came to work and threw up. She had a terrible time, while I just breezed through it—no problems with my weight, my legs, nausea.

"And, generally, the other male executives at work were quite accepting of my pregnancy. I was the first senior officer in a decade to be pregnant, and I found it worked best to stay low key about it all. One thing you learn when you work with men comfortably is to not deal with things too seriously, to not get offended by things that might offend other people. You can't afford it. I believe the differences between men and women don't matter in the business world. I think you can be a woman and be just as competent and successful as any man, and still retain your womanliness. Of course, you can be clear that you are upset when things are inappropriate.

"For example, I was working on a deal in Chicago and when all the executives went up to the dining room for lunch a Chicago lawyer turned to me and said, 'I'm sorry. You can't come with us. Women aren't allowed in that room.' I had to go off somewhere else to eat, and I was really angry about that, and I let them know it—in a firm way. But, on the other hand, when people ask you fifty times a day how you're feeling, they mean well. If you get angry about it, it's just a waste of time.

"As I grew bigger, one of my male colleagues used to say, '*Please* sit down. *Please* sit down. Take it easy. *Do not* come into my office, I'll come to yours.' Another male secretary said to me one day, 'Gee, aren't you overdue?' It was a Tuesday and I said, 'No, I'm not due until Friday.' The poor guy almost fell out of his chair. But because I was relaxed about it, they stayed more relaxed about it, and everyone took it pretty well.

"I used to joke with the office manager, who was very uptight. I would say, 'You know that white table in the conference room—I hope you've saved that for me.' He would laugh and say, 'Yes, they've got the water boiling.' In the hospital, he sent me a flower arrangement, and it was exactly like all the ones we have in the office. He went to the same florist with the same order. He was *trying* to adapt; I found the whole thing amusing.

"My work is very important to me, and I took little time off. For both babies, I worked the previous Fridays and had them on Mondays that were holidays—which I thought was good planning on my part. The first time, we had gone to visit friends in the mountains for the weekend, and I said to my woman friend, 'I'll never know when I go into labor, because I don't know what it feels like,' and she said, 'Oh, it's just like having bad cramps,' and I said, 'Oh, that's what I have.' That night I went to the hospital.

"I had both babies with natural childbirth. The first time, I had long labor—fourteen hours—because he was in 'sunnyside up' and they had to turn him around. The second time, I assumed it would be the same story, but it took less than two hours and the baby came flying right out! Frank and I saw the whole thing. I had bought a pair of glasses to wear in the delivery room because you're not supposed to wear contact lenses, and after the second baby was born Frank said, 'Honey, do you want your glasses now?' I said, 'Glasses? I never had time to get my lenses out!'

"I stayed home with Daniel for five weeks, and with Chloe for ten days, but I didn't particularly like staying home and taking care of them full time. When I was pregnant the first time, a friend asked, 'Aren't you going to take some time off before the baby comes?' I said, 'What for?' She said, 'To get the baby's room ready.' I said, 'What would I do the next day?' That's just not my idea of the way you do things. I need too high a level of activity to just stay home. By my standards, many of my friends who are housewives don't *do* anything—that is, they are busy and occupied, and yet their day just seems to go along with nothing *happening* in it.

"I have a housekeeper-governess who comes in week days and stays until I get home from work. She is a wonderful woman, and I'm glad I can afford her. On the other hand, everybody has some measure of guilt about leaving their children: It's a built-in guarantee. And it gets more difficult as they get older. It gets difficult when they start crying as you walk out the door, even though I know for a fact that the minute the door's closed and they see the crying hasn't done any good, they stop.

"But, because my children have never felt threatening to me—in fact, they have inspired me in many ways—when I am home I find I *want* to spend time with them. Because Frank and I are away from them all day, we really enjoy them, we really have fun with them, when we're home. When Daniel was one year old we wanted to go away for a vacation, but we found we never got around to making the arrangements. Suddenly we realized that the reason was because we did not want to leave our child. So I called up our baby-sitter, who was a nursing student, and her vacation time coincided with ours, so we instantly made plans for all four of us to go away, and that worked out beautifully.

"I also find that it's easier to be patient when you're only home a few hours a day. You can be amused by things that might otherwise make you really angry. Daniel threw all the laundry down the stairs the other night—all the *clean* laundry, the bath towels, sheets, pillow cases—and he was squealing with laughter. I wasn't pleased about it, and I closed him in his room for a few minutes, but it was hard to keep a straight face—it really was funny, and he didn't mean to be destructive. It was funny because it wasn't the ninetieth time I had watched him do it. Frank and I were trying to reprimand him and hold back our laughter at the same time.

"We are both aware that the children have done more than simply make our marriage better—they have added another layer to the relationship. Of course, they have cut into our time alone—but they're there because we *want* them around. I don't think either of us minds at all the attention the other one gives to the children. I don't think there's any jealousy over that. The chances are that when we're together, we're either both taking care of them, or one of us is taking care of them so the other can do something—there's nothing particularly competitive about it.

"Neither of us feels we have our own personalities, our own *raison d'être*, invested in them. I think the more time you spend with people, the more tolerant you become of the differences among people—including your own children. The older you are, the better you feel about yourself. And the better you feel about yourself, the more comfortable you are with other people's personalities and differences. With maturity, you learn to be flexible, to be tolerant—you have a wisdom that creates a good setting for kids. And you can have a better relationship with your children because there is less stress, and you can make accommodations.

"I am assuming, of course, that as you get older you don't get too attached to *things*, so that your life becomes too rigid, too inflexible, to adapt to changes that children bring. I was never particularly rigid. For example, I can tolerate a rather great amount of dirt and dishevelment in the house—so it hasn't been particularly difficult for me to adjust. But, I am not a thinker about these kinds of things. I am an instinctive person. I feel instinctively that if you have a household that is run the right way—if you have a warm, loving family with a certain measure of discipline— then your kids will come out okay.

"Another of the keys to enjoying children—especially if you work—is to have essentially a basic organized habit. If I stayed home all the time, I would fill my day with projects and committees. I was an arts and crafts counselor in college, so I like to putter. And I like to handle a multitude of things at once. Maybe I survive so well because I do things very fast. My friends know if I say I'm going to do something, the time between when I say it and when I do it is very short. If I say, 'I'm going to get Daniel a bulletin board,' you know the first day I don't have a lunch date I'll be out getting him a bulletin board. And if you don't think he should have one, you must say so right away.

"You have to be good at either doing lots of things simultaneously, or learning to do things very quickly—which means you give up a level of fine tuning to just get things done. You also have to be very good at relying on other people to do things: If you can't delegate and have to do everything yourself, it's harder to survive.

Last summer, I had to go away for a week-long seminar in San Francisco, and it required planning up and down the line. Frank was in the middle of a big trial, and he left the house at eight each morning and got home at ten each night. So my housekeeper came at 6:30 each morning, and my baby-sitter showed up at four, and my mother came at five—and they did just fine. I had five days' worth of frozen dinners in the freezer—it was an intricate system of survival. I guess we could have been less organized, and they would have gotten along just fine. But it meant I didn't have to worry. I would call home every night, and Daniel would answer the phone, say, 'Hi, mommy, grandma's here' and hang up on me! So I knew everything was under control.

"Daniel adores his grandparents. They add an enormous amount to his life. Grandparents can be completely nondisciplinary, benevolent adults. They devote 100 per cent of their attention to their grandchildren when they're around because it's a special occasion, and they're not trying to get anything else done—I think that's very good for kids, it makes them feel good about themselves to have that kind of attention.

"Part of my attitude toward my own children comes from my parents, who made a concerted effort to rear me to be independent. My mother worked almost all my life, either for money or as a full-time volunteer. She is an active, smart lady—Phi Beta Kappa, straight A's in college—and she, like me, got married at an age that was late for her time: She was twenty-eight years old. She and I have very different personality traits—we used to fight all the time.

But she was an excellent mother and she is a fantastic grandmother.

"She always wanted grandchildren, but she didn't put any pressure on me to have children younger, or, even, to get married. Both she and my father exhibited enormous self-restraint, although I'm sure they felt as if they were going around with tape over their mouths, dying about my single and childless state. But they never said a single word. They are very savvy people, and they just thought it would be inappropriate to bring it up—but it must have been a great strain. I have no doubt that I would have trouble exhibiting the same tact. I have enough trouble restraining myself with my peers who have chosen to not have children—ever. I know they have made intelligent choices, and I should accept it. But—you know how people who are happily married always want their unmarried friends to get married—well, it's the same kind of phenomenon. If you waited to have children, and find you really like them, and you receive a lot of pleasure from them, then you don't want anybody else to miss out on it."